THE ART AND SCIENCE
OF REMINISCING

THE ART AND SCIENCE OF REMINISCING: Theory, Research, Methods, and Applications

Edited by

Barbara K. Haight
Medical University of South Carolina
Charleston, South Carolina, USA

Jeffrey D. Webster
Department of Psychology
Langara College
Vancouver, British Columbia, Canada

Taylor & Francis
Publishers since 1798

USA	Publishing Office:	Taylor & Francis
		1101 Vermont Avenue, N.W., Suite 200
		Washington, DC 20005-3521
		Tel: (202) 289-2174
		Fax: (202) 289-3665
	Distribution Center:	Taylor & Francis
		1900 Frost Road, Suite 101
		Bristol, PA 19007-1598
		Tel: (215) 785-5800
		Fax: (215) 785-5515
UK		Taylor & Francis Ltd.
		4 John St.
		London WC1N 2ET
		Tel: 071 405 2237
		Fax: 071 831 2035

THE ART AND SCIENCE OF REMINISCING: Theory, Research, Methods, and Applications

1 2 3 4 5 6 7 8 9 0   BRBR   9 8 7 6 5 4

This book was set in Times Roman by Princeton Editorial Associates. The editors were Christine Williams, Holly Seltzer, and Deborah Klenotic; the prepress supervisor was Miriam Gonzalez. Cover design by Michelle M. Fleitz. Printing and binding by Braun-Brumfield, Inc.

A CIP catalog record for this book is available from the British Library.
♾ The paper in this publication meets the requirements of the ANSI Standard Z39.48-1984 (Permanence of Paper)

Library of Congress Cataloging-in-Publication Data

The art and science of reminiscing : theory, research, methods, and
    applications / edited by Barbara K. Haight and Jeffrey D. Webster.
        p. cm.
    Includes bibliographical references and index.

    1. Reminiscing.   2. Reminiscing in old age.   3. Autobiographical
memory.   I. Haight, Barbara K.   II. Webster, Jeffrey D. (Jeffrey Dean)
BF378.R44A78   1995
153.1'2—dc20   94-43253
                                                                                      CIP

ISBN 1-56032-298-5

To Barrett, the wind beneath my wings.—B.K.H.
To Mom and Dad, of course, for giving me memories worth reminiscing about.—J.D.W.

Contents

Contributors   xiii

Foreword: The Life Review   xvii
Robert N. Butler

Preface   xxiii

PART 1: THEORY   1

CHAPTER 1   An Integrated Review of Reminiscence   3
Barbara K. Haight and Shirley Hendrix

    Data Collection   4
    Scholarly Discussion (Theory)   4
    Research   6
    Methods   7
    Applications   8
    Summary   8
    Appendix   9

CHAPTER 2   The Processes of Adaptive Reminiscences   23
             Paul T. P. Wong

             Taxonomy of Reminiscence   24
             Adaptive Processes of Reminiscence   29
             Conclusions   35

CHAPTER 3   Reminiscing as a Process of Social Construction   37
             John A. Meacham

             Philosophy of History   38
             Social Construction of Memories   43

CHAPTER 4   A Conceptual Model of Socialization and Agentic
             Trait Factors That Mediate the Development of
             Reminiscence Styles and Their Health Outcomes   49
             P. S. Fry

             The Model   54
             Discussion   58
             Conclusion   60

CHAPTER 5   The Individual's Life History as a Formative
             Experience to Aging   61
             Bo Hagberg

             Purpose of the Present Study   63
             Method   64
             Results   65
             Discussion   70
             Conclusion   75

PART 2: RESEARCH

                                                               77

CHAPTER 6   Reminiscence and the Oldest Old   79
             Sharan B. Merriam

             The Georgia Centenarian Study   80
             Frequency and Uses of Reminiscence   81
             The Life Review   84
             Memories and Future Ambitions   86
             Conclusion   87

CHAPTER 7   Adult Age Differences in Reminiscence Functions   89
               Jeffrey D. Webster

               Method   91
               Results   93
               Discussion   95
               Conclusion   102

CHAPTER 8   A Qualitative Look at Reminiscing: Using the
               Autobiographical Memory Coding Tool   103
               Christine R. Kovach

               Measurement by Content Analysis   105
               Using the Autobiographical Memory Coding Tool   107
               Discussion   115
               Conclusion   122

CHAPTER 9   An Exploratory Analysis of the Content and
               Structure of the Life Review   123
               Brian de Vries, John A. Blando, and
               Lawrence J. Walker

               Background and Introduction   123
               Life Events   124
               Integrative Complexity and Life Events   126
               Objectives of the Present Study   127
               Method   127
               Results   129
               Discussion   134
               Conclusion   137

CHAPTER 10   Group Reminiscence: Evaluating Short- and
               Long-Term Effects   139
               M. J. Stones, Christine Rattenbury, and
               Albert Kozma

               Study 1: Why Community Residents Participate in
                 Reminiscence   140
               Study 2: Effects of a Reminiscence Intervention
                 on the Cognitively Impaired   142
               Study 3: Reminiscence in a Nursing Home   144
               Study 4: Maintenance and Implications of Therapeutic Effects   146
               Conclusion   150

PART 3: METHODS   151

CHAPTER 11   Themes and Props: Adjuncts for Reminiscence
                Therapy Groups   153
             Irene Burnside

             Themes   153
             Props   158
             Guidelines   162
             Conclusion   163

CHAPTER 12   Method and Uses of the Guided Autobiography   165
             Brian de Vries, James E. Birren, and
                Donna E. Deutchman

             The Method   166
             Overview of the Process   166
             Guiding Themes   167
             The Group Process   169
             The Group and Its Facilitator   170
             Problematic Circumstances in the Group Process   171
             Benefits of Participation   172
             Research   173
             Special Applications of Guided Autobiography   175
             Conclusion   175
             Appendix   176

CHAPTER 13   The Linchpins of a Successful Life Review:
                Structure, Evaluation, and Individuality   179
             Barbara K. Haight, Peter Coleman, and Kris Lord

             Life Review   180
             Linchpins of the Life Review   181
             Research Background   182
             Testing the Process   185
             Conclusion   189
             Appendix   189

CHAPTER 14   Finding Common Ground and Mutual Social Support
                Through Reminiscing and Telling One's Story   193
             Howard Iver Thorsheim and Bruce Roberts

             Key Concepts   194
             The Need   194
             Possible Methods to Encourage Telling One's Story   198
             Encouraging Telling One's Story Among Elders   200

Illustration of an Empowering Method to Encourage
   "Telling One's Story"   202
Conclusion   204

CHAPTER 15   Using Reminiscence Interviews for Stress
   Management in the Medical Setting   205
   Bruce Rybarczyk

Rationale for Developing a Reminiscence Approach   205
Two Variations of the Reminiscence Interview   208
Initial Study Using the Two Interviews   210
Follow-Up Study   213
Summary of the Research Findings   216
Future Directions   217

PART 4: APPLICATIONS

PART 4: APPLICATIONS   219

CHAPTER 16   Reminiscence Interventions for the Treatment
   of Depression in Older Adults   221
   Lisa M. Watt and Philippe Cappeliez

Development of Reminiscence as a Therapeutic Intervention   221
Reminiscence and Cognitive Models of Depression   223
Conclusion   231

CHAPTER 17   Evaluating the Impact of Reminiscence on Older
   People with Dementia   233
   Bob Woods and Fionnuala McKiernan

Empirical Studies   235
Integration and Conclusions   239
Practical Issues and Applications   241
Conclusion   242

CHAPTER 18   Reminiscence in Psychotherapy with the Elderly:
   Telling and Retelling Their Stories   243
   Linda L. Viney

The Power of the Stories of the Elderly   244
Reminiscence as a Source of Confirmation   246
Personal Construct Story Retelling Therapy for the Elderly   246
Three Elderly Clients' Use of Reminiscence in Their
   Storytelling Therapy   248
Reminiscence in Psychotherapy with the Elderly:
   Some Reflections   254

CHAPTER 19   Differential Effects of Oral and Written
                         Reminiscence in the Elderly   255
                 Edmund Sherman

                 Oral Versus Written Reminiscence   257
                 Method   258
                 Results   261
                 Discussion   263
                 Conclusion   264

CHAPTER 20   Finding Meaning in Memories:
                 The American Association of Retired Persons'
                 Reminiscence Program   265
                 Betty Davis

                 History of the Program   265
                 Description of the Reminiscence Program   266
                 Implementing the Reminiscence Program   267
                 Conclusion   271
                 Appendix   272

CHAPTER 21   Memory Lane Milestones: Progress in
                 Reminiscence Definition and Classification   273
                 Jeffrey D. Webster and Barbara K. Haight

                 Reminiscence: What It Is and What It Is Not   275
                 Taxonomies of Reminiscence Functions   278
                 Future Directions   284
                 Conclusion   285

References   287
Index   315

Contributors

JAMES E. BIRREN, Ph.D.
Associate Director
Borun Center for Gerontological Research
School of Medicine
University of California
Los Angeles, CA 90024

JOHN A. BLANDO, Ph.D.
Consultant
School of Family and Nutritional Science
University of British Columbia
Vancouver, British Columbia V6T 1W5
Canada

IRENE BURNSIDE, R.N., Ph.D.
Adjunct Professor
School of Nursing
San Diego State University
San Diego, CA 92182

ROBERT N. BUTLER, M.D.
Chairman and Brookdale Professor
  of Geriatrics and Adult Development
Mount Sinai Medical Center
New York, NY 10029

PHILIPPE CAPPELIEZ, Ph.D.
Associate Professor
School of Psychology
University of Ottawa
Ottawa, Ontario K1N 6N5
Canada

PETER COLEMAN, Ph.D.
Professor of Social Gerontology
Geriatric Medicine
University of Southampton
Southampton S09 4XY
United Kingdom

BETTY DAVIS, R.N., B.S.
Senior Program Specialist
Reminiscence Program
American Association of Retired Persons
Washington, DC 20049

DONNA E. DEUTCHMAN, B.A.
Associate Director for Development of
UCLA/JHA
Borun Center for Gerontological Research
School of Medicine
University of California
Los Angeles, CA 90024

BRIAN de VRIES, Ph.D.
Assistant Professor
School of Family and Nutritional Science
University of British Columbia
Vancouver, British Columbia V6T 1W5
Canada

P. S. FRY, Ph.D.
Visiting Professor of Psychology and
Research Affiliate at the Centre on
Aging
University of Victoria
Victoria, British Columbia V8W 3P5
Canada

BO HAGBERG, Ph.D.
Professor
University of Lund
Gerontology Research Center
S-222 20 Lund
Sweden

BARBARA K. HAIGHT, R.N.C., Dr.P.H.
Professor of Nursing
Medical University of South Carolina
Charleston, SC 29425

SHIRLEY HENDRIX, R.N., M.S.N.
Research Nurse
Medical University of South Carolina
Charleston, SC 29425

CHRISTINE R. KOVACH, R.N., Ph.D.
Assistant Professor
College of Nursing

Marquette University
Milwaukee, WI 53233

ALBERT KOZMA, Ph.D.
Co-Director
Gerontology Center
Memorial University of Newfoundland
St. John's, Newfoundland A1B 3X9
Canada

KRIS LORD, B.A., B. Sc.
Lecturer in Psychology and Counsellor
Salisbury College
Salisbury, Wiltshire SP1 2LW
United Kingdom

FIONNUALA McKIERNAN, Ph.D.
Clinical Psychologist
Camden & Islington
Community Health Services
N.H.S. Trust
United Kingdom

JOHN A. MEACHAM, Ph.D.
Professor of Psychology
State University of New York at Buffalo
Buffalo, NY 14260

SHARAN B. MERRIAM, Ed.D.
Professor, Adult and Continuing Education
University of Georgia
Athens, GA 30602

CHRISTINE RATTENBURY, Ph.D.
Clinical Psychologist
Gerontology Center
Memorial University of Newfoundland
St. John's, Newfoundland A1B 3X9
Canada

BRUCE ROBERTS, Ph.D.
Professor of Psychology
St. Olaf College
Northfield, MN 55057

BRUCE RYBARCZYK, Ph.D.
Assistant Professor
Department of Psychology and Social
Science

Rush Presbyterian-St. Luke's Medical
   Center
Chicago, IL 60612

EDMUND SHERMAN, Ph.D.
Professor of Social Welfare
Ringel Institute of Gerontology
State University of New York at Albany
Albany, NY 12222

M. J. STONES, Ph.D.
Department of Health Studies and
   Gerontology
University of Waterloo
Waterloo, Ontario N2L 391
Canada

HOWARD IVER THORSHEIM, Ph.D.
Professor of Psychology
St. Olaf College
Northfield, MN 55057

LINDA L. VINEY, Ph.D.
Director
Department of Psychology
University of Wollongong
Wollongong, NSW 2500
Australia

LAWRENCE J. WALKER, Ph.D.
Professor
Department of Psychology

University of British Columbia
Vancouver, British Columbia
   V6T 1W5
Canada

LISA M. WATT, M.A.Sc.
Graduate Student
School of Psychology
University of Ottawa
Ottawa, Ontario K1N 6N5
Canada

JEFFREY D. WEBSTER, M.Ed.
Psychology Instructor
Department of Psychology
Langara College
Vancouver, British Columbia
   V5Y 2Z6
Canada

PAUL T. P. WONG, Ph.D.
Professor of Psychology
Trent University
Peterborough, Ontario K9J 7BS
Canada

BOB WOODS, M.A., M.Sc., F.B.Ps.S.
Senior Lecturer in Psychology
Department of Psychology
University College of London
London WC1E 6BT
United Kingdom

Foreword: The Life Review

In 1961 I first presented the concept of the life review (Butler, 1961), which I built over several years (Butler, 1963, 1974). I saw reminiscence in the aged as part of a normal life review process brought about by the realization of approaching dissolution and death. It is characterized by the progressive return to consciousness of past experiences, particularly the resurgence of unresolved conflicts. These conflicts may be reviewed again and reintegrated. If the reintegration is successful, it may give new significance to the older person's life and prepare him or her for death by mitigating fear and anxiety.

This is a process that occurs in all persons in the final years of their lives, although they may not be totally aware of it and may, in part, defend themselves from realizing its presence. Life review is spontaneous and unselective, and also occurs in other age groups. However, the emphasis on putting one's life in order is most intense in old age.

In late life, people have a particularly vivid imagination and memory for the past and can recall with sudden and remarkable clarity early life events. There is renewed ability to free-associate and bring up material from the unconscious. Individuals realize that their own personal myths of invulnerability and immortality can no longer be maintained. All of this results in the reassessment of life, which can bring about depression, acceptance, or satisfaction.

The life review may occur in the forms of light nostalgia, mild expressions of regret, and storytelling. Often the person will tell his or her life story to anyone who will listen. At other times it is conducted in silent monologue without witnesses. In many ways, the life review is similar to the psychotherapeutic situation in which a person reviews his or her life in order to understand present circumstances.

Sometimes in the process of reviewing his or her life, a person may experience a sense of regret that becomes increasingly painful. In severe forms the regret can generate anxiety, guilt, despair, and depression. In extreme cases, if a person is unable to resolve problems or accept them, terror, panic, and even suicide can result. The most tragic outcome of a life review is the feeling that one's life has been a total waste.

On the other end of the spectrum, some of the positive outcomes of reviewing one's life include the righting of old wrongs, reconciliation with enemies, acceptance of mortality, a sense of serenity, pride in accomplishment, and a feeling of having done one's best. Life review gives people an opportunity to reflect on what to do with the time they have left and to work out emotional and material legacies. People become ready, but are in no hurry, to die. The serenity, philosophical development, and wisdom that are observed in some older people may be, in fact, a reflection of the successful resolution of their life conflicts.

A lively capacity to exist in the present is usually associated with these more positive responses, including the direct enjoyment of such elemental pleasures as nature, children, shapes, colors, warmth, love, and humor. One may become more capable of mutuality—a comfortable acceptance of the life cycle, the universe, and the generations. Creative works may result, such as memories, works of art, and music. People may put together family albums and scrapbooks and study their genealogies.

It is often difficult for younger persons, including mental health personnel, to listen thoughtfully to the reminiscences of older people. We have been taught that this nostalgia represents "living in the past" and a preoccupation with the self. It is often seen as boring, meaningless, and time-consuming chatter. Quite to the contrary, this reminiscence has a constructive purpose. It is part of a natural healing process, and it represents one of the underlying human capacities on which all psychotherapy depends. The life review should be recognized as a necessary and healthy process in daily life as well as a useful tool in the mental health care of older people.

In 1963 I published the most formal presentation of "The Life Review: The Interpretation of Reminiscence in the Aged" (Butler, 1963). At the time reminiscence was regarded by many psychiatrists and psychologists as a sign of pathology; indeed, it was considered a sign of senile dementia by some. I disagreed with this prevailing point of view because of my experience as a principal investigator in the National Institute of Mental Health's Human Aging study of community-residing, healthy older persons (Birren, Butler, Greenhouse, Sokoloff, & Yarrow, 1963), whose reminiscences I had found were often fascinating and in no sense reflected pathology. I also noticed that their reminiscences revolved around various life conflicts, and after much reflection, a literature search, and discussion with others, I refined and built upon my original formulation of 1961. I presented the concept before my scientific colleagues at the National Institute of Mental Health's Laboratory of Clinical Science, which was, and still is, predominantly biomedical and not behavioral in orientation. Nonetheless, my presentation was well received.

I submitted my paper to the journal *Psychiatry,* which published it some months later in 1963. It never occurred to me at the time that this work would have such an impact on the fields of gerontology, geriatrics, nursing, social work, psychology, art, history, occupational therapy, and to some extent, psychiatry itself. It became the basis of various doctoral theses in the United States and abroad. Some of these concerned the psychology of human development in later life, rather than therapy. The American Association of Retired Persons later developed a reminiscence program (see Chap. 20), and similar programs exist in Great Britain and Japan. Many nurses and social workers have employed either life review or reminiscence therapy. Other psychotherapists, art therapists, and occupational therapists also employ the life review in their work.

My colleague, Myrna I. Lewis, and I wrote about life review therapy in 1974 (Lewis & Butler, 1974). Life review therapy is a more structured and purposive concept than simple reminiscence. It includes an extensive autobiography of the older person and testimony from his or her family members. Such memoirs can be preserved by writing, tape recording, or videotaping them. Family photo albums, scrapbooks, genealogies and other memorabilia, as well as pilgrimages back to places important in their lives, all evoke crucial memories, responses, and understanding in patients. A summation of one's life work or a summary of feelings about parenting by some means can be useful. The goals and consequences of these steps include a reexamination of one's life that may result in expiation of guilt, the resolution of intrapsychic conflicts, the reconciliation of disturbed family relationships, the transmission of knowledge and values to those who follow, and the renewal of ideals of citizenship and the responsibility for creating a meaningful life.

Lieberman and Tobin (1983) have confirmed that reminiscence is crucial to the emotional well-being of an older person, helping to resolve past conflicts and enabling the development of a coherent life history. Handbooks for composing a personal autobiography are available to aid nonprofessional writers in exploring and describing their histories and lives. These accounts form a valuable first-person historical source for use by families, sociologists, cultural historians, and others, in addition to providing therapeutic benefits and satisfaction for the authors of these works. The concept of life review has been bolstered by an increasing interest in the United States in finding one's ethnic "roots". In fact, a significant percentage of tourism relates to people who are tracing their heritage. The United States is populated by people from no fewer than 134 backgrounds. Fifty million, or 22 percent of the population, claim English lineage, and 49 million trace their lineage to Germany. The next most numerous ethnic groups are, respectively, Irish, African-American, French, Italian, Scots, Polish, Mexican, and American Indian.

My simple observation three decades ago that no one should write reminiscence off as a sign of senility and pathology is now perceived as a contribution to the developmental psychology of late life, a mode of historiography, and a potentially valuable therapy. Attempts are still being made to conceptualize more clearly reminiscence and the life review. Unfortunately, I have had very little opportunity to pursue the subject myself beyond an abortive effort in the 1960s and 1970s to collect comprehensive life reviews or autobiographies from middle-aged and older creative persons. During that time period I published a paper on creativity (Butler, 1976) and placed these taped and typed memoirs in the archives of the American Psychiatric Association. But beyond that I have neither studied nor speculated further on either the life review or creativity.

The field of the life review, such as it is, has grown in several directions. For example, it has influenced our concept of oral history, which predates written history, of course, in virtually every culture and is part of the oral tradition. Herodotus, the father of the art of history, certainly employed oral histories. Much more recently Allan Nevisn, the American historian, helped found and implement the oral history program at Columbia University, which derived from his seminal book, *Gateway to History* (Nevisn, 1938). Without the oral tradition, the field of anthropology would be greatly limited. Individual life histories can also contribute to the understanding of specific historical periods, such as the economic depression of the 1930s, as illustrated by the works of Glen Elder and Studs Turkel. The Foxfire Books of Elliot Wiggington also demonstrate how brief oral histories can preserve knowledge of various skills that are disappearing.

Another line of growth related to the life review is human development, in terms of intellectual and personal growth, and wisdom. James Birren, Paul Baltes, and others have worked in this area. Death, the catalyst of the life review, and its impact on late life have also received some attention.

The next line of growth related to life review is more directly therapeutic. It has evolved with the help of nurses such as Patricia Ebersole and Irene Burnside, and in James Birren's work on the therapeutic autobiography, which posits that meditation on one's past, one's relationships, and one's place in the universe has therapeutic implications. Life review therapy may be seen as an inexpensive "alternative therapy". It can be carried out in an individual or group therapy setting. But, like any therapeutic approach, it can also have a dark side. Family memories can be very powerful. Emotional events in a family, such as loss of a loved one through war or suicide or dispossession from one's home because of economic setbacks, can leave a profound mark. Such events may be concealed as family secrets, but then resurface unexpectedly through the process of life review. The results can be very painful as well as therapeutic.

Where should the study of life review proceed from here? First, it is essential that we understand and clearly define the various terms we use, such as personal narrative, autobiography, life review, and reminiscence. These terms require further qualification and conceptualization. Perhaps most importantly, they need operational clarification for purposes of undertaking specific quantitative studies—so long as it is understood that certain concepts such as the life review defy absolute quantification. Webster and Haight tackle this important issue in the concluding chapter of this book.

The use of life review in history is noted in Emerson's statement that "history is a collection of biographies". We need biographies not only from the rich, famous, and powerful but also from people in everyday life to understand human behavior in our great multi-ethnic and multi-cultural society. For example, in collaboration with Margaret Mead, we helped to set up a program on "kin and communities" with the Smithsonian Institution in 1976, and collected life histories on the Mall in Washington, D.C., that summer. Similarly, we would also do well to have life reviews from those who immigrate to our land, where they have sought either economic opportunity or political asylum. John Meacham makes a similar observation in Chap. 5 of this book. Rita Dove, Pulitzer Prize winner and American poet-laureate, was quoted in *The New York Times* (May 19, 1993, p. C15) as saying, "If only the sun-drenched celebrities are being noticed and worshiped then our children are going to have a tough time seeing value in the shadows, where the thinkers, probers and scientists are who are keeping society together."

From the point of view of human development, we seek both richer qualitative and quantitative data, particularly focused on creativity and wisdom. These two topics are as important as they are elusive to human understanding and any additional information that helps us to understand these two positive human qualities is welcome.

The therapeutic use of life review and of all psychotherapies may be endangered now because of the trend toward containment of health-care costs, which may favor medication in psychiatric treatment over "talking" therapies. Nonetheless, communication and relationship are quintessential to human understanding and the resolution of conflicts. It seems unlikely that medications alone can ever accomplish those goals. As one's life nears an end, the opportunity to confront lifetime conflicts and acts of omission and commission, which warrant guilt as well as opportunities for atonement, resolution, and reconciliation, is precious because this is the last opportunity one has.

Robert N. Butler

Preface

This book was written to provide a definitive resource for teachers, students, clinicians, and researchers who work in the field of reminiscing, as well as those interested in ecologically valid forms of memory. As such, it will find its place as a text or supplementary text in upper division nursing, psychology, social work, and gerontology courses, as well as a general resource for researchers and practitioners. Many of the chapters will also strike a responsive chord in a general audience interested in examining their own life histories.

Although recognition of reminiscing as a potentially adaptive process can be traced back 30 years to the seminal work of Robert Butler, there has been little effort to consolidate the work and paint a complete picture of reminiscing as an entity. Very few edited volumes on reminiscence exist and their primary mandate was neither a representative sampling nor an integrative review of the field. *The Art and Science of Reminiscing: Theory, Research, Methods, and Applications* presents reminiscing as an overall topic and examines the theory and research of reminiscing while discussing the different ways of conducting the process and reporting ways in which practitioners have applied the methodology. This is a seminal effort to provide a variety of viewpoints in one place, to encourage varied arguments as to what is and what is not reminiscing, and to summarize and provide directions for the future.

The contributors to this book, many of whom are pioneers and leading figures in the field, are well known for their solid and innovative reminiscence research and were invited to contribute their thoughts for that reason. Thus, this book provides the thinking of respected experts with guidance for the future. It is an exciting first attempt at combining varied viewpoints to reach a gestalt in reminiscing.

There are several unique features to this book. First, the contributors represent a multidisciplinary group. Unlike the interesting and helpful effort by Boranto (1993) in which virtually all authors are clinicians, this volume includes by design representatives of psychiatry, psychology, gerontology, nursing, and community advocacy. It is a sign of the growing maturity of the field, and a strength of this book, that a multidisciplinary perspective is a reality rather than a concept to which we only pay lip service.

Second, this is a multinational effort. Contributors come from Australia, Canada, England, Sweden, and the United States. Clearly, the power, drama, and utility of reminiscing know no geographic borders. As we note in the concluding chapter, what part cultural differences may play in the process, function, and outcome of reminiscing remains to be systematically documented. A first step in this direction is to illustrate the international interest in reminiscence and then to examine the convergences/divergences that emerge.

Third, this is a multisectional effort. Cognizant of the breadth of interest that reminiscence researchers manifest, we have included articles spanning the spectrum of interest from conceptual model building to the nuts and bolts of organizing and conducting actual reminiscence groups. We have divided the book into sections examining theory, research, methods, and applications. These sections are convenient organizational divisions but are somewhat artificial. They do seem to faithfully represent, however, the scope and particular interests of individuals in the field. Similarly, the assignment of chapters to specific divisions artificially "pigeonholes" them. There is often overlap within articles between research and theory, for instance, or methods and applications. Our intent is not to perpetuate boundaries between subareas of reminiscence investigation, but only to illustrate the diversity of interests inherent in the field.

Finally, we are honored to have the man responsible for the interest in the field, Robert Butler, provide us with a historical context and his personal view of reminiscing in the Foreword. Surprised that a simple clinical observation could spawn such a vibrant research field, Butler illustrates how work in reminiscence has grown to touch and inform related academic disciplines. Butler reiterates his earlier views on the life review and notes several issues that the field still has not adequately addressed. Hopefully, this volume will begin to address some of these needs, particularly those of clarification.

THEORY

In this section, contributors examine reminiscence from a theoretical perspective. Haight and Hendrix review the empirical work in the field, providing us with a sense of the scope and vigor of reminiscence research. Referring to an earlier review that reported most of the work to the end of the 1980s, they detail the work in the 1990s by dividing it into the four sections of theory, research, methods, and applications. An excellent annotated reference list is at the end of their chapter for the personal use of the reader.

Wong's taxonomy of reminiscence types provides a theoretical framework for investigating many avenues of aging, including those leading to a successful outcome. He provides an overview of six types of reminiscence accompanied by example vignettes of each type and scoring rationale and criteria. Wong notes how current self-configurations, or schemas, are malleable and how current schemas and memories influence one another.

Meacham takes the reconstructive nature of reminiscing and places it firmly in a broad social context. He argues that the process of reminiscing is not an individualistic one, but rather is a process of social construction. The meaningfulness of recalled memories is negotiated via social exchange in a reciprocal fashion. When there is a convergence of interpretation of memories, then Meacham argues that this bolsters our confidence in the "trans-contextual" meaningfulness of the memories of those events.

In the following chapter, Fry proposes a model of reminiscence that brings conceptual clarity to the field and establishes a framework for research that has testable hypotheses. As such, it lends much needed rigor to the area. The model investigates how an individual's reminiscence style has both antecedents in the form of a constellation of agentic traits and consequences in the form of diverse health outcomes. Her articulation of this transactional model reinforces our appreciation of the dynamic, multifaceted nature of reminiscing.

Hagberg examines the relationship between reminiscence, well-being, and retirement. He illustrates the interactive nature of recall and how memories are reconstructed in resonance with current emotional and psychological needs. His findings and discussion nicely dovetail with empirical work and theoretical thinking in the area of autobiographical memory currently being investigated by experimental psychologists. As Webster and Cappeliez (1993) note, these two areas of research can inform each other, and Hagberg's work is an example of a bridging study.

RESEARCH

The research section includes cutting-edge projects that focus on relatively unexplored dimensions of reminiscence. Merriam describes reminiscence in the oldest old, centenarians, a population about which we know little. She refutes one of Butler's earlier statements that reminiscence is a universal process in older people and postulates that if this were so, her study population would all have participated in a life review. In a comparison of centenarians with 60- and 80-year-olds, she found no age differences in the frequency of reminiscence and concluded that there is nothing particularly unique about the functions of reminiscence across these age ranges.

Webster investigates multiple functions of reminiscence across the life span. In a unique, large scale study of subjects ranging in age from 17–91, he discusses age and gender differences in the Reminiscence Functions Scale (RFS). Like Merriam, Webster found no age differences for the total amount of reminiscence, although interesting age differences occurred for the individual factor scores with older adults scoring higher on some but lower on others compared to younger adults. Webster cautions against adopting a "gerocentric" focus and argues for a life-span perspective.

Kovach shares an Autobiographical Memory Coding Tool (AMCT), which, like Wong and Watt (1991), employs a qualitative content analysis of transcribed tapes. She determined that reminiscences were of two broad types. Validating interpretations confirmed or verified that the person had lived a fruitful life while lamenting interpretations involved negative appraisals of past events. Kovach provides a clear and comprehensive description of the use and scoring character-istics of the AMCT and provides suggestions for its use in clinical settings.

de Vries, Blando, and Walker continue the qualitative theme evident in Ko-vach's contribution with an exploratory analysis of the content and structure of life's events. Young, middle-aged, and older adults nominated and then discussed significant life events. Transcripts were analyzed for "integratial complexity," an information processing variable. Perhaps surprisingly, there were more similari-ties than there were differences in the form and substance taken by the life review across both age and gender.

Finally, Stones, Rattenbury, and Kozma summarize the findings from three short-term and one long-term reminiscence projects. These authors detail the advantages and disadvantages of using various outcome measures, particularly levels of mood and happiness, when applied in diverse settings (e.g., institutional versus community living). A rather dramatic finding, enabled by their 18-month follow-up study, concerned differences in morbidity and mortality rates, with participants in reminiscence groups outliving control subjects.

METHODS

This section provides ways of using reminiscence in practice as well as in research. Its focus is on the many ways we can entice, coax, and stimulate reminiscences in various forms. The authors in this section describe their own methods of practicing reminis-cence for replication by both researchers and practitioners.

Burnside describes her experiental knowledge base in group work. She dis-cusses the use of props and themes as ways to elicit memories from groups. Particularly helpful is a timeline that recalls major events over the older person's life span. A discussion of "too many" props serves as instruction for practitioners just beginning groups.

de Vries, Birren, and Deutchman share their procedure for conducting autobiographical groups, one way of using reminiscence. Using a well-proven, structured approach, these authors clarify the rationale for, and steps involved in, conducting guided autobiography groups. A series of thematic branching points is used as a stimulus for reminiscence that is first written in journal form and then shared in the group setting.

Haight, Coleman, and Lord describe the linchpins of a therapeutic life review and share the research base for this methodology. They report the success of a small pilot study in the United Kingdom using these techniques: Case studies and descriptions of certain life events are particularly powerful and poignant and fully illustrate the therapeutic value of a life review.

Another method of reminiscing, called Telling One's Story, uses Kelly's framework as a guideline. Thorsheim and Roberts view telling one's story as a unique way to meet self-expression needs in people of all varieties. They share helpful key concepts for conducting the process and again provide an international view with their Norwegian experiences. Particularly useful is their description of storytelling as a way of establishing common ground and finding social support. They, too, describe their methodology for the use of practitioners and researchers interested in doing reminiscence.

Rybarcyzk presents the use of reminiscence in a medical setting and describes two different interventions, a life experience interview and a life challenges interview. The challenge reminiscing intervention helps people cope and reduces stress before surgery very effectively. Rybarcyzk's intervention is short and uses volunteers. The use of volunteers may be helpful for others looking for a cost-effective way of conducting these processes. He makes a very interesting point concerning volunteer differences as he notes that most of the improvement found in patients was the work of two particularly skilled counselors.

APPLICATIONS

The applications section provides a world view of ways to use reminiscence for populations who are depressed, demented, bereaved, and/or aging well. Contributors to this section provide a true multinational mix with examples of reminiscence applications in Australia, Canada, the United Kingdom, and the United States.

Watt and Cappeliez have an interest in treating depression with reminiscence. Using the typologies developed by Watt and Wong in an earlier paper and enlarged by Wong in his chapter, they suggest that both integrative and instrumental reminiscence may be useful in treating depression. Watt and Cappeliez discuss concepts such as coping, resources, and internal guidelines and make a strong argument for the use of reminiscence with depressed populations.

Woods and McKiernan focus on the use of reminiscence with patients who have dementia. Their literature review shows the promise of reminiscence as a way to provide personhood to people afflicted with dementia. The same review also highlights the paucity of research with this population while creating an enticing potential. From their experience in practice and an integration of the literature, they generously provide practical tips and applications for those of us thinking of using reminiscence as an intervention with this population.

Viney speaks of older people telling and retelling their stories. She offers powerful vignettes showing the use of reminiscence in psychotherapy. Particularly poignant are the case studies describing personal construct therapy with the bereaved, withdrawn, and dying. Viney argues that stories help develop and maintain identities, provide guidance, create order, and empower us. By renegotiating the meaning of stories, the therapist can help create more constructive frames of reference for the client.

Sherman describes both oral and written reminiscence in groups. He contrasts these two methods of recall very well for those of us trying to decide how to use the tool of reminiscence. His chapter answers and raises questions for practitioners. He concludes with the idea that written reminiscence can be effectively incorporated into an oral reminiscence group with beneficial effects.

Finally, Davis talks about the nationwide reminiscence program in the United States that is sponsored by the American Association of Retired Persons (AARP). For ten years, the program has trained volunteers to reminisce with isolated homebound older persons as a way to effectively communicate with them. Davis' clear directions will be helpful to other organizations and nations wanting to implement similar programs. Most importantly, it is interesting to see that such a large scale program is possible.

In the concluding chapter, we tackle the seemingly intractable problem of concept clarification. Terms that are conceptually related and often used synonymously are contrasted along five broad dimensions. This preliminary exercise helps clarify both the similarities and differences between terms such as life review, reminiscence, and narrative.

Recent taxonomies of reminiscence functions are also detailed and compared as well as directions for future research. While admitting that there are still obstacles to surmount, we nevertheless optimistically conclude that the recent advances documented in this book promise a vital, expansive future for reminiscence research and practice.

Barbara K. Haight
Jeffrey D. Webster

Part One

Theory

This section presents a selection of scholarly work that begins to develop a theory of reminiscence. As a basis for the work, Haight and Hendrix present a detailed review of the literature in the field since 1990, conveniently divided into the same sections as this book, a ready resource. They also cite a previous reference for those who wish to review the work from 1963, when Butler first coined the term "life review," to 1990.

Wong then offers a taxonomy of reminiscence helpful to practitioners and researchers who wish to classify their own style of reminiscence and compare it to others. His work is a fine first step toward greater communication among those in various fields who use reminiscence interventions.

Meacham argues for viewing reminiscence from a social construction perspective. He sees reminiscing as a social process having social functions and states that the social construction of meaningful memories is not a simple matter; rather it depends on negotiating the meaning of memories with others who have a broad range of experience and age.

Fry proposes a framework for research that examines an individual's reminiscence style based on agenetic traits. Fry incorporates Wong's taxonomy into her concepts by hypothesizing relationships among the agenetic traits of optimism, humor, empathy, and openness and integrating and instrumental types of reminiscence.

Hagberg concludes the section with a view of the individual's life history as a formative experience and agrees with Fry's discussion that perceptions of old age differ depending on the unique personality structure of an individual.

Reading this section will allow one to see a theory of reminiscence emerging, a theory of different styles that are influenced by many variables.

Chapter 1

An Integrated Review of Reminiscence

Barbara K. Haight
Shirley Hendrix

This chapter builds on an earlier integrated review of reminiscing that was praised for its useful format and criticized for its narrow focus (Haight, 1991). Responding to the critiques, in this chapter we use the integrated format while broadening the outlook. The review is categorized into four sections. In the Theory (Scholarly Discussion) section, we review the development of concepts and tools, as well as theory and reviews. In the Research section, we review quantitative and qualitative research with both individuals and groups. Papers that provide directions for using the life story are reviewed in the Methods section, and reports of programs that have used the life story are considered in the Applications section. However, as stated in the Preface, the use of the life story is growing so swiftly and the field is widening so rapidly that this review does not include all categories of the life story. Specifically, autobiography, biography, and oral history are not a part of this review. To be included in this review, a report had to meet the following criteria:

1   It was published in 1990–1993.
2   It was published in a refereed journal.

3 It contains the following keywords: *reminiscence, remembering, life review,* or *life story.*

DATA COLLECTION

Interest in reminiscing has increased remarkably in the past 3 years. Whereas approximately 130 articles were published between 1960 and 1990 (Haight, 1991), from 1990 through 1993, there were 68 published articles—1991 was a banner year, with a total of 23 articles. The articles are changing from chiefly serendipitous reports of reminiscing to more formal reports of theory development (Wong & Watt, 1991), concept development (Burnside & Haight, 1992), tool development (Webster, 1993), and experimental research (Haight & Dias, 1992). Qualitative research (Kovach, 1991b) contributes a more in-depth picture of the field and is key to increasing our understanding of the use of reminiscence. The field of reminiscing is beginning to grow, coalesce, and make a great contribution to interpreting the way individuals live their lives.

The work of 1990–1993 divides easily into four categories that reflect the structure of this book. First and foremost is the Scholarly Discussion section, which includes concept and tool development, as well as theory and reviews. The number of scholarly discussions available reflects a healthy tendency among authors to examine past beliefs and contribute new ideas. The Research section includes both quantitative and qualitative studies. Research has examined not only outcomes, but also content, meaning, and themes in people's life stories. The Methods section records different ways of using recall and past memory. Finally, the Applications section presents reports of successful reminiscence programs. Figure 1 depicts the reported literature divided into these four categories. For the first time, research and scholarship constitute more than half the field.

There is also another group of scholars who use reminiscence to study lives for autobiographical accounts and oral histories to capture the essence of history that would otherwise be lost. Although this research is related and equally important, it is not included in this review. The field is growing so rapidly that a specific focus was needed to make the review manageable.

SCHOLARLY DISCUSSION (THEORY)

The reviews published in the 1990s seem more goal directed and purposive than earlier reviews. Burnside (1990) examined the literature with the view of using reminiscence as an independent nursing intervention. Haight (1991) took a similar approach, examining the extent to which the literature could be used as a basis for practice. She concurred with earlier reviewers that there was a need to use common labels when talking about the use of past memory. As a group, previous and present reviewers stressed the need for more in-depth research. Kovach (1990) looked at the problems and promise of earlier studies and Burnside, Haight, and

Kovach made recommendations for change. Webster and Cappeliez (1993) added to the field with a selective review of both clinical/reminiscence and experimental/autobiographical memory domains, noting the conceptual overlap between the two areas. They pointed out neglected areas of reminiscence research, such as age and personality difference. They also offered a definition of reminiscence.

The reviewers thus speak to the growth of scholarly thought on the use of reminiscence and the need for researchers and practitioners to be speaking the same language.

Falling under the rubric of theory or concept development is the work of scholars trying to identify "kinds of reminiscence." Wong and Watt (1991) created a typology of styles of reminiscing. Although their work was a great contribution to the literature, it would have been greater if they had used existing labels in their typology or, at least, talked about how the labels they used were related to or different from existing labels. They did further research on the types of reminiscence that contribute to successful and unsuccessful aging, showing the scholarly use of their labels (Watt & Wong, 1991).

Kovach presented a model of reminiscence to guide researchers and clinicians and developed a coding tool in which quantitative content analysis procedures are used to code memories into two different typologies, validating or lamenting (Kovach, 1991c, 1993). With the construction of his Reminiscence Functions Scale (RFS), Webster (1993) also created typologies. The RFS was normed on a variety of age groups, and the typologies created by Webster were related to those of Wong and Watt (see last chapter). Over time, reviewers and researchers have encouraged scholars to use common labels and meanings so that we all begin to speak the same language. The use of the same labels would have made these studies a great deal more useful.

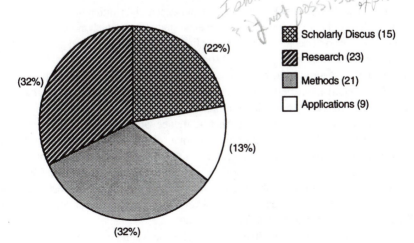

Figure 1   Types of articles on reminiscence published in 1990–1993.

In another use of reminiscence, Staudinger, Smith, and Baltes (1992) adapted the life review as a way to understand wisdom-related knowledge in women. They concluded that the wisdom-related perspective of analysis has great promise in enriching the study of life review, particularly when it is intertwined with personality development. Martin (1991) used the same approach to investigate life themes, experiences, and personality styles in older adults. Both Martin and Staudinger et al. demonstrated the richness of data in the life story that can be used by both researchers and clinicians to understand people and aging.

Coleman (1991) looked at the meaning of reminiscence in late life. He concluded that reminiscence is not an exclusive characteristic of old age, but rather a necessary tool to bring sense and order to one's life across the life span. In some ways, Merriam (1993a) agreed with Coleman when she challenged Butler's statement that life review was universal and reported no correlation between approaching death and life review as a universal process.

Burnside and Haight (1992) analyzed reminiscence and life review jointly in an effort to show the differences and similarities between the two concepts. They also wrote an article explaining the differences in the two concepts when used as nursing interventions (Haight & Burnside, 1993). Perhaps their efforts will help both practitioners and researchers to describe their methodologies more clearly and again contribute to a common language.

RESEARCH

Approximately 22 researchers examined the art and science of reminiscing in 1990–1993. Some reported reminiscing in groups and some with individuals; some explored their topic qualitatively and others, quantitatively. All contributed to an increased understanding.

Haight and Dias (1992) conducted reminiscence eight different ways and then tested each modality in a controlled experimental study to see which modality was most effective in lowering depression and raising life satisfaction, psychological well-being, and self-esteem. Their study was the only one that compared many types of reminiscing interventions to determine the best method for producing a therapeutic outcome.

Fry (1991a) identified those who reminisce often and pleasantly. Other researchers compared those who reminisced successfully with those who reminisced unsuccessfully and found that sentience and openness contributed to frequent and satisfactory reminiscing. Fishman (1992) established a significant relationship between high ego integrity and low death anxiety but was not able to find a relationship between life review and ego integrity. In contrast, Taft and Nehrke (1990) reported the absence of a relationship between ego integrity and of reminiscence other than life review; however, when the style of reminiscence was life review, there was a significant association.

Still others tried to establish a relationship between ego integrity and reminiscing and failed. Cook (1991) used group reminiscence as an intervention to increase ego integrity and found no significant increase. Neither did Bramlett and

Gueldner (1993). In the Bramlett and Gueldner study, there was an increase in power from pre-test to post-test, but there were no differences based on the reminiscing intervention. In a last look at ego development, Beaton (1991) found that ego development did not explain differences in reminiscing style.

Other researchers examined reminiscence as an intervention. Rybarczyk and Auerbach (1990) found that patients could use reminiscence successfully to cope with anxiety before surgery. Pietrukowicz and Johnson (1991) successfully used reminiscence to influence in a positive direction the attitudes of nurse aides caring for older people. Two other researchers, Youssef (1990) and Stevens-Ratchford (1993), used reminiscence successfully to lower depression and raise self-esteem in groups of older people. Finally, Haight (1992a) found that the therapeutic effects of a life review lasted for at least a year.

Two other researchers looked at outcomes in different ways. Botella and Feixas (1992–93) found the guided autobiography to be an adequate therapeutic tool to promote the reconstruction of experience in older adults. Sherman (1991) found that cherished objects influenced reminiscence and were also correlated with higher mood scores.

Qualitative research contributed to the understanding of the function and forms of reminiscence. David (1990) conducted a content analysis of life review tapes and suggested that researchers need to consider the social context when studying reminiscence as an adaptive factor. Kovach (1991a, 1991d) identified lamenting and validating as two major reminiscence themes. In the second manuscript on reminiscence behavior, using the same sample, she described two sources of variability contained in reminiscing: engagement, meaning involvement, and diversity, meaning the type of reminiscence. Kovach's contributions would have been more valuable as a complete piece if she had included all the information in one article.

Luborsky (1993) supported Fry's (1991a) findings when he found that non-depressed persons were more flexible than depressed persons in reporting their lives. Wallace (1992) refuted Butler's psychodevelopmental explanation of life review, arguing that reminiscence is more socially activated.

METHODS

There were numerous reports on methods, not experimentally tested, that authors created as ways to help clients use the past. Moore (1992) described the use of reminiscing in weekly sessions with groups. Phair and Elsey (1990) described settings such as schools where reminiscence can be successfully used. Lashley suggested the use of the nursing process for dealing with painful memories (Lashley, 1993) and described a case study using a religious perspective (Lashley, 1992). Magee (1991) suggested the use of metaphors in life review groups, and Lowenthal and Marrazzo (1990) described a method they called *milestoning* to cue and evoke positive memories. Perhaps at this stage research has shown the efficacy of reminiscing, and practitioners are exploring various uses of the modality.

In several case reports, Crose (1990) showed that gestalt techniques used with life review aided ego integration. Adams (1991) provided a lesson plan for nurses and specified activities through which one could examine one's personal life. Aranda (1990) described the life review as a way for professionals to access culture-related information.

Boggs and Leptak (1991) proposed other ways of evoking memories, such as drama. Molloy and Bramwell (1991), while warning us that life history is not beneficial to all people, offered ways to conduct the process.

Poetry is still another way to evoke the life review, as Edwards (1990) suggested. Forrest (1990) described reminiscence therapy in Scotland that in-volved the use of commercial tapes, slides, and flash cards, while Haight and Burnside (1992), offered specific directions for conducting either a life review or a reminiscence intervention.

McAllister (1990) described sources and products useful in eliciting reminis-cence, and McCloskey (1990) suggested that music could be used to evoke old memories, especially for those with cognitive impairment. Peachey (1992) created specific life review questions, and Waters (1990) described further techniques for using reminiscence in groups and suggested ways to maximize the positive impact of this intervention. Wolf (1990) suggested that examination of nontraditional lives would provide more information on aging.

APPLICATIONS

Not only were authors prolific in suggesting methods for conducting the reminis-cence process, but they also reported many successful reminiscence programs. Schindler (1992) spoke of the need to assist older people who have experienced trauma, such as the Holocaust, to recall the past. Before the victims died, they needed to assuage their guilt because they had survived and talk about the horror. Reminiscence was used by Hewett, Asamen, and Dietch (1991) to help people cope with daily living in a nursing home, by H. Ross (1990) to change caregivers' attitudes, by Newbern (1992) as a research tool, and by Wholihan (1992) with hospice patients. Woodhouse (1992) used reminiscence to help female substance abusers make the reality of their lives more visible. Galassie (1991) used the act of recall to understand gays and lesbians. Reminiscence was also found to be useful in helping women understand themselves (Giltinan, 1990) and as a method of family therapy (DeGenova, 1991). Thus the ways of reminiscing and their appli-cations are many and varied.

SUMMARY

Interest in the life story as a research tool, a therapeutic intervention, and a human phenomenon continues to grow. With continued work of the caliber of that reviewed herein, the methodology will be clear, the interventions defined, and the value of the life story appreciated.

Appendix: Reminiscence Included in Present Review

Article	Content
Scholarly Discussions	
Black, G., & Haight, B. (1992). Integrality as a holistic framework for the life-review process. *Holistic Nurse Practitioner, 7,* 7–15.	Used Erikson's developmental theory and Butler's life review theory in discussing life review as a developmental task and its use as an intervention by nurses. Presented a conflict reintegration model.
Burnside, I. (1990a). Reminiscence: An independent nursing intervention for the elderly. *Issues in Mental Health Nursing, 11,* 33–48.	Described the current use of reminiscence by nurses. Emphasized the need for interaction among reminiscence theory, research, and nursing practice.
Burnside, I., & Haight, B. (1992). Reminiscence and life review: Analyzing each concept. *Journal of Advanced Nursing, 17,* 855–862.	Analyzed the differences between the concepts of life review and reminiscence and provided directions for implementation of each concept by nurses in research and practice.
Coleman, P. (1991). Ageing and life history: The meaning of reminiscence in late life. *Sociological Review* (Monograph), *37,* 120–143.	Discussed whether there are, in later life, special psychological influences on the construction of life histories. Also examined the theoretical viewpoints of reminiscence functions, the characteristics and consequences of types of reminiscing, and the interaction of social history and individual development.
Haight, B. (1991). Reminiscing: The state of the art as a basis for practice. *International Journal of Aging and Human Development, 33,* 1–32.	Reviewed life review and reminiscing literature from 1960 to 1990. Made recommendations for research and practice.
Haight, B., & Burnside, I. (1993). Reminiscence and life review: Explaining the differences. *Archives of Psychiatric Nursing, 7,* 91–98.	Described the differences between life review and reminiscence. Compared goals, theoretical bases, nurse and client roles, processes, and outcomes.
Kovach, C. (1990). Promise and problems in reminiscence research. *Journal of Gerontological Nursing, 16,* 10–14.	Reviewed research literature on use of reminiscing with elderly people.

Appendix: Reminiscence Included in Present Review *(Continued)*

Article	Content
Kovach, C. (1991c). Reminiscence: Exploring the origins, processes, and consequences. *Nursing Forum, 26,* 14–20.	Reported reminiscence model to integrate current knowledge of reminiscence process and guide future research.
Kovach, C. (1993). Development and testing of the Autobiographical Memory Coding Tool. *Journal of Advanced Nursing, 18,* 669–674.	Reported the Autobiographical Memory Coding Tool, designed to measure quantitatively from qualitative material.
Lamme, S., & Baars, J. (1993). Including social factors in the analysis of reminiscence in elderly individuals. *International Journal of Aging and Human Development, 37,* 297–311.	Discussed use of reminiscence by elderly people. Suggested that a contextualist theory expanded to include sociological life course theory will contribute to the development of a framework for analysis of reminiscent behavior in elderly people.
Martin, P. (1991). Life patterns and age styles in older adults. *International Journal of Aging and Human Development, 32,* 289–302.	Used Thomae's cognitive theory of aging in an exploratory study of age fates and age styles. Demonstrated the three life patterns recognized in three case studies.
Staudinger, U., Smith, J., & Baltes, P. (1992). Wisdom-related knowledge in a life review task: Age differences and the role of professional specialization. *Psychology and Aging, 7,* 271–281.	Investigated differences in old and young professional women's knowledge of fundamental life pragmatics through a life review task. Recommended life review as a viable method of accessing life knowledge.
Webster, J. (1993). Construction and validation of the Reminiscence Functions Scale. *Journal of Gerontology, 48,* 256–262.	Developed a scale to measure reminiscence function. Used the scale with 710 volunteers and identified seven factors. Demonstrated the scale's reliability and validity.
Webster, J., & Cappeliez, P. (1993). Reminiscence and autobiographical memory: Complementary contexts for cognitive aging research. *Developmental Review, 13,* 54–91.	Reviewed research from clinical/reminiscence and experimental/autobiographical memory domains with a view to integration. Proposed new directions for cognitive aging research.

Appendix: Reminiscence Included in Present Review *(Continued)*

Article	Content
Watt, L., & Wong, P. (1990). A taxonomy of reminiscence and therapeutic implications. *Journal of Gerontological Social Work, 16,* 37–57.	Reported on the development of a taxonomy of reminiscence and described six major types of reminiscence: integrative, instrumental, transmissive, narrative, escapist, and obsessive. Discussed the therapeutic implications of using this taxonomy in reminiscence therapy with elderly people.

Research

Article	Content
Bacher, E., Kindler, S., Scheler, G., & Lerer, B. (1991). Reminiscing as a technique in the group psychotherapy of depression: A comparative study. *British Journal of Clinical Psychology, 30,* 375–377.	Investigated the efficacy of reminiscence in group psychotherapy with clinically depressed hospitalized patients. Patients rated visual analog depression scale, three subjectively rated visual analog scales by psychiatrist. Divided the sample into two groups. The control group received traditional group psychotherapy, while the experimental group received reminiscence group therapy. $N = 22$. Found a significant decrease of depression in the reminiscing group.
Beaton, S. (1991). Styles of reminiscence and ego development of older women residing in long-term care settings. *International Journal of Aging and Human Development, 32,* 53–63.	Investigated the relationship between the style of reminiscence an older person used when recounting his or her life story and the level of the person's ego development. Performed content analysis of taped interviews using Fallot's scoring system and independently scored Washington University Sentence Completion Test for Ego Development (WUSCTED). Taped one interview for completion of WUSCTED and then invited subject to tell life story. $N = 75$ women residing in long-term care facilities. Found some support that ego development accounts for differences in reminiscence styles. Found unclear results about level to which ego development explains style of reminiscence.
Botella, L., & Feixas, G. (1992–93). The autobiographical group: A tool for the reconstruction of past life experience with the aged. *International Journal of Aging and Human Development, 36,* 303–319.	Examined the Guided Autobiography Group (GAG) as a therapeutic tool for preventive psychological intervention with elderly people. Performed pre- and post-test repertory grid analysis. Analyzed autobiographical texts using Feixas's method. Conducted 12 weekly 90-min guided autobiographical group sessions. $N = 18$: 8 = experimental, 10 = control (elderly volunteers at a recreational society).

Appendix: Reminiscence Included in Present Review *(Continued)*

Article	Content
	Found that participation in the GAG produced a significant, positive change in construing processes.
Bramlett, M., & Gueldner, S. (1993). Reminiscence: A viable option to enhance power in elders. *Clinical Nurse Specialist, 7,* 68–74.	Investigated the usefulness of reminiscent storytelling as a therapeutic modality to enhance the sense of power in well elderly.
	Administered Power as Knowing Participation in Change Scale, Version II, as pre-test and post-tests 1 and 2.
	Conducted three 1-hr audiotaped group reminiscence sessions for experimental subjects; control subjects were tested without intervention.
	N = 81 independently living, well elderly people.
	Found no significant differences between experimental and control groups at pre-test and post-test 1, or post-test 2.
Cook, E. (1991). The effects of reminiscence on psychological measures of ego integrity in elderly nursing home residents. *Archives of Psychiatric Nursing, 5,* 292–298.	Investigated the efficacy of a reminiscence group in increasing ego integrity in elderly nursing home residents.
	Administered the LSI-A, GDS, and RSE scales as pre- and post-tests to experimental and control groups.
	Conducted 16 weekly 1-hr group reminiscence sessions for two experimental groups and the same number of sessions for a control group that focused only on current topics; another control group was only pre- and post-tested. N = 56 nursing home residents.
	Found no significant differences for increased ego integrity for the experimental groups, although a trend was seen in the direction of the hypothesis.
David, D. (1990). Reminiscence, adaptation, and social context in old age. *International Journal of Aging and Human Development, 30,* 175–188.	Explored the interaction among social factors, reminiscence, and adaptation in old age.
	Performed content analysis of taped interviews and administered a self-rated scale.
	N = 43 residents of retirement communities.
	Found that high peer contact was associated with adaptive memories, but the direction of the link between peer contact and memory was reversed between the sexes.
Fishman, S. (1992). Relationships among an older adult's life review, ego integrity, and death anxiety. *International Psychogeriatrics, 4,* 267–277.	Explored the relationship among life review, ego integrity, and death anxiety in older adults.
	Mailed or administered the Life Review Questionnaire; Adult Ego Development Scale; Death Anxiety Scale, including the Death Preparation Scale.
	N = 115 (65% return rate).

Appendix: Reminiscence Included in Present Review *(Continued)*

Article	Content
	Found no positive relationship between life review and ego integrity and only partial support for a negative relationship between life review and death anxiety; however, there was a significant relationship between a high level of ego integrity and a lowered death anxiety level.
Fry, P. (1991). Individual differences in reminiscence among older adults: Predictors of frequency and pleasantness ratings of reminiscence activity. *International Journal of Aging and Human Development, 33,* 311–326.	Examined the psychosocial correlates of frequency and pleasantness ratings of reminiscence in a sample of elderly people.
	Administered the Reminiscence Questionnaire, the Life Attitude Profile, Bradburn's Affect Balance Scale, the Personality Research Form, the ES scale of the Minnesota Multiphasic Personality Inventory, the Geriatric Depression Scale, the Life Experience Survey, a measure of activities of daily living, a social support measure, and the Cornell Medical Health Index.
	$N = 70$ community residents in semisheltered housing.
	Found that community or nursing home living did not contribute to the wide variation in self-reported reminiscing; frequency of reminiscence and pleasantness of reminiscence were not significantly correlated.
Haight, B. (1992). Long-term effects of a structured life review process. *Journal of Gerontology: Psychological Sciences, 47,* 312–315.	Examined the long-term effects of life review on the psychological well-being of homebound elderly people.
	Administered the Life Satisfaction Index—A, Bradburn's Affect Balance Scale, Zung's Depression Scale, and the Activities of Daily Living Scale.
	Revisited subjects 1 year after intervention with individual structured evaluative life review to administer the scales.
	$N = 35$.
	Found no significant change in any variable after 1 year but found some small trends for lasting effects of some outcome measures.
Haight, B., & Dias, J. (1992). Examining key variables in selected reminiscing modalities. *International Psychogeriatrics, 4* (Suppl. 2), 279–290.	Examined the variables underlying selected reminiscing processes to determine those that contributed to well-being.
	Administered the Life Satisfaction Index—A, Bradburn's Affect Balance Scale, Rosenberg Self-Esteem Scale, and the Beck Depression Inventory.

Appendix: Reminiscence Included in Present Review *(Continued)*

Article	Content
	Randomly assigned subjects living independently, in retirement settings, and in nursing homes to one of five reminiscence modalities in a group or individual situation. Each modality consisted of six weekly 1-hr sessions.
	$N = 240$.
	Found that individuality, structure, and evaluation contributed to the therapeutic effectiveness of life review.
Kovach, C. (1991a). Content analysis of reminiscences of elderly women. *Research in Nursing & Health, 14,* 287–295.	Examined how reminiscers interpret past experience to obtain a clearer concept of reminiscence.
	Performed content analysis using idea unit as unit of analysis.
	Conducted 30-min taped semistructured interviews.
	$N = 21$ elderly women in a day-care center.
	Grouped the themes revealed by the analysis into two main categories: validating and lamenting.
Kovach, C. (1991d). Reminiscence behavior: An empirical exploration. *Journal of Gerontological Nursing, 17,* 23–28.	Examined attributes and variations in reminiscing behavior.
	Performed content analysis of transcribed interviews to discover patterns and variations in reminiscing behavior.
	Conducted 30-min taped semistructured interviews.
	$N = 21$ elderly women in a day-care center.
	Found two sources of variability in reminiscing behavior: engagement and diversity.
Kovach, C. (1991b). Reminiscence: A closer look at content. *Issues in Mental Health Nursing, 12,* 193–204.	Gave the subject more control over the content of reminiscing in order to learn more about the concept of reminiscence.
	Performed content analysis of transcribed interviews divided into idea units.
	Conducted 30-min taped semistructured interviews.
	$N = 21$ elderly women in a day-care center.
	Found that subjects reminisced most about what they had done in their lives and frequently about relationships and people in their lives; they reminisced infrequently about possessions.
Luborsky, M. (1993). The romance with personal meaning in gerontology: Cultural aspects of life themes. *The Gerontologist, 33,* 445–452.	Examined the validity of the assumption that life story telling is beneficial as well as the basic traits of the life story itself.
	Performed content analysis of transcripts using a case comparison method to assess the main orienting image and the temporal sequence of topics.
	Conducted interviews using a standardized method developed to elicit life history through the use of a pair of contrasting images to structure the story.

Appendix: Reminiscence Included in Present Review *(Continued)*

Article	Content
	N = 16 elderly people, evenly divided between depressed and nondepressed, at an urban geriatric center.
	Found statistical differences (*p* = .0069, Fisher Exact Probability Test) between depressed and nondepressed in organizing image and topic sequence; also found differences in complexity.
Merriam, S. (1993). Butler's life review: How universal is it? *International Journal of Aging and Human Development, 37,* 163–175.	Examined commonly held assumptions about life review.
	Administered a life review questionnaire in a battery of tests.
	N = 289 elderly.
	Found that life review was not precipitated by the approach of the end of life and was not a universal process.
Pietrukowicz, M., & Johnson, M. (1991). Using life histories to individualize nursing home staff attitudes toward residents. *The Gerontologist, 31,* 102–106.	Examined whether a positive summary of a resident's life history on the chart would counter staff's stereotypic attitudes and result in more personalized staff–resident interactions.
	Administered the Aging Semantic Differential Adjective Checklist pre- and post-test.
	Randomly assigned staff of two nursing homes to control group or group who read anonymous resident's chart with or without life history.
	N = 43.
	Found that the life history caused aides to perceive residents in a more positive manner.
Rybarczyk, B., & Auerbach, S. (1990). Reminiscence interviews as stress management interventions for older patients undergoing surgery. *The Gerontologist, 30,* 522–528.	Evaluated the efficacy of reminiscence interviews for stress management prior to major surgery and assessed the effectiveness of older compared with younger interviewers.
	Administered the State–Trait Anxiety Inventory, the Coping Self-Efficacy Inventory, and physiological and postoperative adjustment measures.
	Conducted 45- to 60-min individual interview that followed one of four protocols.
	N = 104 male patients scheduled for surgery within 24 hr.
	Found that reminiscence interviews were effective presurgical interventions compared with nonreminiscence placebos and routine hospital procedures; peer interviewers were overall more effective than younger interviewers.

Appendix: Reminiscence Included in Present Review *(Continued)*

Article	Content
Sherman, E. (1991). Reminiscentia: Cherished objects as memorabilia in late-life reminiscence. *International Journal of Aging and Human Development, 33,* 89–100.	Systematically examined (a) the connection between reminiscence and objects, (b) what objects stirred recollection, and (c) whether the objects were cherished. Administered Affect-Balance Scale and classified objects according to Csikszentmihalyi and Rochberg-Halton categories. Administered a 6-page questionnaire to volunteers at four senior centers and then provided a brief clarification interview. $N = 100$ elderly people. Found significant differences between men and women on a number of objects and reminiscence variables and a significant positive relationship between pleasant reminiscing and mood score; varied results were found for effects and types of objects.
Stevens-Ratchford, R. (1993). The effect of life review reminiscence activities on depression and self-esteem in older adults. *American Journal of Occupational Therapy, 47,* 413–420.	Investigated the effects of life review reminiscence activities on reported depression and self-esteem. Administered Rosenberg Self-Esteem Survey and the Beck Depression Inventory. Randomly assigned male and female subjects to either a control group who received only pre- and post-testing or a group who received a structured, six-session (3 weeks) life review reminiscence activities intervention with slides, presentations, music, writing, and discussion. $N = 24$ elderly living independently in a retirement community. Found no significant difference between the two groups for depression or self-esteem.
Taft, L., & Nehrke, M. (1990). Reminiscence, life review, and ego integrity in nursing home residents. *International Journal of Aging and Human Development, 30,* 189–196.	Explored the relationship between intra- and interpersonal frequency of reminiscence and uses of three dimensions of reminiscence described by Romaniuk. Administered a reminiscence questionnaire and an ego integrity scale; subjects responded to questions as asked by interviewer. $N = 30$ well nursing home residents. Found no significant relationship between frequency of reminiscence and ego integrity, but found significant correlations between the life review dimensions of reminiscence and ego integrity and between age and ego integrity.

Appendix: Reminiscence Included in Present Review *(Continued)*

Article	Content
Wallace, J. (1992). Reconsidering the life review: The social construction of talk about the past. *The Gerontologist, 32,* 120–125.	Investigated how respondents constructed and communicated life stories.
	Performed secondary analysis of content of taped interviews focusing on process of story production.
	Performed secondary analysis of 30-min to 3-hr unstructured interviews with near-centenarians who had been invited to tell how they accounted for their longevity.
	N = 30.
	Found that stories were told by elderly to specific audiences for specific reasons, not as an automatic storytelling or life review process.
Wong, P., & Watt, L. (1991). What types of reminiscence are associated with successful aging? *Psychology and Aging, 6,* 272–279.	Examined the validity of a reminiscence taxonomy and whether certain adaptive types of reminiscence are associated with successful aging.
	Administered scales measuring mental status, health status, and adjustment status.
	Performed content analysis of transcribed interviews using the paragraph as the basic coding unit.
	Conducted individual interviews using critical-incident approach for reminiscence.
	N = 71 elderly living in the community and institutions.
	Found that successful agers demonstrated more integrative and instrumental reminiscence and less obsessive reminiscence than did unsuccessful agers.
Youssef, F. (1990). The impact of group reminiscence counseling on a depressed elderly population. *Nurse Practitioner, 15,* 32–38.	Assessed the effects of group reminiscence on the levels of depression in elderly women in nursing homes.
	Administered the Beck Depression Inventory.
	Randomly assigned subjects to one control group or one of two intervention groups who received six unstructured, closed reminiscence group sessions.
	N = 60.
	Found no significant differences between the groups, but did find relatively large absolute changes in the two experimental groups.

Methods

Article	Content
Adams, J. (1991). Professional development module P2: Human biography—a personal approach. *Nursing Times, 87* (25), i–viii.	Created a lesson plan for an open learning course for nurses. Nurses used self life review to develop better professional understanding of patients' individuality.

Appendix: Reminiscence Included in Present Review *(Continued)*

Article	Content
Aranda, M. (1990). Culture friendly services for Latino elders. *Generations, 14,* 55–57.	Offered bilingual and bicultural mental health services to outpatients in a predominantly Latino neighborhood; services included a type of genealogical life review that nurtured family knowledge and understanding.
Boggs, D., & Leptak, J. (1991). Life review among senior citizens as a product of drama. *Educational Gerontology, 17,* 239–246.	Conducted an exploratory study to examine substance of life review and use of drama as a vehicle to facilitate life review. Performed content analysis of taped interviews after 13 volunteers attended a play related to senior citizens issues. Most denied reminiscing, but most also engaged in active reflection on their lives during the interview.
Burnside, I. (1993). Themes in reminiscence groups with older women. *International Journal of Aging and Human Development, 37,* 177–189.	Reviewed articles on the use of themes in reminiscence groups and reported data from one of three studies in which specific themes were used for older women.
Crose, R. (1990). Reviewing the past in the here and now: Using gestalt therapy techniques with life review. *Journal of Mental Health Counseling, 12,* 279–287.	Presented case reports on use of gestalt therapy in conjunction with life review for older adults. Older clients responded similarly to other clients.
Edwards, M. (1990). Poetry: Vehicle for retrospection and delight. *Generations, 14,* 61–62.	Reported use of poetry in a group setting in a convalescent center to evoke feelings that led to reminiscence.
Forrest, M. (1990). Reminiscence therapy in a Scottish hospital. *Health Libraries Review, 7,* 69–72.	Reported on open reminiscence groups led by a librarian in a hospital who used commercial tapes, slides, and flashcards to promote recall followed by reminiscing. Nine weekly 90- to 120-min sessions were conducted separately with male and female patients. Program was subjectively evaluated to be highly beneficial to patients.
Gropper, E. (1991). Reminiscence therapy as a nursing intervention. *Advancing Clinical Care, 6,* 26, 41.	Presented two case studies in which reminiscence was used as an emotionally supportive intervention with individuals who experienced trauma.
Haight, B., & Burnside, I. (1992). Clinical outlook: Reminiscence and life review: Conducting the processes. *Journal of Gerontological Nursing, 18,* 39–42.	Differentiated between processes of reminiscence and life review. Presented effective ways to conduct each modality to assist gerontological nurses who use these interventions.

Appendix: Reminiscence Included in Present Review *(Continued)*

Article	Content
Lashley, M. (1992). Reminiscence: A biblical basis for telling our stories. *Journal of Christian Nursing, 9,* 4–8.	Presented a case study in which personal storytelling was encouraged to help an elderly nursing home resident realize her worth.
Lashley, M. (1993). The painful side of reminiscence. *Geriatric Nursing, 14,* 138–141.	Described the nursing process used to deal with painful memories evoked during life review/reminiscence intervention.
Lowenthal, R., & Marrazzo, R. (1990). Milestoning: Evoking memories for resocialization through group reminiscence. *The Gerontologist, 30,* 269–272.	Conducted weekly reminiscence-milestoning sessions in a psychiatric center rehabilitation unit with groups of 5–9 with one facilitator or 10–16 with cofacilitators. Sensory stimulators, cueing, and modeling were used to evoke positive reminiscences. Groups were held over period of 9 years. No controlled testing was done, but subjective evaluation was positive.
Magee, J. (1991). Using metaphors in life review groups to empower shame-driven older adults. *Activities, Adaptation, and Aging, 16,* 19–30.	Described use of life review groups to help older adults in different settings transcend their poor self-esteem.
McAllister, C. (1990). Materials for reminiscence. *Health Libraries Review, 7,* 120–122.	Commented on the value of reminiscence and types of products or sources to enhance effectiveness of reminiscence groups.
McCloskey, L. (1990). The silent heart sings. *Generations, 14,* 63–65.	Discussed results of a program combining music with reminiscence and life review that was used with individuals and groups with cognitive impairment or terminal illness.
Molloy, G., & Bramwell, L. (1991). The life history process: Is it useful? *Perspectives, 15,* 12–15.	Studied the usefulness of encouraging older institutionalized adults to tape record their life history using memory aides and photographs with or without interviewers. Overall, participants' comments were positive, but some comments indicated that the life history process is not beneficial for all elderly people.
Moore, B. (1992). Reminiscing therapy: A CNS intervention. *Clinical Nurse Specialist, 6,* 170–173.	Reported on a reminiscing group in a retirement village initiated as a requirement of a clinical nurse specialist course. Positive written evaluations by group caused retirement home to engage facilitator to continue group.
Peachey, N. (1992). Helping the elderly person resolve integrity versus despair. *Perspectives in Psychiatric Care, 28,* 29–30.	Described how nurses can use life review to help elderly clients focus on positive aspects of their life experiences.

Appendix: Reminiscence Included in Present Review *(Continued)*

Article	Content
Phair, L., & Elsey, I. (1990). Sharing memories. *Nursing Times, 86,* 50–52.	Reported on settings amenable to reminiscing.
Waters, E. (1990). The life review: Strategies for working with individuals and groups. *Journal of Mental Health Counseling, 12,* 270–278.	Reported on techniques of conducting life review with individuals, groups, and families that may maximize the positive impact of the life experience.
Wolf, M. (1990). The call to vocation: Life histories of elderly religious women. *International Journal of Aging and Human Development, 31,* 197–203.	Reported three life histories from a larger study to illustrate personal choices throughout the life span of elderly Catholic nuns.

Applications

Article	Content
DeGenova, M. (1991). Elderly life review therapy: A Bowen approach. *American Journal of Family Therapy, 19,* 160–166.	Presented a case study of use of Butler's life review theory and Bowen's family systems theory to assist an elderly woman understand her present situation and come to terms with unresolved conflicts of the past.
Galassie, F. (1991). A life-review workshop for gay and lesbian elders. *Journal of Gerontological Social Work, 16,* 75–86.	Described a workshop designed to help gay and lesbian people in their sixth and seventh decades assess and integrate their homosexual histories into their whole life stories.
Giltinan, J. (1990). Using life review to facilitate self-actualization in elderly women. *Gerontology & Geriatrics Education, 10,* 75–83.	Described the use of life review discussions with a group of independently living elderly women at a senior citizens center to facilitate continued growth and expansion of participants' inner lives.
Hewett, L., Asamen, J., & Dietch, J. (1991). Group reminiscence with nursing home residents. *Clinical Gerontologist, 10,* 69–72.	Reported on the effectiveness of group reminiscence with a nursing home population. Found mixed results: Reminiscence had positive use for resolution of daily living issues but appeared to be demoralizing for those elderly who had had little opportunity to change their lives.
Newbern, V. (1992). Sharing the memories: The value of reminiscence as a research tool. *Journal of Gerontological Nursing, 18,* 13–18.	Presented findings on the value of reminiscence for personal growth from a larger study of health self-care practices used by women in the South, 1900–1945. Presented three case examples and discussed implications for the use of reminiscence in nursing practice.

Appendix: Reminiscence Included in Present Review *(Continued)*

Article	Content
Ross, H. (1990). Lesson of life. *Geriatric Nursing, 11,* 274–275.	Described the effects of a state geriatric training program designed to help nurses, social workers, and mental health aides examine the influence of life review on their attitudes toward elderly people. Found positive changes in workers' attitudes and sensitivity toward older people.
Schindler, R. (1992). Silences: Helping elderly Holocaust victims deal with the past. *International Journal of Aging and Human Development, 35,* 243–252.	Reported on use of assisted reminiscence to help elderly people who had an urgent need to share a difficult past experience with children and grandchildren. For this group, it was the Holocaust.
Wholihan, D. (1992). The value of reminiscence in hospice care. *American Journal of Hospice and Palliative Care, 9,* 33–35.	Reviewed use of reminiscence therapy with hospice patients and proposed guidelines for its use to affirm these persons' self-worth and sense of uniqueness and help them face death more peacefully.
Woodhouse, L. (1992). Women with jagged edges: Voices from a culture of substance abuse. *Qualitative Heath Research, 2,* 262–281.	Described an exploratory study in which life history was used to help women who were substance abusers make the reality of their lives more visible. Positive effects were expressed by the women, and the meanings the women ascribed to the experiences of their lives were illuminated.

Chapter 2

The Processes of Adaptive Reminiscence

Paul T. P. Wong

The past affects us more than we generally realize. Our perceptions are colored by past experiences. Even our values, life-styles, and the choices we make spring from our unique past history. Whether we are resilient or vulnerable to stress, whether we are resourceful or inadequate in coping, often has its roots in early childhood experiences.

Whereas the causal role of early experience in personality development is widely recognized, there is little agreement as to how the present is shaped by the past. Diverse theoretical formulations tend to emphasize different underlying mechanisms. Learning theorists focus almost exclusively on environmental impact and conditioning. Psychoanalysts pay special attention to early childhood experience and unconscious motives. Recent research on reminiscence, life review, and autobiographical memory has revealed the importance of conscious, cognitive mechanisms.

Our past can be both a burden and a resource. The emotional baggage and the scars we carry can sap our energy and reduce our sense of well-being. Defective self-concepts and irrational beliefs based on faulty negative memories can further hinder us from effective functioning. But the vast reservoir of memories can also serve as a storehouse of wisdom, meaning, and solace. This chapter is concerned mainly with the adaptive aspects of reminiscence.

Different from other types of memory, reminiscence serves our psychosocial rather than informational needs. Butler (1963) revolutionized our view of reminiscence by proposing that memory can be a source of mastery, wisdom, and gratification in old age. Therefore, remembering the past not only empowers individuals for the present, but also prepares them for the future. Butler's life review interpretation of reminiscence opened up a whole new field of research (see Foreword).

However, research on the adaptive benefits of reminiscence has not always yielded consistent results. One way to reconcile the seemingly contradictory findings is to recognize that reminiscence is multidimensional and that only certain types of reminiscence are adaptive. With Watt, I recently identified six types of reminiscence—integrative, instrumental, transmissive, narrative, escapist, and obsessive—and reported that only the first two types are associated with successful aging (Wong & Watt, 1991).

The response to our paper has been most gratifying. Numerous graduate students from North America and Europe have inquired about the procedure of coding and classifying reminiscence. Therapists have inquired how they may apply such a classification to help their clients to live fully in spite of the burden and traumas of the past. In this chapter, I address these queries, but the main thrust is on the adaptive processes of integrative and instrumental reminiscence.

TAXONOMY OF REMINISCENCE

Integrative Reminiscence

The main ingredients of integrative reminiscences are acceptance of self and others, conflict resolution and reconciliation, a sense of meaning and self-worth, and the integration of the present and past. The following are examples of integrative reminiscence:

Accepting one's past as significant and worthwhile: "I have had a wonderful life"; "I'm satisfied with the way my life has turned out."
Accepting negative past experiences and integrating them with the present: "When I was young, my father deserted the family. We were very poor, but we stuck together and loved each other as a family. I believe that this hardship in my childhood has made me a better person."
Reconciling reality with ideal: "I always wanted to be a writer, but I discovered that I just don't have the talent, so I became an editor."
Reconciling past conflicts and accepting those who have hurt one in the past: "When I was a teenager my parents broke up, and both remarried. I was very resentful because they did not seem to care about my feelings or needs. But as I grow older and look back I understand that they were really not compatible with

each other. They had suffered for many years before their divorce. Now I'm on good terms with both sets of parents."

Recalling experiences and lessons that have contributed to the development of personal values and meaning: "My father was a medical missionary. He was a godly man and provided a good role model for all his children. I'm grateful for the important values that I learned from him and have kept through all my life."

Achieving a sense of coherence in the past and the present: "I have experienced many difficulties and much suffering. It is my faith in God that has carried me through and given me a sense of meaning. I was brought up in a large family. My parents were devout Christians. They really lived out their faith. I think that they are really part of my life and my children's lives."

Instrumental Reminiscence

Instrumental reminiscence can be defined by three kinds of statements:

Remembering past plans and goal-directed activities: "Ever since I was a child, I always dreamed about becoming a nurse. I had to work several years to save up money and I had to talk to my parents on many occasions until they finally agreed to let me leave home and move to the city to study nursing. But I'll tell you, it was worth it."

Drawing from past experience to solve present problems: "During the Great Depression, life was very hard. There were very few jobs and money was difficult to come by. But we learned to survive by budgeting and making do without many things. The lessons I learned in those years have really helped me in trying to live on my old age pension."

Recalling how one coped with past difficulties: "I think the worst experience was the day I found out I had tuberculosis. The doctors wanted to take out the lung. They said it was the only hope I had but I refused. I was damned if those germs were going to get me, so I practiced a positive mental attitude. Two years later I had recuperated. I think what helped my progress most was my state of mind."

Transmissive Reminiscence

Transmissive reminiscence is similar to storytelling and oral history. It is the recounting of past events with the purpose of instructing or entertaining the listener. It can be inferred from references to the practices of a bygone era and statements about the lessons one has learned from one's past experiences:

Sharing traditional values and cultural heritage: "We were always taught to respect our elders. So when my parents were alive, I always gave them lots of money to spend, I took good care of them and they stayed with us until they died. I have taught my own children the same way and I hope they will look after us during our last years."

Sharing personal wisdom or lessons learned in one's past: "For most of my adult life, I was a drunk. I lost my job, I lost all my friends, and worst of all I abandoned my wife and children. Finally, I woke up in the hospital without remembering how I got there. That day I knew I had to change or I would be dead. Through the help of AA I was able to break free from alcohol and I haven't touched a drink in 20 years. That's why whenever I have the opportunity I tell young people about the dangers of drinking."

Both kinds of transmissive reminiscence presuppose an audience. In most cases, the listener is a younger person who may benefit from such knowledge. A common example would be grandparents' teaching their grandchildren moral lessons through stories from their family's history or personal experience.

Escapist Reminiscence

Escapist reminiscence is also referred to as defensive reminiscence. Whenever one seeks comfort from people and events that inhabit one's memory landscapes, one is engaged in escapist reminiscence. It is evident in statements that glorify the past and deprecate the present.

Boasting exaggeratedly about past achievements: "You wouldn't believe how tough we were in the war when you look at me now. Let me tell you about the day when we were flying over enemy territory when all of a sudden we were overwhelmed by a squadron of German planes. We killed a bunch of them, but eventually the Germans got all my buddies and I was the only one left. My plane was riddled with bullets, I was shot twice in the leg, and I was completely outnumbered. I thought about bailing out, but then I remembered why I was there—to defend democracy and the freedom of those counting on us at home. So I stayed, and I fought, and I killed all those Germans. Never was there such a fight. It's guys like me that have given you the type of life you lead today."

This is not an example of transmissive reminiscence because of the illusion of self-importance exemplified by the last two sentences. The fact that this heroic act was frequently referred to with relish throughout the interview confirmed that this veteran indulged in escapist reminiscence.

Exaggerating the pleasant aspects of the past and desiring to return to "the good old days": "My husband and I had some really great times together. We had so much fun going on camping trips, fishing. . . . My memories of the many cities we have visited are as vivid as if I was there right now. The sights, sounds and smells are so beautiful and fill me with longing to have those times back. Life is so very bland and lackluster now—my memories are what keeps me going."

There is a strong tendency to recall selectively pleasant aspects of the past and overlook negative events. Dwelling on the good old days allows a person to escape from present realities. Such flight to the past is similar to daydreaming or

fantasizing about the future. It can be psychologically beneficial because it provides a source of happiness and a buffer against present stress. When the present
is painful and the future looks bleak, the past becomes the only source of solace.
Furthermore, memories of self as someone who was loved and valued enable one
to maintain a positive self-concept when everything conspires to destroy one's
self-esteem. But escapist reminiscence has its drawbacks when it is carried to the
extent of interfering with present functioning.

Obsessive Reminiscence

Obsessive reminiscence is characterized by persistent rumination on unpleasant
past events. It is often accompanied by feelings of guilt, shame, resentment, or
despair. Another characteristic of an obsessive reminiscence is that it tends to be
repeated like a broken record. It reflects a failure to integrate problematic past
experiences with the more positive aspects of life.

Confessing guilt, bitterness, or disappointment: "My husband died when I
was away for two days visiting my friends in the West. He fell in the bathtub and
eventually died because there was no one there to help him. It has been years now
but I still cannot forgive myself for leaving him home alone for two days. This
terrible thing would never have happened had I stayed with him."

Obsessive reminiscence causes inner pain, which serves as a warning that all
is not well within one's psychic system. The cause is typically some past trauma
or unresolved conflict. Obsessive reminiscence is an inner cry for healing.

While this type of reminiscence is generally associated with poor mental
health, it can also be adaptive for two reasons. First, it calls attention to the
unfinished business and provides the motivation for healing. Second, it may
reflect an intense inner struggle that is necessary for recovery. Integration is
generally preceded by the working through of obsessive memories.

Narrative Reminiscence

Narrative reminiscence is more descriptive than interpretative or evaluative. It
consists of either bare-thread statements of autobiographical facts or the recounting of past episodes with embellishment.

Providing a simple autobiographical sketch: "I was born in Aberdeen,
Scotland in 1920. I got married right after the Second World War to my sweetheart
from school. We moved to Canada in the early 1950s, and my first job in Canada
was working as a technician at CGE in Peterborough."
**Providing anecdotes from the past in the absence of psychological evalua-
tions present in the other categories of reminiscence:** "Every winter my dad
used to flood the side lawn and we would have a skating carnival. We were all

dressed up in different costumes, and dad was always a clown. And dad would take all the little girls for a skate. Then we'd come in and have cocoa and sandwiches."

This is not a case of transmissive reminiscence because it is neither a general description of a bygone era nor a moral lesson.

Guidelines for Coding Reminiscence

A three-stage procedure may be used to code reminiscences.

Stage 1   First, the reminiscence data are divided into paragraphs, which serve as the units of analysis.

If data are based on diaries or autobiographies, paragraphs already exist. In the case of tape-recorded and transcribed oral reminiscence, paragraphs can be identified using simple rules of English style. Each paragraph must have at least one complete sentence and a self-contained idea. Typically, a paragraph begins with a topic sentence, which is elaborated in one or more sentences, and ends with a summary of the main point.

Whenever the interviewer asks a question that introduces a new topic, it usually marks the beginning of a new paragraph. It is also helpful to pay attention to the flow and pauses of the interviewee's speech while coding paragraphs.

The main purpose of using the paragraph as the unit of content analysis is that each paragraph conveys a complete thought. It does not make a great deal of difference in the coding process whether the reminiscence is divided into two or three large paragraphs or five or six smaller paragraphs, as long as each paragraph is classified correctly.

Stage 2   In the second stage, each unit is assessed for the presence of one of the six types of reminiscence. In classifying reminiscence, the therapist should focus not on isolated sentences, but on the main idea in each paragraph. For example, in the case of a woman wrestling with the meaning of the untimely death of her husband, the entire process of grieving and eventual acceptance would constitute an integrative reminiscence, not just the single statement indicating acceptance.

Another important consideration is the overall pattern of reminiscence. In the case of obsessive reminiscence, it is the repetitive nature of certain negative sentiments that reveals an obsession with past troubles. Similarly, it is the disproportional and recurrent remembrance of the good old days that identifies a reminiscence as escapist. Thus, the classifying of each unit should be done in the context of the entire reminiscence transcript, which helps clarify the meaning of each paragraph.

Stage 3   In the third stage, each subject is given a score for each of the six types of reminiscence. These scores represent the total number of words devoted to each type of reminiscence. This quantitative measure enables the researcher to investigate the relationships between different types of reminiscence and other psychological variables. In addition, therapists may use this measure to assess the progress of reminiscence therapy by monitoring the increased use of adaptive types of reminiscence and decreased use of maladaptive types.

ADAPTIVE PROCESSES OF REMINISCENCE

It is beyond the scope of this chapter to discuss all the adaptive functions of reminiscence and their underlying mechanisms. Lieberman and Tobin (1983) identified three functions of reminiscence: (a) To maintain the self-concept in the midst of change and decline, through mythmaking; (b) to serve as a resource of consolation and gratification; and (c) to resolve past conflict and achieve meaning for the remaining years. My own analysis focuses on the particular adaptive functions of integrative and instrumental reminiscence.

Functions of Integrative Reminiscence

One of the most important functions of reminiscence is to help the individual achieve ego integrity. According to Erikson (1959, 1963, 1982), ego integrity is the cumulative product of having successfully resolved the earlier stages of development. It is "reaping of the benefits of a life richly spent, not only in the storehouse of memories, but in the fruition of problems worked through, plans executed, mediation undertaken, suffering survived" (Ulanov, 1981, p. 113).

The attainment of ego integrity is a lifelong process, according to Erikson. It depends on successful management of developmental conflicts, acceptance of one's life cycle without regrets, and harmonization of different stages of life without fear of death. The hallmark of ego integrity is wisdom.

Butler's (1975) view of ego integrity is less ambitious:

> It is a quality of "serenity" and "wisdom" derived from resolving personal conflicts, reviewing one's life and finding it acceptable and gratifying, and viewing death with equanimity. One's life does not have to have been a "success" in the popular sense of that word in order to be gratifying. People take pride in a feeling of having done their best, of having met challenge and difficulty and sometimes from simply having survived against terrible odds. (p. 417)

The life review, according to Butler, is the primary mechanism whereby ego integrity is achieved.

Ego integrity may be conceptualized as the development of positive but realistic self-schemas. In the struggle for survival, we need a self-concept that has stood the test of time and enables us to cope with the demands of the present and the uncertainties of the future.

Ego integrity involves the integration of various self-schemas in such a way that we have a clear sense of coherence and identity. This cannot be achieved by mythmaking and denying the negative aspects of our past. Nor can it be attained by reclaiming the innocence of childhood. Ego integrity requires a longitudinal perspective and honest examinations of one's entire life history.

I agree with Butler that the mechanism responsible for ego integrity is the life review. It is a long and arduous process, which involves confronting, making sense of, and working through painful past experiences. It is also a dynamic process, because it requires revisions of self-schemas so that we can incorporate both the negative and positive aspects of the past into a self-concept that approximates the kind of person we want to be.

Wisdom is the crowning achievement of the search for ego integrity. Wisdom is demonstrated in learning to accept the self with all its defects and failures. Wisdom is also manifested in having a sense of meaning, purpose, and coherence in the midst of adversities and relentless change.

One of the major sources of confusion in the reminiscence literature is the failure to clarify the concept of life review. Although there is some consensus that life review is evaluative, the distinction between active life review and the actualization of life review has not been recognized.

Strictly speaking, life review is an active, ongoing process. Life review is said to be actualized when one has resolved most of the past conflicts and has more or less achieved integrity and all that remains to be done is an occasional fine-tuning. Once the major work of life review has been successfully completed, it will be manifested in integrative reminiscence.

Whenever the literature mentions life review, it typically means active life review. For example, Molinari and Reichlin (1984–85) observed, that

> In contrast to simple storytelling, life review reminiscence is personal and intense, representing an active grappling with the past in order to come to terms with it. Conflict is a natural part of life review, reflecting as it does a set of contents and an internal process that is evoked through the recollection of experiences that remain unresolved. (p. 82)

In a similar vein, Horacek (1977) emphasized the problem-solving aspect of life review: "Life review offers an opportunity to understand and accept personal weaknesses and past misdeeds and to take responsibility for our actions. There is the chance to resolve longstanding conflicts, to restore relationships with a spouse, children, relatives, and friends" (p. 104).

What these writers have in mind is clearly the problem-solving process of active life review. When individuals are still in the throes of working through unresolved conflicts, a high level of reminiscence is to be expected.

Active life review tends to be triggered by major transitions or personal crises. Although active life review is adaptive, in the short run it can be painful and may have an adverse impact on one's well-being and life satisfaction.

Although conflict resolution has been the main focus of the life review literature, the search for self-worth and self-identity may be equally important. A conflict-free life can be boring and meaningless. Similarly, a past devoid of problems may also be shallow and empty. Resolution of all past conflicts does not necessarily confirm the value of one's existence. That is why in active life review, people are seeking something that imbues their past with a sense of meaning and significance. They need the validation that they have not lived in vain.

Related to the search for meaning and self-worth is the quest for self-identity. People want to know who they are. There must be, at the very core of their being, some basic, irreducible, and immutable elements that define who they are.

The foundation of self-identity often lies buried, however. It is only by excavating layers and layers of memories that we can get to the beginnings from which our self has evolved. Having stripped away the persona and discovered what we are really like, we can work toward self-acceptance. Without the self-knowledge gained through active life review, self-affirmation means self-deception.

Thus, active life review attempts to answer a number of fundamental questions we ask about ourselves: Why do I feel so insecure? What have I done that I am ashamed of? Why do I have such a poor self-concept? What do I really want in life? What is my ultimate purpose in life? Is my life meaningful? These are difficult questions that demand a great deal of soul searching.

Active life review is also the self's adaptive response to past traumas, because if there is no confronting and working through of painful memories, there can be no healing and restoration. The presence of an obsessive memory indicates the need for or the failure of active life review.

The preceding analysis indicates why it is important to distinguish between the active life review and actualized life review. It is a distinction between process and product, which may have very different psychological correlates. Without this distinction, it would be difficult to predict and interpret the relationship between life review and various outcome measures.

Integrative reminiscence indicates the actualization of life review: The individual not only has resolved past conflicts, but also has achieved personal significance and self-acceptance. This type of reminiscence should be associated with healthy and happy aging (Wong & Watt, 1991).

The cognitive processes of active life review involve the following:

Search of early memories: This is especially important in working through memories related to feelings of shame, guilt, and anger. Basically, it is the process of confronting past traumas and unresolved conflicts in order to recognize the events and forces that have shaped one's present condition.

Reconstruction of memories: The past seldom intrudes into the present without distorting it. In restructuring one's life history, the mind actively seeks to fill in missing gaps and rearrange events so that life begins to make sense and take on personal significance.

Revision of self-schemas: The revision of self-schemas is the major part of working through the past. In this process, one has to revise existing schemas and beliefs in such a way that the negative sides of the past are integrated with the positive aspects.

Search for personal meaning: This process includes searching for past experiences and acquired values that make life meaningful (Wong, 1989).

In essence, the main function of active life review is to achieve and protect ego integrity. Active life review includes processes that serve one's need for coherence, meaning, identity, and self-esteem and facilitate the struggle to be free from psychic pain and conflict.

Functions of Instrumental Reminiscence: Preserving the Sense of Mastery

To be effective in dealing with the exigencies of life, one needs a sense of mastery and competence. Otherwise, even small problems seem unsurmountable, and one is constantly threatened by feelings of inferiority and insecurity.

A backlog of successes is important in building confidence, but success alone is not sufficient. People can be very successful by objective criteria but still feel haunted by a sense of inferiority, which is rooted in early experience.

From the perspective of reminiscence therapy, early memories are useful in identifying possible causes of negative schemas about the self and others. Numerous therapeutic benefits will flow from the revision of mistaken schemas. At the very least, acceptance of one's limitations and weaknesses removes the need for relying on unadaptive defense mechanisms to overcome feelings of inferiority. As we survey the wreckage from the past—all the futile struggles and all the broken dreams—we begin to see ourselves in stark nakedness. All of a sudden, we realize that we are not as smart as we thought, and that we may not have what it takes to be what we have always wanted to be.

By giving up fictitious goals of superiority, one is freed from both the illusion of success and the burden of failure. One recognizes the absurdity and futility of such misguided aspirations as saving the whole world. At this point, dreams of glory give way to more realistic life goals (Adler, 1958).

By revising self-schemas, we also learn to adopt realistic strategies to cope with the demands of life. Once we have identified the internal and external obstacles and differentiated the controllable and uncontrollable forces, we are able to use appropriate strategies to cope with various demands.

A sense of mastery is needed in every stage of development. Erikson (1963) believed that mastery is a major source of satisfaction and proposed that the desire to achieve autonomy begins in early childhood. The subsequent developmental tasks to achieve initiative, competence, and generativity are all related to the need for mastery. Both Adler (1927/1957, 1958) and Fromm (1947) postulated that people possess an innate drive to overcome helplessness experienced in childhood through mastery over their environment.

The mastery motivation is beneficial because it mediates adaptive behaviors, such as problem solving and persistence. According to Bandura's (1977, 1981) self-efficacy theory, people's perception that they can effect changes in their environment increases their ability to cope and leads to greater persistence in the face of adversity. People who perceive that outcomes are independent of their behaviors are likely to become helpless and vulnerable to depression (Seligman, 1975).

However, an excessive need for control because of an unresolved inferiority complex can be destructive. Attempts to dominate and intrude into other people's territories can ruin relationships. The tendency to control the uncontrollable can create unnecessary frustration, anxiety, and hostility (Wong, 1992; Wong & Sproule, 1984).

The task of maintaining a sense of agency and mastery becomes increasingly difficult in later years. Regardless of how we glorify the golden age, sooner or later the harsh realities of aging descend on all of us. Unless we die prematurely, the relentless aging process does not leave anyone unscathed.

Old age can be a breeding ground for feelings of inferiority because of diminished coping resources and the chronicity of age-related problems. We feel helpless when there is no cure to health problems and when our memories are failing us. We are made to feel inferior when we have to ask others to do things we used to do well. These feelings may be compounded by memories of childhood situations associated with feelings of inferiority.

The illusion of control also plays an important role in bolstering one's sense of competence (Lefcourt, 1976; Taylor & Brown, 1988). It has been suggested that the active mastery of middle age changes into a more passive mode, or even a magic mode of mastery in old age (Neugarten & Gutmann, 1958). In their desire for greater mastery, the elderly's perception of personal control may become highly inflated; sometimes their perceived control may be based on wishful thinking and fantasy.

There are many ways to preserve a sense of mastery through reminiscence. One way is to recall career achievements. Several investigators (e.g., Butler, 1963) have recognized the value of summarizing one's life work. Others may not be interested in our resume when we are out of the job market, but it is for our own mental health that we know what we have done with our lives in spite of the limitations. At the very least, it gives an account of how we have spent our productive years. If we have not fared too badly in spite of the many constraints, we can derive certain measures of satisfaction.

Magee (1988a) observed that

When older adults confront current problems, many regularly review their lives for instances of successful problem-solving conduct. These precedents support their self-concept as competent people and serve as a model of effective behavior that they can adapt to their current situations. (p. 9).

Such recollections serve not only as a motivation for mastery, but also as a source of wisdom.

Even when dealing with the problem of bereavement, it is helpful to learn from past experience. "Methods used to adjust to past losses, however, are probably the most important factor defining acceptance of one's own death. By recounting past crises and their resolutions, the aged gain access to their most effective coping skills" (K. King, 1984, p. 282).

By reminiscing about a time of strength and accomplishment, we reassure ourselves and others that we are the same competent person. This sense of sameness and consistency reinforces the construction of the self as a functioning, effective problem solver. Such a self-identity fosters self-esteem.

There is now considerable evidence that instrumental coping is beneficial (Billings & Moos, 1981; Folkman, Lazarus, Pimley, & Novacek, 1987; Lazarus & Folkman, 1984). Instrumental reminiscence can be regarded as remembering the past use of instrumental coping.

A sense of mastery cannot be maintained solely by memories of past achievements. There is the need to find new activities and involvements in later years. Commitment to meaningful work can lessen our pains and provide a surge of energy.

It is through looking back that we learn what we have always wanted to do. We are more likely to feel that we are engaged in something meaningful when there has been a lifelong commitment. Finding meaningful work in old age is a main ingredient of mastery.

Unfortunately, declining health will eventually force us to give up many activities. However, we need not become less active, because we can switch to activities that are more in line with our inner needs and physical constraints. As we grow older, we tend to become more inner oriented and spiritually minded. We should always explore and discover activities that make us feel competent and fulfilled.

Reminiscing, whether in the form of writing an autobiography or sharing recollections with friends, is an activity that capitalizes on the strength of the elderly. It requires a minimum of physical energy and provides inner resources for living.

To promote a sense of mastery, a two-prong approach is needed in reminiscence therapy. On the one hand, we need to help clients become aware of their inferiority complex, fictitious life goals, and the self-destructive strategies they used in their attempts to overcome inferiority. On the other hand, we need to encourage them to recall past accomplishments and successes in achieving life goals. Such instrumental reminiscence helps maintain a sense of continuity and mastery.

There are at least three processes whereby instrumental reminiscence contributes to healthy aging:

Access to problem-solving skills: Instrumental reminiscence ensures that one's actions and decisions benefit from accumulated wisdom and experience in coping with the demands of everyday life.

Search for realistic tasks: We learn what we can do and cannot do only by examining our track record. Learning to pursue realistic goals and activities not only frees us from unnecessary frustration, but also gives us a sense of competence.

Summarizing past achievements: Reviewing instances of successful problem solving and accomplishments provides a firm foundation of mastery and resourcefulness.

Both instrumental reminiscence and commitment to meaningful activities are needed to keep us afloat in the face of continued decline and loss in old age. If we have done it before, we can do it again in overcoming the challenges of life.

CONCLUSIONS

Memories can cut both ways—they can depress us or elevate our spirit; they can bind us or set us free. When the power to recall is properly channeled, reminiscence can help maintain a sense of integrity and mastery.

I have focused on the adaptive processes of integrative and instrumental reminiscence in this chapter. Most of these processes are cognitive in nature. The most difficult and painful processes involve confronting and reconstructing the past and revising one's schemas. Only through these processes can one develop a realistic, yet positive, self-concept in spite of past negative events, present difficulties, and future uncertainties.

The other adaptive processes of reminiscence concern the use of memory as an inner resource. Our memory storage provides us with a constant supply of wisdom, inspiration, and personal meaning. Thus, as a resource, memory not only expands our coping capabilities, but also helps us maintain a positive self-concept.

When reminiscence takes place in a group setting, it also serves the social support function; I have discussed the adaptive benefits of social reminiscence elsewhere (Wong, 1991).

Reminiscence yields many practical implications for therapy (Watt & Wong, 1990). In this chapter, I have identified only several adaptive processes which may be employed in a therapeutic context.

Chapter 3

Reminiscing as a Process of
Social Construction

John A. Meacham

At the heart of this chapter is the thesis that remembering is better understood as a social process than as an individual process. Yet the constructs of learning and memory, especially as they have been conceived individualistically, have provided the conceptual and methodological foundation for much of contemporary psychology, while topics such as group mind and archaic memories typically have been relegated to the fringe. Thus the question of in what sense remembering is better understood as a social process deserves more than a brief response. Drawing on the ideas of Vygotsky (1978), Habermas (1984; see also McCarthy, 1981), and others, I have argued on several occasions for the importance of social, cultural, and historical contexts to our understanding of remembering (Meacham, 1972, 1980, 1988, 1992). In this chapter, I refrain from merely retracing these arguments and instead explore the social nature of remembering from a new perspective, one that is particularly relevant to our understanding of reminiscing.

Reminiscing is concerned with the remembrance, often in a casual way, of something that is long past (Haight, 1991; Perrotta & Meacham, 1981–82). This

I am grateful to John C. Mohawk for conversations that led to ideas presented in this chapter.

focus on the past is clearly shared with the discipline of history, and so it is appropriate to adopt the study of history as a heuristic standpoint from which to consider the functions and processes of remembering and reminiscing and whether they are better understood individualistically or socially, culturally, and historically.

PHILOSOPHY OF HISTORY

Much of the late 19th century approach to history was a reaction to and a transcendence of the early 19th century positivist approach to the study of history, according to which the task of historians was to describe history exactly as it occurred (Walsh, 1967). The positivist approach to the study of history was beneficial in stimulating the collection of historical records, texts, and so forth, but the expectation that detailed descriptions of historical events would provide a base from which more general laws paralleling those of the natural sciences could be deduced was not fulfilled.

Instead, the task traditionally taken up by historians, in response to what Walsh (1967) described as the morally outrageous notion that history has no rhyme or reason, has been to search for meaning and purpose in the sequence of historical events. For example, early speculations on the meaning of history centered on the role of providence and, during the Enlightenment, on the idea of progress. Other meanings within history were advanced by Herder, who maintained that history reflected progress toward a more complete humanity; Hegel, for whom history was the dialectical unfolding of absolute spirit; and Marx, for whom history was a reflection of material, economic relations. Vico's early suggestion that societies and cultures pass through cycles was articulated in histories such as Spengler's *Decline of the West,* in which history was conceived as an overlapping of cycles of growth and decay of independent civilizations, and Toynbee's comparative study of civilizations, *A Study of History.*

The speculative philosophy of history did not extend, for the most part, beyond the close of the 19th century, as the task for historians came to be seen as less one of finding the meaning in history than one of understanding, in a critical, reflective manner, how it is that historians construct meaning and attribute it to history. Thus for Walsh (1967), history was important not for its presentation of objective, past events, but for the opportunity it provides for each new generation "to write its histories afresh" (p. 109) within the context of its present activities. It is noteworthy that at a time when historians were already shifting from a speculative to a critical perspective on history, psychologists and, in particular, experimentalists interested in memory, were embracing positivism in an attempt to imitate the methodology of the natural sciences.

All histories are thus constructed from particular, even moral, perspectives (Walsh, 1967). To choose among them on objective grounds can be difficult, if not impossible, and so the appeal must be primarily to our values and beliefs about what is reasonable in human behavior. Thus, for example, the current debate over multiculturalism in the American educational system is not, primarily, a debate over any objective facts of history, but rather a debate over who gets to tell their story (for whoever tells the story of history likely leaves everyone else's story out) and who has the power to control which story gets told and which story is silenced. Opponents of multiculturalism are concerned that the story of Western civilization and its values continue to be told and heard; advocates of multiculturalism are concerned that this is a story of a particular elite that "has its blind spots, its absences, its systematic pattern of exclusion and discrimination" (Kalantzis & Cope, 1992, p. B3) and its "silences about women and racial and ethnic divisions in American society" (Kessler-Harris, 1992, p. B3). The impact on the field of history of much scholarship since the 1960s on the lives of ordinary people, the history of everyday life, and the history of social groups and the cultures, ideologies, and social relationships that unite and divide them is seen in the publication of the three-volume *Encyclopedia of American Social History* (Winkler, 1993).

This brief review of how the discipline of history has oriented itself toward the past provides several perspectives that can be adopted as standpoints from which to consider the functions and processes of remembering and reminiscing: (1) describing history exactly as it happened, (2) discovering the true meaning in history, (3) constructing meaning and attributing it to history, and (4) negotiating who gets to tell their story and whose stories are left out of history. This general sequence is recognizable as similar to the ontogenesis of knowledge, in its movement from absolutist perspectives on events and their interpretation, through relativistic perspectives on what can be known, to an understanding that knowledge is the outcome of a process of inquiry involving many individuals (cf. P. M. King, Kitchener, Davison, Parker, & Wood, 1983).

Remembering Events Exactly as They Happened (First Standpoint)

A glance through a contemporary textbook on remembering reveals terms such as *storage, retrieval, recall, recognition, decay, interference,* and *forgetting.* These and similar terms convey the traditional perspective on remembering, within which the primary issue is whether memories are accurate. The criterion of accuracy is the extent to which a particular memory corresponds with the event in the past that is the basis for the memory. Typically, a researcher is present at the past event or otherwise is able to establish, independently of the memory, the nature of the event. If appropriate storage and retrieval processes occur, then the memory is accurate; if there is decay, interference, or forgetting, then the memory is not accurate or is missing. Analogous to the positivist approach to history, this perspective on remembering is one of remembering events exactly as they happened.

Within this traditional perspective on remembering, remembering processes are conceived individualistically, that is, as residing within the mind of a single person. This is ironic, for by locating remembering processes within each individual mind, this perspective would at first appear to privilege the individual and grant the individual authority over his or her own memories. Yet, in practice, it is the authority of the original event and of the researcher that are paramount, and not the individual's memory. The deemphasis of the individual rememberer is revealed in an often-cited section from Woodworth and Schlosberg's (1954) *Experimental Psychology*:

> Such aids in memorizing [as relying on familiar items and patterns] are naturally regarded with much favor by O [the organism], but E [the experimenter] would like to be rid of them. They make the learning task less uniform and introduce variability and unreliability into the qualitative results. Besides, E wants to study the formation of new associations, not O's clever utilization of old ones. (p. 708)

Typically, the issues that are significant within other perspectives on remembering—that is, what the memories mean, who has the authority to determine whether the memories are accurate, and whose memories are these—do not arise.

Although this emphasis on remembering events exactly as they happened might be appropriate in some limited contexts, for example, in the classroom when rote memorization of schoolwork is required and in the courtroom, its usefulness in understanding reminiscing can certainly be challenged. The accuracy perspective on reminiscing leads family members, friends, and therapists to respond to an individual's reminiscences by questioning their validity, that is, by asking whether the reminiscences correspond to actual past events in the person's life or are merely fantasies and fabrications. Because remembering processes are considered to be located within the mind of a single individual, when a person's memories are judged to be inaccurate and, by implication, his or her remembering processes are found to be faulty, then it is the person who is considered to be lacking. Indeed, to the extent that family members and others believe that they have better access to the actual past events, for example, from their own study of history or from the standpoint of what they wish to believe about past events, the reminiscences of the individual are seen as redundant and without value, except as they might confirm what is already known. In such a context, to reminisce is to expose oneself needlessly and perhaps foolishly to evaluation and possible rejection by others. Thus conceptualizing reminiscing as the remembering of events exactly as they happened does not lead to a sympathetic understanding of reminiscing.

Discovering the Meaning of Memories (Second Standpoint)

In some contemporary textbooks on remembering, one can also find such terms as *recoding, schemas, reconstruction,* and *gist.* These terms indicate a perspective on remembering that is less concerned with verbatim recall than with whether the individual can recall the main points and meaning of past events or information that was presented. Remembering is understood not as a process by which the individual stores and retrieves an exact copy of the original information or event, but rather as a process by which the individual uses a few pieces of fact to reconstruct a coherent and meaningful memory. The person might actually be incorrect in the recall of certain facts, yet through inferential reasoning arrive at a good understanding of the gist of the original event. Of course, this process can also lead to distortions, as the individual strives to construct memories that make sense within the context of present needs, motives, and circumstances. Analogous to the speculative approach to history, this approach to remembering is one of discovering within the memories the true meaning of the original events.

Like the positivist perspective, the speculative perspective on remembering conceives of remembering processes as individualistic, seeing the reconstruction of memories as taking place within the mind of a single person. And, like the positivist approach, it appears to privilege the individual, who, in constructing a memory, discovers whatever meaning is associated with the original events, but in actuality is concerned more with the likelihood of distortion in the individual's reconstruction and the extent to which the individual's present needs, motives, and circumstances stand in the way of his or her ability to discover the true meaning. Reiff and Sheerer (1959) made this point with a nice example:

> Each time, the event is placed into a differently structured personal frame of reference of an evergrowing autobiography, which in turn affects the respective remembering in a different way. A girl who married at twenty may at thirty remember chiefly the dress she wore at her wedding; at forty, the food consumed at the wedding breakfast; at fifty, the fact that her uncle sent a stingy present. (p. 39)

This example raises the issue of the extent to which memories can be a guide to the true meaning of the original events, given that they are always distorted by present circumstances.

This reconstructive perspective on remembering appears at first to attribute greater importance to the personal meanings that individuals discover in their own memories of events than to rote recall. However, in practice, this perspective leads family members, friends, and therapists to respond to an individual's reminiscences by focusing on the subjective nature of the memories and thus on the likelihood that the individual's needs, motives, and circumstances have introduced distortions into his or her memories. Although the individual may have constructed one meaning, some counselors and therapists will remain unconvinced, without additional corroborating evidence, that this is the true meaning of the original events. They remain committed to the view that behind the memories there still lies some set of facts that might be apprehended and might be called on in the discovery of the true meaning of the original events. Whatever meaning the individual might have constructed for him- or herself in the course of reminiscing remains subordinate to the supposed true meaning. In such a context, to reminisce is to expose oneself to the charges that one's interpretation of the original events reflects merely personal biases and that, in reminiscing, one has failed to distinguish the objective facts from one's subjective interpretation of them. Thus conceptualizing reminiscing as the discovery of meaning, conceived individualistically, leads to no more sympathetic an understanding of reminiscing than does conceptualizing reminiscing as the remembering of events exactly as they happened.

Constructing the Meaning of Memories (Third Standpoint)

At this point, it may be helpful to introduce a metaphor to clarify the distinction between discovering the meaning of memories versus constructing the meaning of memories. Suppose in the geometry of points and lines we let points represent facts or true copies of past events and let lines represent the meanings of those original events. Given only two data points to graph, any number of curved lines can be drawn connecting them; however, as the number of data points increases, the curve of a line that is fitted to the points is increasingly constrained. Similarly, given only a few remembered details regarding the past events, it is possible to discover a large number of meanings that might link the events in a coherent fashion; as the number of factual details that are remembered increases, so the meaning that is discovered becomes a closer approximation to the true meaning. To consider remembering from the standpoint of the discovery of meaning (the second standpoint) is to assume that some points are initially given and that they determine the range of possible meanings that might be discovered; although remembering is considered a reconstructive process, the process is one of reconstructing, discovering, or uncovering whatever true meaning has already been determined by the facts of the matter.

In contrast, to consider remembering from the standpoint of the construction of meaning (the third standpoint) is to assume that it is not the points that are initially given but rather the line. Once a line has been drawn, the locations of all the points are necessarily determined by the shape of the line. The implication for remembering is that a meaning, once constructed, has the power not merely to shape but indeed to bring into existence specific remembered details that appear to serve as support for the meaning. Analogous to the critical approach to history, the process is one of construction of meaning and subsequent attribution of this meaning to past events. The potential for this process is underscored by the current controversy over recall of repressed memories of childhood sexual abuse. Loftus (1993), for example, while cautioning that "the fact that false memories can be planted tells nothing about whether a given memory of child sexual abuse is false or not" (p. 533), nevertheless makes clear that there are a variety of processes through which individuals can come to have specific memories of events that in fact never happened; such processes include hypnosis, pressure for social acceptance, hearing the stories of those who actually experienced trauma, and "the use of protracted imagining of events and authority figures establishing the authenticity of these events" (p. 533).

When the construction of the meaning of memories is considered from an individualistic standpoint, we are confronted immediately with the same problem of relativism with which philosophers of history have been confronted. If that which we remember reflects merely the meanings we have constructed in the light of current needs, motivations, and circumstances, how can we know which memories are true and should be accepted and which are false and should be rejected? How can we distinguish in our own mental experience between valid memories and mere fantasies or reflections of what others have told us? How can we distinguish in the reported experiences of others between true memories and fantasies, fabrications, and projections? How can we distinguish among our own reminiscences or those of others between memories that should be accepted as valid and worthy and memories that are symptomatic of delusion and dysfunction? B. M. Ross (1991) has provided a detailed and thoughtful exploration of these and similar issues in autobiographical remembering, to which there appear to be no simple solutions. Nor have historians, psychologists, or philosophers come up with a simple solution to the problem of relativism (Chandler, 1987; P. M. King et al., 1983).

SOCIAL CONSTRUCTION OF MEMORIES

I have no simple solution to offer, either, but I do believe that the problems of relativism are made worse when remembering is conceived individualistically and made more tractable when remembering is conceived as a social process having social functions. When one individual draws a line, the locations of all the points on the line are determined by the shape of the line; however, when two or more individuals draw lines that intersect, the points established by the intersections are distinguishable from the points that lie merely on one line or the other. When one individual constructs a narrative that links past events in a meaningful way, his or her family, friends, and therapist might reasonably question whether the interpretation of those events is valid outside of the context within which the person has constructed the narrative. However, when two or more individuals, each constructing narratives that are meaningful in their own lives, find that there is an intersection of their interpretations of past events, not only these individuals but also others can have greater confidence in the transcontextual meaningfulness of the memories of those events. The social construction of meaningful memories of past events is not a simple matter and depends on negotiating the meaning of memories with other persons of a broad range of ages and experiences; I have presented a more detailed discussion of this topic elsewhere (Meacham, 1992).

There are a number of additional senses, beyond the social validation of meaning, in which remembering and reminiscing are social and not individual in nature (Meacham, 1972, 1980, 1988, 1992; B. M. Ross, 1991). Certainly, social stereotypes and attitudes, including biases and prejudices, guide the constructive process of remembering, particularly when inferences are required to fill in gaps in the narrative of what can be recalled. A third sense is that the construction of memories is guided by social identifications, for example, one's membership in a family, social class, religion, ethnicity, race, nationality, or gender. It is in this third sense—that all individuals are necessarily members of groups—that Halbwachs (cited by B. M. Ross, 1991), for example, argued that all memory is collective.

A fourth way in which remembering is social is that it occurs not in isolation, but instead while the individual is in dialogue with others. These social interactions are reciprocal in that others guide the reminiscer's remembering process through their questions, prompts, and reactions while the reminiscer attempts to enlist listeners in cooperative action through transmitting information about the past and through provoking in listeners feelings similar to those the reminiscer is experiencing. Even when one is remembering in isolation from others, one is actually engaged in an implicit dialogue, according to Ong (cited by B. M. Ross, 1991), who noted, that "even to talk to yourself you have to pretend that you are two people" (p. 179). For Vygotsky (1978), all the higher mental functions, including remembering, are social in their development and in their nature.

Thus remembering and reminiscing may be considered from the standpoint of the construction of meaning, which when understood individualistically leads to problems of relativism but when understood socially leads to a more appropriate understanding. From the individualistic perspective, why should family members, friends, and therapists value reminiscences that they believe to be constructed in an ad hoc, solipsistic manner? One might find the reminiscences a useful guide to an individual's current motivations and feelings, but this is not the same as valuing the reminiscences per se. By implication, why should an individual who is reminiscing in such a manner be valued? From the social perspective, however, the reminiscences that are constructed are valued (a) because they reflect the remembering individual's membership in and identification with significant social groups, (b) because they arouse similar feelings in others and incite them to cooperative action (Meacham, 1992), and (c) because the constructed meanings of the memories can be validated through dialogue with others. (Greater validity is achieved when the constructed meanings are negotiated with many individuals representing a broad range of ages and experiences; see Meacham, 1992.) The points or memories determined by one individual who is constructing a line or a meaningful narrative have little value; value accrues when the lines or meaningful narratives constructed by two or more individuals intersect to yield shared reminiscences that become the basis for further dialogue, shared feelings, and co-operative action (Meacham, 1992).

In this chapter, I have discussed the construction of meaning prior to arguing for the social nature of this construction; yet constructive processes and social processes are complementary. Indeed, the social nature of remembering requires that the processes of remembering be constructive rather than merely entail the storage and retrieval of accurate copies of past events. Suppose remembering was not a constructive process; we would be in continual conflict with each other as we held fast to our convictions that our own, individual memories were the only faithful copies of past events. Because remembering is a constructive process, however, we are able to remember in dialogue with other persons, not only blurring and merging our memories to produce a unified remembrance but also sharpening and strengthening our memories to produce more valid recollections. In summary, reminiscing is better conceived (a) as a social than as an individualistic process, (b) as a constructive process than as storage and retrieval of true copies of events, and (c) as a matter of the coherence and meaningfulness of memories within present social and motivational contexts than as a question of correspondence of memories to past events.

Whose Memories Are These? (Fourth Standpoint)

My brief review at the beginning of this chapter of how the discipline of history has oriented itself toward the past included the observation that in the current debate over multiculturalism in the American educational system the primary concern has been negotiating which groups get to tell their story and whose story will be left out of history. Kessler-Harris (1992) suggested that "we need to see the struggle over multiculturalism as a tug of war over who gets to create the public culture" (p. B7). At the same time, the philosophy of history has developed far beyond its early concern with history as it really happened toward a greater concern with the process of inquiry that historians use.

Reminiscing is a process of social construction similar in many respects to how historians do history. Among the similarities are

- A shared concern with the past;
- A focus less on facts than on patterns, interpretations, and meanings;
- An interest in determining which facts and interpretations are, in some sense, true; and
- A recognition that the use of the past as a tool to understand the present, not an understanding of the past per se, is the goal (see B. M. Ross, 1991, for more similarities).

Metaphorically, reminiscing as a process of social construction takes place when two or more individuals each draw lines that intersect and the points established by the intersections are viewed by family members, friends, and therapists as memories whose meaningfulness has thus been established across contexts. But what conclusions might be drawn if the lines do not intersect? If the two reminiscing individuals stand in positions of relative equality to each other, they can negotiate the difference between them—I'll advance my line a few inches, if you'll advance yours a few inches; I'll agree to shift my meaning toward yours, if you'll shift yours toward mine—for, under conditions of equality, the goal is to maintain and strengthen friendship and the possibilities for cooperative action (Meacham, 1992). To maximize the validity of what is socially constructed, it is thus essential that the sharing of reminiscences and the negotiation of meaning take place under conditions of equality.

Reminiscing becomes problematic when it occurs under conditions of relative inequality in power, which is, of course, what the debate over multiculturalism is about: Those who have been in cultural ascendance have been accustomed to drawing the line that defines a meaningful sequence of historical events; those who have been less powerful have had to settle for a sense of history and personal identity defined at best by those few points at which their own interests intersect with the dominant culture's "a priori" line of history.

To give just one example, Oklahoma, the state with the largest (but still a minority) Native American population, recently celebrated the centennial of the great land rush of 1893, when 100,000 pioneers scrambled for land that had been set aside for members of the Cherokee Nation (B. Johnson, 1993, p. A7). A Native American spokesperson remarked that to celebrate the devastation of the native people of Oklahoma was analogous to Germans celebrating the Holocaust. Another added, "I don't think that ever occurs to people because they don't think of Oklahoma as being Indian territory where many different native peoples lived before statehood." The president of the Centennial Foundation replied, "History is history. We can't change it. We need to make sure it is told as accurately as it can be." This exchange provides an unfortunate illustration of the existence of conflicting views on the philosophy of history: the construction of meaning and, in response, describing history exactly as it happened.

I can surmise that a line of history that would be meaningful for Native Americans would include such events as the Indian Removal Act of 1830, according to which all the Indian peoples living in the Eastern United States were forced to relocate to areas west of the Mississippi River. Tens of thousands died of disease, starvation, and exposure as they were escorted by the army along the Trail of Tears or shortly after they arrived in Indian Territory. The year 1890 marks the massacre of the surrounded and essentially defenseless families camped at Wounded Knee, South Dakota. With the Indian Reorganization Act of 1934, the federal government abandoned its philosophy of forcing the assimilation of Native Americans in favor of a pluralist philosophy, restoring the right of Native Americans to govern themselves. In 1970, the American Indian Movement (AIM) was formed, with the purpose of working for the protection of Native American sovereignty and the protection of treaty rights.

My point in listing these dates is that none is likely to be on the line of history defined by the powerful, White majority. And traditionally what has counted as history, and what has counted as historical events worth remembering, has been to a large extent a matter of who first draws the line that establishes a meaningful sequence of historical events, as well as who has the power to insist that others, including women and minorities, have to find their own histories and identities in intersections with that first-drawn line or not at all, for no provision is made for meaningful events of history that might lie off the first-drawn line. What multiculturalism is about is recognizing the many, diverse lines of history that are represented within our society and striving to weave these lines together into a meaningful societal history that accords equal respect to each of the lines.

What implications does this discussion of inequality, power, and who first draws the line of history have for our understanding of reminiscing? At first, one might respond that individuals who reminisce are, after all, free to reminisce about whatever they wish; who knows or cares whether the memories are accurate? However, this response stems, as I have attempted to show, from an individualistic perspective on remembering and reminiscence and leads directly to a devaluing not only of what has been remembered, but also of the reminiscer.

If, on the other hand, we accept that reminiscing is a process of social construction, then reminiscing must be not merely influenced by, but indeed fundamentally grounded in, the full range of social relations that exist within our society, including relations of inequality and power along dimensions such as age, gender, social class, race, ethnicity, and religion. Both the process and product of reminiscing will reflect the gendered and age-structured relations of power that exist among family members; the similarities and differences in terms of gender, class, race, ethnicity, and religion that exist among friends and between therapists and clients; and the social psychology of the clinical or research setting. Who within the family structure has the authority to reminisce, to define the significant events of family history and how these are to be interpreted? Is it possible that some therapists reserve for themselves a privileged role, not unlike that of professional historians, in passing judgment on clients' interpretations of their reminiscences?

When reminiscing is understood as a process of social construction, it is not inconsequential that an individual and his or her therapist might be of quite different ages; have lived through quite different historical periods; and interpret the experiences of their lives from the standpoints of quite different identities of gender, race, ethnicity, social class, and religion. These differences cannot be ignored and represent a substantial challenge to the individual and therapist struggling together to accept and value the meanings that have been constructed in the course of reminiscing. What if the therapist finds it impossible to recognize points of intersection with the feelings and the meanings represented by the reminiscences of a particular individual? Perhaps the therapist's range of experiences has been limited by his or her own young age, or social class background, or gender; perhaps another therapist would find it easier to accept and value what is implied by the individual's reminiscences.

The questions that we—family members, friends, therapists—must continually raise as we listen to an individual who is reminiscing are as follows: Whose memories are these? Who is entitled to construct the meaning for the events that are being described? If the meaning is not clear, what steps can be taken, not toward ensuring conformity with someone else's previously established interpretations, but toward ensuring that there can be the greatest number of points of intersecting meaning within the social group?

These suggestions should not be taken as implying that the individual who is reminiscing is always entitled to his or her interpretations and that the most likely abuse of power is by family members, friends, or therapists, for clearly this is not necessarily so. Instead, the main point I wish to make is that consideration of reminiscing needs to be shifted, as was the case in the philosophy of history, from emphases on what is remembered, how accurately it is remembered, and the meaning of what has been remembered toward a greater emphasis on the process of reminiscing. I have argued that this process of reminiscing is not an individualistic process, but instead is a process of social construction. All our reminiscences belong not to individuals, but to the community and to society.

Chapter 4

A Conceptual Model of Socialization and Agentic Trait Factors That Mediate the Development of Reminiscence Styles and Their Health Outcomes

P. S. Fry

After decades of research on developmental processes and the thematic contents of reminiscence among older adults (Haight, 1988; Kaminsky, 1984; Lieberman & Tobin, 1983; Perotta & Meacham, 1981–82), we only now have the beginnings of an understanding of why and how the contents of the life review or recollections of past events become associated with a wide range of therapeutic benefits and positive outcomes. However, despite the extensive range of research and literature concerned with describing the benefits of reminiscence, which include self-esteem development, psychological well-being, and adaptive functioning in later life (Coleman, 1974; R. G. Moore, Watts, & Williams, 1988; Myerhoff & Tufte, 1975; Romaniuk & Romaniuk, 1981; Webster & Young, 1988), the notion that different types of reminiscence styles are associated with different types of personality factors and psychosocial variables (Fry, 1991a; Perotta & Meacham, 1981–82;

The development of this chapter was supported, in part, by a strategic grant to the author from the Social Sciences and Humanities Research Council of Canada (File No. 492-87-0006). The author is grateful to Anne Humenek and Evelyn Doyle for their assistance in the qualitative analyses of the exploratory interview data and to Dr. Mark Kolodziej for his assistance in the analyses of the preliminary statistical data that formed the basis of the conceptual model proposed in this chapter.

Watt & Wong, 1990; Webster & Cappeliez, 1993) and lead to a wide range of positive and negative adaptations and health outcomes (Fry, 1991a; Wong & Watt, 1991) has only recently begun to gain currency among researchers and professionals. Along with other life cycle researchers (e.g., Lieberman & Falk, 1971; Sperbeck, 1982), I have examined the differential relationships between the frequency and pleasantness of reminiscence and personality traits (e.g., sentience, will to meaning, and understanding), sociodemographic factors (e.g., education levels and income levels), and a range of health outcomes (severity of health problems, poor perceptions of social support availability, depression, and lack of life satisfaction) (Fry, 1991a).

Although there is still a dearth of empirical studies on the relationships among reminiscence, personality factors, and therapeutic outcomes (for a review of those that do exist, see Thornton & Brotchie, 1987), the majority of practitioners of reminiscence intervention have remained faithful to the overall assumption that all forms of reminiscence incontrovertibly lead to therapeutic efficacy. More recently, however, research done by Wong and Watt (1991) on the typologies of reminiscence has shown that different types of reminiscence (integrative, instrumental, escapist, and obsessive) are differentially adaptive or unadaptive and are differentially linked with successful and unsuccessful aging outcomes. This research has been instrumental in shaking the assumption that therapeutic efficacy follows from all types of reminiscence. For example, Wong and Watt (1991) have drawn attention to the possibility that certain types of reminiscence styles (e.g., the escapist and obsessive styles), if maintained or encouraged in therapeutic intervention with elderly individuals, may have detrimental and negative outcomes with respect to successful aging patterns. Conversely, instrumental and integrative types of reminiscence are more closely related to positive and successful aging patterns (Wong & Watt, 1991). It is important to bear in mind that integrative and instrumental types of reminiscence are seen to have as their main therapeutic function the achievement of a sense of meaning, coherence, and reconciliation with regard to one's past and often involve processes such as working through one's feelings of guilt, failure, and depression. In contrast, obsessive and escapist reminiscence styles are seen to have as their main therapeutic function the expression of unresolved conflict, guilt, embarrassment, and shame associated with memories of past events.

However, previous research has not examined the direct or indirect relationships between an individual's reminiscence style and the psychosocial variables, motivational beliefs, and early environmental conditions characteristic of his or her functioning. Nor has previous research examined, within a protracted time framework, the direct or indirect relationship between specific reminiscence styles and health outcomes in terms of psychological and physical well-being.

In inferential data that I have collected in a number of recent exploratory studies using samples of elderly persons (Fry, 1983, 1990a, 1991a, 1991b, 1993), I examined sets of correlational links among older individuals' reminiscence styles and various psychosocial variables and health outcomes. These links are shown in Figure 1. In this chapter, I present a conceptual framework within which I propose that the frequency and pleasantness of reminiscence are determined, in part, by distal negative and positive organizational behaviors and sociodemographic characteristics of the individual. At a subsequent stage in the conceptual framework, I postulate that the concurrent and multiple interactions of these aforementioned variables with personality traits, motivational systems, and environmental modifying conditions contribute to shaping the individual's reminiscence style(s) and ultimately become associated with positive or negative outcomes in terms of physical and psychological well-being and self-efficacy. Whether the distal and proximal antecedents and consequents of reminiscence style(s) are related to health outcomes causally or correlationally, or whether these variables have direct or indirect effects on outcomes, is far from clear yet; nor are we at a stage in the formulation of a conceptual model of reminiscence development at which we can propose specific directional hypotheses. One underlying

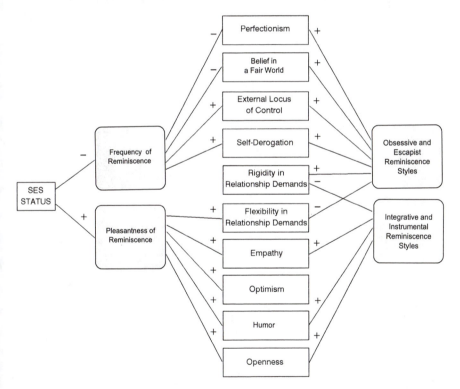

Figure 1 Hypothesized correlational links among reminiscence styles, psychosocial variables, and positive and negative health outcomes. A plus sign indicates a positive correlation significant at the .05 level; a minus sign indicates a negative correlation significant at the .05 level; SES = Socioeconomic status.

assumption of the present conceptual model is that use of a path analysis structural equation statistical modeling technique allows the interactions of various antecedent and consequent factors that influence reminiscence styles and their outcomes to be studied concurrently and within a prospective design.

A closer examination of the interactional framework proposed in Figure 2 suggests that to the extent an individual's agentic traits (e.g., empathy, openness, optimism, and humor) interact with motivational beliefs of flexibility in relationships and an internal locus of control, the individual is more likely to use instrumental and integrative reminiscence styles to resolve feelings of guilt, failure, and loss associated with the past. Therefore, it may be hypothesized that the individual's reminiscence styles will either directly or indirectly be an influential precursor of outcomes in terms of physical and psychological health and well-being (see Figure 2).

In contrast, closer examination of the interactional framework presented in Figure 3 suggests that the agentic traits of perfectionism, self-derogation, and self-blame and related motivational beliefs in a just and fair world may evolve into a disengagement with reality, further inhibiting the individual's recollections of pleasurable events of the past. Thus, obsessive and escapist types of reminiscence not only may be linked with unpleasant recollections of past events, but also may

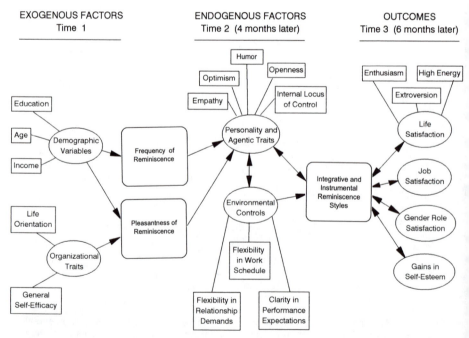

Figure 2 Correlational links among agentic traits, instrumental and integrative reminiscence styles, and positive health outcomes.

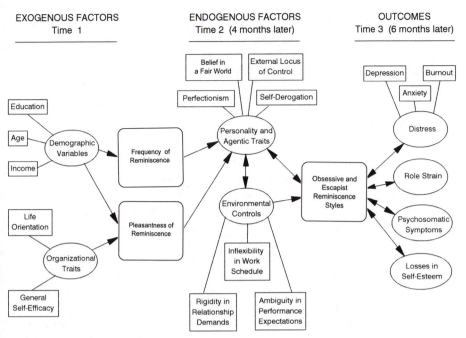

EXOGENOUS FACTORS
Time 1

ENDOGENOUS FACTORS
Time 2 (4 months later)

OUTCOMES
Time 3 (6 months later)

Figure 3 Correlational links among agentic traits, obsessive and escapist reminiscence styles, and negative health outcomes.

become a long-term cover-up for deep-seated guilt and remorse. Obsessive and escapist styles or types of reminiscence may therefore become either causally or correlationally linked to negative physical and psychological health outcomes (Webster, 1993).

Considering that several reviews of the reminiscence function (e.g., Molinari & Reichlin, 1984–85; Romaniuk, 1981; Romaniuk & Romaniuk, 1981; Thornton & Brotchie, 1987) and a few empirical studies (e.g., Fry, 1983, 1991a; Haight, 1988; Wong & Watt, 1991) have noted the widespread use of reminiscence among older adults in both the natural environment and institutional settings, it is not surprising that researchers and practitioners have become increasingly interested in examining the multiple links among influential antecedents, precursors, and consequents of reminiscence and their causally or correlationally related influence on shaping the therapeutic efficacy, or lack thereof, of reminiscence.

A detailed review of the literature revealed no previous attempt to propose a conceptual model of the assumed multiple interactions between and among distal and proximal factors and among exogenous and endogenous variables that may be directly or indirectly instrumental in shaping older individuals' reminiscence styles. Nor does there currently exist a transactional model of the relationship between habitual reminiscence styles and their direct or indirect influences on health outcomes.

In this chapter, I propose one such conceptual model (the tenability of which may be the subject of future research) embedded in a path analysis structural equation model and combined with a qualitative methodology for assessing the contents of phenomenologically approached life review interviews with older adults.

THE MODEL

Consistent with earlier hypotheses (J. E. Birren, 1987; Coleman, 1986; Lieberman & Tobin, 1983; Wong & Watt, 1991), the present conceptual model proposes that reminiscence types or styles that become habitual to older adults are multidimensional and multidirectional in their origins and effects.

The conceptual model, comprehensively explicated in Figures 2 and 3, proposes that a path analysis structural equation procedure be used to examine the multiple links and sequences between the distal and proximal factors that influence (a) the frequency and pleasantness of reminiscence activity reported by individuals and (b) the types of reminiscence that become habitual to individuals. The model proposes that people's individuated socialization histories first shape the frequency and degree of pleasantness with which they recall past events. Later interactions of these distal factors with people's agentic traits, motivational beliefs, and locus of control may be modified by environmental controls and become linked, either causally or correlationally, with the types or styles of reminiscence that individuals learn to use habitually. The conceptual model presented in Figures 2 and 3 postulates further that older adults' habitual reminiscence styles are related, at least correlationally, to specific health and well-being outcomes.

The bottom line proposed in the conceptual model is that the direct and indirect links or associations of various reminiscence styles with health and well-being outcomes should be studied at three stages and be examined both within a protracted time framework and within a prospective, as opposed to retrospective, research design.

Stage 1

At Stage 1, the model proposes that only antecedent variables should be assessed. Despite conflicting viewpoints and inconsistent findings about factors explaining the why, when, and how of the reminiscence phenomenon (J. E. Birren, 1987; J. E. Birren & Hedlund, 1987; Disch, 1988; Haight, 1988), the notion that the frequency and pleasantness of reminiscence are linked with early sociodemographic characteristics of individuals has only recently begun to gain currency among researchers (Fry, 1983, 1991a; Webster, 1994a). More specifically, it is proposed that at Stage 1, the exogenous conditions of demographic variables (i.e., age, educational level, income, and occupational and marital status) should be assessed, along with organizational traits (i.e., perceptions of self-efficacy and positive life orientation) that the individual is assumed to have acquired in the early stages of development. The selection of sociodemographic variables and organizational tendencies as antecedent factors of reminiscence types is based on my recent exploratory findings (Fry, 1990b) derived from using a direct test of the path analysis technique and a qualitative analysis of the contents of reminiscence. The path coefficients in the model presented in Figure 1 were estimated using the traditional procedure of ordinary least squares (Hunter, Gerbing, Cohen, & Nicol, 1980). A detailed description of the routine paths found is beyond the purview of this chapter. The results of the path analyses demonstrated that the models presented in Figures 2 and 3 were partially consistent with the data, as shown in Figure 1. However, the chi-square test for overall goodness of fit indicated no significant differences between the model and the data, reinforcing the notion that the model, as conceptualized, is at least minimally tenable and provides a good fit for future research.

The assessments in Stage 1 point to the indirect role that background factors play in mediating the frequency with which older adults reminisce and pleasantness of their reminiscences.

Stage 2

At Stage 2, two sets of endogenous variables—agentic traits and environmental controls—mediate the relationship between frequency and pleasantness of reminiscence assessed at Stage 1 and the types or styles of reminiscence assessed at Stage 2. The notion that a wide range of agentic traits (e.g., openness, exhibitionism, sociability, sentience, self-derogation, and self-blame) are linked with the reminiscence activity has been proposed and supported by a number of previous researchers (Fry, 1991a; Sperbeck, 1982; Webster, 1994a; Webster & Cappeliez, 1993). In the present conceptual model, I further postulate that a constellation of agentic traits, including optimism, humor, empathy, openness, and self-confidence (see Fig. 2), is further linked correlationally, if not causally, with the integrating and instrumental types of reminiscence taxonomies identified by Wong and Watt (1991). A different constellation of agentic traits, including perfectionism, self-derogation, self-blame, and an inflexible belief in a just world (see Fig. 3), is related to obsessive and escapist typologies of reminiscence. Using a differential-population subject selection procedure, I (Fry, 1991a) conducted in-depth interviews with 32 elderly women (from a wide range of socioeconomic backgrounds) selected from a total pool of 160 elderly persons. These 32 elderly subjects had been previously identified as having high ratings on measures of perfectionism, self-derogation, self-blame, and belief in a just world. Similar interviews were conducted with another sample of 21 elderly women (selected from a wide range of socioeconomic backgrounds) who had high ratings on measures of humor, optimism, openness, and sociability. By encouraging life review procedures as vehicles for self-disclosure and self-reportings, I was able to perform a content analysis of the phenomenologically approached interviews. Using a path-analysis-generated correlational matrix, I (Fry, 1991a) was able to identify a framework of correlational links among the elderly women's background characteristics, their agentic traits, their environmental conditions, and their types or styles of reminiscence. These correlational data turned out to be consistent with the broad perspectives of other researchers (e.g., Lefcourt & Martin, 1986; Nekanda-Trepka, 1984; Nezu, Nezu, & Blissett, 1988) who have argued that high self-expectations of work combined with perfectionistic standards, self-critical attitudes, self-derogatory cognitions, lack of humor and optimism, a belief in a just world, and a "just desserts" life orientation, ultimately promote unadaptive aging. These and similar constellations of agentic traits and motivational belief systems have generally been recognized by both theorists and researchers (Fassinger, 1990; Lerner, 1980; MacLean & Chown, 1988) to be mediators of the manner in which older adults review and assess their life attainments. Such individuals also report health outcomes such as role strain, depression, and burnout (Fry, 1991a).

My exploratory qualitative data, supplemented by other indirectly related statistical inference data from related studies with samples of older adults (e.g., Fry, 1990a, 1991a, 1991b, 1993) served as the basis for the comprehensive conceptual model portrayed in Figures 2 and 3. In Figure 2, for example, there is a graphic portrayal of the links and/or direct and indirect effects that background factors, agentic traits, and environmental conditions are hypothesized to have on the development of integrative and instrumental reminiscence styles. Similarly, Figure 3 shows the links among background factors, agentic traits, and environmental conditions that are hypothesized to contribute to obsessive and escapist reminiscence styles.

At Stage 2, it is postulated, agentic traits and environmental conditions interact further to exert direct or indirect influence on the reminiscence styles to which individuals become habituated. The suggestion is that individuals with different agentic traits use different types of reminiscence to accept, reject, or confront their past successes and failures, to make meaning of their life's goals, or to respond to the nurturant and hostile elements of their environment. A constellation of environmental control factors is introduced in the model with a view to assessing modifying conditions of the environment, such as certainty or specificity in the expectancies for role performance, rigidity or flexibility in work performance and schedules, and levels of control available to the individual.

Stage 3

Stage 3 of the model calls for assessment of the long-term health outcomes associated with the individual's reminiscence style. Distressing health outcomes such as depression, anxiety, burnout, role strain, low self-esteem, and a high level of psychosomatic symptoms are hypothesized to be associated with obsessive or escapist styles of reminiscence (see Figure 3). Such a prediction is predicated on the assumption that in a general population of older men and women lacking status, control, and social and financial supports, ambiguity in work expectancies and age-related roles increases the potential for the depressive and guilt-ridden reminiscence associated with an obsessive style. In contrast, positive health outcomes such as life satisfaction, gender role satisfaction, and gains in self-esteem are hypothesized to be associated with integrative and instrumental types of reminiscence (see Figure 2). (For further discussion, see Fry, 1986.)

A Longitudinal and Prospective Framework

In the total equation model proposed at Stages 1, 2, and 3 we are concerned with assessing both the direct and indirect influences of the exogenous and endogenous variables that affect (a) first on the individual's frequency and pleasantness ratings of reminiscence and (b) the individual's development of a specific reminiscence style. Consistent with the thinking of previous researchers (Rodin, Timko, & Harris, 1985; Schulz, 1976; Slivinske & Fitch, 1987; Wong & Watt, 1991), the model distinguishes integrative and instrumental types of reminiscence from obsessive and escapist types and links the latter more closely with low self-worth, a less goal-directed orientation toward the past and present, and an external locus of control orientation. In contrast, the integrative and instrumental reminiscence styles reflect an internal locus of control that appears to be linked with life satisfaction, the relative absence of psychosomatic symptoms, and subjective good health. A plausible explanation for why negative health outcomes are associated with an external locus of control has been provided by Reid (1984) and R. P. Smith et al. (1988), who contended that individuals with an external locus of control have a greater dependence on external conditions and other persons to meet their health care needs. The theoretical conceptualization behind the locus-of-control influences on reminiscence styles is also the work of Aronoff and Wilson (1985) and Fry, Slivinske, and Fitch (1989). These researchers have argued that individuals with an external locus of control tend to reduce their feelings of self-deprecation by being unstructured in their reminiscence style. They are generally rambling in their descriptions of life-events, and they have a tendency to recall past events and experiences in a much less goal-directed way than do individuals with an internal locus of control. It is not surprising, therefore, that the obsessive style of reminiscence in individuals becomes associated more closely with negative health outcomes such as anxiety, distress, role strain, and burnout (see Figure 3).

In summary, the conceptual model presented in Figures 2 and 3 contains two sets of antecedents—demographics and organizational orientations—that are assumed to be linked to the frequency and pleasantness ratings of reminiscence. Although not fully explicated in the conceptual model, the notion of a scarcity hypothesis (Baruch, Beiner, & Barnett, 1987; Kirchmeyer, 1992) is implied, suggesting that high social status and financial security may insulate men and women from the need to reminisce frequently or to review unpleasant past events. At Stage 2 of the model, two sets of mediating variables—agentic traits and environmental conditions—are proposed to shape two categories of reminiscence style (integrating or instrumental vs. obsessive or escapist). Four sets of outcomes—distress, life satisfaction, role strain, and self-esteem gains/ losses (see Stage 3)—are linked with the two broad categories of reminiscence styles. The double-headed arrows reflect the correlations between and among the exogenous and endogenous factors and the single-headed arrows indicate potential linkages with the next stage of development. In some cases, there are reciprocal relationships. For example, at Stage 2 agentic traits are assumed to shape reminiscence types, which in turn are assumed to modify the agentic traits. It is important to note that the model is conceptualized within a prospective framework in that Stage 1 variables are assessed 4 months before Stage 2 variables are assessed, which in turn are assessed 6 months before Stage 3 variables are assessed.

DISCUSSION

Although a myriad of potentially adaptive functions of reminiscence have been postulated in the literature (e.g., improving self-esteem, coping with depression, self-understanding, and death preparation) (Fry, 1990a), in practice there remain several important obstacles to progress in pinning down the types or styles of reminiscence that older adults use in the natural environment and determining to what extent these reminiscence types or styles should be encouraged or discouraged in therapy. The most common obstacle to understanding the positive or negative effects of a reminiscence intervention is the lack of empirically based knowledge of the distal and proximal conditions that function as antecedents or consequents to shape the negative or positive outcomes of the reminiscence intervention. In this chapter, I have argued that the lack of a conceptual model of the holistic and multidimensional aspects of reminiscence development has made it difficult for researchers to examine the multiplicity of effects that reminiscence interventions may have on elders' physical and mental well-being. I have proposed a plausible conceptual model, the tenability and validity of which need to be established more explicitly through future research.

The present model has the potential to provide a richer and broader explication of the links among the internal and external factors that differentially shape older adults' reminiscence styles; reminiscence styles, in turn, differentially shape health outcomes. The model not only draws attention to the adaptive and unadaptive functions of individuals' habitual reminiscence styles, but also clearly implicates the influence of people's agentic traits, locus-of-control orientations, and environmental conditions. The bottom line proposed in the conceptual model is that there are many routes to therapeutically positive outcomes of reminiscence intervention in the later years of life, along which agentic traits and reminiscence styles form major way stations.

Implications for Therapy

Although the next important step is the designing of experimentally controlled studies to test the theoretical implications of changing individuals' unadaptive reminiscence styles, there are already some exploratory data that have broad implications for therapy.

The therapeutic efficacy of a reminiscence intervention can be enhanced by drawing participants' attention to the agentic traits and the environmental conditions that are impinging on their reminiscence styles in the natural environment. The suggestion is that the direction of these influences on the individual can be changed by therapists working, by design, to modify the unstructured approach they have frequently used in reminiscence therapy, such as permitting reminiscers to reminisce phenomenologically without making any deliberate attempt to structure the reminiscence processes or to reinterpret the affects or contents of the reminiscences (Fry, 1983).

In reminiscence therapy, clients' attention should be directed more consciously to the affective components or contents of reminiscences, particularly obsessive and escapist reminiscences, which appear to be linked, correlationally at least, to negative health outcomes. In other words, the therapeutic efficacy of reminiscence intervention can be potentially enhanced by encouraging people who use obsessive–escapist reminiscing to pay closer attention to affects of guilt, shame, self-derogation, self-blame, and rigid perfectionism, which are frequently pervasive in their reminiscences. Individuals who are depressed; have low self-esteem; or often show symptoms of distress, burnout, and role strain should be encouraged to attend to the negative affects such as self-derogation in their inner speech and private reminiscences and to their self-imposed perfectionistic standards (Fry, 1991b). Therapists who use reminiscence therapy procedures should bear in mind that the absence of agentic traits such as empathy or the presence of traits such as perfectionism and self-blame in some individuals may promote the feeling that others are avoiding interpersonal contact with them. Such a view may frequently create elements of uncertainty and a sense of rejection in individuals who may have deficits in empathic skills (Koestner, Franz, & Weinberger, 1990; Straker & Jacobson, 1981) and excesses of perfectionism and self-derogation (Mudrack, 1990). In the interest of avoiding the threatening possibility that unpredictable and potentially harmful forces are controlling their clients' lives, therapists can enhance the therapeutic efficacy of reminiscence intervention by encouraging clients to reminisce more on life experiences that were pleasant and provided a sense of personal meaning, personal fulfillment, and achievement. In addition, the model points to the potential for using reminiscence intervention to reduce clients' symptoms of distress, burnout, and role strain by helping them to acquire some measure of subjective control over their agentic traits and some degree of behavioral control over the demands and pressures of their environment.

In summary, it is hoped that the present conceptual model of reminiscence development will open up new avenues of research and broaden the potential scope of reminiscence therapies. The conceptual model suggests that if the links between distal and proximal factors that affect reminiscence styles are to be properly understood, they should be studied over a protracted period of time and within a prospective design. Therapists who use reminiscence intervention are cautioned against prematurely accepting the notion that all reminiscence therapies used in clinical practice lead to some measure of self-efficacy in their clients. The mediational model I have proposed suggests that the net impact of certain reminiscence styles on the individual's health and well-being could well be detrimental, if not destructive. Therapists thus have to integrate the knowledge from the diverse areas of interactions and see how this new knowledge interfaces with their present understanding of the efficacy of reminiscence intervention.

CONCLUSION

The proposed transactional model, represents a cross-germination of ideas previously presented by personality theorists who have studied the influence of locus-of-control orientations and personality traits on health outcomes. Although substantial empirical data are needed to support the proposed links among individuals' personality traits, their motivational systems, and their reminiscence styles, the model suggests that reminiscence style is an influential precursor of health outcome. It is my hope that the conceptual underpinnings of the dynamic framework proposed in this chapter will advance our understanding of how reminiscence styles develop and ultimately come to be associated with several other phenomenological functions, such as improving self-esteem, coping with depression, and understanding the meaning and value of life.

Chapter 5

The Individual's Life History as a Formative Experience to Aging

Bo Hagberg

It is generally agreed that a person's life experiences have consequences for his or her subsequent mode of living. This statement is substantiated by argument from various theoretical standpoints. Positivists state that experiences are added or compiled in an ever widening conglomerate of knowledge. Learning theorists state that experience is gathered by selective reinforcement of occurrences.

Developmental theorists presuppose stages that the individual should successfully pass to fulfill his or her potential. Dynamic psychologists and psychoanalysts emphasize the significance of fixations at different points in early life that could lead to neurotic reactions or deformation of character if they are not negotiated at a later stage. Life span developmental theorists suggest that the accumulation of experience eventually leads to maturity, wisdom, and "good aging." All of these theoretical formulations are characteristic of the prospective approach.

However, the life history as told at old age is a retrospective approach that contains both fact and fiction. Earlier experiences are perceived, selected, remembered, or used with a reconstructive purpose to form the life history or biography of the individual. For many people, identity at old age comes from and is sustained by the content of their life history. The essence of the development over the years is the continuity—that is, one's position in old age is as much as possible a preservation and fulfillment of one's earlier life content. Thus, at any point in life the telling of a life history is a retrospective phenomenon. As such, it is best studied from the phenomenological perspective of Husserl (1965). The application of the phenomenological approach in psychology has been formulated by Ryff (1986) as the assessment of the individual's subjective impressions or experiences and examination of how they relate to external behavior and social circumstances. Gatchel and Mears (1982) expressed the objective in phenomenological research as a focus on consciousness and the individual's unique perception of a material or objective reality. Reality is a private affair. The appearance of things in the mind is more important than whatever actuality exists apart from human awareness. Descriptions and analyses of reality are made according to the individual's unique frame of reference.

Taking both prospective and retrospective views of the life history into account, we have a situation in which a construct—human consciousness—that is formed as a consequence of occurrences during a life span is set to reflect these same occurrences, i.e., subjectively selected life events. The events as they have developed during a lifetime have a direct relationship to the fundamental causal model of personality formation in dynamic personality theory. This theoretical perspective tells us that life experiences form habits of behavior or misbehavior that we summarize in a construct we call *personality*. Consequently, people's perceptions of old age differ depending on the unique personality structure that has formed in them on the basis of their particular life histories. Therefore, in addition to taking a phenomenological approach to the life history, it is also necessary to bear in mind the personality of the person telling the life history. In line with psychoanalytic thinking, hypotheses can then be formed about the relationship between a person's life history report and his or her personality characteristics (Hagberg, Samuelsson, Lindberg, & Dehlin, 1991). At a general level, a relationship (i.e., the relation between reminiscing and mental status at the time of autobiographic report) could be assumed to exist between the reported life history both in terms of content, evaluation and way of telling on one side and maturity levels defined by development stages (Erikson, 1982), or degree of neuroticism (Eysenck & Eysenck, 1969) or coping capacities (Lazarus & Folkman, 1984).

Related to the personality of the person who is telling his or her life history is the condition of the person when reporting. Mood, mental health, and physical health all influence the mode of the life history report and especially the evaluation of its content. Furthermore, the significance of the person's life history to his or her present situation must be considered. Few studies have compared the relevance of the happening to the memory of the same occurrence. Field (1989) made that comparison and concluded that the significance of each aspect depended on the outcome criteria. When outcome was defined as present mental health and well-being, the subjective life report was far more important than the authentic occurrence in predicting present well-being.

PURPOSE OF THE PRESENT STUDY

The purpose of the present study was to explore the relationship between biographical report and satisfaction with a current life event, taking into account the present mental status as well as the personality of individuals in a healthy sample. Specifically, I examined the influence of current retirement experiences and personality characteristics on individuals' life histories.

Life history is a very broad concept. It includes many kinds of experiences, and therefore a limitation of the content was necessary. The focus of the present study was the impact of social interaction over the lifetime. It is well known from psychodynamic research that one of the strongest influences on the development of the self-image as well as other personality characteristics is one's relationships to significant others. Thus in the present study, recording of the life history was geared toward subjects' reporting on significant others and evaluating their relationships to these persons. A general model for the theoretical analysis is presented in Figure 1. As is usual in most autobiographical studies, the prospective path in the model is assumed and cannot be supported by data from the present retrospective study.

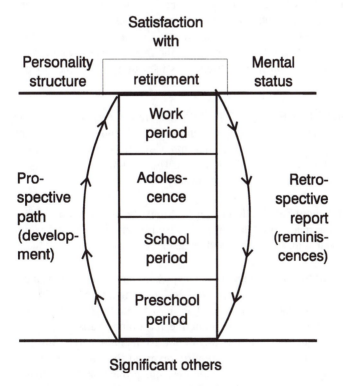

Figure 1   Hypothetical model of retirement satisfaction.

METHOD

Subjects

Eighteen randomly sampled 70-year-old men and women participating in a larger autobiographical study were interviewed and tested with the same design as used with 40 healthy 73-year-old volunteers in a study of the efficacy of selenium consumption. All subjects completed questionnaires on their health and mental status and were tested for cognition and personality. They were also interviewed on their life history and present well-being as pensioners. Mental status was assessed after each interview.

Measures

The life history report focused on the person's relationships to significant others during different periods of his or her life and the person's evaluation of these relationships. Satisfaction with retirement concerned the emotional, economical, and practical adaptation to retirement. Present mood, physical health, and psychological health were evaluated on the basis of responses to psychometric tests, questionnaires, and interviews on cognition and personality and the assessment by the interviewer of neurosis, coping, locus of control, stress vulnerability, engagement, and life-style. For convenience, the material was divided in three blocks: (a) life history report, (b) retirement satisfaction report, and (c) present-status assessment.

Life History Report   The life history report was obtained during a semistructured interview covering childhood, school, adolescence, and the work period. Subjects assessed their relationship with significant others from previous life periods as positive, negative, or neutral. These summary evaluations were used as basic units for the analyses of life history.

Retirement Satisfaction Report   Similarly, an evaluation of the retirement period was made after the subjects talked about the practical, emotional, and economical adjustments they had made to retirement.

Present-Status Assessment   The present-status assessment included many measures. Cognitive functions were tested using a word definition list (Wechsler, 1981) as a measure of verbal ability and Koh's Block Design test (Wechsler, 1981) as a measure of inductive reasoning. Personality was evaluated using a projective test, the meta-contrast technique (G. Smith & Nyman, 1961). Factor analysis of the reports revealed the following five dimensions for description of personality: depression, projection, compulsive behavior, anxiety, and regressive behavior.

Coping capacity was assessed during the interview as how well the individual was handling periods of own illnesses; the disease of a close relative; separation from spouse by either divorce or death; and, for those who had adult children, separation from children. All persons were found to have experienced at least one of these stresses. The outcome of each stressful event was evaluated by the interviewer on a three-point scale (+ = good handling, 0 = ordinary handling, – = bad handling). Locus of control in relation to coping capacity was also assessed during the interview, through inquiring whether the person believed the outcome came about by his or her own doing or another person's doing.

Life-style was described according to Zetterberg's (1977) taxonomy, which includes working person, family person, social person, consumer person, nature person, religious person, or physical person. Judgments of stress vulnerability and commitment were made on the basis of the person's overall behavior during the interview. To assess neurosis, depression, physical health, and psychological health, the interviewer used Swedish translations and adaptations of the Cornell Medical Index and the Columbia Adult Health Inventory (Nyman & Marke, 1958).

RESULTS

The overall correlations between the evaluation of the four life history periods and the individual's assessment of retirement satisfaction showed that a positive life history evaluation correlated with a positive retirement evaluation. Specifically, it was found that the earlier the life period reminisced, the more positive its relationship to retirement satisfaction: $r = .45$ for the childhood period, .31 for the school period, .26 for the adolescence period, and .06 for the work period. Thus, there is a gradual decrease over life periods as they relate to retirement satisfaction.

When the relationships between life history report and status at examination were examined, the same general trend was found. Reports from earlier periods in life showed high and often significant correlations with all of the status variables except cognition (see Table 1). Low and nonsignificant correlations were found between life history report and verbal ability and inductive reasoning. However, it could be argued that the life history report depends on individual competence at the time of interview. To examine this possibility, I considered some cases with contrasting good and bad cognitive ability (Table 2) and coping capacity (Table 3), that is, the best and worse cases.

Table 2 shows the life history reports of persons with high and low cognitive performance. As may be seen, there were practically no differences in the evaluations of the relationships in any of the life periods, and generally the evaluations were positive. Quite the opposite was found when two individual cases with good and poor coping capacity were compared, as Table 3 shows. Different evaluations were given for all life history periods; that is, the good coper offered positive reports, and the poor coper offered negative reports.

Table 1 Correlations Between Assessments of Life Periods and Present-Status Variables

| Life history period | Cognitive ability | | | Present-Status Variable | | | | |
	Verbal	Inductive	Coping	Psycho-logical health	Physical health	Depres-sion	Neurosis	Personality structure
Childhood	.02	.13	.68	−.47	−.34	−.34	−.43	−.42
School	.05	.07	.41	−.16	−.22	−.17	−.31	−.48
Adolescence	.17	.02	.23	−.28	−.35	−.16	−.05	−.22
Work	.11	.11	−.28	−.13	−.09	−.10	−.12	−.05

Confidence limits: $r = 25$ $p < .05$ and $r = .32$ $p < .01$.

Table 2 Life History Report in Relation to Individuals with Different Verbal and Inductive Cognitive Capacity*

| Life history period | Cognition | | |
	High verbal/inductive ability	Low inductive ability	Low verbal ability
Childhood			
Mother	+	+	+
Father	+	+	+
Siblings	2,+	3,+	2,+
Report	+	+	+
Assessment	+	+	+
School			
Teachers	+	+	+
Friends	+	+	+
Performance	+	+	0
Need of help	−	−	−
Parents	+	+	+
Report	+	+	0
Assessment	+	+	−
Adolescence			
Military service	+	−	−
Fiancé/fiancee	−	−	Yes,+
Living at home	+	+	+
Parents	+	+	+
Report	+	+	0
Assessment	+	+	+
Work			
Job change	6	6	2
Job adjustment	+	+	+
Superior	+	+	+
Work mates	+	+	+
Health problems	−	+	−
Report	+	+	+
Assessment	+	+	0

*(+, −, and 0 indicate positive, negative, or neutral evaluation of the relation and period. The numbers refer to numbers of siblings or job changes.)

Table 3 Life History of Two Cases with Good and Bad Coping Capacity

Life history period	Coping +	Coping −
Childhood		
Mother	+	0
Father	+	0
Siblings	6,+	1,0
Report	+	−
Assessment	+	−
School		
Teachers	+	0
Friends	+	0
Performance	+	0
Need of help	+	+
Parents	+	0
Report	+	−
Assessment	+	−
Adolescence		
Military service	−	Yes,−
Fiancé/fiancee	−	−
Living at home	No	Yes
Parents	+	0
Report	−	+
Assessment	−	+
Work		
Job change	5	2
Job adjustment	+	0
Superior	−	0
Work mates	+	0
Health problems	No	Yes
Report	−	+
Assessment	−	0

In various degrees, this was also the case for other status variables and personality characteristics. Thus, marked differences in life history reports were found depending on individual differences in all components of mental status except for cognition, that is, coping capacity, psychological health, and personality structure.

I further analyzed the influence of mental status on life history report and retirement satisfaction by partialing out the effect of mental status variables on the relationship between life history report and retirement satisfaction for each life period reminisced. Starting with cognition, the bivariate correlation between childhood report and retirement satisfaction was .45. When cognitive capacity was held constant, the relationship remained the same or .47. This was also the case regarding the reports about the school, adolescence, and working periods. Thus, cognition seemed to have no effect at all on the relationship between life history report and retirement satisfaction. Also, the common variance for these variables and cognition was close to zero.

In contrast, when coping was held constant, the relationship between life history report and retirement satisfaction dramatically changed. The correlations were .45, .31, .26, and .06 for the childhood, school, adolescence, and work life periods. Partialing out coping capacity reduced the correlation between childhood and adolescence to zero or close to zero. I found that coping shared almost all variance with both life history report and retirement satisfaction and also correlated significantly with both in the childhood and school periods. For all periods, coping correlated positively with the retirement satisfaction, but it correlated only with the childhood and school periods of the life history report. No other status variables—psychological health, physical health, depression, neurosis, or personality structure—were capable of changing the relationship between life history report and retirement satisfaction to the same extent that coping did.

The results from the bivariate analyses thus clearly show that retirement satisfaction was related to subjects' perception of some life periods and to some characteristics in subjects at the time they reported their life history.

To identify which combination of periods from the life history report discriminated persons who were satisfied with retirement from persons who were not, I performed a stepwise discriminant analysis with retirement satisfaction as the independent variable and the life periods as potential discriminators. The results showed that positive evaluations of relationships to significant others during childhood and adolescence characterized 76% of the individuals who were satisfied with their retirement. Neither evaluation of the school period nor evaluation of the working period entered the prediction. The prediction was significant at $p < .001$.

I also tested the multivariate relationship between mental status and retirement satisfaction using a stepwise discriminant analysis. Of the 11 status variables, 3—coping capacity, neuroticism, and degree of depression—identified 70% of the individuals who were satisfied with their retirement ($p < .01$).

When the relevant parts of the two domains of life history report and mental status, as defined by discriminant analyses, were indexed and correlated to retirement satisfaction, there was a strong positive correlation between retirement satisfaction and a positive evaluation of relationships in childhood and adolescence ($r = .50$). Negative relationships during the same periods were related to less successful coping, more neuroticism, and more depressive traits ($r = -.61$). Consequently, there was also a negative relationship between these characteristics and retirement satisfaction ($r = -.54$).

The crucial issue, finally, was to examine more closely the causal relationships among the three domains. Thus, the separate parts of the preceding analysis were tested in a causal model using SYSTAT/EZPATH (Steiger, 1989). The results from the correlation analysis led me to believe that the life history report was affected by the retirement satisfaction; which was in turn affected by present state and personality; which in turn were, at least hypothetically, determined by the life history experience. This structural model of the interrelationships among the endogenous variables (latent variables) and their related measurement variables was tested on the present data, and the results are shown in Figure 2.

The model fit the data well, with a nonsignificant result ($p = .21$) and a goodness-of-fit index of .956. However, to achieve this fit, the model had to be modified in relation to the original hypothesis so that present state is now said to depend on retirement satisfaction. This revision was probably made necessary by the fact that both coping and depression were reported by the subject and only neuroticism was assessed externally. The original hypothesis presupposed an independent assessment of status.

The main conclusion to be drawn from the dependency model is that satisfaction with retirement in terms of practical, economical, and emotional adaptation is linked to a positive report of one's relationships to significant others in one's childhood and adolescence. A second conclusion is that this satisfaction with retirement is reflected in a positive present mental status. And finally, one's evaluations of one's relationships to significant others during childhood and adolescence probably reflect the formation of elements in one's personality that are of significance for one's present well-being.

In addition, most of the variance in retirement satisfaction was attributable to the life history evaluation, whereas less than half was attributable to present status. Furthermore, of the four life periods, only two—childhood and adolescence—

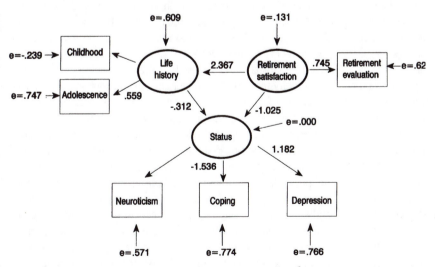

Figure 2 Structural model of retirement satisfaction. Note: $\chi^2(5, N = 51) = 7.09$, $p = .21$; goodness-of-fit index = .956; adjusted goodness-of-fit index = .816; and e = errors of measurement.

were of relevance, and of these two, childhood was twice as important as adolescence. The model also shows that the memory of those life periods was more important than present mental status. In terms of present mental status, there was a different significance among the qualities of mental status, with the most important quality being coping capacity, followed by depression and neuroticism.

DISCUSSION

In general terms, the correlations and the results of the discriminant analysis in the present study confirm the notions that a person's life history is one of the determinants of how the person will experience old age and that crucial experiences during critical periods of life are important to personality formation in terms of neuroses, coping capacity, and depressive signs. The hypothesized relationship between those qualities and satisfaction with retirement was not verified in the dependency model, probably because of the retrospective design of the study. However, it seems clear that in such a design one reflection of present satisfaction is the mental state of the individual. Perhaps the most salient feature of the model is the link from the present situation backward to a remembrance of valued relationships in critical past life periods. These past evaluations also brought forward personality structures that had crucial impacts on present mental state, which by implication would be a determinant of present well-being.

The significance of the subjective life history report for well-being in old age is supported by the results from a number of studies (J. E. Birren & Deutchman, 1991; Butler, 1964; Field, 1989; Ryff, 1986; Ryff & Essex, 1992). In addition, the present results point to some periods of special importance in this regard, namely, childhood and adolescence. Focusing on a particular aspect of the life history such as the attachment to important persons, the evaluation of such a relationship in a retrospective review is assumed to be important first of all for the preservation of personality characteristics, but also for the experience of life satisfaction (Bowlby, 1986). The present findings support such an assumption and specify the periods of importance to be childhood and adolescence, which relate to present life satisfaction both directly as reminiscences and indirectly by way of the reminiscing effects on mental status and personality.

In general, a positive life history report also leads to a positive old age evaluation. It is reasonable to believe that this finding to some extent reflects the factual side of the relationship between what actually passed and its effects on personality formation and supports the continuity principle. Sometimes this relationship goes over the formative effects of the life history on the perceiver's personality structure. Coping capacities, degree of neurosis, and depression substantially alter the relationship between the life history report and old age evaluation, whereas cognition, locus of control, stress vulnerability, and degree of commitment did not alter it or altered it substantially less. The present findings are consistent with both the life span psychology concept of continuity in development (Schaie & Willis, 1991) and the deterministic view of personality formation (Erikson, 1982).

These results raise a number of theoretical and principal questions. Differences in memorability of life periods have been found (Rubin, Wetzler, & Nebes, 1986), and most memories reported in old age are from the adolescence period (Fromholt & Larsen, 1991), whereas memories from the working period are less frequent, a profile that well agrees with the present results. It has been suggested that the greater emotionality embedded in memories from childhood and adolescence periods explains the difference (A. Freud, 1936).

The significance of controlling for the authenticity of memories has been discussed. Do we need to know what actually happened? Is the memory a reconstruction or a reproduction? It has been questioned whether all memories are reproductive (Barclay, 1988; Linton, 1986) ever since Bartlett (1932) and later Neisser (1967) argued that memory is mainly a constructive process. The main issue has been to identify the reconstructive mechanism and determine its consequences for the individual and his or her well-being (Rubin et al., 1986). The present results suggest that the reproductive process interacts with the beholder to create an experience against which the present situation is perceived as favorable. Such a conclusion was supported by Fitzgerald (1986), who promoted the idea that memory schemata change as the experience changes, and by Piaget (1926), who argued that memory schemata change with development. Both statements support the reconstructive position.

A favored hypothesis regarding autobiographical memories is that most memories come from the recent past and that there is a continuous decrease of memory of the distant past. Fromholt and Larsen (1991) and Rubin et al. (1986) have demonstrated the opposite: They found that with increasing age and increasing number of memories, memories come from the childhood and the adolescence periods. The present results confirm such a finding, with the qualification that the school period was a low-frequency memory period.

So far, the present results fit well with previous findings. However, a crucial question that arises from the present analysis is why the satisfied retirees evaluated their childhood and adolescence relationships more positively than did the dissatisfied retirees. There are at least three options to consider. First, they may have experienced good childhood and adolescence periods, which they now remember with pleasure, and this memory augments present feelings of well-being and satisfaction.

Second, taking the reconstructive position to its extreme, reevaluation of memories of a negative nature most likely contributes to an increase of satisfaction in old age for individuals so disposed. This view probably coincides with selectivity in perception. Maybe individuals are quite particular for different reasons about which version of a memory to cherish.

Third, from a dynamic point of view, access to memories, especially the negative ones, might be low if there is a high level of psychological defense in the individual. This would favor the memorability of positive aspects of relationships to significant others, and the result would express an optimal regulation of flow into the conscious presence of experiences that can benefit the individual in terms of bringing satisfaction and psychological well-being.

The design of the study does not allow any statements that favor a prospective conclusion, that is, that circumstances produce effects on status and retirement satisfaction. However, from a retrospective and phenomenological standpoint, the results support the hypothesis that one's perception of particular periods of one's life history adds to one's retirement satisfaction but one's present status can, in various degrees, interfere with this mechanism. Open for speculation is the link among life history report, present status, and retirement satisfaction; is it experience, perception, memory, or the accessibility of memories that determines the present status of the individual? Depending on one's theoretical standpoint, each explanation seems as good as the others.

Maybe there is also a fourth option. The link over status (i.e., how the memory of experience is filtered through the present mental status of an individual with unique personality characteristics) would favor a psychodynamic standpoint, whereby the unconscious experience is also considered. Although the memory of, for example, a parental relationship in childhood is positive, there may be other episodes not remembered but of a negative emotional quality that affect one's sense of well-being in old age. According to the psychodynamic paradigm, those unconscious episodes are as important as the conscious ones in affecting the individual. Maybe it is at this point that the neurotic component (Figure 2) in present status is active, in order to increase well-being by the so-called secondary gain mechanisms. This leads to the conclusion that from the reality at the bottom of the experience, an authentic reminiscence process reconstructs and selects good memories, and in some cases on top of this there is a neurotic reality falsification process that converts negative memories into positive ones in order to allow them to enter consciousness. If they are not in any way acceptable, they remain repressed and thus unaccessible for reminiscence. Such a line of thought is even more pregnant when one considers the depressive component of present status (Figure 2). An unhappy relationship with a caring person in childhood could, even if not recognized, be a starting point for depressive reactions for individuals with a depressive inclination (anaclitic depression). This means that although a positive childhood relationship with, for example, a mother is consciously remembered, subconsciously a negative feeling can be harbored that reduces the present satisfaction with life. So, reminiscing means making the blend of remembering and not remembering optimal for the present purpose of well-being.

Now, turning to the psychotherapeutic experience, it is generally agreed that an indication for psychotherapeutic reconstructive work is at hand when one is anxious for a reason that one cannot identify or remember. The discomfort is supposed to come from an unrecognized memory's emotional component that uncritically invades one's conscience. Disarming the complex to reach the goal of relief of anxiety can be said to be the purpose of psychotherapy in this case. We know that for many elderly, telling their life story maintains their identity and increases their well-being by reducing their apprehension in daily life (Haight, 1992a). It is conceivable that a process that mimics the psychotherapeutic work is achieved by individuals themselves, without outside help. The lifelong experience and knowledge can be an asset to the elderly in this process (Haight, 1992a).

Still another explanation seems possible. Maybe old people remember in a different way than do young people. C. Adams (1991), for instance, found that adolescents' story recall was reproductive and text based, whereas adults' recall was more reconstructive and interpretative. Furthermore, the adults summarized the story's psychological and metaphoric meanings. These results seem to illustrate Schopenhauer's thesis that "The first forty years of life furnish text, while the remaining thirty supply the commentary; without the commentary, we are unable to understand aright the true sense of coherence of the text, together with the moral it contains" (C. Adams, 1991, p. 323). If there is such a difference, old people have a special competence when treating memories that make them especially important as contributors to satisfaction with life. This suggests that it is how, rather than what, we remember that adds to retirement satisfaction and well-being. It is also reasonable to assume that the more of this special competence of remembering that is in effect, the more likely it is that integrity is achieved (Erikson, 1982).

The relationship between biography and retirement satisfaction, adjustment to aging, or psychological growth shows similarities to the relationship between life history and personality formation in a dynamic psychological perspective. A similar mechanism can be hypothesized on two sides of the triangular model in Figure 2; that is, the experiences that once created the personality structure also seem to be needed to uphold the function of that structure, as can be seen in the mental status at examination. Furthermore, there is a similarity between the content on both sides. The autobiographical report was focused on the relationships with significant others in different life span periods. Reminiscing fed the individual with memories of attachment and an evaluation of how the individual's need for attachment was met in different periods of life. The present results showed two periods to be crucial: childhood and adolescence. In these two periods, the relationships to primary caregivers and friends were generally agreed to be of great importance for the individuation process, laying the foundation for the person's future identity and mental status.

The relationships in the model can be viewed from different time perspectives: the present tense, i.e., the retiree's view of his present life and the mental status of the retiree. The past tense, i.e., the experiences from the different life periods. When looked on from the retiree's point of view, we find a report heavily dependent on his or her reminiscences. When we look at the results from a life period perspective, the deterministic aspect is prominent, i.e., how previous experience determines later perception. Finally, when looked at from the present status of the retirees, the formative potentialities of different life periods in shaping the individual personality structure are prominent. This line of argument is supported by Rappaport, Enrich, and Wilson (1982), who advocated the importance of a total temporal perspective to the promotion of healthy development over the life span, and Rowe (1982), who stated that people give meaning to the present in terms of our past and future perspectives.

Rosenmayr (1979) repeatedly analyzed the relationship between past experience and present status. His basic assumption was that life satisfaction depends on the meaning one gives to the life situation and that meaning can only be given to the present in reflection of the past. Moreover, self-discovery and self-presentation, as well as self-differentiation, are created through one's relationships with significant others. In this way, a coalition is obtained between life course theories and the interactionists regarding how the individual identity is shaped and retained over time. Even though the formative consequences of life events are recognized from a prospective point of view, an additive attitude whereby different elements of deprivation have been added up to a state of "cumulative deprivation" in old age (Rosenmayr & Majce, 1978) does not seem to account for the retrospective role of reminiscences. A successive reformulation of the interpretation of previous experience that is a central feature of the reminiscing process interposes a window or a latitude between the historical event and its representation in the present, with implications for the present sense of well-being and life satisfaction. This process is similar to the therapeutic process, wherein critical incidences in previous experiences are made conscious, critically evaluated, and reformulated either to change the structure of the perceiver (the psychoanalytically oriented psychotherapy) or to reconstruct the previous experience so that it has a less detrimental influence on the individual's present status. With this complementary interpretation of the autobiographical process in mind, we can argue that reminiscing is also a form of self-therapy in which the person takes advantage of the possibility of reevaluating previous experience to the benefit of his or her present status in terms of self-reflection and identity refinement. Such a line of argument would also explain the seeming paradox that those with a prospectively recorded disadvantaged development not always in old age are those who are most dissatisfied with their present condition. Comparing the interviewer's assessment of the life review report with the subject's own evaluation, there are an almost total disagreement in a number of cases. While the reviewer may see a life under most dissatisfying conditions, the subject evaluates the life review positively.

Maybe the difference has to do with how much work the individual is prepared to invest in his or her life history, together with his or her capacity to make something out of it. From this point of view, one's handling of one's life story can be related to the results of recent creativity research. In a study of creative artists, G. Smith and Carlsson (1990) found a unique relationship between the creative artist and his or her autobiography. Mainly, the creative artist has a much closer relationship to the emotional parts of his or her childhood memories, especially concerning significant others. Thus, they are not remembered but are actually experienced, still with their emotional quality present. Remarkably, in highly creative artists, both positive and negative, happy and unhappy, memories are available, whereas in less creative artists it is either one or the other type of memory. Creativity most likely is one component of life satisfaction, and the present results imply that the use of the past in the present is a way of potentiating previous experiences to benefit the present, in this case in terms of thinking creatively and, by implication, increasing life satisfaction.

CONCLUSION

Considering the interaction of the whole triangle, life story–mental status–life satisfaction, and taking into account the phenomenological approach, the parallel to psychodynamic psychotherapeutic treatment models is obvious, even though phenomenology is an approach to the study of individuals, rather than a specific theoretical foundation. Phenomenology has been most extensively used in clinical work with a therapeutic context, where it is important to understand individuals' subjective experiences. As in psychotherapy, it is the phenomenological aspect of the life history that is of interest. It conveys the meaning that the individual attributes to events that have passed. Maybe it is not the same meaning that was true when the experience took place, but it is the meaning that the experience has come to hold at the present.

Again, it may be important to distinguish between adaptive and maladaptive preconstructs (Gergen & Gergen, 1983), that is, concepts that influence one's present feelings, motivations, and cognition in ways that are beneficial to one and concepts that have detrimental effects. Both types of constructs might be more or less central and represent the core of the individual's self-image continuously supported by his or her life story. Other parts of the self may be more vulnerable to change that is induced by reconstructing the life story. From a psychotherapeutic perspective, a reevaluation of central past experiences, such as relationships with significant others, can bring about a change in mental status and ultimately in well-being and life satisfaction, which in turn is expected to have a positive outcome on one's present state. For central hard-core items such as neurotic reaction or depressive insufficiency, psychotherapeutic counseling may be needed, but in other areas, such as self-image and self-confidence, an interest in and a positive attitude toward one's own life story may be sufficient intervention to increase present well-being and life satisfaction in old age. The present analysis gives clear support to such a statement. In Birren's (1993) terminology, the telling of one's life story may be the poor person's psychotherapy.

Part Two

Research

Merriam begins the research section with a report on a study of the reminiscences of the oldest old. Her findings refute Butler's statement that reminiscing is a universal occurrence in older people: Only 41% of the centenarians she interviewed had conducted a life review, as did 50% of the 60 year olds. Perhaps this is a cohort difference, and as society begins to value the telling of the life story, more individuals will review their lives.

Webster's research supports Merriam's. Studying an even younger sample, Webster found that, in some instances, teens reminisced as much as adults did, particularly for problem solving and understanding one's identity. This research encourages those who use reminiscence therapeutically to consider it from a life span perspective and use it with younger people.

Qualitative research is well represented in this section, with the work of Kovach and of de Vries, Blando, and Walker. Kovach presents the Autobiographical Memory Coding Tool for the use of future researchers wanting to analyze life stories. de Vries et al. report the use of a qualitative technique to analyze the structure and content of life events. Again, the analysis was made across the life span, continuing the trend of using life story methodology with younger people. Both studies encourage us to examine personality traits, style of reminiscing, and age at which the life story is researched.

Stones, Rattenbury, and Kozma looked at the short- and long-term effects of group reminiscing. In their chapter, they provide an excellent overview of outcome measures and share a startling and encouraging outcome: Happiness was maintained over a prolonged period in the reminiscence group and actually contributed to a longer life span and decreased physical illness.

Chapter 6

Reminiscence and the Oldest Old

Sharan B. Merriam

As evidenced by the range of topics covered in this book, reminiscence is an intriguing yet complex phenomenon to understand. Although it is a behavior that individuals of all ages engage in, it is also commonly thought to serve a special function in late life. Many researchers in the past 25 years have sought to understand how reminiscence might function as an adaptive mechanism to relieve stress, enhance self-esteem, increase life satisfaction, ward off depression, and so on.

Unfortunately, the research as a whole has proven inconclusive with respect to both reminiscing's adaptive value and its relationship with increasing age (Merriam, 1980; Molinari & Reichlin, 1984–85; Romaniuk, 1981; Thornton & Brotchie, 1987). For example, although it is commonly thought that older adults reminisce more than younger people, this is not consistently borne out in the literature. For example, Cameron (1972) reported that adults of all ages thought

The research reported in this chapter was supported by National Institute of Mental Health Grant R0143435. The author thanks Principal Investigators Leonard Poon, Gloria Clayton, and Peter Martin for making this research possible and for their assistance in data collection and analysis.

about the future twice as frequently as they thought about the past; Hyland and Ackerman (1988) found that middle-aged subjects reminisced less frequently than did younger or older subjects; and Merriam and Cross (1982) found no age differences in the frequency of reminiscence among young, middle-aged, and older adults. On the other hand, Taft and Nehrke (1990) found a relationship among life review, age, and ego integrity, and Lieberman and Tobin (1983), comparing older and middle-aged respondents, found that the older adults "spent significantly more time discussing the past than [did] their middle-aged counterparts" (p. 282). They concluded that "the elderly invest more of themselves in their past than [do] younger people" (p. 282).

Particularly associated with older adulthood is the life review form of reminiscence. First proposed by Butler in 1963, the life review involves evaluation, analysis, and reorganization of past experiences; it is therapeutic work, as opposed to a simple recalling of the past for enjoyment or storytelling. In fact, Butler stated that "the life review is not synonymous with, but includes reminiscence" (p. 67). It is most often (though not exclusively) precipitated by "the realization of approaching dissolution and death" (Butler, p. 66). Butler (1974) wrote that "only in old age can one experience a personal sense of the entire life cycle" and "old age inaugurate[s] the process of the life review" (p. 534).

Although much of the research on reminiscence has involved older adults, very little data have been collected from the oldest old, especially those born more than a century ago. Although some study samples have included participants in their 80s, 90s and 100s, only one study has focused on the memories of centenarians. In a study of interview data from 276 centenarians, Costa and Kastenbaum (1967) found that successful recall of three different types of past memories (earliest memory, most salient historical event, and most exciting event) predicted the presence of future ambitions. Echoing Butler, they concluded that a centenarian's "reservoir of memories helps sustain his present moment of existence and also aids him in creating a perspective in preparation for his eventual death" (Costa & Kastenbaum, p. 15).

The Georgia Centenarian Study, involving centenarians, 80-year-olds, and 60-year-olds, provided an opportunity for us to examine some common notions about reminiscence and life review. The study also yielded some other fascinating data. For example, when asked to reminisce about the most notable historical event they could remember, the centenarians talked about the sinking of the *Titanic,* having talked to President *Theodore* Roosevelt, the first telephone, and Booker T. Washington's speech. This chapter presents an overview of the findings from the Georgia Centenarian Study with regard to aging, reminiscence, and life review.

THE GEORGIA CENTENARIAN STUDY

The Georgia Centenarian Study was begun in 1988 with a grant from the National Institute of Mental Health. The overall purpose of the study was to determine how psychosocial factors combine to contribute to successful adaptation in the oldest old (see Poon, 1992). Eighty-year-olds and 60-year-olds were included in the study because it was thought that different patterns of adaptation might emerge from different cohorts. The focus of the study being on successful adaptation, each participant had to reside in the community and be cognitively intact. A community-dwelling person was defined as anyone who was self-sufficient or partially self-sufficient and was living in the community and not in a custodial institution. Persons who lived in their own home, the home of relatives, a group or old-age home, or a life-care community were defined as community dwellers. Intact cognitive status was defined as not being demented or disoriented; the Mini-Mental Status Examination was used as a screening tool at the time of recruitment (Folstein, Folstein, & McHugh, 1975).

Centenarians were identified and recruited by referrals from state and local agencies, community organizations, and the media. Eighty- and 60-year-olds were recruited from probability samples generated by the University of Georgia Survey Research Center. Overall, the final sample consisted of 107 centenarians, 93 eighty-year-olds, and 91 sixty-year-olds. Seventy percent of the sample was white, and 30% was black. Sixty-seven percent was female.

The reminiscence component of the Centenarian Study consisted of a three-part instrument included in the test battery administered to all participants. The centenarians were tested individually in their homes; the interviewer read the individual items to them and recorded their responses. Most of the 80- and 60-year-olds were tested in centralized locations around the state.

In an exploration of the simple reminiscence behavior of the centenarians, the first part of the reminiscence instrument consisted of a question eliciting the frequency of occurrence of reminiscence and a 17-item Uses of Reminiscence scale. The second component of the instrument contained four questions about the life review type of reminiscence (whether they had conducted a life review; whether they had done so more than once, and, if so, when; what precipitated the review; and whether they were satisfied with their life). The third section asked the same four questions used by Costa and Kastenbaum (1967) in order to replicate their study. These questions elicited earliest memory, most exciting event, most salient historical event, and future ambitions. The rest of this chapter presents a brief overview of the findings.

FREQUENCY AND USES OF REMINISCENCE

The frequency with which the three age groups reminisced was determined by asking them "How often do your thoughts and conversations turn to past experiences and events?" and having them respond on a 5-point scale from *never* (1) to *very often* (5). There were no significant differences among the three groups in frequency of reminiscence. The group means for the 60- and 80-year-olds were identical (3.35) and the group mean for the centenarians only slightly (but not significantly) higher (3.47). This finding seems to add support to the uncoupling of age and reminiscing.

Several studies, however, have found links between frequency of reminiscence and dependent measures such as depression (McMahon & Rhudick, 1967), life satisfaction (Haight, 1988; Havighurst & Glasser, 1972, Hyland & Ackerman, 1988), and self-concept (C. N. Lewis, 1971). Since the Centenarian Study was interested in successful adaptation, a number of instruments designed to explore different dimensions of adaptation were included in the study (see Poon, 1992). Thus, there was an opportunity to assess the relationships between frequency of reminiscence and several dependent measures. Specifically, correlation coefficients were used to examine the relationships between frequency of reminiscence and life satisfaction (Neugarten's Life Satisfaction Index), depression (Geriatric Depression Screening Scale), morale (Bradburn's Affect Balance Scale), and coping (Health and Daily Living Scale) (Bradburn, 1969; Center for the Study of Aging and Human Development, 1978; Lawton, 1975; Neugarten, Havighurst, & Tobin, 1961). Statistically significant correlations were found between frequency of reminiscence and depression and between frequency of reminiscence and coping with a health issue. However, because the amount of variance explained by these relationships was negligible (approximately 2%), these relationships were not considered meaningful, despite their statistical significance.

To explore further how centenarians might make use of reminiscence, the 17-item Uses of Reminiscence scale was constructed for the study. The 17 items were read to centenarians as follows: "People think about or talk about their past for many different reasons. Do you think about or talk about your past in order to . . ." Answers to each item were recorded on a 5-point Likert-type scale from *no, never* (1) to *yes, very often* (5). The 17 items can be found in Table 1.

Responses to the items were factor-analyzed using a principal-components analysis followed by varimax rotation. As can be seen in Table 1, the procedure yielded three factors that together explained 55.8% of the total variance. Factor 1, termed Therapeutic, consisted of the most items (9) and explained most of the variance. Factor 2, Informative, consisted of 5 items, and Factor 3, Enjoyment, consisted of 2 items. Only one of the 17 items—"get relief from boredom"—failed to load on a factor.

Clearly, for the centenarians, the predominant use of reminiscence was therapeutic. The items in Factor 1 reflect coping with life's problems, an effort to understand oneself, and the work involved in Butler's life review. Item 14, "Put your life in order"; Item 15, "Deal with knowing your life is finite"; and Item 17, "Deal with unpleasant or troublesome memories," all loaded solidly into Factor 1 and reflect aspects of the life review. This form of reminiscence has been identified by nearly all writers and researchers as separate from other forms. Clements (1982) used the term *therapeutic* to distinguish between life review and recreational reminiscing, and Moody (1988b) wrote that the therapeutic use of reminiscence offers "an opportunity for personal integration, psychological healing, and self-actualization" (p. 9).

The second factor, Informative, reflects what Coleman (1986a) identified as the *informative* or *storytelling* function of reminiscence. More recently, Moody

Table 1   Factor Loadings of the 17 Items on the Uses of Reminiscence Scale

Item	Statement	Factor 1: Therapeutic	Factor 2: Informative	Factor 3: Enjoyment
10	Get over feeling lonesome	.73	.03	.27
12	Understand life	.73	.36	.05
15	Life is finite	.72	.23	−.03
14	Put life in order	.69	.43	.06
6	Understand self better	.67	.19	.15
7	Cope with loss	.65	.25	.29
16	Help relax	.65	.12	.38
17	Deal with troublesome memories	.61	.38	.28
11	Help accept changes	.59	.47	.04
9	Make future plans	.26	.69	.04
13	Deal with a present problem	.42	.67	−.03
8	Tell of accomplishments	.18	.63	.24
5	Entertain others	.07	.60	.41
2	Teach others about the past	.17	.55	.28
1	Relive a pleasant experience	.02	.15	.74
3	Lift spirits	.30	.17	.66
4	Relief from boredom	.44	.14	.46

(1988b) has written about what he called the *educational/cultural transmission* form of reminiscence, used for "passing on values or lessons of the past" (pp. 14–15). Item 2, "Teach others about the past," speaks directly to this purpose. Item 5, "Entertain others," and Item 8, "Tell of your accomplishments," suggest the storytelling component. The other two items that loaded on this factor, "Deal with a present problem" and "Make future plans," indicate a sense of time, suggesting that, by reminiscing, the reminiscer can locate him- or herself within historical time. Costa and Kastenbaum (1967) speculated that in centenarians, the ability to differentiate among past experiences would be indicative of a healthy outlook on the present and the future, and they were able to support this assumption in their study of 276 centenarians.

Yet another distinct function of reminiscence is represented by the third factor, Enjoyment. "Relive a pleasant experience" and "Lift your spirits" clustered to suggest a light-hearted, past-the-time-of-day type of reminiscence. This is closest to what Coleman (1986a) called *simple reminiscence* and Clements (1982) identified as a recreational use of reminiscence.

The factor structure presented in this chapter is based on data from the 107 centenarians only, but identical analyses were undertaken with data for the 80- and 60-year-olds and from the entire sample combined. Interestingly, the same three-factor solution emerged (see Merriam, 1993b). These analyses suggest two conclusions. First, there is nothing particularly different about centenarians' reminiscence behavior, in terms of either frequency or function, from that of adults as much as 40 years younger. Second, reminiscence is a multidimensional construct. Although the three distinct factors found in this study have been proposed by other writers, there is little empirical research to verify their existence. In fact, much of the research on reminiscence is confounded by the fact that different types of reminiscence behavior are not distinguished from each other. *Life review, simple reminiscence, oral history, guided autobiography,* and a host of other terms are used interchangeably in the literature. This may account in part for the inconclusive findings regarding reminiscence's value as an educational or therapeutic intervention.

THE LIFE REVIEW

Since Butler (1963) proposed the term *life review* more than 30 years ago, the notion that older persons review their lives in the face of approaching death has become entrenched in both the literature and practice of gerontology. In 1963, Butler described the life review as "a naturally occurring, universal mental process characterized by the progressive return to consciousness of past experiences, and, particularly, the resurgence of unresolved conflicts; simultaneously, and normally, these revived experiences and conflicts can be surveyed and reintegrated" (p. 66). The life review is most commonly, although not exclusively, triggered by "the realization of approaching dissolution and death" (Butler, p. 66). It is most likely to occur in the aged, Butler speculated, because they are nearer to death, because they are retired and thus have more time for self-reflection, and because "the customary defensive operation provided by work has been removed" (p. 67). Although life review may occur earlier, "it takes on a striking intensity in early old age" and "then begins to abate in the 70s and 80s" (M. I. Lewis & Butler, 1974, pp. 165, 169).

I was able to test two assumptions that undergird the concept of the life review using data from the Georgia Centenarian Study (see Merriam, 1993a). First, I reasoned that if the life review were a universal process, all the centenarians, if not all the 80-year-olds and many 60-year-olds, would have conducted a life review. Second, if, for the reasons just stated, the older people are, the more likely they are to have engaged in a life review, then all the centenarians—the oldest old and those closest to death—at some point would have reviewed their lives.

To examine these assumptions, I asked the following question of all participants: "Some people review and *evaluate* their past in order to get an overall picture of their life. This is called the life review. Have you reviewed, or are you currently reviewing your life?" Respondents could answer *yes, no,* or *currently reviewing.* As can be seen in Table 2, 46.4% ($n = 134$) of the total sample said they had not reviewed their lives. When the responses to this question were examined by age cohort, a surprising 43.8% of the centenarians, 44.7% of the 80-year-olds,

Table 2   Percent of Centenarians, 80-Year-Olds and 60-Year-Olds Who Had Conducted a Life Review

Age	Had not conducted a review ($n = 134$)	Had conducted a review ($n = 105$)	Were currently reviewing ($n = 50$)
100 ($n = 105$)			
%	43.8	41	15.2
n	46	43	16
80 ($n = 94$)			
%	44.7	41.5	13.7
n	42	39	13
60 ($n = 90$)			
%	51.1	25.6	23.3
n	46	23	21

and 51.1% of the 60-year-olds said they had not reviewed their lives. A chi-square test revealed that the differences among the three age groups were not significant.

Participants who *had* conducted a life review were asked, "What caused you to begin reviewing your life?" A wide range of answers were reported. For a few, the life review was caused by a major life event, such as the death of a spouse, the children's leaving home, or retirement. For others, the life review was precipitated by a prompt ("Prayer," "When young people ask questions," or "When someone mentions someone I know") or by a generalized need ("Thinking how life could get better," "Not being able to do things for myself," "Making important decisions," and "Life changes"). A number of respondents indicated that, for them, life review was a continuous process. "Have done it since I was young," stated one centenarian. Thinking about the past is an "ever-daily experience," said another. Still others could identify no particular cause: "Don't know what causes it; I think about the past and present a lot," one respondent said. "Just getting older" and "Things in daily life," said others. No single cause was cited by the majority of respondents, and no one alluded, directly or indirectly, to his or her impending death as the reason for engaging in a life review.

The centenarians' life review behaviors clearly call into question Butler's (1963) contention that life review is a universal process. One might speculate that these centenarians were unable to recall having conducted a life review; however, a criterion for participating in this study was cognitive competence. Furthermore, the life review questions were part of a longer instrument on reminiscence that required the participants to answer numerous questions about recalling the past.

Lieberman and Tobin (1983), who also found that more than half of their sample had not reviewed their lives, suggested that the life review might be a process that

> demands high levels of inner skills not necessarily characteristic of most people . . . [and that] perhaps we have been in error in assuming that the special skills needed to carry out a successful life review—a lifelong habit of introspection and heightened preoccupation with themes of mortality and immortality—are characteristic of most men and women. (pp. 309, 310)

I also speculated that perhaps nearly half the participants had not reviewed their life because they were satisfied with their past life. When asked the question "Are you satisfied with your past life?", 87.4% of the total sample said they were, and 12.5% either said no or indicated they were not totally satisfied, making comments such as "There are things I would change." However, an analysis of these data along with the preceding data revealed that being satisfied with one's past life was independent of having conducted a life review.

The present findings also call into question the notion that the life review is prompted by the realization of approaching death. The centenarians who reported having reviewed their lives gave a wide range of reasons for doing so, suggesting that there are many possible motivators.

These findings suggest that the claims that life review is universal and is initiated by the awareness of approaching death need to be reexamined. Perhaps attention could be focused on how the life review functions for those who have a need to engage in it and how it might be a socially or culturally bound phenomenon (Moody, 1988b; Tarman, 1988).

MEMORIES AND FUTURE AMBITIONS

As I noted earlier, I could find only one other study on centenarians' recall of past events. Using interview data collected on 276 centenarians by the Social Security Administration, Costa and Kastenbaum (1967) investigated the relationship between being able to recall past events and having future ambitions. Using a systems framework, they speculated that "the organization of centenarians' memories" could be thought of as "a subsystem of a more general psychological system" (Costa & Kastenbaum, p. 11). The more differentiated this subsystem, implying "a finer articulation, or separation, among past experiences" (Costa & Kastenbaum, p. 11), the better a centenarian would be able to create "a perspective on his [or her] present and future" (Costa & Kastenbaum, p. 15). Four items from the Social Security Administration's questionnaire were used in the analysis: the earliest memory, the most salient historical event, the most exciting event, and whether the respondent had any unrealized ambitions. Costa and Kastenbaum found a statistically significant correlation between level of differentiation and future ambition. That is, respondents who could recall all three types of past events were also more likely to respond to the future ambition question.

The Georgia Centenarian Study provided an opportunity to replicate Costa and Kastenbaum's (1967) investigation. The same four questions were asked of the Georgia centenarians, and data were analyzed in a similar manner; for details, see Merriam, Martin, Adkins, & Poon (in press). For the Georgia centenarians, no significant relationship was found between the ability to recall three types of past events and statement of a future ambition.

The inability to replicate Costa and Kastenbaum's (1967) findings might be due to several factors. First, the samples were from cohorts born approximately 30 years apart. In addition, 70% of Costa and Kastenbaum's centenarians were male, compared with 26% of the Georgia sample. The percentages of participants who responded to the questions also differed significantly. In Costa and Kastenbaum's study, 22% did not respond to the earliest-memory question, 52% did not identify a salient historical event, and 44% could not recall the most exciting event in their life. The respective percentages for the Georgia group were 10%, 12%, and 17%. Similarly, whereas 77.3% of the Georgia centenarians were able to recall all three memories, only 30.8% of Costa and Kastenbaum's centenarians were able to do so. Differences in data collection techniques may explain the differences in response rate between the two samples and, in turn, our inability to replicate their results. Because of the large percentages of subjects who did not respond to the three memory items in Costa and Kastenbaum's study, their results need to be interpreted with caution. Our study, based on a more complete data set, revealed no significant relationship between ability to recall past memories and statement of future ambitions.

The lack of significance with a more complete data set challenges the theoretical assumptions underlying Costa and Kastenbaum's (1967) study. Although it seems reasonable that the ability to differentiate among past memories would predict the ability to have a perspective on the present and future, one might not necessarily presuppose the other. That is, one person may be able to recall the past quite well but not be particularly future oriented; another person may be oriented toward the present or future. It might also be unrealistic to expect centenarians, who have few years left to live, to have "unrealized future ambitions." Finally, time perspective itself might be conceptualized in different ways. For example, it could be hypothesized that a sense of self with an identifiable past, present, and future is indicative of good mental health. Furthermore, as some reminiscence research has already suggested, recalling the past might be an adaptive mechanism for present and future problem solving.

CONCLUSION

Despite the inconclusiveness of empirical research findings, numerous personal experiences and testimonials to the value of reminiscence are common in the literature. Research is important for both uncovering misconceptions and providing a solid foundation for practitioners who see reminiscence as a means of facilitating late-life growth and development. The Georgia Centenarian Study offered an opportunity to explore some common assumptions about reminiscence, life review, and aging. The findings from this study contribute to the knowledge base on reminiscence and life review in several ways.

First, if in fact older persons reminiscence more than younger ones, and if older adults are more likely to engage in a life review (because they are closer to death), then centenarians should be the most involved of any age group in both of these behaviors. Although I did not assess the reminiscence behavior of young people in this study, a substantial age range was represented, that is, between the very young old (some would say late middle age) 60-year-olds and the oldest old centenarians. No statistically significant age group differences were found. Given the 40-year age range of the sample (60 to centenarians), these findings should call into question the notion that older persons necessarily reminisce more than younger adults. The same was also true of the life review—there were no significant differences among the centenarians, 80-year-olds, and 60-year-olds who stated they had reviewed or were currently reviewing their lives. An even more intriguing finding with regard to the life review is that it was far less than universal, as Butler (1963) claimed. Only a little more than half (56.2%) of the centenarians reported that they had reviewed or were currently reviewing their lives.

A second major contribution of the present study is that it underscores the need for both researchers who investigate reminiscence and practitioners who use it as an intervention to clarify their concepts. Reminiscence appears to be a multidimensional construct that has very discrete functions. Three were uncovered in this study: a therapeutic function closely akin to the life review; an informative, or storytelling, function; and an enjoyment or recreational function. Various types of reminiscence have been delineated previously in the literature. However, the plethora of terms being used to describe reminiscence behavior and the number of researchers who fail to define or distinguish the type of reminiscence they are investigating have hindered the usefulness of this phenomenon in aging research and practice. The lack of significant links between reminiscence and particular dependent measures (as was found in this study) may well be a function of how the phenomenon is conceptualized. Whether one evokes the past to obtain pleasure and enjoyment, to put one's life in order, or to pass on the lessons of the past might make a great deal of difference in whether the desired outcomes of the use of reminiscence are achieved.

In conclusion, much remains to be investigated with regard to the nature and functions of reminiscence. Careful attention in the future to conceptualizing the phenomenon and examining the assumptions underlying it will help us maximize the potential of reminiscence as an educational and therapeutic intervention.

Chapter 7

Adult Age Differences in Reminiscence Functions

Jeffrey D. Webster

Reminiscence appears to be universal at all ages after middle childhood. It can occur as soon as a child begins to remember things. A 10-year-old child reminisces. (Havighurst & Glasser, 1972, p. 245)

Given this provocative claim, it is somewhat surprising that no systematic attention has been paid to possible similarities or differences in reminiscence behavior among persons across the life span. Although a few researchers (e.g., Kiernat, 1983; Webster & Young, 1988) have explicitly stated that a life span perspective is warranted in the study of reminiscence, developmental differences in this domain have been virtually ignored.

Until very recently, the vast majority of studies have excluded subjects younger than their mid-50s, thereby eliminating the possibility of basic age comparisons. Despite the lack of corroborating empirical evidence, most laypersons, and many authors, apparently subscribe to the notion that reminiscence is the bailiwick of elderly adults. Erikson, Erikson, and Kivnick (1986), for instance, stated that a willingness to remember the past is old age specific. Ironically, the few claims that reminiscence is a natural process manifested even in children, such as Havighurst and Glasser's statement and Magee's (1988a) claim that "reminiscing generally becomes 'second nature' after seven years of age" (p. 1) are also empirically unsubstantiated.

A small but cohesive body of evidence, however, has recently begun to challenge the age-specific assumptions implicit in reminiscence research. Some of this evidence is in the form of literature reviews (e.g., Romaniuk, 1981; Thornton & Brotchie, 1987; Webster & Cappeliez, 1993) in which reviewers have found no evidence, in the form of controlled studies, of a uniform and universal increase in reminiscence behavior in elderly adults.

In terms of the empirical evidence, there are only a handful of published studies that have included adults of all ages, and they have typically focused on simple reminiscence frequency, rather than function. Merriam and Cross (1982) investigated age differences on measures of simple reminiscence frequency in adults ranging in age from 18 to 90 and found that older and younger adults scored higher than middle-aged adults and closer to each other than to the middle-aged subjects. Hyland and Ackerman (1988) found that their younger subjects reported more frequent reminiscence than did their middle-aged subjects and that the frequency with which the younger subjects reminisced was similar to older adults' frequency of reminiscing. Romaniuk and Romaniuk (1983) reported an overall lack of age differences in several facets of the contents of reminiscence. Specifically, there were no age differences in (a) the frequency of recalled transitional or nontransitional life events, (b) the preponderance of positive affect, (c) the primary character of the reminiscence, and (d) the redundancy of memories recalled. Although there were some differences between young and elderly subjects on some aspects (e.g., mean age of memories retrieved), these results call into question the ostensible age-specific nature of reminiscence. Finally, I (Webster, 1994) recently found that gender (females higher) and personality (openness to experience higher), but not age, were significant predictors of simple reminiscence frequency in a sample of adults ranging in age from 18 to 81. Although few in number, these studies—Hyland and Ackerman (1988), Merriam and Cross (1982), Romaniuk and Romaniuk (1983), and Webster (1994)—generally show that younger and older adults tend to reminisce with similarly high frequency and to reminisce more frequently than middle-aged adults.

Recently, Staudinger and her colleagues (e.g., Staudinger, 1989; Staudinger, Smith, & Baltes, 1992) and de Vries, Blando, and Walker (see Chapter 9) have examined life review reminiscence as a context for the emergence and manifestation of wisdom (e.g., Staudinger et al., 1992) and have examined the structure and content of life review (e.g., de Vries, Bluck, & J. E. Birren, 1993). For both sets of investigators, findings included a lack of age differences for global measures, with some minor age differences emerging in finer grained analyses. Furthermore, in a conference paper, Weenolsen (1986) reported that most of her female subjects stated that they had engaged in the life review process before the age of 30. These findings and the apparent similarity in simple reminiscence frequency between younger and older adults suggest that what may be unique at a more advanced age is less simple frequency than function. That is, the goal of memory retrieval, of which reminiscence is the means, may serve different purposes as we grow older.

In this chapter, I present evidence that explicitly tests the above speculation. I assessed adult age differences on a measure of reminiscence functions across the life course, in an effort to establish a database against which developmental questions can be gauged. To my knowledge, this study is the first of its kind.

METHOD

Subjects

The subjects in the present study were the same subjects used in a larger project to develop a reliable and valid psychometric instrument of reminiscence function, the Reminiscence Functions Scale (RFS; Webster, 1993). For a description of the data collection procedure, readers are referred to the 1993 article.

Subjects consisted of a diverse convenience sample, including 289 males and 421 females ranging in age from 17 to 91 years ($M = 45.76$, $SD = 21.69$). The subjects' level of education ranged from those with no formal schooling whatsoever to those with at least some postgraduate work ($M = 12.57$ years, $SD = 2.58$). Self-perceived health scores ranged from 1, representing *very poor* to 7, represent-

Table 1   Demographic Characteristics of Sample

	Age group								
Variable	Teens	20s	30s	40s	50s	60s	70s	80s[a]	Total Sample
Gender									
Male	31	32	39	38	41	44	44	20	289
Female	88	73	47	39	39	58	58	18	421
Age									
M	18.3	22.5	34.2	44.4	53.8	64.6	73.1	83.2	45.7
SD	0.6	2.6	2.7	2.6	2.7	2.8	2.6	2.8	21.6
Education									
M	12.5	13.1	13.5	13.4	13.4	12.0	11.3	10.3	12.6
SD	0.6	1.0	1.9	2.4	2.5	3.4	3.7	2.9	2.6
Health									
M	5.3	5.3	5.2	4.9	5.2	5.1	4.8	4.9	5.1
SD	1.1	1.2	1.1	1.3	0.9	1.3	1.6	1.7	1.3

[a]One 91-year-old man was included in the 80s decade.

ing *excellent* (*M* = 5.09, *SD* = 1.27). Table 1 presents a breakdown of the demographic variables for the sample as a whole as well as by decade group.

Measures

The RFS is a 43-item questionnaire in which subjects indicate on a 6-point scale how often they reminisce with a particular function in mind (Webster, 1993). Subjects read the following introduction:

> At different points throughout their lives, most adults think about their past. Recalling earlier times can happen spontaneously or deliberately, privately or with other people, and may involve remembering both happy and sad episodes. The process of recalling memories from our personal past is called reminiscence, an activity engaged in by adults of all ages.
>
> This questionnaire concerns the why, or functions, of reminiscence. That is, what purpose does reminiscence fulfil, or, what goal does retrieving certain memories help you accomplish?

The 43 items were randomly ordered in the questionnaire and presented as completions to the stem: "When I reminisce it is:". For example, an item following from the stem might read: "to pass the time during idle or restless hours." Responses ranged from *never* (1) to *very frequently* (6).

The RFS consists of seven factors, representing the various functions of reminiscence over the life course. The seven factors (with abbreviated sample items in parentheses) are as follows:

1   Boredom Reduction ("to reduce boredom"),
2   Death Preparation ("because I feel less fearful of death after I finish reminiscing"),
3   Identity/Problem Solving ("to try to understand myself better"),
4   Conversation ("to create ease of conversation"),
5   Intimacy Maintenance ("to keep alive the memory of a dead loved one"),
6   Bitterness Revival ("to keep memories of old hurts fresh in my mind"),
7   Teach/Inform ("to teach younger persons about cultural values").

Reliability

Internal consistency scores computed using coefficient alpha for all items demonstrate that the RFS has good internal consistency. Scores ranged from .79 for Conversation to .89 for Identity/Problem Solving (mean alpha = .84, *SD* = .04).

Validity

The RFS's predictive validity was assessed by examining its relationship to Costa and McCrae's (1985) personality dimensions Neuroticism, Extraversion, and Openness to Experience. A separate validation sample was drawn from students at Langara College (see Webster, 1993, for complete details). As hypothesized, Bitterness Revival correlated with Neuroticism ($n = 120$, $r = .42$, $p < .01$, one-tailed), Conversation correlated with Extraversion ($n = 123$, $r = .33$, $p < .01$, one-tailed), and Identity/Problem Solving correlated with Openness ($n = 120$, $r = .18$, $p < .05$, one-tailed).

RESULTS

A total RFS score was computed for all subjects by summing across all seven function scores. A 2 (sex) × 8 (age) analysis of variance (ANOVA) was performed with the RFS total score serving as the dependent variable. Results indicated a main effect for sex, $F(1, 693) = 3.87$, $p < .05$, with women scoring, on average, higher than men. No effect was found for age, $F(7, 693) = .923$, $p = .488$. The Sex × Age interaction was also nonsignificant, $F(7, 693) = .552$, $p = .795$. Figure 1 shows the relationship between age and total RFS score.

A 2 (sex) × 8 (age) between-subjects multivariate analysis of variance (MANOVA) was performed with the seven RFS factors serving as the dependent variables. SPSS/PC+ (version 4.0) computer software (Norusis, 1990) was used for the analysis. The use of Wilks's lambda criteria for the overall MANOVA revealed main effects for both sex, $F(1, 693) = 6.52$, $p < .0001$, and age, $F(7, 693) = 12.47$, $p < .0001$. The Sex × Age interaction, however, was not significant, $F(7, 693) = 1.09$, $p = .298$.

The results of univariate F tests for both sex and age effects on all seven RFS factors are reported in Table 2.

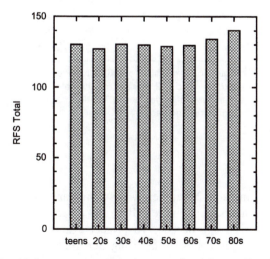

Figure 1 Relationship between age and total score on Reminiscence Function Scale (RFS).

Table 2 Univariate *F*s and Significance Levels for all Factors on Reminiscence Function Scale by Sex and Age

Factor/variable	F	p
Boredom Reduction		
Sex	.83	.36
Age	8.04	<.0001
Death Preparation		
Sex	.17	.68
Age	18.24	<.0001
Identity/Problem Solving		
Sex	12.99	<.0001
Age	6.90	<.0001
Conversation		
Sex	4.74	<.05
Age	1.30	.25
Intimacy Maintenance		
Sex	12.75	<.0001
Age	8.96	<.0001
Bitterness Revival		
Sex	2.21	.14
Age	5.97	<.0001
Teach/Inform		
Sex	.25	.62
Age	26.19	<.0001

Note. For sex, *df*s = 1 and 693; for age, *df*s = 7 and 693. For the multivariate analysis of variance, $N = 709$ because of one missing case.

Age Effects

It can be seen from Table 2 that there were significant age effects on all RFS factors, except Conversation. Figure 2 illustrates the relationship between each RFS factor and each age decade. To protect against Type I error rate, I performed all multiple comparisons using Scheffe's procedure and set the alpha criterion at .05.

Figure 2a shows a U-shaped relationship between age and Boredom Reduction, with teenagers scoring higher than all other age groups except for the 20- and 80-year-olds. The 20-year-olds scored higher than the 50-year-olds.

Figure 2b illustrates the relationship between age and Death Preparation. A clear, monotonically increasing linear function was evident, with the 80-year-olds outscoring all younger cohorts, with the exception of the 70-year-olds. The 70-year-olds scored higher than the teenagers and 20- and 30-year-olds. Both the 60- and 50-year-olds scored higher than the teenagers and 20-year-olds.

Figure 2c depicts the relationship between age and Identity/Problem Solving. There was a tendency for adults in the first half of life (i.e., adolescence through the 40s) to use this function more often than adults in the latter half of life (i.e., the 50s through the 80s). Specifically, teens, 20-year-olds, and 30-year-olds scored higher than did both the 70- and 60-year-olds.

Figure 2d depicts the nonsignificant relationship between age and Conversation—all age groups scored at approximately the same level. No two age groups were significantly different from each other on this factor.

The relationship between age and Intimacy Maintenance is shown in Figure 2e. Except for the teenagers, who scored at approximately the same mean level as the 40- and 50-year-olds, there was a monotonicallly increasing linear trend, with the 70- and 80-year-olds scoring higher than both the 20- and 30-year-olds. The 60-year-olds scored higher than the 20-year-olds.

Figure 2f illustrates the effects of age on Bitterness Revival. There was an overall trend for the younger adults to score higher than their older counterparts on this function. Only the teenagers, however, were reliably different from the 60- and 70-year-olds.

Finally, the relationship between age and Teach/Inform is shown in Figure 2g. There appeared to be a steady increase in the use of reminiscence to teach or inform from adolescence through the 30s, after which the frequency with which reminiscence was used for this purpose was virtually even across the decades. Specifically, the 70-, 60-, and 50-year-olds scored higher than the teenagers and 20- and 30-year-olds, while the 80-, 40-, and 30-year-olds scored higher than the teenagers and 20-year-olds.

Sex Effects

As can be seen from Table 2, gender had significant effects on three of the RFS functions: Identity/Problem Solving, Conversation, and Intimacy Maintenance. Women scored higher than men on all three factors.

DISCUSSION

More than two decades ago, Havighurst and Glasser (1972) exhorted their fellow researchers to "study reminiscence throughout the life cycle, to describe it empirically, and to discover its functions in human development" (p. 245). The present

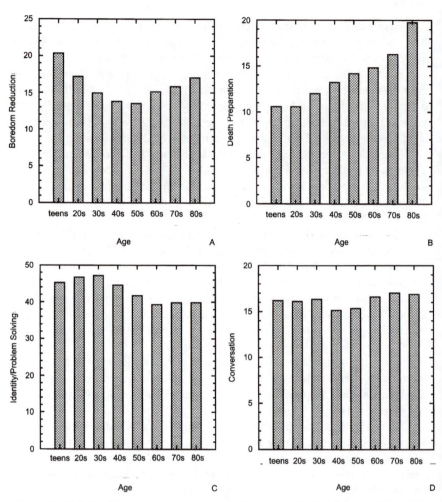

Figure 2 Relationships between age and the factors on the Reminiscence Functions Scale.

study provides a sound foundation for movement in this direction. The current findings, based as they are on a large and demographically diverse sample, provide a much needed database that serves as a foil for unsupported statements in the literature. Anecdotal claims concerning the putative increased association between age and reminiscence behavior can now be objectively assessed.

Age/Cohort Differences

Given the potential range of scores for the RFS as a whole (i.e., 43–258) and the relatively large number of discrete age categories represented in the sample (teens

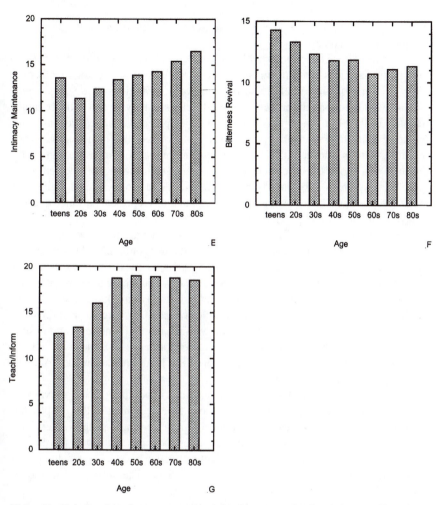

Figure 2   Relationships between age and the factors on the Reminiscence Functions Scale (*Continued*)

to 80-year-olds), the similarity among the total RFS scores (see Figure 1) of all the age groups is remarkable. The lack of age differences in total RFS scores provides compelling empirical evidence that reminiscence is a life span process that begins quite early in life, complementing the findings of the studies of reminiscence frequency and the dimensions of life review discussed in the introduction to this chapter.

The findings are paradoxical, however, in that they provide evidence both for and against age differences, the latter in the guise of the RFS total score and the former when the total score is divided into composite subscale, or factor, scores. The evidence strongly suggests that the global construct of reminiscence may be relatively age invariant, but specific reminiscence functions are used with greater frequency at certain ages.

Our results enable us to provide a clear description of age differences using one particular measure. Unfortunately, because of our cross-sectional methodology, it is impossible to determine the relative contributions of developmental change versus cohorts differences to these findings. It may be that cohort characteristics of the "Me generation" mask true developmental changes. For instance, younger adults may score at a similar level to older adults on certain measures not because there is true stability in a particular reminiscence dimension, but rather because of a cohort-specific social norm of increased introspection and self-analysis. The explanation for the observed differences, therefore, awaits longitudinal analyses. For now, the following post hoc explanations represent educated guesses informed by theory and previous research.

The finding of a curvilinear relationship between age and the use of reminiscence to reduce boredom, whereby younger and older adults scored higher in this use of reminiscence than did middle-aged adults, is most likely explained in prosaic, rather than theoretical, terms. Specifically, younger and older adults, the former students and the latter most likely retired, simply have more free time than middle-aged adults who must juggle multiple occupational, parental, and financial considerations. Such responsibilities require much more of a present- and future-oriented focus. Hence, the increased use of reminiscence as a means of killing time seen in the younger and older age groups is a luxury not afforded as often to midlife adults pressed for time.

Of greater theoretical interest and practical importance is the curvilinear nature of the relationship itself. As discussed at the beginning of this chapter the vast majority of studies have chronologically truncated their samples to exclude younger adults. Had we adopted the same circumvention strategy in the present study, the conclusion for Boredom Reduction would have been that there is a monotonic, linear increase with age from the 50s on. The benefits of including subjects from all age groups is clear.

Butler's (1963) notion that the life review facilitates an elderly person's acceptance of impending death received support from the finding of an increase with age in the use of reminiscence in the service of preparing for death. This finding is consistent with the notion that elderly adults, in general being closer to death than their younger counterparts, would engage in reviewing their past more frequently in an effort to put their house in order before they die. In fact, it can be seen from Figure 2b that the 80-year-olds were approximately twice as likely to reminisce for this purpose than the teenagers and 20-year-olds.

In an exploratory study conducted more than 20 years ago, Lieberman and Falk (1971) suggested that middle-aged adults were more likely than elderly adults to use reminiscence as a problem-solving tool. The present results lend qualified support to their suggestion, in that the adults 60 years or older scored lower than did all the other age groups in this regard. Unfortunately, it is impossible to identify whether the identity or the problem-solving aspect of the Identity/Problem Solving factor was responsible for this finding. As I have noted elsewhere, there is some reason to suspect that identity and problem solving may be separate factors manifesting divergent developmental trajectories (Webster, 1993). In fact, recent work (Webster, 1994) has documented the separation of the Identity/Problem Solving factor into two separate factors.

As Table 2 and Figure 2d show, there was no difference in the frequency with which the different age groups used reminiscence for the purpose of conversation. Apparently, younger adults are just as likely as elderly adults to engage in "Remember the time we" conversations. This finding contrasts with the related work of Boden and Bielby (1983), who found that elderly adults were more likely than young adults to recall the past spontaneously in the presence of strangers. As a means of engaging a new acquaintance in a novel situation, elderly adults invoked the past as a resource (e.g., "The last time I was in a situation like this was 1942 in a Navy recruiting office"). Younger adults (at least the students in Boden and Bielby's study), in contrast, are more likely to talk about current events when engaging a stranger whom they perceive as being similar to themselves (e.g., "What courses are you taking this semester?"). Perhaps conversational reminiscence is a multipurpose tool for older adults in many situations but is more context specific (i.e., is used with friends and family) for younger adults who have less of a shared history from which to establish contact with strangers.

Maintaining intimacy is a function of reminiscence that serves to keep alive the memory of a significant other who is no longer available to the reminiscer. The unavailability can be the result of several factors, such as geographic distance or estrangement, but, as assessed in the RFS, it is primarily due to death (e.g., "to remember someone who has passed away"). Hence, it is not surprising that a steady increase in the use of this function was found in the present sample from the 20s on, since the older one becomes, the more likely one has lost a friend or family member to death.

The teenagers, however, were the exception to this general pattern, using reminiscence as a means of maintaining intimacy almost as frequently as the 40- and 50-year olds used it for this purpose. One suspects that the teens' targets of reminiscence were still alive, perhaps being girlfriends or boyfriends from whom they were separated. As one 19-year-old male wrote in an earlier pilot study, "Sometimes when I'm alone and I hear a certain song on the radio, I think of the good times I've had with a friend (girl) over the summer, and hence, think about that person" (parentheses in original). This is not to suggest that adolescents do not reminisce about persons who have died. A deceased grandparent with whom the adolescent was very close would be an obvious example of a target of reminiscence. Further work in which persons were explicitly asked who they reminisce about would help clarify this issue.

In an earlier pilot study of the RFS, one subject admitted reminiscing "over old hurts, like picking at a scab on a wound." Akin to the probing of a painful tooth, there seems to exist a propensity to occasionally retrieve hurtful episodes from our past. In *The Gates of Ivory*, novelist Margaret Drabble (1992) wrote, "Offenses twenty years old are held up to the light, shaken, and savaged" (p. 35). The RFS Bitterness Revival factor captures the essence of this type of reminiscence. The decline in the use of this function with age suggests that as we become older, we are better able to attenuate the negative impact of bitter memories. Perhaps time reduces the immediate sting of a real or imagined slight that occurred long ago. Older adults may be more willing to surrender the acrimonious emotions associated with painful memories, which may serve primarily to sap one's psychological resources. Interesting connections between this finding and related areas of cognitive aging research are apparent. For example, is the willingness to let go of bitter memories *enabled* by relativistic thinking, a cognitive skill that is assumed to be integral to the postformal operational thought manifested by some elderly adults (e.g., Sinnott, 1984)? Or perhaps less use of reminiscence to revive Bitterness, reflecting an appreciation of the contextualism and relativism of life's events, represents a precursor to or facet of wisdom (e.g., Staudinger et al., 1992).

Finally, the use of reminiscence to Teach/Inform seems to tap into both negative and positive stereotypes of reminiscence. In the former case, unwilling but captive youths are forced to hear for the thousandth time grandpa's story of how tough it was in the Great Depression. In the latter scenario, eager grandchildren anticipate the funny stories a grandparent shares about the old days. Although there is an age-related change evident in this function, one suspects that the asymptote is due more to parenthood than to age. That is, dependent children are natural targets to whom parents and grandparents tell entertaining or informative stories. Nonparents, in comparison, must rely on younger siblings or impressionable peers, who constitute a much smaller potential audience. Although this certainly occurs (as evidenced by mean scores of approximately 13 for the teenagers and 20-year-olds combined), the opportunities to teach and inform others increase with age. Nevertheless, the current pattern of age differences is consistent with Erikson's (1963) notion that generativity—that is, an outward-focused concern for guiding and mentoring succeeding generations—is most salient beginning in the 40s. That younger adults also engaged in this process in our study is consistent with Peterson and Stewart's (1993) findings that younger adults engaged in generative behaviors. Further research needs to tease out the potentially confounding effects of age and the probability of having children.

Gender Differences

The present finding of sex differences in the purposes of reminiscing are consistent with other studies of the dimensions of simple reminiscence frequency (eg., Merriam & Cross, 1982; Webster, 1994) in which it was found that women generally reminisced more frequently than men. In the present study, three RFS functions—Identity/Problem Solving, Conversation, and Intimacy Maintenance—were differentiated on the basis of gender, with women scoring higher on all three measures.

Two areas of research can help explain the obtained gender differences. First, one can argue that there is a thematic quality to the identity/problem solving, conversation, and intimacy maintenance purposes of reminiscence. Findings from recent feminist scholarship concerning the embeddedness of women's identity in a social network (e.g., Belenky, Clinchy, Goldberger, & Tarule, 1986; Gilligan, 1982; Mac Crae, 1990) have an important bearing here. Specifically, it has been advanced that women define themselves in terms of reciprocal interpersonal relationships in which understanding and nurturance are integral components. Women's "different voices" develop as a function of verbal exchange, that is, of talking, hearing, and empathizing with an intimate. In short, a woman's sense of identity is enmeshed in, and oriented toward, intimate social relationships. This caring, expressive orientation contrasts with an instrumental, autonomous identity seeking that is supposedly more characteristic of men. For men, identity precedes intimacy; for women, they are coincidental.

Rosenthal (1987), for example, discussed the role of the "family comforter," which was ascribed to women 60% of the time in her sample. Attributes assigned more often to female comforters than to male comforters, included being sympathetic and a good listener (i.e., expressive). Men were seen as better at giving technical advice (i.e., instrumental). Women seem to perform the valuable family function of kin keeper, which perhaps includes keeping memories of family members, deceased and otherwise, safe and accessible (i.e., maintaining intimacy).

The present findings, at least superficially, seem to map onto this framework. That is, identity/problem solving is tied to (dependent on?) intimacy maintenance, both of which interact with, and are partially enabled by, conversation. If the pattern of sex differences had been different and unrelated (e.g., if women scored higher on the Boredom Reduction and Teach/Inform factors), we would be hard pressed to discern a unifying framework. The current findings, however, parallel the framework emerging from one area of research on the psychology of women.

The current findings are also consistent with research on the development of autobiographical memories in childhood. For instance, Fivush and Reese (1992) have shown that parents tend to engage their young daughters in elaborative forms of narrative conversations about the past and, in contrast, tend to engage their young sons in repetitive forms of narrative conversations about the past. The former style involves a richly detailed, evaluative form of reminiscence that the child and parent cocreate. It emphasizes the social nature of memories; the broader contextual framework in which they are supported; and the enjoyable, intimate nature of their shared retrieval. The latter style, by comparison, has a more pragmatic focus, wherein the adult attempts to elicit correct autobiographical facts from the child in shorter, repetitive questioning forms of interaction. These relatively consistent dyadic differences in narrative conversational style suggest that gender differences in the skill of reminiscing are taught very early in life. As Reese and Fivush (1993) concluded, "daughters may very well grow up to value reminiscence more than sons and to produce more elaborate personal narratives" (p. 605).

CONCLUSION

Reminiscence is a multidimensional construct, and it serves myriad purposes for adults of all ages. Remembering one's personal past is a normative process triggered by a constellation of life events that clearly are not limited to old-age-specific exigencies. These findings clearly qualify, if not invalidate, claims concerning the timing and elicitation of reminiscence made in the literature.

It is quite probable that people use specific reminiscence functions differentially on the basis of many variables (e.g., sex, health, personality, and life events), rather than age alone. Future investigations with the RFS (Webster, 1993) or other psychometrically sound instruments need to examine the relative contributions of these other variables. The results of such studies will allow us to situate reminiscence functions in a clearer theoretical and pragmatic perspective.

Chapter 8

A Qualitative Look at Reminiscing: Using the Autobiographical Memory Coding Tool

Christine R. Kovach

Methodological difficulties have hampered much of the research on reminiscence. This chapter presents one measurement approach that uses content analysis of reminiscence interview data. A brief background discussion of conceptual issues should serve as a helpful prelude to understanding the measurement approach.

The empirical findings regarding reminiscence are plagued by contradictions and low correlation coefficients. Most researchers have conceptualized reminiscence in vague and broad terms as "the act or habit of thinking about or relating past experiences, especially those considered personally most significant" (McMahon & Rhudick, 1967, p. 65).

The measurement of reminiscence has been imprecise and inconsistent and often has entailed simply a count of sentence units that refer to the past. Surely an understanding of the meaning of the activity of reminiscing cannot come from these vague and superficial conceptualizations and operationalizations.

In an attempt to understand the nature of the cognitive process of reminiscing, I undertook a qualitative study with 21 elderly women over age 65 (Kovach, 1991a). In-depth examination of more than 400 pages of reminiscence transcripts revealed that the women primarily verbalized personally significant autobiographical memories. Descriptions of events and people such as movie stars, of books, or of sports of the era were extremely rare unless the event had personal significance or connection for the reminiscer (e.g., going to hear Frank Sinatra sing with a group of girlfriends or being a competent player on the high school basketball team). In addition, the reminiscing about the events was often accompanied by explicit or implied interpretations of the events (Kovach, 1991b).

The interpretations made by the women were classified as validating or lamenting (see Figure 1). Validating interpretations confirmed that the person had lived a fruitful life, and lamenting interpretations involved negative interpretations of past events. Themes from the data that pertained to the validating interpretations

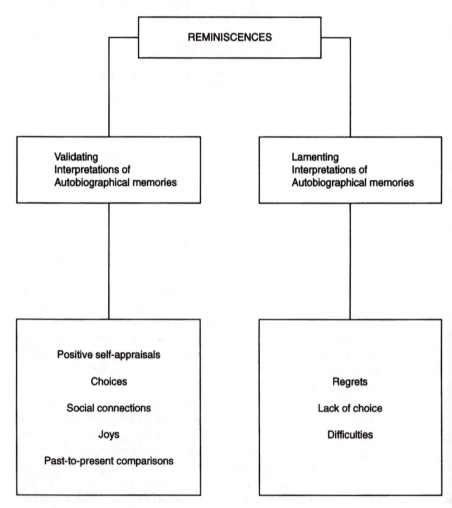

Figure 1 Autobiographical memory categories and themes.

were (a) positive self-appraisals; (b) having had the opportunity to make choices in one's life; (c) having experienced positive social connections; (d) having experienced life occurrences that were interesting, joyous, or unique; and (e) comparing the past with the present in a manner that depreciated the present and praised the past. Themes from the data that reflected lamenting interpretations were (a) regrets, (b) having lacked choice about the events in one's life; and (c) having had difficulties in one's life (Kovach, 1991a).

The finding that reminiscences contained a variety of interpretations of auto-biographical memories is important for several reasons. It suggests that people use memories from the past as a part of some cognitive work. This notion is consistent with reconstructive cognitive theories that state that memories are more often a reconstruction than a reproduction. This belief is supported by multiple studies demonstrating that reminiscences are often distortions of past events even though the reminiscers believe in the veracity of their personal memories (Barclay & Wellman, 1986; Brewer, 1986; Rubin, Wetzler, & Nebes, 1986). Even more compelling was the finding that almost all of the reminiscers verbalized one to three dominant themes as they reminisced and that these themes remained stable over time (Kovach, 1991a, 1993). For example, one person verbalized primarily regrets and social connections, and another person had positive self-appraisals and joys as dominant themes. The presence of dominant themes suggests that the construction of autobiographical memory interpretations may serve an important role in helping people to maintain or attain a sense of personal existential meaning. This notion is consistent with Csikszentmihalyi and Beattie's (1979) notion that autobiographical memories form an affective and cognitive gestalt that serves to maintain a sense of self-worth, organize interactions with the environment, and facilitate adaptive behaviors.

The discoveries that the elderly women's reminiscing included fairly explicit and stable interpretations of the autobiographical memories and that there was considerable variability between subjects reminiscing opens the door to the potential for more focused and in-depth examination of the cognitive process of reminiscing. In order for the science to advance, however, a consistent method of measuring autobiographical memories is needed.

MEASUREMENT BY CONTENT ANALYSIS

Measuring meanings or interpretations is a complex task and yet one that must be undertaken if our understanding of reminiscence is to move beyond the superficial and benign. Krippendorf (1993) has said that a credible content analysis cannot just objectively analyze the words that are present, but must discern the cognitive models being used. Unraveling the frameworks by which people live requires that logical and validated inferences be made from the text. The dangers inherent in this type of endeavor are that the measurement will not meet the scientific standards of rigor that have come to be expected and that the inferences will not be valid reflections of the meaning behind the syntactical symbol.

Currently, qualitative researchers are debating what constitutes credible qualitative research and what constitutes journalism or a lack of scientific rigor. Much qualitative research has been deemed to be superficial, lacking in logic, or simply a fitting of the researcher's a priori notions onto the data collected. But the content analysis and qualitative methods literatures are equivocal on what *is* credible scientific inquiry. In other words, there is more than one right way to do a content analysis. Each investigator must determine the methods that are most appropriate for meeting the purposes of the inquiry.

Overview of the Development and Testing of the Autobiographical Memory Coding Tool

The development and testing of the Autobiographical Memory Coding Tool (AMCT) are explained in detail elsewhere (Kovach, 1993). I undertook the development of the tool because of my strong belief that content analysis was a credible method, and perhaps, the only possible method, of acquiring the in-depth data needed to advance science in this field. I developed systematic, time-consuming steps for conducting the analysis to generate valid and reliable indicators of symbolic content.

The reliability indices for the AMCT obtained in several studies have been quite good. For the decision of whether a subject was a validating or lamenting reminiscer, intercoder reliability estimates, calculated as percentage of agreement, were .93, .93, and .95. Intercoder reliability estimates for determining whether a theme was dominant for a reminiscer were .83, .83, and .86. A test–retest reliability estimate of four randomly selected transcripts coded twice over a 2-week interval yielded 100% agreement on the coding of dominant themes and of validating and lamenting categories (Kovach, 1993).

Content validity was assessed by a gerontological clinical nurse specialist and a psychiatric clinical nurse specialist, both of whom used reminiscence therapy in their practice. Also, 18 reminiscence transcripts from two other studies were analyzed to determine whether the categories reflect the range and variations in interpretations of autobiographical memories. Refinement and expansion of the tool based on these activities have been ongoing (Kovach, 1993).

The Reminiscence Interview

The AMCT may be used on autobiographical memory data obtained in group or individual reminiscence sessions in which various interview strategies were used. It may be used after a single reminiscence session or after multiple interview sessions.

My experience reminiscing with many older adults has provided some guidelines for obtaining rich, unbiased data. Frail older adults tend to reminisce for no longer than 30–40 min, after which time, they tend to change the topic to the present or future, or want to end the interview and move on to another activity. Surprisingly, older adults generally begin engaged reminiscing quite readily. There is usually no need to spend preliminary sessions developing a relationship with the subject.

One potential bias in reminiscence interviews is that the resulting data will be confabulated as a by-product of the interaction between the reminiscer and the interviewer. Ideally, to avoid this bias, a researcher would ask the subject to reminisce about whatever he or she wishes and would not interrupt the flow of memories. However, I have found that frail older adults do need periodic questions and probes throughout the interview to assist them in continuing to verbalize their reminiscences. Even though researchers are, in general, interested in giving subjects as much control over their reminiscing as possible, semistructured interview questions are probably needed. Value-laden questions should not be used; only neutral and silent probes should be used. A reactivity effect may be avoided by beginning interviews with instructions such as follows:

> I am interested in listening to your reminiscences . . . memories from the past which you recollect. I have no expectations about the kinds of things you will reminisce about. I would like you to reminisce about whatever you wish. Occasionally, I may ask you a question to encourage you to continue reminiscing, but I would like you to reminisce about whatever you want to reminisce about. Tell me the memories from the past that come to mind.

Reminiscences from different life periods (e.g., childhood and young adulthood) as well as about particular topics (e.g., school, sports, and holidays) should be elicited. When a reminiscer focuses on one time of life or a particular experience, the interviewer should continue to focus on that topic until it is closed by the reminiscer or naturally comes to an end. If there is any question of whether a statement refers to an event that occurred 5 or more years in the past, the reminiscer should be asked how long ago the experience or event occurred.

USING THE AUTOBIOGRAPHICAL MEMORY CODING TOOL

In this section, the procedures for conducting the content analysis are presented in specific systematic steps. Background information is presented to clarify and explain procedures in more depth. Measuring autobiographical memory interpretations from transcribed interview data involves the following steps:

1   Delineating the units of analysis.
2   Deleting units that do not refer to the past.
3   Coding the data as one of the eight autobiographical memory themes or as neutral/informative recall.

4   Identifying dominant themes.
5   Classifying themes into validating and lamenting categories.

Step 1: Delineating the Units of Analysis

Background   In a content analysis, one of the most fundamental and important decisions is into which basic unit of analysis the text will be divided. Molecular approaches to dividing text rely on a specific word, sentence, or line. The molecular approach tends to reduce observations to more concrete and specific activities and tends to have a higher reliability than does a molar approach to analysis (Weber, 1985). A molecular approach to dividing reminiscence transcripts would result in losing sight of the activities that are at the heart of the inquiry, namely, the significance of past personal events to the interviewee and the interviewee's interpretations of them.

The meaningful unit of analysis for understanding the interpretations or significance of past personal events is the idea unit. An *idea unit* is a constellation of words or statements that relate to the same central meaning or chief end of a particular action or situation (Barclay & Hodges, 1987). Idea units are delineated through a study of events, contexts, and meanings.

My experience with the AMCT coding system indicates that fairly extensive practice coding "pilot" transcripts is necessary to achieve acceptable reliability in both dividing the units and coding the data (Step 3). If untrained, two coders will make similar divisions, but, often, one coder will divide the transcripts into units that are too small. This is dangerous because the data can lose its meaningfulness. Coders need to immerse themselves in the data and be practiced in understanding and using the definitions of events, contexts, and meanings. Units of analysis can show great variation in length. One page of transcript could have four units of analysis, or two pages could make up one unit. A researcher may decide to weight these units differently or may decide that substantively, the length of time a reminiscer spent describing an event and interpreting that event is of little meaning.

The importance of frequency counts and weighting to content analysis is hotly debated. Each research situation needs to be judged individually and with prudence. Frequency counts are often credible and helpful tools in content analysis. Quantitative content analysis assumes that the frequency of occurrence of a content attribute is a basis for inferences. This assumption should not be made without forethought about the conceptual veracity of frequency as a measure of the intensity of that specific variable.

Researchers studying autobiographical memory have found that quantitative approaches to content analysis are credible. In several studies using the AMCT (Kovach, 1987, 1991a, 1993) I have found similar frequency distributions of verbalizing both categories and themes, supporting the usefulness of frequency counts in the coding of reminiscence transcripts.

Definitions   The list below provides definitions of key terms.

Autobiographical memories—the recollections and cognitive reconstructions of personal experiences that occurred 5 or more years in the past.

Events—topics or experiences that are logically connected and intelligible. An event is a unit that makes sense and is meaningful to the person recalling it.

Context—the perceived setting in which an event or a series of events is nested. Contexts may be physical, psychological, or social. A physical context is a particular place. A social context refers to the social setting in which an event occurred. A psychological context is the cognitive context that the person characterizes as his or her state of mind at the time of recall.

Meanings—interpretations of contextualized event. The significance the event holds for the individual.

Procedure: Step 1   At least two coders should perform the initial phase of Step 1 and should perform it independently of one another. At the end of Step 1, the coders should work together to perform a procedure called consensual analysis, described later.

The coders begin by reading the entire transcript straight through. In the next reading, they begin examining the text for the event that is central to the communication. In pencil, they make a vertical line (|) at the beginning of each new event and a dot (•) at the end of each event. Contexts have not been useful for dividing the transcripts into units of analysis.

Once the units are divided according to events, each unit is reread and divided into smaller units if the meaning or interpretation of the event changes. For example, if a woman begins reminiscing about when she cared for her sick husband by describing the difficulties of the experience and ends this topic by saying how thankful she was to have shared these months with her husband, she has provided two interpretations of one event. One unit ends at the point where she completes her descriptions of the difficulties, and the second unit begins where her interpretation of the event is more positive.

The units are divided not on the basis of what the interviewer has said, but rather on what the subject has said. No slashes or dots should appear on lines of transcript that were spoken by the interviewer.

After all of the transcripts are divided into units of analysis, at least one other person is needed to perform a procedure known as *consensual analysis*. In this procedure, each page of the transcript is read by the coders and at least one other person, who must reach consensual agreement regarding where each unit begins and ends. When a disagreement exists, all parties have an equal voice in making final decisions. Slashes and dots are moved as needed.

Step 2: Deleting Units That Do Not Refer to the Past

Background   Five years has been arbitrarily chosen by the research community as the cutoff for reminiscence responses, the neurophysiological mechanisms involved in memory being insufficiently understood to allow a more precise estimate of when a memory may be considered to be tapping a remote event. When reading transcripts, it is uncommon for it to be unclear whether an event occurred within the last 5 years. It is, however, helpful for the interviewer conducting the reminiscing session to ask the subject when an event occurred if there is any uncertainty.

Procedure: Step 2   The coder reads through each transcript and, when a unit refers to events that occurred within the past 5 years or involve the present or future, writes *NR* (not a reminiscence) in the lefthand column and places a vertical line alongside the NR that runs the length of the text. The NR notation and vertical line serve to block off the portions of text that are not a reminiscence and eliminate them from further analysis.

Step 3: Code the Data as One of the Eight Autobiographical Memory Themes or as Neutral/ Informative Recall

Background   The AMCT conceptualizes the interpretations of autobiographical memories as either validating or lamenting. Five themes capture the validating style of interpreting autobiographical memories; three themes indicate the lamenting style. These themes are depicted in Figure 1 and emerged from a qualitative study reported elsewhere (Kovach, 1991a).

It is important for the coders to be familiar with the definitions of the themes and variations in each theme. They need to read through and become familiar with the autobiographical memory thematic dictionary (Table 1) and the variations in each theme (Tables 2–9). These are used to code the data.

Another code that is used is *neutral/informative recall,* and it is assigned to units that contain either a brief recall of information or a neutral description of an event. Because these units contain no explicit or implicit interpretation of events, it is not possible to assign meanings to them.

Procedure: Step 3   The coders read each unit of analysis individually. They determine the meaning of the unit by referring to the autobiographical memory dictionary or the list of variations in each theme. Once the theme of the unit has

Table 1 Autobiographical Memory Thematic Dictionary

Code	Theme
1	POSITIVE SELF-APPRAISAL—reminiscent units in which a positive evaluation of the self was evident or a personal accomplishment was described.
2	CHOICES—reminiscent units in which the person explicitly stated or implied that life occurrences were dependent on personal behavior or commitments versus being the result of luck, chance, fate, or power beyond the person's control.
3	SOCIAL CONNECTIONS—reminiscent units in which the person described a personal positive relationship, having received support from others, or being associated with someone who is accomplished or skilled.
4	JOYS—reminiscent units in which the person described having experienced interesting pleasurable, unique, or entertaining life occurrences.
5	PAST-TO-PRESENT COMPARISONS—reminiscent units in which the person expressed that the past was better than the present through a depreciation of the present and an expression of praise for the past.
6	REGRETS—reminiscent units in which the reminiscer expressed remorse or rebuked him- or herself for acts or commissions.
7	LACK OF CHOICE—reminiscent units in which the person expressed not having had the opportunity to make choices about the events in his or her life or not having had control over the negative events in his or her life.
8	DIFFICULTIES—reminiscent units in which the person described experiences of the past as bad in some way or as involving losses.
9	NEUTRAL/INFORMATIVE RECALL—units that contain either a brief recall of information or a neutral description of an event.

been determined, or it has been determined that the unit is a neutral/informative recall, the appropriate code number (from the thematic dictionary) is placed in the righthand column next to that unit of transcript. There is no need to write out the name of the theme—the code number will suffice.

If a unit can be coded as two themes, the unit should be examined more carefully. It may need to be divided into two units of analysis. If this is determined to be the problem, the coders write REVISED UNIT in the righthand column and proceed with coding.

Often, the confusion involves units that can be coded as both a joy and another validating theme or units that can be coded as both a difficulty and another lamenting theme. Further study of the unit is needed. Usually, even though such units contain descriptions of joyous or difficult events, they also contain an explicit expression of regret, opportunity for choice or lack thereof, social connectedness, praise for the past, or a positive self-appraisal. This expression is the explicit interpretation of the event and is the primary meaning of the unit. These units should therefore be coded under the one theme that captures the primary meaning of the unit. This will result in all of the themes being mutually exclusive.

Table 2   Definition of and Variation in Positive Self-Appraisals

POSITIVE SELF-APPRAISAL—reminiscent units in which a positive evaluation of
the self was evident or a personal accomplishment was described.
Positive self-appraisals included
  Qualities of the reminiscer
    having been smart
    having been energetic
    having been pretty
    having been a leader
    having possessed a good temperament
    having been kind
    having been creative
    having had a good figure
    having had personal initiative (e.g., to work hard, to find a job, to practice
      music, to do chores)
    having been well-dressed
    having had an athletic physique
  Accomplishments of the reminiscer
    having overcome a fear or vice
    having kept a clean house
    having managed to remain married
    having met obligations or provided support to children, husband, parents
    having been a good wife/husband
    having been a good mother/father
    having been competent (e.g., at work, school, athletics, cooking, dancing,
      game playing, carpentry, musical instruments, military service,
      volunteerism, leadership, finances)
    having handled crises or emergency situations well
    having been well educated
    having been involved in community service

If, after careful thought, a determination cannot be made about which of the
nine codes to assign to a unit, a question mark (?) is placed in the righthand
column of the transcript next to that unit. This unit will be eliminated from further
analysis, but the number and percentage of units that were coded thus should be
reported.

Coding of the transcripts should be mutually exhaustive. Text should be
coded as

  Not a reminiscence (NR)
  Cannot determine (?)
  Neutral/informative recall (9)
  One of the eight autobiographical memory themes (1–8)

Examples of autobiographical memory themes coded from reminiscence transcripts are presented in Table 10.

Table 3   Definition of and Variations in Choices

CHOICES—reminiscent units in which the person explicitly stated or implied that life occurrences were dependent on personal behavior or commitments versus being the result of luck, chance, fate, or power beyond the person's control.
Choices involved
Nonconformance
 defying boss, colleagues at work
 going against rules at work/school
 not adhering to religious laws/traditions
 disagreeing with a person in a powerful position
 violating codes
Commitments
 remaining faithful to husband
 not remarrying
 adhering to religious laws/traditions
 accepting children and their choices
 not mixing with boys of other faiths
 never riding a motorcycle again
 not burdening children with caregiving
 not drinking or smoking
 bettering myself
Alternative/optional choices
 marry/not to marry
 move/not move
 education: leave school, stay in school, study a particular subject
 travel: take a vacation, return to homeland
 employment: take a new job, remain with a job, work harder, work less
 change churches or not
 change emphasis in ministry or not
 take entrance exam or not

Step 4: Identifying Dominant Themes

A dominant theme is a theme that occurs in a transcript at a frequency that is twice what would be expected by chance. To determine which themes may be dominant, it is necessary to develop a frequency distribution of autobiographical memory themes (see Table 11). To calculate the percentage of units that would be twice what would be expected by chance for Subject 1 in Table 11, I calculated the total number of units that were analyzed as themes; this equaled 18. Eighteen was divided by 8 (the number of possible themes) to obtain the expected distribution by chance, 2.25. Twice the expected distribution is 4.50. The number 4.5 is rounded up to 5, and thus all themes that were verbalized in 5 or more units would be considered dominant. Positive self-appraisals and past-to-present comparisons were dominant themes for Subject 1. Positive self-appraisals and difficulties were dominant themes for Subject 2. The dominant themes are determined for each coded transcript.

Table 4   Definition of and Variations in Social Connections

SOCIAL CONNECTIONS—reminiscent units in which the person described a
   personal positive relationship, having received support from others, or being
   associated with someone who is accomplished or skilled.
Social connections included
  Positive relationships with
    parents
    siblings
    boyfriend
    husband
    children
    fellow employees
    employers
    in-laws
    friends
    family
    teachers
    minister
    grandchildren
    great-grandchildren
    aunts
    uncles
  Having received support from others
    money
    clothing
    food
    cultural growth
    care during illness
    affidavit to escape Holocaust
    defense from "bullies"
    friendship
    assistance during crises
  Being associated with someone who is accomplished or skilled
    husband
    parents
    children

$$\text{Distribution that would be expected by chance} = \frac{\text{Total no. of units}}{\text{No. of themes (8)}}$$

Step 5: Classifying Themes into Validating and Lamenting Categories

Procedure: Step 5   Frequency distributions are developed for both the validating and lamenting categories of themes (see Table 12). Examinations of frequency distributions for validating and lamenting interpretations have shown similar patterns of skewness. On the basis on these examinations, I have

Table 5   Definition of and Variations in Joys

JOYS—reminiscent units in which the person described having experienced interesting, pleasurable, unique, or entertaining life occurrences.
Joys included
Interesting/entertaining occurrences
work activities
school activities
moving experiences
humorous incidents
weather incidents
home appliances/conveniences
firefighting
precocious-childhood occurrences
Pleasurable occurrences
vacation experiences
dancing
dating
shopping
Sunday car rides
sports
games
learning experiences
church picnics
holidays
Unique occurrences
accidents
injuries
illnesses
attaining a unique work position
relationship
possession
military events

divided percentage distributions into thirds. Transcripts that fall into the top third of the validating distribution may be considered to be from a validating reminiscer. Transcripts that fall into the top two thirds of the lamenting distribution may be considered to be from a lamenting reminiscer. In Table 12, Subjects 2 and 5 had greater than 33% of their transcripts coded as lamenting and therefore may be considered lamenting reminiscers. Subjects 1, 3, and 4 had greater than 66% of their transcript coded as validating and may be considered validating reminiscers.

DISCUSSION

The time and effort required to perform a content analysis using the AMCT allow more precise research on autobiographical memories and reminiscence. This

Table 6 Definition of and Variations in Past-to-Present Comparisons

PAST-TO-PRESENT COMPARISONS—reminiscent units in which the person expressed that the past was better than the present through a depreciation of the present and an expression of praise for the past.

Comparisons of the past to the present included

People in the past were

friendlier

less spoiled

not as wasteful

more supportive

more interested in religion

less fanatical about religious beliefs

harder working

better

children studied harder

people were less rebellious

children "minded"

In the social fabric of the past

dances were better

schools were better

there were no drug problems

there was less emphasis on sex

churchgoing was more social

things were made to last longer

it was safer

there was less emphasis on money

it was less crowded

there was more school loyalty

police were more dedicated

Table 7 Definition of and Variations in Regrets

REGRETS—reminiscent units in which the reminiscer expressed remorse or rebuked him- or herself over acts or omissions.

Regrets involved

not leaving job/leaving job

not getting own home

living with in-laws

losing photographs

running from home

marrying husband

marrying at a young age

having worked so hard

leaving school

having done a certain type of work

having missed out on opportunities/activities because had to work

leaving church

moving

having a child early in marriage

leaving pastoral ministry

Table 8   Definition of and Variations in Lack of Choice

LACK OF CHOICE—reminiscent units in which the person expressed not having
    had the opportunity to make choices about events in his or her life or not having
    had control over negative events in his or her life.
Lack of choice involved
    No opportunity to choose
        doing certain work-related tasks
        going to work at a young age
        working hard
        leaving the country
        losing possessions
        missing school frequently
        leaving work
        going to continuation school
        having caesarean deliveries
        having to study
        having to leave husband
        having to adhere to religious practices/laws
        having to give up farm
        having to live with few comforts/leisure opportunities
        work hours
        leaving home at a young age
        date of marriage
        work duties
        having to stay in school
    Lack of control over negative events
        injury caused by supervisor at work
        landlord's refusal to let them move into apartment
        inability to get a nice wedding dress
        husband's never seeing his grandchildren
        inability to have children
        inability to get desired job
        son's divorce
        bridge built in front of house

discussion focuses on some possible uses for data coded through the extensive
procedure of the AMCT.

Tests of the usefulness of various clinical interventions may be facilitated by
coding data as validating or lamenting. People who verbalize mainly regrets,
losses, and difficulties may benefit from a psychoanalytically guided reworking of
these memories or a life review therapy. People verbalize mainly validating
interpretations may benefit from sharing these memories through the lighter
psychosocial reminiscence intervention.

Currently, there are no empirically based guidelines on who might benefit from
either life review or reminiscence interventions. The variability in people's interpretations of their autobiographical memories suggests that memories may serve different
functions for different people or that the process of reminiscing might be different.

Table 9   Definition of and Variations in Difficulties

DIFFICULTIES—reminiscent units in which the person described experiences of the past as bad in some way or as involving losses.

Difficulties involved

Relationships
  being odd one in family
  having boyfriend marry someone else
  leaving husband
  not receiving support from others
  being in a bad marriage

Negative occurrences/losses
  death of a relative
  illness/injury of self, loved one
  being physically attacked
  being confronted by a snake
  missing childhood fun
  Great Depression
  being raised without a father
  financial situation
  work/school
  labor/delivery
  loss of possessions
  Holocaust
  bad relocation/traveling experiences
  taking care of sick relative
  difficulty raising children
  son's mental retardation
  being beaten by father
  public speaking
  dangerous experiences
  being excluded from the military
  father's alcoholism
  missing fun holidays

People may also use memories differently at different stages in their life. By examining the effects of reminiscing interventions on people with various needs, in various stages of life and with various interpretations of memories, caregivers can develop expertise in matching the qualities and needs of the reminiscer to specific interventions.

For the person who verbalizes primarily validating interpretations, reminiscence may serve to remind him or her of past accomplishments, past successes at coping with life's stresses, and success at sustaining meaningful relationships with others. Reminiscing may help the elderly cope with an awareness of their mortality by confirming that they lived a rich and full life. People who are currently experiencing difficult times may find that past-to-present comparisons help them cope with the present bad times because this type of reminiscing confirms that

Table 10   Examples of Autobiographical Memory Themes

Positive Self-Appraisal

"Nick told me, he said, 'If you are a piece worker if you make over a quota you get paid for this piece work.' I tried. You know they give me the regular amount and I asked the one across from me how much she made. I think it was a few dollars more. I says I'm gonna try. I did try hard and I only made a nickel. I said, 'for a nickel, no way.' So I slow down again. And then as time went on I kept on saying, 'if could do it I'm gonna try, I'm gonna try.' Well I started, ya know, 50 cents more and worked my way up."

Choices

"My sister and I went on with our schooling, I was deciding on being a physical recreation teacher or physical therapist. I chose therapy. Therapy seemed more interesting than doing games and sports all day."

Social Connections

"He came and he was such a nice gentleman. So we went on and he says, 'Where do you want to go?' He said, 'Wanna go get a glass of beer or get a drink someplace?' And well, I said, 'I'll tell ya, I don't drink and I'd just as soon go get an ice cream soda or something.' So that hit the spot with him right then and there. He says, 'Oh, that's fine' so we went and had an ice cream soda and we talked. So he stayed at a motel downtown, so I took a streetcar and went back home. So then he called me to see if I got home all right. I said, 'Fine.' My God, he went back to New Jersey and every day I got 3 or 4 letters air mail, special delivery. And in one month I married him. One month I married my husband and we were never separated outside of having babies or having operations."

Joys

"Oh, I played tennis every single day of my life. And then I started golf and golf was my chief pleasure. I played golf until I was in my 70's. And bridge, contract bridge was my very best love. I used to ice skate a lot. I was always the last one on the skating rink, I used to love it so."

Past-to-Present Comparisons

"I can't understand it now—the young ones saying, 'I want to work but I can't find nothing to do.' I said, 'Well, but it's funny to me when I was workin', I could get more work than I wanted to do.' If you want to work you can. When I ride around I see the signs out: Help Wanted. So there's something to do if you want to work. Better than sittin' home waitin' on a handout."

Regrets

"I got the job then I got a telegram from Northeast: 'Come back to work.' Then I got another telegram, 'Please come back.' You know I regretted it. Because they were making such good money, not in clothing, you didn't make that much, and I stayed. I would've got a good Social Security check from Northeast. That I regret, that I regret."

Lack of Choice

"I was supposed to go to East High and I couldn't because my father died and I had to get out and work and take care of my mother. I cried so hard. I wanted to go on with my schooling."

Difficulties

"My first marriage I was too young. I didn't live with him six months. We waited until my parents was out in the field and then we snuck out. My mother didn't live but for two weeks. Next time, before I could write she had passed. It worried me. Oh, honey, it worried me because I decided not to let her know I was leaving. It sure did, honey, it worried me."

Table 11 Frequency of Reminiscence Units for Each Subject by Theme

Subject	Positive self-appraisal		Choices		Social connections		Joys		Past-to-present comparisons		Regrets		Choice		Difficulties		Total
	No.	%	No.	%	No.	%	No.	%	No.	%	No.	%	No.	%	No.	%	no.
1	7	39	2	11	0	0	1	6	6	33	1	6	0	0	1	6	18
2	10	42	0	0	2	8	1	4	1	4	1	4	1	4	7	30	24
3	10	55	0	0	1	5	5	29	0	0	2	11	0	0	0	0	18
4	3	10	8	26	13	42	4	12	0	0	0	0	0	0	3	10	31
5	7	22	0	0	2	6	3	9	2	6	4	12	6	18	9	21	33

Table 12 Frequency of Reminiscence Units for Each Subject by Lamenting and Validating Category

Subject	Validating		Lamenting	
	No.	%	No.	%
1	16	89	2	11
2	15	63	9	37
3	16	89	2	11
4	28	90	3	10
5	14	42	19	58

they have seen and been a part of the best of life. During times of transition or crisis, past experiences may be used to interpret current experiences and thus function in an adaptive and problem-solving capacity. These processes may help the person maintain his or her self-concept through the life span.

Dominant themes may be similar to the self-schemata described by Markus (1977). Self-schemata are cognitive generalizations about the self that are rooted in past experiences and organize and guide the processing of self-referenced information contained in an individual's social experience. Csikszentimihalyi and Beattie (1979) also spoke of life themes that are rooted in existential concerns from earlier years of life and consist of affective and cognitive gestalts that influence behavior.

Dominant themes may be studied and linked with other concepts, such as mood, stress and adaptation, self-esteem, and quality of life. People may make use of memories not only at different periods of their life, but also under different situations. Examining under what conditions reminiscence is a constructive or a destructive cognitive occurrence will aid explanation of the functions of both reminiscence and autobiographical memories.

Autobiographical memories contribute to the self-referent database that each person possesses. This database may be used to construct and reconstruct knowledge about the self that will influence self-concept, self-esteem, and behaviors. By studying the relationship of dominant themes to self-esteem, mood, and behavior over time, as well as during periods of stability and transition, researchers can begin to explain these links so theory can be further developed and refined.

Recent work by several authors has led to different conceptualizations of reminiscence themes. Future work will be assisted if scholars can begin to use the same terminology and can reach agreement on conceptual definitions. In the following brief discussion, I attempt to discern conceptual similarities and differences among the schemata of several authors.

Watt and Wong (1991) used qualitative techniques to develop a taxonomy of six reminiscence types based on function of reminiscence: integrative, instrumental, transmissive, narrative, escapist, and obsessive. Webster (1993), used quantitative factor analysis to delineate seven reminiscence factors: boredom reduction, death preparation, identity/problem solving, conversation, intimacy maintenance, bitterness revival, and teach/inform. Webster's categories are similar to those of Watt and Wong in that they not only describe attributes of reminiscence, but also assign a functional quality to each theme.

Merriam (1989) discerned four components that make up the structure of simple reminiscence: selection, immersion, withdrawal, and closure. She described the process of reminiscing from the selection of a past experience as material for reminiscence to withdrawal from immersion in the particular past event. Understanding this cognitive process may help us explain the dynamics of memory selection and retrieval, as well as why certain memories are dismissed.

The AMCT is different from these three conceptualizations in that it measures interpretations of autobiographical memories that are verbalized while the person reminisces. Interpretations are the meaning the reminiscer attributes to an event. It is my hope that this tool will lead to a better understanding of the function of reminiscing through a study of the links of autobiographical memory interpretations to other variables under different conditions.

CONCLUSION

I hope that as the AMCT continues to be used, it will be refined and possibly expanded. There is also a need for further methodological work, especially in providing empirical support for the validity of the AMCT. Content analysis and qualitative inquiry are two research areas that are continuing to evolve. As research strategies, both are challenges to use effectively, but they hold promise for revealing the complexities of the human condition.

Chapter 9

An Exploratory Analysis of the Content and Structure of the Life Review

Brian de Vries
John A. Blando
Lawrence J. Walker

We examined the content and structure of the life reviews of a sample of women and men across the adult life span. Content was operationalized as the number of events that individuals identified from their past and their evaluation of them; structure was operationalized as integrative complexity (Baker-Brown et al., 1992), an information-processing variable assessing the cognitive structure underlying thought. The primary aim of this investigation was the exploration of these events and their cognitive representation—this *substance* of life review—by age and gender.

BACKGROUND AND INTRODUCTION

Life review (and its many variants) is seen to be a major psychosocial task of later life (e.g., Erikson, 1968) and has enjoyed significant attention in the gerontology

Preparation of this chapter was supported by a grant from the Social Sciences and Humanities Research Council of Canada to the first author. We thank Susan Bluck for her data coding assistance.

literature as a meaningful and adaptive process in the later years (e.g., Coleman, 1986b; Webster & Cappeliez, 1993). In their attempts to chart the origins of the interest in this construct, researchers most often point to Butler's (1963) seminal presentation of the life review. Life review has been reported to be initiated by an awareness of approaching dissolution and death and to be an inevitable response to the ability loss of aging (Buhler, 1933); it is more persistent in times of transition and crisis (M. Lowenthal, Thurnher, & Chiriboga, 1975). The vast majority of research studies in the area of life review have addressed themselves to analyses of the therapeutic benefits of life review for older individuals, yielding, overall, equivocal results (e.g., Merriam, 1980; Thornton & Brotchie, 1987; Wong & Watt, 1991). This disappointing yield has led some authors (e.g., Webster & Young, 1988) to call for a focus on the process or the structure and substance of life review, rather than its adaptive value.

The alleged age specificity of life review has also recently been questioned (Thornton & Brotchie, 1987; Webster & Young, 1988). M. I. Lewis and Butler (1974) have suggested that life review can occur at all ages, although it takes on a striking intensity and clarity in early old age. M. Lowenthal et al. (1975) found that roughly 14% of students, 33% of newlyweds, 44% of middle-aged parents, and 12% of preretirees were engaged in an active and evaluative review of specific past events and experiences. The early works of Buhler (e.g., 1933) and Erikson (e.g., 1968) and others also reveal that at particular times over the course of a life the individual's past becomes particularly salient. These conceptual and empirical accounts suggest that life review is perhaps better understood as a life span process and not confined to the later years (e.g., Webster & Cappeliez, 1993).

Also surprising by its relative absence in the literature is the role of gender in the analysis of life review. The different "voices" with which women and men "speak" have been the subject of much recent discussion with younger samples (e.g., Gilligan, 1982), and researchers in the areas of personality and social psychology have begun to address men's and women's memories of past relationships. Along such lines, Harvey, Flannery, and Morgan (1986) and M. Ross and Holmberg (1992) found that women reported more vivid memories of relationships than men. In the present research, we sought to explore the roles of gender and age in the manifestation (e.g., the "shape") of life review.

LIFE EVENTS

Butler (1963) spoke of the life review as comprising an understanding of the nature and forces shaping life, such as previous experiences and their meanings and life events and their effects. The interpretation, reinterpretation, and eventual integration of the salient events of a life are the essence of a coherent personal narrative (e.g., J. E. Birren & Hedlund, 1987; Bruner, 1987; Cohler, 1982; Gergen & Gergen, 1986; McAdams, 1985; Runyan, 1984). The examination of the ways in which individuals present and understand the important events of their lives is an examination of the constituents of the life review.

Surprisingly little empirical attention has been paid to life events in this context. M. Lowenthal et al. (1975) interviewed men and women from across the life span and asked them to describe the timing, nature, and evaluation of past life events. They reported that older participants perceived their past events more negatively and that younger participants reported a markedly higher proportion of life events linked with changes in life satisfaction. Romaniuk and Romaniuk (1983) examined age differences in the retrospective nature and significance of transitional life events for women and men across the life course. Martin and Smyer (1990) examined the number and type of life events construed by different cohorts of individuals. The findings of these two studies revealed more overall similarities than differences, although there were differences in type and placement of events as a function of age.

The empirical interest in life events largely resides in the literature on stress and adaptation (Holmes & Rahe, 1967; Janis, 1958; Lazarus, 1966; Selye, 1956). Holmes and Rahe are probably the best known investigators to have pursued systematically the idea that events that require change, adaptation, or adjustment are associated with, and may cause, a wide range of human disorders. In the more than 20 years since the initial presentation of the Social Readjustment Rating Scale (SRRS; Holmes & Rahe, 1967), a voluminous literature on how life events influence health, adjustment, and well-being, along with criticism of this approach, has emerged (e.g., Perkins, 1982; Rabkin, 1980).

Researchers have attempted to examine the mechanisms of this influence by describing the properties of life events. Thoits (1983), in particular, has identified the primary affective dimensions of life events: undesirability, event magnitude or intensity, uncontrollability, and unpredictability. Undesirability appears to be the most crucial dimension of events, often implicated in the etiology of psychological disturbance. The contrast between major and minor events (i.e., event magnitude or intensity) has been most commonly noted by researchers examining depressive outcomes. Brown and Harris (1978), for example, distinguished between severe and nonsevere events and found the former to be more common among clinically depressed patients. However, even when the number of undesirable events is controlled, Thoits (1983) found that event intensity exerted a significant and unique influence. Thoits also has claimed that uncontrollable events are associated with disturbance probably because they are typically those for which individuals are not responsible or that could not have been prevented. Vinokur and Caplan (1986) and others (e.g., Seligman, 1975) have also made the link between mental health and perceived responsibility for life events.

Related to the issues of control and responsibility are the issues of anticipation and predictability. Neugarten (1970), for example, claimed that the salience of life events lies in their timing. She claimed that it is the unanticipated (e.g., the death of a child), not the anticipated (e.g., the birth of a child), that is likely to represent the traumatic event and to require greater adjustment. It is worth noting that the individual's appraisal of adjustment has rarely been assessed and instead has been inferred on the basis of scores on measures of depression and other psychological functioning.

INTEGRATIVE COMPLEXITY AND LIFE EVENTS

The impact of significant life events is not restricted to health and well-being and may also be seen in cognitive functioning, as evidenced in the integrative complexity literature. Integrative complexity is a dimension of information processing built on the hierarchical components of differentiation (the assessment of multiple, independent perceptions on, or dimensions of, a given stimulus) and integration (the interaction among the differentiated parts and pieces). Integrative complexity provides for an analysis of the structure underlying thought as represented in verbal and written materials and has been assessed in a wide array of contexts, including the public statements of international political leaders and policymakers (Suedfeld & Tetlock, 1977), the writings of famous authors (Porter & Suedfeld, 1981), and the discussions of death and dying in the life reviews of men and women from across the adult life span (de Vries, Bluck, & J. E. Birren, 1993). Integrative complexity is a state-oriented derivative of the trait theory of conceptual complexity (Suedfeld, Tetlock, & Streufert, 1992). The premise is that individuals have customary levels of complexity of thought (including upper and lower boundaries) that, at any given time, are influenced by various environmental, physiological, and psychological conditions (Suedfeld & Bluck, 1993).

A number of archival studies have identified "disruptive stress effects," one of which is a reduction in integrative complexity that accompanies stressful events. Suedfeld and Tetlock (1977), for example, found that the complexity of communications between international decision makers decreased as countries in conflict moved closer to war. Individual governmental leaders and social elites showed similar patterns as a function of war-related stresses (Ballard, 1982). The decrease in integrative complexity with impending death (called "terminal drop") is further evidence of the disruptive stress hypothesis (Porter & Suedfeld, 1981; Suedfeld & Piedrahita, 1984).

Suedfeld and Bluck (1993), however, reported that the men, and not the women, in their study responded to negative life events with *increased* complexity—no complexity changes were seen with positive events. They attributed these results to differences between personal stressors and societal stressors, with the latter being more dramatic and associated with, among other things, less perceived control and therefore having a greater impact on complexity. Positive events require no such adaptation. The gender difference was interpreted as representing different patterns of coping. To date, there has been no assessment of the levels of complexity associated with retrospective appraisals of life events.

OBJECTIVES OF THE PRESENT STUDY

The present study was an application of the integrative complexity and subjective life events literatures to a life span conception of life review. Life events may be seen to be the markers or mileposts of a life that provide the shape and substance of the life review. Integrative complexity provides a window on the cognitive structural representations of these events. In the context of these overlapping areas, several empirical questions arise:

1   What roles do age and gender play in the number of and evaluative ratings of subjective life events? That is, how does the alleged age expertise associated with life review manifest itself in the reporting of life events?
2   What are the cognitive representations of these events and how do they vary by age, gender, and evaluative ratings? That is, how are events that have been characterized as undesirable, intense, uncontrollable, or unanticipated represented in the terms of integrative complexity?

METHOD

Participants

Participants were 30 men and 30 women, drawn in equal numbers from three age groups: young, middle-aged, and old. The sample comprised primarily middle-income Caucasian American, with minority Asian American and Native American representation. Education levels ranged from 8 to 20 years. The mean ages for the three groups were 21.2, 41.9, and 72.7 years, respectively, and did not differ by gender.

Measures

Individual participants were asked to consider their entire lives from birth to the present in terms of the significant and important events they had experienced. They were told that "significant and important" was best defined by them in the context of their lives and that there were no restrictions placed on, or expectations about, the number or type of events.

To cue for a consideration of events over time, the Rappaport Time Line was provided to each participant (H. Rappaport, Enrich, & Wilson, 1985). The time line is a 12-inch line placed vertically on a plain piece of paper anchored and labeled at one end with the word BIRTH and at the other end with the word DEATH. Participants were asked to locate themselves at present on this dimension of time and to roughly chart the events of their past. Participants then completed the Life Event Identification and Evaluation Table. This measure was intended to elicit brief descriptions and evaluations of the significant events indicated on the time line. This table comprised a series of columns with the following headings: Event Label, Age of Event, Pleasantness–Unpleasantness Rating, Outcome Desirability–Undesirability Rating, Intensity, Responsibility, Anticipation, and Adjustment Rating. Under the first column, participants were requested to write a brief description of the events of their lives. Row by row, then, that is, event by event, individuals were asked to respond to these events by way of the following measures:

age at which the event occurred;
whether the event was very pleasant, pleasant, both pleasant and unpleasant, unpleasant, or very unpleasant;
whether the outcome of the event was very desirable, desirable, both desirable and undesirable, undesirable, or very undesirable;
the degree of emotional intensity;
the amount of responsibility the individual felt he or she had in the event;
the extent to which the individual felt he or she has been able to adjust to it (or has resolved the event in some cognitive way); and
the extent to which the event was anticipated.

Intensity, responsibility, adjustment, and anticipation were rated on a 5-point scale (after Vinokur & Caplan, 1986) from *not at all* (1) to *a great deal or extreme* (5).

The adjectives provided for responding to the pleasantness–unpleasantness of the event and to the desirability–undesirability of the outcome were purposely presented in a different format from that used for the other evaluations, reflecting suggestions made by Vinokur and Caplan (1986) and Vinokur and Selzer (1975). Pleasantness–unpleasantness and desirability–undesirability referred, respectively, to the event itself and to the outcome; all other dimensions of evaluation referred specifically and solely to the event itself. Intensity was used as an assessment of event magnitude. Responsibility was included as a measure of control after Vinokur and Caplan (1986). Anticipation was modeled after Neugarten's (1970) assertion (supported by Vinokur and Caplan) that events become crises or critical and significant to the extent that they are unanticipated. Adjustment was included as a dimension to reflect an appraisal of the ongoing cognitive effort and the resolution, in a psychological sense, of the event.

The participants were individually interviewed in a single session of an average of 40 min (range = 25–90 min). These interviews were tape-recorded for subsequent transcription and scoring. Participants were asked variations of the following questions: "Why is this an event of significance for you? What is it about this event that makes it of significance or importance to you?" The interview, then, was the narrative life review: each participant's event-by-event analysis of his or her entire life.

Scoring

The discussions of significance for each of the life events were coded for level of integrative complexity according to the standard scoring procedures (Baker-Brown et al., 1992). The basic scoring unit in integrative complexity is the paragraph, defined as two or more sentences dealing with one specific topic. The scoring system provides a 7-point continuum. A score of 1 reflects a categorical, all-or-nothing approach to information processing or the perception of only a single acceptable perspective or dimension (i.e., lack of differentiation); a score of 3 represents recognition of multiple, legitimate alternative ways of perceiving an issue (i.e., differentiation); a score of 5 reflects the generation of combinatorial or interactive positions (i.e., basic integration); a score of 7 recognizes multiple, embedded levels of schemata (i.e., high integration). Scores of 2, 4, and 6 represent transition points between the major scores.

Paragraphs are considered unscorable if the sentences are incoherent, purely descriptive (as opposed to evaluative), cliches, quotations from someone else, or satire (Baker-Brown et al., 1992). These event discussions were blindly scored by event, not by subject, one paragraph at a time (i.e., the first event for all of the subjects was scored first, then the second event for all subjects was scored, then the third, and so on). Only 4 of the 840 event discussions were classified as unscorable. Thus each event received a single score that was the measure used in analyses. A mean score also was calculated. Interjudge reliability was assessed by a second independent rater who scored a random sample of 147 paragraphs (representing the event discussions of 20% of the sample). Interjudge reliability was found to be $r = .82$; there was 86% agreement between the two raters.

RESULTS

Number of Life Events

We initially examined the data in terms of the number of events recalled by this life span sample of men and women. A 2 (gender) × 3 (age group) analysis of variance (ANOVA) was conducted with number of events as the dependent variable. Overall, individuals identified an average of 14 events (range = 1–35). A significant main effect was uncovered for the age group variable, $F(2, 54) = 4.277$, $p < .02$. The older participants (i.e., both the old and middle-aged groups) identified a greater number of events than did the younger participants: $M = 16.7$, 14.5, and 10.5, respectively. A marginally significant gender main effect was also noted: Women tended to identify a greater number of events than did men, with means of 15.5 and 12.2, respectively, $F(1, 54) = 3.617$, $p = .05$.

Type and Evaluation of Life Events

The types of events generated covered a wide variety of topics and paralleled those identified by standardized lists such as the SRRS (Holmes & Rahe, 1967). For example, the most frequently identified events were moving (i.e., relocation and immigration), marriage or the start of a romantic commitment, issues of schooling (including beginning and graduation), and issues of career (including beginning, changing, and retiring from a career). Other prominent events were illness, injury, family issues (e.g., divorce and marriages of siblings), births and deaths, and episodes of personal growth (e.g., therapy, lessons learned, and joining Alcoholics Anonymous).

There was also a significant number of relatively unique life events, events unlike those found on standardized lists. These included giving a child up for adoption, coming out or sexual realization, quitting piano lessons, attempting suicide, writing a book, attending Expo '86, becoming a vegetarian, and having an abortion. A comparison of the impact of these unique and normative life events on the life review is beyond the scope of this chapter, but it would certainly be a worthy enterprise.

To characterize their distribution, we categorized events as a function of their ratings and expressed them as percentages of the individuals' overall event number. Three categories were computed on each dimension to reflect meaningfully distinct levels. The mean percentages of events that were classified as pleasant (including very pleasant), unpleasant (including very unpleasant), and both pleasant and unpleasant were 55.2%, 27.9%, and 16.9%, respectively. An ANOVA revealed neither age nor gender differences in these percentages. A similar analysis conducted on the outcome desirability–undesirability dimension revealed a similar pattern. Overall, 71.1% of the event outcomes were rated as desirable (including very desirable); 15.6%, as undesirable (including very undesirable); and 13.3%, as both desirable and undesirable. Again, there were neither age nor gender differences in these rating percentages.

Mean percentages reflecting low (i.e., "not at all" and "just a little"), moderate, and high (i.e., "quite a bit" and "a great deal or extreme") categorizations of participant ratings on intensity, responsibility, adjustment, and anticipation are

presented in Table 1. The only dimension on which there were significant differences was anticipation, for which there was a three-way interaction, $F(4, 108) =$
2.59, $p < .05$. Analyses of simple main effects revealed that whereas in the young
and old groups, men had a greater proportion of highly anticipated events than did
women, in the middle-aged group, the reverse was true.

Complexity of Life Events

We first examined the complexity data in terms of the mean event complexity
scores as a function of age group and gender. No significant differences were
noted in this 2 (gender) × 3 (age group) ANOVA—men and women of all ages
used similar levels of overall complexity ($M = 2.56$) in discussing the events of
their past. This mean level reflects rudimentary differentiation and is consistent
with mean levels reported for other groups (e.g., de Vries et al., 1993; de Vries &
Walker, 1987; Suedfeld & Bluck, 1993).

Event complexity scores were also analyzed by age and gender as well as in
terms of the ratings on the Life Event Identification and Evaluation Table. As
might be expected, the correlation between the pleasantness and desirability
ratings was very high ($r = .75$, $p < .001$), so these ratings were combined and
called "positive." The unpleasant and undesirable ratings were combined and
called "negative." In pre-tests, complexity scores associated with ratings of "both"
on the pleasantness and desirability dimensions did not differ from those associated with ratings of unpleasant and very unpleasant and undesirable and very
undesirable, respectively. In addition, complexity scores associated with moderate
ratings and those associated with high ratings on the dimensions of intensity,
responsibility, adjustment, and anticipation did not differ from one another. For
parsimony and clarity, then, the analyses reported here are based on complexity

Table 1   Percentage of Life Events Rated Low, Moderate, or High in Intensity, Responsibility, Adjustment, and Anticipation

Dimension	Low	Moderate	High
Intensity (high > moderate > low)[a]	10.7	20.3	69.0
Responsibility (high > low > moderate)	30.3	12.6	57.1
Adjustment (high > moderate > low)	10.2	18.4	71.4
Anticipation (high > low > moderate)	35.2	22.6	43.2

[a] Scheffé multiple comparisons are in parentheses.

scores reflecting positive versus negative (including "both") ratings and low versus high (including moderate) ratings on intensity, responsibility, adjustment, and anticipation. The complexity scores represent the mean of those complexity scores associated with these dichotomized ratings.

A 2 (gender) × 3 (age group) × 2 (rating: positive vs. negative) ANOVA with repeated measures on the last factor yielded a highly significant main effect for the rating variable, $F(1, 52) = 114.983$, $p < .001$. Negative events were described in more complex ways than were positive events. A three-way interaction was also revealed, $F(2, 52) = 7.117$, $p < .005$ (see Figure 1). Analyses of simple main effects revealed that young and middle-aged women and men all followed this pattern in their descriptions of negative and positive events. In the oldest group, the men only described negative events in more complex ways than positive events.

A similar 2 (gender) × 3 (age group) × 2 (rating: low vs. high intensity) ANOVA with repeated measures on the last factor was conducted for the intensity rating and yielded a main effect for the rating factor, $F(1, 28) = 4.245$, $p < .05$. High intensity ($M = 2.51$) events were discussed in more complex terms than were low intensity ($M = 2.20$) events. A 2 (gender) × 3 (age group) × 2 (rating: low vs. high adjustment) ANOVA with repeated measures on the last factor was also conducted for the adjustment rating. A marginally significant main effect was found for the rating factor, $F(1, 30) = 3.913$, $p = .06$. The tendency was for those events to which there was only minimal adjustment to be higher in complexity ($M = 2.94$) than those events to which there was significant adjustment ($M = 2.36$). In both of the preceding analyses, cell sizes were substantially reduced (by roughly half), throwing into question the reliability of these effects (recall that participants must have at least one event that is rated both high and low on any particular dimension to be included in these repeated-measures analyses).

A 2 (gender) × 3 (age group) × 2 (rating: low vs. high responsibility) ANOVA with repeated measures on the last factor was conducted to examine complexity differences associated with ratings of responsibility. This analysis yielded a main effect for the rating variable, $F(1, 49) = 9.165$, $p < .005$. Events for which the individuals had little responsibility were understood in more complex ways than were events for which the individuals had greater responsibility: $M = 2.77$ vs. 2.42.

A 2 (gender) × 3 (age group) × 2 (rating: low vs. high anticipation) ANOVA with repeated measures on the last factor was conducted to examine complexity differences associated with the anticipation of an event. Again, a main effect was found for the rating variable, $F(1, 46) = 35.245$, $p < .001$. Events that had been unexpected were understood in more complex terms than were events that had been expected: $M = 2.99$ vs. 2.44. This main effect was qualified, however, by a three-way interaction, $F(2, 46) = 6.053$, $p < .005$. Analyses of simple main effects revealed a pattern similar to the interaction described in Figure 1: Unanticipated

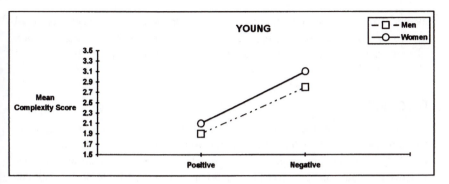

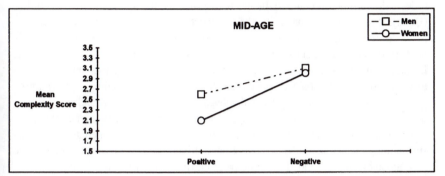

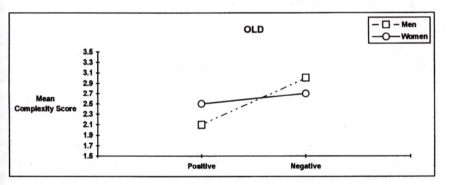

Figure 1 Mean complexity scores for positive and negative events as a function of gender and age group.

events were discussed in more complex terms than were anticipated events for all groups except older women, for whom there was no difference. Furthermore, older men were more complex than were older women in their discussions of unanticipated events.

DISCUSSION

The present study yielded several interesting and provocative findings with regard to the form and substance of the life review for women and men across the life span. In our study, older participants, that is, those from both the old and middle-aged groups, reported a greater number of past life events than did young participants. Perhaps this reflects differential exposure to the normative (history and age-graded) events of life (Baltes, 1987). For example, as might be expected, more older than younger participants discussed career issues (e.g., age-graded or those biological and social determinants of development); surprisingly, the inverse was not true for issues of schooling. Immigration was mentioned with greater frequency by older participants (e.g., history-graded or those influences associated with historical time), although relocation or moving was mentioned almost equally by all age groups. Births and deaths were mentioned more often by the middle-aged and old groups (e.g., age-graded). Relationship issues were mentioned more often by the young and middle-aged groups. Issues surrounding the acquisition or loss of either a driver's license or an automobile were mentioned by younger and older participants and not at all by those in the middle years (e.g., age-graded). Older participants mentioned with greater frequency illness and/or injury (e.g., age-graded) as well as war (e.g., history-graded). Younger participants recalled sports activities with greater frequency.

There was a general trend to favor more normative markers as the events of a life. Perhaps this was a demand characteristic of the task; alternatively, perhaps this was a way for the participants to understand their life as having evolved in a reasonable, orderly, or systematic fashion. That older adults had in larger proportion experienced these normative life markers may underlie the greater number of events identified in their life reviews.

There was a marginally significant tendency for women to report a greater number of events than men. Gilligan (1982) has written about women's embeddedness in relationships and their orientation to interdependence. It was perhaps as a consequence of their role obligations and connectedness to others in their social environment that the women reported a greater number of events (i.e., including the events of others). Along such lines, relationship events, leaving home, and births and deaths were reported with greater frequency by women (but only middle-aged and older women) than by men. This result reinforces the work of Harvey et al. (1986) and M. Ross and Holmberg (1992), who reported that women had more vivid memories of relationships.

The events identified were primarily of a pleasant and desirable nature. This was true across the age groups and for both men and women and is consistent with previous research on the self-concept. Greenwald (1980), for example, noted the general tendency for individuals to remember more good than bad personal experiences and more successes than failures. Greenwald called this "benefectance" and defined it as the tendency for people to perceive themselves as effective in achieving what they desire and avoiding what they do not desire. Tesser and Campbell (1982) referred to this as the motivation to maintain a positive self-evaluation.

This is not to say, however, that these events were of a trivial or unimportant nature. The vast majority of events were rated as high intensity. Furthermore, the majority of events were ones for which individuals felt considerable responsibility and events to which they felt they had adjusted. The pattern on ratings of anticipation was less clear: High event anticipation was more characteristic of men than of women in the young and old groups, but the reverse was true for the middle-aged group. Does this suggest a certain approach to life that might characterize the genders differently over the life span or across cohorts? Perhaps the relational characteristics of women's events render such events generally less predictable, or perhaps men generally desire a more ordered account of their lives. The break in such an interpretation occasioned by the middle years is intriguing and merits further attention.

No age or gender differences were noted in the overall complexity levels with which the life events were discussed. It might have been predicted that the alleged (e.g., M. I. Lewis & Butler, 1974) intensity and clarity of life review in old age might manifest itself in increased complexity, as a measure of cognitive sophistication; previous research (e.g., de Vries et al., 1993) suggests that discussions of issues within an individual's realm of experience or sphere of expertise, broadly defined, are represented by greater complexity than are discussions of more foreign issues. One's own life and events are certainly areas of individual expertise—areas that are independent of age and gender boundaries.

Differences, however, emerged in the finer analyses of complexity levels associated with event ratings. Recall that positive events were discussed in more simplistic ways than were negative events, not unlike the results reported by Suedfeld and Bluck (1993). Negative events may require some cognitive finessing on the part of the individual in order to eliminate or minimize the associated dissonance or anxiety. Perhaps this additional expenditure of cognitive energy in the search for understanding and meaning is rewarded or manifested by increased complexity in the recollection of such events. A similar interpretation may be offered for the finding of increased complexity with higher levels of intensity. It could also be that negative affect is associated with greater stimulus clarity or salience than is positive affect (e.g., "Never look a gift horse in the mouth").

Tetlock's (1984) analysis of cognitive style and political belief systems is relevant here. Tetlock suggested that adherents to ideologies that highly value both freedom and equality are under greater pressure to consider policy issues in more integratively complex terms than are advocates of ideologies that place a greater weight on only one value. Tetlock called this the value pluralism model. Perhaps the process of accounting for negativity in a predominantly positive framework is analogous to adhering to an ideology in which two values are equally esteemed. The combination of negative and positive is likely to elicit greater complexity than is either alone (e.g., de Vries & Walker, 1987).

In the present study, however, this pattern was qualified by the fact that it did not apply to the older women of the sample, for whom there was no difference between positive and negative events, again parallel to the findings of Suedfeld and Bluck (1993). The older women engaged more consistent cognitive structures in the analysis of both the positive and negative events of their lives, in contrast to the greater variability of the older men's cognitive structures. Perhaps this suggests an age- and gender-related difference in the search for meaning that is manifested in the recall and representation of events. Perhaps this is representative of gender-related differences in coping styles in later life. One thing is certain— gender is a relevant variable for further examinations of the life review with older samples.

The association between low event responsibility and high complexity indicates that individuals used greater complexity to describe events that happened to them than to describe events that they made happen, independent of age. Perhaps events that were not of an individual's own doing required greater cognitive effort in the accounting procedures; individuals may have felt a need to justify the events and their role in them. This might also account for the tendency toward higher complexity of descriptions of events characterized by lower adjustment and vice versa. The implication is that lower adjustment implies continued effort at understanding or acceptance of the event (i.e., a Zeigarnik effect), the cognitive "work" associated with greater complexity.

The main effect on the anticipation dimension assumed a similar form and may be similarly understood as supporting Neugarten's (1970) assertion that unanticipated events are the ones likely to introduce dissonance. Perhaps the resolution of dissonance, over time, manifests itself in greater complexity (i.e., the result of the search for meaning and understanding). This pattern, however, did not represent the experiences of the older women in the present sample, for whom anticipated and unanticipated events did not differ in terms of complexity. Perhaps the recall of unanticipated events (i.e., discussing the ways in which life and events are unpredictable), which were also fewer in number, has a greater negative impact on information processing, as represented in decreased complexity, on women than it does on men. Is it something in the telling of the story or in the reconstruction of the event? Alternatively, perhaps this finding, taken in conjunction with the similar finding on the positivity–negativity dimension, suggests a certain impartiality and objectivity—a sense of having seen it all—on the part of older women in the life review. Again, this provocative finding underscores the relevance of gender as a variable influencing the form and context of the life review.

CONCLUSION

We examined the life review, operationalized in terms of life event identification and elaboration, in a sample of women and men from across the adult life span. Overall, there were more similarities than differences in the form and substance of the life review. The recalled events, were, for the most part, positive and intense, and ones for which individuals felt responsible and to which they had adjusted. They tended to entail issues of education, career, relationship beginnings and endings, illness, and relocation. Negative events were discussed in more complex ways than were positive events, and greater complexity was also associated with high intensity, low adjustment, low responsibility, and low anticipation.

Age differences along with marginally significant gender differences, were evident in the number of events. Gender and age interacted in the rating of anticipation and the complexity associated with positive and negative events, as well as anticipated and unanticipated events. That both of these complexity findings assumed the same form is striking.

The main effect of age on number of events reviewed is not surprising and fulfills implicit expectations. But certainly the alleged age expertise associated with the life review is more than numerical. The results of the finer complexity analyses suggest this. The differences, however, are not linear increases—they are more subtle and complex. Future research should attend to these classes of differences with a more refined approach to understanding the roles of age and gender in the life review.

Chapter 10

Group Reminiscence: Evaluating Short- and Long-Term Effects

M. J. Stones
Christine Rattenbury
Albert Kozma

In this chapter, we review four studies of group reminiscence intervention we conducted and report on the implications of the results for research and practice. The issues we address are (a) the factors that motivate adherence to a group reminiscence regimen, (b) the benefits of participation, (c) the limitations of measures frequently used to evaluate outcome, (d) participant characteristics related to outcome success, and (e) the temporal progression of therapeutic change.

Because all four studies used similar forms of intervention, we shall describe the general procedure and design characteristics at the outset. Our format for reminiscence was what Sherman (1987) termed "conventional"; that is, we provided participants with topics for discussion and encouraged (but did not pressure) them to share their memories with the group. The topics covered a life stage spectrum from childhood to adolescent to early adulthood to midlife to late-life experiences. Photographs or objects relevant to the topic of each session were sometimes used to prompt discussion. Consistent with the approach of M. I. Lewis

The research reported in this chapter was supported by funding from Social Sciences and Humanities Research Council of Canada to the senior author.

and Butler (1974), the facilitator used an open and friendly manner to encourage spontaneity but did not direct the discussion toward experiential or problem-oriented modes. Different facilitators were used in the four studies, each either trained or experienced in the role. Effects related to the intervention were measured mainly with the SENOTS battery (Stones & Kozma, 1989), which comprises reliable and validated scales of happiness (the Memorial University of Newfoundland Scale of Happiness [MUNSH]), activity limitation, activity level, physical symptomatology, and financial hardship. All the assessment data were collected in standardized interviews and, whenever possible, by someone other than the facilitator.

The four studies differed in purpose, duration, and the characteristics of the participants (Table 1). In three studies of fairly brief duration (1 month) we examined issues of participation, outcome evaluation, and the processes of therapeutic change. In the fourth study, we examined the maintenance of therapeutic effectiveness throughout a prolonged intervention (18 months) along with the implications for morbidity and mortality. Two of the studies, including the long-duration study, were carried out in nursing homes, with the residents screened for communication and cognitive deficits and randomly assigned to treatment or control conditions. In the other two investigations, cognitively impaired clients at a day hospital and healthy residents of apartment complexes for seniors were studied. We report on the latter two studies first.

STUDY 1: WHY COMMUNITY RESIDENTS PARTICIPATE IN REMINISCENCE

Why do people participate in reminiscence therapy? An answer may be sought by examining the kinds of therapeutic change reported. A literature review showed

Table 1   Design Characteristics of the Four Studies

Study	Type of design	Groups	N	Mean age	Population	Duration
1	Baseline comparison of measures	Two reminiscence groups	19	74	Community residence	1 month
2	Experimental (pre/post)	Two reminiscence groups	8	67	Day hospital	1 month
		No-treatment group	9	64		
3	Experimental (pre/post)	Reminiscence group	8	85	Nursing home	1 month
		Current-topics group	8	83		
		No-treatment group	8	87		
4	Experimental (three assessments)	Reminiscence group	75	83	Five nursing homes	18 months
		Control group	101	83		

that although most of the early studies of reminiscence therapy are prescientific in methodology, the reported changes were mainly confined to aspects of psychological well-being (Rattenbury & Stones, 1989). This construct has been indexed by scales termed affect, happiness, life satisfaction, morale, etc.; however, the clearest demarcation is between measures that are relatively intransigent to environmental variability (termed here as happiness) and mood measures, which are responsive to environmental change (Kozma, Stone, Stones, Hannah, & McNeil, 1990).

The more rigorous of the early studies used happiness measures as the dependent variables but provided no evidence of therapeutic gain among community residents (Perotta & Meacham, 1981–82; Sherman, 1987). The use of happiness as an index of outcome is unfortunate because such measures, being strongly influenced by personality or temperament, tend toward stability despite changing life conditions (Costa, McCrae, & Zonderman, 1987; Stones & Kozma, 1986a). In fact, most community residents of any age claim to be happy, with the mean level of happiness lying well beyond the midpoint and near the ceiling (Heady & Wearing, 1988; Stones & Kozma, 1991). As a consequence, the potential for therapeutic gain is largely curtailed. Unlike institution residents, who typically score much lower (Stones & Kozma, 1989), the hope of higher happiness seems an improbable reason for community residents to participate in reminiscence groups, and happiness indexes may be insensitive to monitor therapeutic change. So why do community residents participate at all?

The following are some probable reasons: (a) Participants are self-selected from the lower end of the happiness continuum, (b) motivating factors include the hope to benefit from attributes of psychological well-being other than happiness, and (c) factors extrinsic to psychological well-being motivate participation (e.g., Sherman, 1987, attributed the low attrition rate in his study to the payments received by participants). The hypothesis tested in Study 1 contrasted the former two possibilities (Stones, Ivany, & Kozma, 1994) in a study with unpaid volunteers.

The hypothesis derived from a model of psychological well-being in which happiness and mood are governed by steady-state principles, with happiness representing the usual (or average) level of mood (Stones & Kozma, 1991). If mood falls below the usual level indicated by the happiness score, a probable reason is acute distress of environmental origin. The hope to rectify acute distress may motivate participation in a community-based reminiscence group.

We tested this hypothesis using 19 volunteers from two apartment complexes for seniors. They were recruited by means of posters placed on notice boards advertising the opportunity to participate in a reminiscence group, an information brochure delivered to each apartment, information sessions with groups of residents, and direct solicitation. As shown in Table 1, the mean age of residents who signed to participate was 74 years, with the group at one complex comprising 8 women and 1 man, and the group at the other comprising 9 women and 1 man.

During the week preceding the first reminiscence session, all participants were assessed on the Memorial University Mood Scale (MUMS) measure of mood (McNeil, Stones, Kozma, & Andres, 1994); the MUNSH measure of happiness; and measures of activity limitation, activity level, and physical symptomatology. On the basis of the participants' wishes, the reminiscence sessions were of 45 min duration and were held weekly.

The participants' scores on all the baseline measures were well inside the normative ranges previously obtained with samples of senior apartment dwellers of comparable age. The mean MUNSH and MUMS scores lay at distances 78% and 81%, respectively, along the effective ranges on the scales. However, attendance over the four sessions was not high, with only half the participants attending half or more of the sessions. Probably the main reason for the low attendance rate was the high number of attractive alternative activities available during the brief summer period in which the sessions were held.

The data were analyzed by stepwise multiple regression, with sessions as the dependent variable. The independent variables were demographics (age, sex, and residence), the scales, and the difference score between standardized MUMS and MUNSH estimates—indexing their relative effect. Only the difference score gained entry in the regression (beta = −.54, $p < .02$).

To the extent that happiness indexes the usual level of mood, a baseline mood lower than happiness suggests acute distress. The finding that attendance was higher among participants with a lower baseline mood than happiness is consistent with the hypothesis that reminiscence group participation in a community context is motivated by a hope to alleviate acute distress. However, two cautions are necessary. First, the findings, being the first to address this issue and based on limited sampling, require replication. Second, factors other than acute distress may motivate participation in a chronically depressing institutional context.

STUDY 2: EFFECTS OF A REMINISCENCE INTERVENTION ON THE COGNITIVELY IMPAIRED

Study 1 raises questions about whether happiness indexes are sufficient outcome measures in community-based interventions. The concern relates not to their validity, but rather to their sensitivity with samples who are approaching ceiling levels at baseline. However, questions of validity can arise if the people measured are cognitively impaired.

Baines, Saxby, and Ehlert (1987) and Goldwasser, Auerbach, and Harkins (1987) included happiness scales to evaluate the effects of reminiscence groups comprising cognitively impaired participants, but the findings were inconclusive. Although happiness scales are relatively free from threats to validity such as social desirability bias and response-set effect (yea/nay saying) among cognitively competent respondents (Kozma & Stones, 1987, 1988), response-set effect is corre-

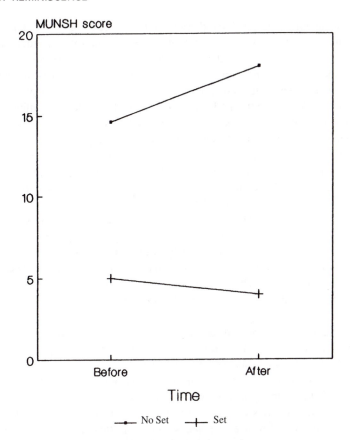

Figure 1 Mean MUNSH scores before and after the intervention period for participants with or without response-set.

lated with low education, low socioeconomic status, and low cognitive performance (Kozma, Stones, & McNeil, 1991; Moum, 1988).

A simple way to estimate response set at the level of the single case was described by Stones (1976, 1977) and adapted for use with the MUNSH (Kozma et al., 1991). If the items on a balanced scale are regarded as independent elements drawn from a common domain, the binomial distribution can be used to generate exact probabilities for the number of yea or nay responses at each level of scale score. With a $p < .05$ probability for rejecting the null hypothesis at either the yea or nay extreme ($p < .10$, two-tailed), the combined statistics from several studies show a prevalence of response-set effect of 7–8% among older respondents.

In Study 2, we examined the effects of a reminiscence intervention with cognitively impaired day hospital patients, paying particular attention to the threat to validity posed by yea/nay saying on the happiness index. The sample comprised

17 persons randomly assigned to either of two reminiscence groups or a no-treatment control condition. As shown in Table 1, the 8 reminiscence group participants (4 men and 4 women) and 9 control group participants (6 men and 3 women) were predominantly in their mid-60s. All participants were at least moderately impaired on a mental status test (Folstein, Folstein, & McHugh, 1975; the group means ranged from 15.8 to 17.1), but none were bedridden or suffered from communication, attention, or behavior disorders that would encumber participation in a reminiscence group. The measures at baseline and post-test comprised the SENOTS battery and mental status test; however, 1 person from each condition was unavailable at post-test because of relocation. The reminiscence groups were facilitated during eight sessions (twice weekly over 1 month) by either of two social workers associated with the day hospital.

The sample's mean MUNSH score at baseline lay at a distance approximately 63% along the effective range on the scale, suggesting the sample as a whole to be moderately unhappy. A multivariate analysis of variance (with time a repeated measure) was computed to determine the effects of group and time on SENOTS scores and mental status. The analysis showed no significant effects of group or time and no interaction effect. These findings provided no evidence for outcome success.

The MUNSH was analyzed for response-set effect among the 15 participants from whom pre-test and post-test measures were available. With a preset probability of .05 at each tail, response set was detected among more than half the participants (2 from the reminiscence groups and 6 from the control group; 6 cases at pre-test, 2 at post-test, and 1 at both; 6 yea sayers and 2 nay sayers). Because both chance and previous empirical research suggest that 10% or fewer in the sample should have shown a response-set effect at this significance level, the evidence is convincing that the MUNSH data for the sample as a whole should be considered invalid. A consequence of response-set effect is that scores on balanced scales, such as the MUNSH, could be expected to converge toward zero. This expectation was confirmed by the finding of lower means for participants with set (5 at pre-test and 4 at post-test) than without set (14.6 at pre-test and 18 at post-test), $F(1, 13) = 6.81, p < .05$ (see Figure 1).

These findings cast doubt on the validity of self-reports to index the level or change in happiness among the cognitively impaired. Moreover, it became apparent after inspection of the sample's responses to the other SENOTS scales that the response-set tendency generalized to the other measures. These findings suggest the need to screen persons with cognitive impairment out of interventions evaluated by self-report or to use outcome indexes other than self-report.

STUDY 3: REMINISCENCE IN A NURSING HOME

Residents of institutions frequently score low on happiness indexes, with the conditions of institutional life believed to be a reason. Rattenbury (1991) located eight studies evaluating the usefulness of reminiscence groups for cognitively unimpaired persons in institutional settings, only one of which used both objective measures and a controlled pre/post design.

Rattenbury and Stones (1989) compared a reminiscence intervention group, a group using a similar format to discuss current topics rather than past events, and a no-treatment control group. As Table 1 shows, the 24 participants were in their 80s. They were determined to be cognitively unimpaired and free from communication deficiencies. Assignment to conditions was randomized. Before and after measures were obtained 2 weeks before and 2 weeks after the 8-session intervention (two sessions per week, each lasting 30 min). The measures included the MUNSH and MUMS to index happiness and mood, an activities inventory (Stones & Kozma, 1986b), and a geriatric rating scale completed by the nursing staff (Meer & Baker, 1966). In addition to the before-and-after battery, a 15-s time-sampling procedure was used to monitor verbal participation within sessions, and the MUMS was administered at the beginning and end of each session.

The findings were as follows:

1   The groups were fully comparable at baseline.

2   Group differences from before to after the intervention were significant only on the MUNSH, with both treatment groups showing gains of equivalent magnitude over the no-treatment group (Figure 2).

3   Verbal participation within the sessions increased over the intervention, with participation significantly correlated with gains on the MUNSH. The MUNSH mean before intervention lay at a distance of 69% along the effective range of scores, indicating only moderate happiness, whereas the postintervention mean for the intervention groups lay at 78%, which is within the usual normative range.

These findings suggest that reminiscing in a group context can have therapeutic effects on the happiness of nursing home residents. However, the finding that the current-topics discussion group showed an equivalent gain to the reminiscence group suggests that reminiscence per se may not be essential to intervention success. Instead, the significant correlation between verbal participation and the change in happiness after the intervention shows the level of participation to have been more important than the content of discussion.

Because of an editorial decision, Rattenbury and Stones (1989) did not report data on the mood measures taken before and after each session in the intervention. However, the findings regarding mood illustrate a temporal progression within the intervention that was relevant to the total therapeutic outcome. Similar to other mood indexes (Mackay, Cox, Burrows, & Lazzerini, 1978), the MUMS comprises Affect and Vigor subscales. Separate analyses of variance were computed for scores obtained on these subscales before and after each session, with weeks of intervention as a repeated factor. Significant effects were obtained for presession affect, $F(3, 42) = 5.86$, $p < .005$, and postsession vigor, $F(3, 42) = 3.16$, $p < .05$. Multiple comparisons

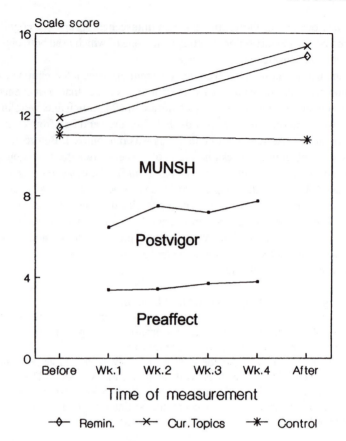

Figure 2   Mean MUNSH scores for the reminiscence (Remin.), current topics (Cur. Topics), and no-treatment control groups before and after intervention and mean presession scores for affect and postsession scores for vigor over Weeks 1–4 of the intervention.

(Newman-Keuls) showed presession affect to be lower at Weeks 1 and 2 than at Weeks 3 and 4 and postsession vigor to be lower at Week 1 than Week 4.

Changes in mood were related to overall therapeutic effects. Only an estimate of the change in presession mood from Weeks 1 and 2 to Weeks 3 and 4 proved predictive of changes on the MUNSH from before to after the intervention ($r = .81$, $p < .01$). This finding shows a continuity to therapeutic change that can be detected after only 2 weeks (Stones, Rattenbury, & Kozma, 1994).

STUDY 4: MAINTENANCE AND IMPLICATIONS OF THERAPEUTIC EFFECTS

Study 3 showed effects on psychological well-being after four reminiscence sessions and indicated that these effects persisted at least 2 weeks beyond the intervention. In Study 4, we examined the maintenance of therapeutic effectiveness during a prolonged (18 months) intervention, along with the implications for morbidity and mortality.

Study 4 included 176 participants from five nursing homes. Table 1 shows a mean age in the eighties. Participants were screened to be ambulatory, free of major speech and hearing deficiencies, and without cognitive impairment. Fifteen residents at each home were randomly assigned to a reminiscence group (23 men and 52 women), and the remainder were assigned to a no treatment condition (27 men and 74 women). The facilitator was the same nurse at all the homes. The weekly sessions were of 30 min duration, barring holidays or special occasions.

The assessment battery comprised the SENOTS scales, administered after 1.5 months (6 sessions), 8.5 months (28 sessions), and 18 months (55 sessions), with a different assessor each time. No pre-test data were collected, because a pilot study at one home showed the residents to be so demoralized that pre-testing threatened their subsequent participation in treatment. Other indexes obtained during the study included a medical chart review, with illnesses categorized according to the International Classification of Diseases (World Health Organization, 1977), and a mental status test to check on cases of cognitive impairment emerging during the study.

Preliminary analyses showed no differences between the reminiscence and control groups with respect to age, gender, or number of diseases. Attendance rate for the reminiscence sessions averaged 83% up until the first assessment, 73% between the first and second assessments, and 70% between the second and third assessments. Correlational analysis was used to evaluate attendance. The most reliable predictor of subsequent attendance was the MUNSH score obtained on an earlier assessment (rs = .27–.37).

The main analyses were a multivariate analysis of variance followed by analyses of variance to clarify significant effects. The analyses were computed for each assessment separately (to assess effects due to group, institution, and gender) and for participants in multiple assessments (to assess the Group × Time interaction). The MUNSH was the only measure from the SENOTS battery to show significance in all the analyses (ps = .05–.005). Figure 3 shows the MUNSH means for the participants in the first (n = 165), second (n = 131), and third (n = 99) assessments and for the 87 residents who participated in all three assessments (reminiscence groups n = 42; control group n = 45). Participants in the reminiscence groups were moderately happy throughout the intervention, whereas residents in the control condition were unhappy. The absence of any significant interaction of group with institution, time, or gender shows the higher MUNSH scores in the reminiscence condition to have been a constant effect. The only other measure to differ between the groups in several analyses was activity limitation. Further analysis of this effect showed it to be present only on four items, three of which begin with the phrase "Health problems prevent me from." One may

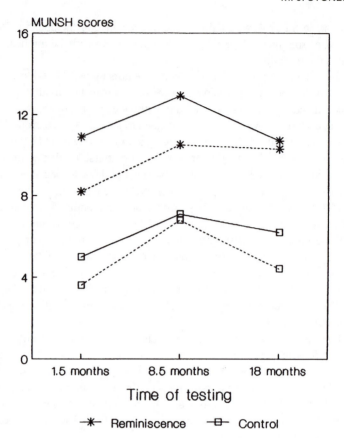

Figure 3 Mean MUNSH scores for the reminiscence and control groups at each discrete time of testing (dotted lines) and for participants present at all three assessments (solid lines).

wonder whether the higher happiness among participants in the reminiscence groups made them less prone to cite ill health as a reason for inactivity.

The reasons for failure to comply with testing were examined. Refusal to comply or absence from the institution at the time of testing accounted for 14% of the total noncompliance and for all the noncompliance at the initial assessment. Sixteen percent of participants in the reminiscence groups failed to comply at the time of the 8.5-month assessment because of physical illness (3%), death (4%), or cognitive impairment (9%), compared with a significantly ($p < .01$) higher proportion of 33% noncompliance in the control condition (13% illness; 11% death; 9% cognitive impairment). As shown in Figure 4, physical morbidity and mortality, but not cognitive impairment, were lower in the reminiscence groups.

Noncompliance was also examined in relation to demographics, disease category, and SENOTS indexes. No evidence was obtained that residents absent

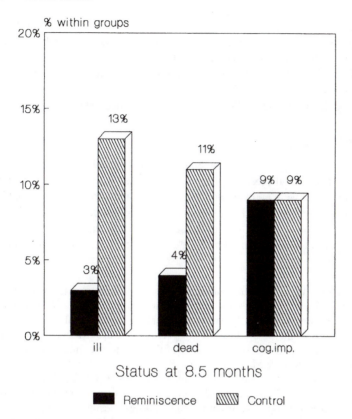

Figure 4 Proportions of the reminiscence and control groups not present at the 8.5-month assessment for reasons of physical illness, cognitive impairment (cog. imp.), or death.

from the 8.5-month assessment were older, differed in gender distribution, or had more disorders recorded in their medical charts than those present—in fact, noncompliance was significantly associated with lower frequencies in the nervous system and musculature disorder categories ($ps < .05$). The SENOTS scores at the 1.5-month assessment were used to predict compliance at 8.5 months. Only the MUNSH showed significant prediction ($p < .01$), with lower scores among residents who were dead or cognitively impaired at 8.5 months.

Analysis of the compliance data at the 18-month assessment showed a mortality of 23% in the reminiscence groups and 37% among the controls. Noncompliance at 18 months was unrelated to demographics or the number or type of diseases but was predicted by lower MUNSH scores ($p < .01$), lower activity levels ($p < .05$), and higher physical symptomatology scores ($p < .01$) at the earlier assessments.

In summary, the findings of Study 4 show the difference in happiness between the reminiscence and no-treatment groups to have been generalized across five nursing homes and to have remained constant over an 18-month intervention. Participants in the reminiscence groups also scored more favorably on certain activity limitation items and were less likely than residents in the control condition to be physically ill or dead 8.5 months into the intervention period. We conclude that happiness was maintained by the reminiscence intervention over a prolonged period and that morbidity and mortality were attenuated over several months.

CONCLUSION

The four studies reported herein have implications for the issues of the methodology, participation, and substantive benefits associated with reminiscence intervention. Studies 1–3 were comparable in sample size and duration to most published reports on reminiscence, whereas Study 4 was considerably broader in scope, duration, and aims. All four studies used objective measures and (apart from Study 1) a controlled design with repeated measurement. The main conclusions are as follows.

1 Of an array of measures including activity limitation, activity level, happiness, mood, objective illness, physical symptomatology, and ratings of function, the measure most consistently to benefit from an institutional intervention was self-reported happiness (Studies 3 and 4). However, the evidence was less convincing that a happiness scale is as useful an outcome index in community interventions (Perotta & Meacham, 1981–82; Sherman, 1987; the present Study 1) or among the cognitively impaired (Baines et al., 1987; Goldwasser et al., 1987; the present Study 2). Researchers should be aware of (previously cited) research on the stability of happiness in community settings (despite life changes) and of the threat to the validity of measures of happiness posed by cognitive deficiency.

2 Attendance related positively to happiness in institutions (Study 4), but to low mood relative to happiness in a community setting (Study 1). This discrepancy may reflect the respective desires by institution and community residents to alleviate chronic versus acute sources of environmental distress.

3 Verbal participation within sessions proved a more potent predictor of outcome success than did the content of discussion (Study 3).

4 Changes in psychological well-being were detected after only four sessions in an institutional intervention (Study 3), with the gain in happiness maintained over at least 18 months (Study 4).

5 The benefits of prolonged intervention included lower morbidity and mortality over several months, with lower mortality predicted by happiness measured at earlier times. The convergence of findings leads us to speculate that the effects on happiness contribute to a postponement of mortality.

Part Three

Methods

In the methods section, the contributors participate in a Show and Tell, sharing their use of old memories in therapy and providing directions for the reader to adopt. Burnside contributes her wealth of experience in describing the use of props and themes in reminiscence. She shares experience-based knowledge, noting that the use of props is particularly valuable for persons with cognitive deficits. This will give others the opportunity to start off a little ahead, instead of using the trial-and-error method.

De Vries, J. E. Birren, and Deutchman provide a method for eliciting an autobiography. Their clearly written piece can serve as a protocol for either research or intervention. Their method is certainly a useful tool for people looking for ways to use the life story. The use of autobiography is becoming more and more common, as a form of both fact finding and intervention.

Haight, Coleman, and Lord combine expertise across continents to examine the therapeutic effect of a structured life review and to provide directions to others who wish to use this structured process. They provide a guideline based on research in the United States and then used and tested in the United Kingdom.

The richness in the use of the life story is further depicted by Thorsheim and Roberts, who see the life story as a means of providing mutual social support. They discuss the key role older people play in maintaining each other's health and see stories as an ideal way to empower older people.

Chapter 11

Themes and Props: Adjuncts for Reminiscence Therapy Groups

Irene Burnside

Two adjuncts to reminiscence therapy groups are themes and props. Both are frequently mentioned in the literature on reminiscence therapy groups, but close examination of the literature reveals precious little to guide the reader who wishes to introduce themes or props in a reminiscence group. Of course, other types of groups might also use them; for example, reality orientation groups (Taulbee, 1986) have used props since their inception, and remotivation groups may combine themes and props consistently during the life of the group (Dennis, 1994). In this chapter, I review the literature on the use of themes and props in reminiscence groups with older adults. I then offer guidelines for their use and pose questions for practice and research.

THEMES

One operational definition of *theme* is "a leader-chosen or member-chosen subject of discourse and discussion which is a unifying dominant idea for a reminiscence group meeting" (Burnside, 1993, p. 180). Another word commonly used in the literature is *topic*.

The earliest detailed list of themes was located in a book about Maggie Kuhn, renowned leader of the Gray Panthers. Kuhn asked older people to jot down their earliest memories and called them the "rudiments of life review" (quoted by Hessel, 1977, p. 34). Some examples were first Christmas, first day in school, first love, first kiss, first illness, and first time hungry. However, these themes were not intended for group work.

Since then, group leaders (including me) have begun themes with the word *first* as an adjective. However, it is not always successful to use "first memory" for a theme, unless one is prepared to deal with the sad memories it may trigger. In the initial meeting of one group, one woman in her late 70s said her first memory was the death of her mother, which set the tone for the rest of the meeting, with the other members following her example and discussing the deaths of loved ones. This unexpected sharing and the subsequent focus by the group on loss, grief, and death made it clear that the theme chosen by the leader had unplanned results.

Selection of Themes

It is not at all clear from the literature what process leaders use to select themes. Occasionally, the group members may choose the themes (D. M. Reed & Cobble, 1986; Youssef, 1990). The most common approach reported in the literature is the life span approach; one term for it is "chronological pattern" (Matteson & Munsat, 1982). Other leaders apparently used a shotgun approach in that the link between the themes of the sessions cannot be made by the reader. The rationale for the use of either approach was lacking in most studies (Burnside, 1993).

Themes are more complex than one realizes, even when one begins a reminiscence group using a protocol delineating specific themes. Themes can be categorized into three types: (a) subtheme, (b) nonrelated theme, and (c) trigger themes (Burnside, 1990a). Subthemes are secondary to the selected meeting theme. For example, a logical subtheme for toys would be games. Nonrelated themes are those that have no obvious connection to the theme being discussed. These may really startle the leader because they are so strange. Even though the memories may not relate in any perceived way to the theme being discussed, something has been retrieved by the person who is sharing.

Trigger themes are more overt. A trigger theme is a word, description, or event shared that continues and expands on the theme under discussion. Triggers often result in introductory comments, such as "That reminds me of" or "A similar thing happened to me." A flashbulb memory is a trigger that creates an immediate, vivid memory in the group members. For example, in a group of people who lived in the United States most of their lives, Kennedy's assassination would be a flashbulb memory (Burnside).

Protocols

Also lacking in the literature is an explanation of what the leader hoped to accomplish by using predesignated themes or a protocol. Protocols regarding themes were explicitly stated by only a few authors (Burnside, 1990a; Cook, 1988; K. King, 1979). More often, they were woven into the fabric of the article and had to be pulled out. It is ironic that descriptions of protocols used by leaders of reminiscence therapy groups are a lacuna in the literature when they are often needed by those who begin reminiscence groups (Burnside & Haight, 1994).

Protocols would help researchers, new group leaders, and students striving to implement reminiscence therapy groups. In the absence of explicit explanations of why themes were used or why particular themes were selected, I suggest that some of the possible reasons for introducing themes are

1 Themes provide structure to the group, helping to reduce the anxiety of both the members and the leader.

2 Themes provide a linchpin for the group meetings, an important method for organizing the group meeting. When the themes are stated ahead of time, members will often do homework and come to the meetings truly prepared to discuss the topics. This strategy can be most helpful to a beginning reminiscence group leader. It also appears to stimulate long-term residents experiencing boredom.

3 Leaders may choose certain themes because of their own interest and curiosity, meeting their own needs instead of the group members' needs, and thereby breaking one of the basic principles of group work.

There are advantages and disadvantages to introducing themes into reminiscence groups; they are listed in Table 1. The greatest advantages are structure and continuity. The disadvantage is that the theme may become a burden, a yoke around the leader's neck because he or she endeavors to keep an entire meeting on a theme that does not get off the ground (Matteson & Munsat, 1982).

Types of Themes

A time line can provide a bonanza of ideas for themes for a group. They are useful because they may conjure up long-forgotten memories, providing ideas about a time span about which older persons can feel they are authorities. Table 2 presents an example of a time line that was designed for older United States residents. A time line for residents of the United Kingdom for world events during 1900–1980 was designed by C. Adams (1991). A leader may wish to include other world events in a multicultural group. In addition, personal time lines for individual members of the group could be constructed (Kuhn, 1977; K. Lukcas, personal communication, June 10, 1992). Genograms are also popular and have been used by nurses (Herth, 1989) and social workers (Ingersoll-Dayton & Arndt, 1990) as a means of eliciting memories, even though the original use of genograms was to

Table 1 Advantages and Disadvantages of the Use of Themes in Reminiscence Groups

Advantages	Disadvantages
• Provide structure and format for group meetings. • Provide continuity, if leader provides link from one meeting to next. • Can be organized for group experience in various ways: in a life span approach, as firsts in elders' lives, or topically (e.g., music, cars, or past events) • Can be switched easily if discussion is not forthcoming. • Can be chosen by either leader or members. • Can suggest props that may be brought to the group. (For women, a doll theme often will result in members' bringing a cherished doll to a group.)	• If the theme is not of interest to members, the leader cannot keep the focus on the theme. • Thoughtful selection is required to provide themes interesting to all members. • Some themes may not be grasped easily by persons with dementia. • Some themes (e.g., wars) may elicit profound sadness. • Careful selection is required for appropriateness for age, gender, geography, and culture.

glean medical information. Genograms could certainly be adapted to reminiscence group work.

Theme Effectiveness

An effective theme is one that catches the interest of the group members and increases their participation—both verbal and nonverbal. In this regard, it can be deemed to be effective therapeutically. A theme could also be effective because of the depth and breadth of the memories discussed.

Once again, the literature fails to provide knowledge about what themes are effective and ineffective themes for various types of groups of older people (e.g., age-, culture-, or residence-based groups) (Rodriguez, 1990). One theme that generates much interest in both men and women in reminiscence groups is a discussion of old cars, most particularly the Model T Ford.

A few years ago, I spoke to a Kiwanis Club in Australia. Immediately, the men thought the purpose of the talk was memory loss and that they would receive tips on how to prevent forgetfulness. (This is not an uncommon occurrence if one uses the word *memory* to describe a group to potential members.) When asked which old car the Australian men remembered the best, the men said exactly what men in groups in the United States had said: "The Model T Ford." The international popularity of that car came as a surprise to me.

Table 2 Time Line That May Suggest Themes for a Reminiscence Group

1900	Hurricane and tidal wave occur in Galveston, Texas—6,000 die
1902	Wilbur and Orville Wright successfully test new glider design
1903	First World Series game takes place
1906	San Francisco earthquake occurs
1908	Ford debuts the $850 Model T as a "motor car for the great multitude"
1910	V-neck first appears and is branded dangerous to health and morals
1913	Mammography is developed
1914	Red and green traffic lights are used for first time in Cleveland, Ohio
1915	Shortwave radio is introduced
1916	First U.S. supermarket opens in Tennessee
1917	United States declares war on Germany
1920	Women's fashion abandons corsets and waistlines, resulting in tubular look
1920	All-purpose tractors come into use, gradually replacing animals and steam-powered farm machinery
1920	Only recorded fatality during major league game occurs—Ray Chapan is killed by a pitch
1921	Local telephone dialing system is offered by Omaha, Nebraska, telephone system
1926	First successful electric phonograph is invented
1926	Talking motion pictures are ushered in with the film "The Jazz Singer"
1927	Charles A. Lindberg completes first transatlantic flight
1927	First iron lung
1928	Lake Okeechobee is swollen by a hurricane—2,000 are killed
1928	Color motion pictures are demonstrated
1930	First long-scale analog computer is built
1934	Adolf Hitler challenges German automakers to develop car; he suggests name Volkswagon
1938	Nylon stockings are invented by DuPont
1941	Pearl Harbor is attacked
1943	Marines take Guadacanal
1944–45	Battle of the Bulge occurs
1945	Battle of Iwo Jima occurs
1945	Atomic bombs are dropped on Hiroshima
1947	Jackie Robinson becomes first black person to play in Major Leagues
1950	U.S. combat forces go to Korea
1950	Color television broadcasting begins in United States
1962	U.S. troops in Vietnam number 12,000
1967	U.S. troops in Vietnam number 480,000
1973	Last U.S. troops are withdrawn from Vietnam

Sources: Nash, 1976; Wetterau, 1990; Williams, 1967.

The most complete list of themes I could locate was compiled by Hamilton (1992). She offered a list of themes that may be used to elicit reminiscence in older persons. The list is presented in Table 3.

PROPS

Because the word *prop* is not defined in the reminiscence group literature, it is important to discuss the other terms writers have used in lieu of the word *prop*. Rodriguez (1990) found that a variety of terms were used to refer to props: *reminiscing stimuli, visual aids, tangible reminders of the past, personal artifacts, antiques of yesteryear, objects, memorabilia, aids in introducing reminiscence, catalysts, relics of the past,* and *evocative materials*. Rodriguez provided the following operational definition of props:

> Items which through their ability to sustain a memory over the passage of time, evoke the recall to mind of long-forgotten persons, events, or scenes which were part of the environment in which one lived during earlier developmental stages. (p. 3)

It should be noted that although Rodriguez did not specify that props were physical items, in her study all props were. She also proposed that memorabilia (props) that stimulate reminiscence in older adults can function as transitional objects; that is, they can effect a transitional phenomenon because the elderly person relates to that time in his or her life that was "characterized by youthfulness, vigor, and autonomy" (Rodriguez, p. 17). The use of transitional objects seems particularly important for older persons who have relocated. Herth (1993) coined a new term for such items, calling them "hope objects."

Props are particularly helpful when the leader needs to provide sensory stimulation or elicit memories in persons who are cognitively impaired. Props, like themes, need to be carefully chosen with the group members in mind. If props

Table 3   General Themes That May Be Used To Elicit Reminiscence

Child-raising customs	Occupation, skills, hobbies
Entertainment (movies, books)	Presidents, politics, elections
Ethnic, cultural, or family tradition	Relationships (pets and relatives)
Fashion	Romance
"Favorites" (Christmas, other holidays)	School days
"Firsts" (car, telephone, date, dress, house)	Significant events (weddings, births, and graduations)
Food preparation	Transportation
Gardens	Travel
Home heath customs	Weather
Medical care and practices	
Music	

Source: Hamilton, 1992, p. 297.

are introduced into a group to support a theme, they may elicit new themes. For instance, if a toy is introduced, it can generate much discussion about a variety of games and toys that the members enjoyed (or were deprived of) as children.

Selection of Props

Props are usually chosen by the leader; however, in a few reported studies, the leaders encouraged group members to bring items to stimulate reminiscence (Dietsche, 1979; Hamilton, 1985; Ingersoll & Goodman, 1983; McMordie & Blom, 1979). If a leader requests props from the group members, the main consideration is not to overload the group with too many objects, particularly if some members have memory loss. Also, if the props are antiques they may be very valuable monetarily. And even if they are not valuable in that regard, rest assured they have great meaning and value to the older person who brought them. It is the leader's responsibility to guard them and treat them with care. Sometimes family members will send props along, so the group leader must be sure they are returned to the correct party intact. I observed one group meeting in which some women began cramming photographs they mistakenly thought were theirs into their purses, which, of course, bent some of the fragile pictures and bent some dispositions as well.

As with themes, group leaders who have used props have not reported their rationales for using props or selecting certain props in the literature. I suggest that some possible reasons are

1   To make group meetings more interesting.
2   To involve the members to a greater degree.
3   To appeal to several senses (e.g., sight, smell, and taste), which is especially important for sensorily deprived individuals.
4   To follow through on a theme. For example, the theme for a reminiscence group of all women could be cooking utensils, and members could bring in a favorite utensil.
5   To provide a group activity with the necessary props to complete the activity. For example, cookie dough or bread dough could be brought in to be shaped and baked during a meeting.
6   To give members greater autonomy and choice in specifying the themes of meetings.

Props can be quite successful when they are properly chosen, but they must appeal to members if they are to elicit reminiscence. According to Rodriguez (1990), both themes and props must be appropriate in four areas: (a) cohort, (b) gender, (c) geography, and (d) culture. When a theme or prop is not successful, one of these factors may have been ignored. Discussing cotton mills in a reminiscence group in the state of Washington, for example, may be courting failure.

My own attempts to use small black-and-white photographs as props have not been successful. Persons with memory loss or vision problems are particularly unable to respond. However, a very special photograph for example, a graduation or wedding photograph, may trigger memories for others.

S. Hendrix (personal communication, June 22, 1992) shared her experience in using what she had deemed were appropriate props for women in their 90s. However, they showed little interest in them. She concluded that perhaps at that age in life, there was an element of self-transcendence (P. G. Reed, 1991). This would possibly tie in with Tornstam's (1989) writing about "gero-transcendence" and "a decrease in interest in material things" (p. 56). The lack of interest was not due to an inappropriateness of the props or to inadequate planning on Hendrix's part. The props were appropriate in all four areas that Rodriguez (1990) described. Hendrix had scoured the area for several antique dolls, hats, kitchen utensils, etc., that she thought would appeal to these elite survivors. There had to have been other reasons for the lack of response. Perhaps there were too many props. Perhaps the women's energy levels were too low. Perhaps the newness of the experience overwhelmed them. Perhaps environmental stimuli or events in the nursing home distracted them. Perhaps we need to ask the women.

Successful Props

Food and beverages usually are failproof—that is, if you remember to omit foods with nuts (they get under the dentures) and bran muffins (they may be healthy, but they are usually too dry). Fresh bread may be brought in, or toast or cookies may be made. Even if the men do not participate in the making and baking, they enjoy the eating and often recall cookies their mothers made. One caution involves introducing sweets if there are members who are diabetics. The surprise element is effective too if the members are never quite sure what the week's treat will be.

Of course, some props easily lend themselves to animated discussions, such as dolls for women and fishing tackle or gear for men. I have found that colognes and shaving lotion work well with the cognitively impaired, because, as mentioned earlier, appealing to many sense modalities can be very effective with this subgroup of participants.

An ideal prop, of course, is one that stirs up memories for all members. However, when some members do not have any memories about a prop, they will often sit quietly, apparently enjoying what other members have to share. For example, elders who were very poor as children may not want to discuss toys that are brought in as props. However, they will usually describe the toys they made when they were children and the games they had played or made up because they had no toys. Those memories more often than not are some of the best shared in a group.

The use of props with alert group members are usually not problematic, but it is a different story when props are introduced in a group of cognitively impaired reminiscers. Then the props must be chosen with great care. Precautions include the following (Burnside, 1994):

1 Do not leave unattended sharp knives or other utensils brought for an activity.
2 Do not introduce or pass around such dangerous props as knives or fish hooks.
3 Clutter can create or increase confusion. Keep the number of props to a minimum; introduce one prop at a time and keep the others out of sight.
4 Do not bring in nonedible items that resemble fruits or vegetables, such as a candle that looks like an edible object or soap that looks like a lemon.
5 Props should be easy to see, hold, or pass around and should not be fragile or breakable.
6 Monitor all props to ensure they are not broken, lost, or misplaced.

Table 4 lists the advantages and disadvantages of introducing props into reminiscence groups. The advantage is that props add interest and stimulate a group. The disadvantages are in finding the appropriate prop. Selecting the prop best suited for a particular group requires careful preparation. Props also require care so that nothing happens to them.

Table 4 Advantages and Disadvantages of Introducing Props in Reminiscence Groups

Advantages	Disadvantages
• Usually elicit immediate response; are excellent triggers.	• If the group includes a wide variety of members, it may be difficult to locate props appropriate for age, gender, geography, and culture of group.
• Are excellent to use with persons with dementia; serve as triggers.	
• May appeal to several senses (e.g., an orange can be seen, touched, eaten).	• Much organization is required to gather props, carry them to meeting, etc.
• Can be used to support a theme selected for the group (e.g., pumpkins for a discussion of Halloween memories).	• For persons with dementia, the prop must be safe (no knives, fishhooks, etc.).
• Can range from simple to complex.	• If entire meeting is based on a prop not well-known to members, little discussion may occur.
• Can range from inexpensive to expensive.	
• May be a "hope object" that renews participants' hope and energizes them (Herth, 1993).	• If prop is valuable or expensive, it must be guarded and cared for.

GUIDELINES

A few guidelines regarding the use of themes and props may help the new leader of a reminiscence group who is feeling anxious about implementing the group.

1 Expect some themes and props to elicit poor response. Either have a second one in mind or, better yet, follow the tangent the group seems to take. The group may be more interested in a related topic or by-product of the theme or prop you introduced.

2 Keep a list of themes and props that you have used successfully to assist you in future groups you may lead.

3 Do not expect the group to reminisce constantly; the topic of conversation will often move from the past to the present or the future, but themes or props can serve the leader well to help refocus the group.

4 Sharing some of your memories may be a method of launching a group meeting. Your memory may set the tone for the meeting, so choose it carefully.

5 Any group requires exquisite organization, and if themes or props are planned, there must be even more careful preparation. A protocol would be useful (Burnside & Haight, 1994); for example, a list of the theme or prop needed for each of a series of meetings may be planned before commencing a group.

6 Expect sadness or tears. War-time memories, as well as favorite-person or -pet themes, especially may cause sadness. Holocaust survivors have powerful traumatic memories, as do former POWs of Vietnam and Korea.

7 You will need to know the cohort group you are leading. Do not bring a prop or suggest a theme that is unfamiliar to them because it is too recent for them.

8 If you accept members ranging in age from 60 to 95, you will have to pay careful attention to the 35-year span. Will the 60-year-old be interested in the themes or props that interest the 95-year-old, and vice versa? Sometimes, leaders' enthusiasm for a theme or prop far exceeds that of the members. Be attuned to members' needs.

9 Bittersweet memories occur (Burnside, 1990a). The reminiscer may relate how a happy situation became painful but then may wish to explain how the pain has been resolved through the years. An example of such a bittersweet memory is the loss of a pet. Be supportive as the reminiscer tells of the bittersweetness.

10 Nonagenarians may not be interested in props (S. Hendrix, personal communication, June 22, 1992); try to determine why this might be and introduce props cautiously to the very very old.

11 A time line of events (e.g., Table 2) can help you decide on appropriate themes for various age groups.

12 State the rationale for each theme chosen to help organize the group overall.

13 Evaluate the effectiveness of the theme or prop through video, feedback from members, or a log written immediately after the meeting.

14 Select a prop that is appropriate to (i.e., safe for) the cognitive level of the group.

15 Introduce only one prop at a time, especially with cognitively impaired persons.

Some questions to ask when considering the use of props or themes with a reminiscence group include What themes (a) do group members suggest when they are asked for ideas? (b) elicit the most discussion? (c) are introduced spontaneously by the older adult group members? (d) work well together when used as a planned intervention? (e) are most effective for what cohort groups? (f) are most effective for hearing impaired? (g) are most effective for cognitively impaired members? (h) do older persons bring most frequently to groups? Finally, how might protocols improve or change the reminiscence therapy group?

CONCLUSION

Themes and props can be introduced separately, or they can be combined. The literature reveals the use of a wide selection of themes and props by group leaders; however, their importance or success has been rarely documented.

It appears that the creativity and historical knowledge of the leader will go a long way toward introducing themes/props that are interesting and stimulating to group members and produce conversation. If a theme or prop does not elicit discussion, the selection may have been a poor choice. The leader needs to determine why.

The introduction of themes or props looks deceptively simple, but, as was pointed out throughout this chapter, the selection of, rationale for, and creative use of a theme or prop are not happenstance. More research in this area is needed to provide group leaders with a better foundation. In addition, the literature on the use of themes and props provides little knowledge about their effectiveness with or importance to group members. As research on reminiscence therapy refines the practice of reminiscence therapy, that can be expected to change.

Chapter 12

Method and Uses of the Guided Autobiography

Brian de Vries
James E. Birren
Donna E. Deutchman

There is a burgeoning interest in exploring autobiographical material. In this chapter, we describe the method and the uses of Guided Autobiography to facilitate the life review. A central premise underlying this approach is that the life review is perhaps most productively done as part of a guided process that directs attention to major life themes. Participating in Guided Autobiography can help individuals recall details of their lives, identify their strengths and weaknesses, develop a sense of coherence about their lives, and accept their lives as they have evolved.

An autobiography is a story of a life, the explanation or interpretation of this life by the individual who has lived it. The term *hermeneutics* is given to the study of interpretation. The study of autobiography is, in a sense, the study of hermeneutics: how people of different age, gender, and eras interpret their lives (Moody, 1988a). For researchers, Guided Autobiography facilitates such interpretation by heightening an individual's awareness of the themes around which his or her life has developed. The content or products of Guided Autobiography are a source of

We thank John A. Blando for his assistance in the preparation of a draft of this chapter.

data about individual development and the social and historical influences on individual lives. Guided Autobiography is perhaps the premier avenue to insights about the way life is experienced from the inside, including the experience of growing old.

THE METHOD

Autobiography is the story of his or her life that an individual fashions from reminiscences of people, events, and emotions. Although all autobiographies may be said to be guided stories or accounts, being dictated by the purposes of the narrator (e.g., to leave an account of the family's history for others, to explain events and their consequences, or to attempt to achieve coherence and insight for personal satisfaction or life justification), Guided Autobiography is a semi-structured, topical, group approach to life review. Guided Autobiography is an educational process of bringing one's understanding of the past into the present in order to integrate the experiences and events of one's lifetime (de Vries, J. E. Birren, & Deutchman, 1990). As such, it combines and extends several of the strengths of other life review techniques.

Guided Autobiography entails a written component, similar to Progoff's (1975) intensive journals, facilitating in-depth and personal reflection, further scrutiny of one's past, and an appreciation of the tapestry of one's life. It also incorporates a group experience, similar to the methods of M. I. Lewis and Butler (1974), enhancing recall, reinforcing participation, and promoting self-esteem (J. E. Birren & Deutchman, 1991).

An unique feature of Guided Autobiography. is its structured nature. This follows from the conviction that certain themes elicit especially salient memories and form common threads that run through the life and bind the fabric of the life story. J. E. Birren (1987) likened this to the productivity of the old fisherman who always seems to catch fish when others fail. When asked why, he says, "I know where the fish are." The themes in Guided Autobiography, the psychological fish, are designed to elicit reminiscence in areas that are likely to be evocative of the important experiences and emotions of a life.

OVERVIEW OF THE PROCESS

Guided Autobiography comprises two steps. Each participant writes autobio-graphical essays on preselected topics and then reads these essays aloud in a group setting. The Guided Autobiographical process is typically and productively com-pleted over the course of 2 weeks, meeting daily for about 2 hours, although other groups have met weekly over 10 weeks or in other schedules.

Groups most often include five to six participants and a facilitator. A number of groups may be conducted simultaneously, as space and number of group facilitators permit. A group that is too large may result in individuals' not having sufficient opportunity to participate meaningfully. A group that is too small may limit the potential for similarities and contrasts to be drawn by group members; too few members may also lead to the dissolution of the group should one or two members be absent or choose to leave. It is generally not recommended that new members be added after the first group meeting. A late addition may disrupt the natural progression of sharing and the development of group cohesion.

In the first meeting of the group, organization and introductions are accomplished. Expansive thinking has been encouraged in the past by asking members at the first session to write 10 words that best describe themselves and identify the 3 that are most descriptive. After finishing the list, members are asked to share their words, and the group engages in a discussion of the implications of such descriptors. This process accustoms the people to expressing personal material in the group and sensitizes them to a strong personal orientation.

Related to such self-descriptors are the metaphors individuals use to describe their lives. These metaphors are also frequently probed at the initial group meeting; for example, members may be asked what animal they think they most resemble, the type of animal they think their friends would say they resemble, and the animal that they would most like to resemble. This focus on ideal, actual, and public interpretations of the self helps the group members become more divergent in their thinking and feel at ease in self-disclosure.

At each subsequent meeting, approximately a half hour is devoted to the discussion of the issues and sensitizing questions of the theme that will guide the following meeting's interaction. The group facilitator distributes and reads aloud the description of the topic and elaborates on some of the sensitizing questions. The goal of introducing these issues and questions is to stimulate thinking and offer alternative perspectives regarding the ways in which a topic may be approached.

The remaining 90–120 min is devoted to the reading of the autobiographical essays. Each individual is allotted approximately 15 min to read and elaborate on his or her essay; an additional 5 min per person is allocated for group discussion. The group facilitator moderates this discussion, ensuring that basic group principles and rules (discussed below) are followed. It has become common practice that the last group meeting also entails a social event (often a shared meal) celebrating the lives that have been shared. Individual groups have often decided to continue meeting on their own or to arrange reunion meetings to update their autobiographies.

GUIDING THEMES

The themes of Guided Autobiography focus group members' thoughts on the central issues of life and the major changes, adaptations, and accommodations that are made over the course of a life. The use of themes works against obsessive rumination in life review; themes expand perspectives and productively channel attention. B. Birren (personal communication, July 14, 1986) likened the Guided

Autobiography to a nine-sided prism refracting the light (the life story) differently, depending on which side (theme) is showing. This is how Guided Autobiography encourages creative and divergent thinking about oneself and one's life.

In Guided Autobiography, participants typically write two-page autobiographical essays on each of nine themes. The themes that have been most often used in the past (and the order in which they have been used) are

1 History of the major branching points in my life;
2 Family history;
3 Career or major life work;
4 The role of money in my life;
5 Health and body image;
6 Loves and hates;
7 Sexual identity, sex roles, and sexual experiences;
8 Experiences with and ideas about death and dying and other losses;
9 Influences, beliefs, and values that provide meaning in my life.

Other elective themes have included the role of music, art, or literature; experiences with stress; social networks and social support; and the role of education.

The themes and accompanying sensitizing questions (as shown in the appendix, page 176) have emerged from 17 years of experience in conducting Guided Autobiography groups throughout North America. The themes represent powerful issues that run through the life course and elicit salient memories, some of which touch on what Magee (1988a) called the "toxic" issues of family development. The sensitizing questions identify issues and promote reminiscences that are important to a life theme. They remind individuals of memories that may not otherwise be readily recalled; they also provide a wider range of perspectives that might be taken in addressing aspects of the life review. The purpose of the questions is to guide and stimulate thought about the issues, rather than place a structure on thinking or elicit specific answers. As an example, the theme "History of the Major Branching Points in Your Life" and its accompanying sensitizing questions follows. A complete list of all the themes and their sensitizing questions has been provided by J. E. Birren and Deutchman (1991).

Group members are guided through the autobiographical process by these themes and questions in a manner that encourages reminiscence and builds understanding and momentum in the group process. The order in which the themes are presented flows from the most basic life issues (e.g., branching points and family) to the more abstract and philosophical issues (e.g., death and dying and meaning in life). Earlier reflection on these basic issues can help stimulate productive reflection on later themes. The organization of the life review around these themes enhances the group process by providing a basis for sharing common feelings and circumstances. Moreover, more sensitive issues (e.g., sex and sexuality) appear later in the process and are shared in a group in which trust has been established.

THE GROUP PROCESS

A central feature of the Guided Autobiography process is the sharing of the life review and the exchange of life stories with other members of the group. The exchange of one's past with other persons reinforces the motivation to participate. Paradoxically, it has been found that what may be difficult to write is sometimes easily expressed in the group context and that new associations may arise from the group discussion (de Vries et al., 1990). J. E. Birren (1987) has suggested that "the facts and the feelings take on a living quality for both readers and listeners as each new session builds upon previous sessions" (p. 75). Participants are enriched by the opportunity to review similarities in experience and develop a sense of the universality of lives (Yalom, 1970). Contrasts between the life stories highlight the range of individual differences and the uniqueness and individuality of human experience.

The group experience provides the opportunity for individuals to see themselves (or their dreams or fears) in the lives of others, recalling events that might have otherwise been forgotten and facilitating the expression of feelings about events that they might have thought were inappropriate. The confidence and trust of the group enhance recall. J. E. Birren and Deutchman (1991) described this aspect as the "Oh phenomenon," wherein a person comes to Guided Autobiography with what he or she perceives to be a dark secret, some act or feeling that has made the person feel separate and unacceptable. Revelation of this secret is often met with little surprise or even similar revelations and social acceptance. In this and other ways, the group assists members who have become stuck at some painful point in the past, providing the social nudge to move them on to new territory.

Group members also serve as agents of support and feedback to one another. Burnside (1994), among others, has suggested that realistic changes may occur as a consequence of group feedback. She further identified that the distribution of attention among group members has the effect of reducing pressure on any one individual and providing support in dealing with what may be painful memories (de Vries et al., 1990). Friendships and confidant relationships develop as individuals share histories and emotions.

Group composition varies as a function of setting and organization. The prototypic group includes women and men from across the adult life span with diverse ethnic and occupational backgrounds; it has been located primarily in a university environment. The age heterogeneity of such groups is seen as a strength, providing opportunities for both young and old to understand more fully family (intergenerational) roles, revealing common elements of and distinct perspectives associated with different life phases, and providing opportunities for older adults to act as mentors to younger persons and for younger persons to benefit from the accumulated experiences of the older adults.

Other groups, however, have successfully consisted of particular cohorts (e.g., older parents who have recently suffered the death of an adult child) and have been located outside of academic institutions (e.g., in religious institutions and community centers).

A key dimension of the group interaction is what J. E. Birren and Deutchman (1991) have termed the *developmental exchange*: the incremental and mutual exchange of personally salient and meaningful information. Participants in the Guided Autobiography move from "tentatively and guardedly alluding to important features of their lives toward an increasingly open sharing of significant personal information" (J. E. Birren & Deutchman, 1991, p. 45). Individuals implicitly take into account the affective value of shared information and trade personal vignettes of equivalent affective value, albeit different content. Over time, the developmental exchange builds on itself and leads to even greater self-disclosure as trust is established and the group forms bonds.

The power of the group experience notwithstanding, writing one's autobiographical statements is an integral part of the Guided Autobiography process. As J. E. Birren and Deutchman (1991) have written, "Personal, private reflection and the motivation to delve deeply into the banks of memory are summoned by the task of writing down one's recollections" (p. 57). Writing serves to stimulate further recall and help one organize one's thoughts. An individual can thus rehearse what will be shared in the group; monitor the developmental exchange of affectively charged material; and highlight experiences that are more central, thereby optimizing his or her time in group interaction. The written word also exists as a permanent record or as a template for the construction of a more comprehensive autobiography.

THE GROUP AND ITS FACILITATOR

The rules, principles, and culture of the group govern its conduct. These rules should be established early in the life of the group, discussed among participants, and modeled by the group facilitator. The following rules are particularly beneficial to Guided Autobiography:

1   A willingness and commitment to participate;
2   Listening actively and attentively when others are sharing;
3   Striving to be supportive of others and accepting of individual differences;
4   Avoiding judgmental statements about the choices other members have made or about their feelings, beliefs, or opinions;
5   Confidentiality (J. E. Birren & Deutchman, 1991).

Clearly, these rules are important and are worth reviewing early in the group experience.

A central core of the group is the facilitator. A group facilitator need not be a health care professional or therapist; "the personal attributes of a successful group facilitator are motivation, warmth, the ability to listen, and the ability to communicate effectively" (J. E. Birren & Deutchman, 1991, p. 26). As de Vries et al. (1990) have proposed, "Facilitators should be supportive and able to define limits, monitoring emotional levels of the group, and defining/promoting the essential nonjudgmental quality of the exchange" (p. 6). Group facilitators should share their own stories minimally and use them selectively as a method of promoting exchange within the group and motivating the group to interact. Nonprofessionals should keep in mind that the goal is to offer the opportunity for individuals to explore their life histories, not to offer group psychotherapy, and thus leaders should not probe into the feelings and emotions of group members beyond those that emerge naturally and are shared readily. Unlike group therapy sessions, Guided Autobiography is not problem centered. The many emotions of life do present themselves in Guided Autobiography. However, they should not be solicited, but should be allowed to emerge naturally, as they do in daily life.

PROBLEMATIC CIRCUMSTANCES IN THE GROUP PROCESS

Problems may arise in conducting Guided Autobiography groups that the facilitator should be aware of and guard against. For example, one of the participants may be trained in a professional orientation that may lead him or her to impose an interpretation on something shared in the group process, for example, a story from an individual's family background or health or even the description of a dream. It should be noted to all members that they should express their insights into their own lives in their own language and metaphors, rather than in expert language, and that group discussion around such insights should be similarly phrased. The facilitator should discourage discussion that emphasizes particular ways of studying or interpreting lives (e.g., Rogerian, Jungian, Freudian, and so on).

There may be a participant who is unduly intrusive in the discussion or who takes up too much time in presenting his or her life story. Rotating the order of reading the themes ameliorates this problem. The time monopolizer is put in a sequence that limits this effect and the sense of a group is introduced. Alternatively (and rarely), an individual may scarcely participate, declining to share a particular theme or withholding emotional affect. As long as the group process is not obstructed, this person is perhaps best left "to harvest those aspects of the Guided Autobiography process with which he or she feels comfortable" (J. E. Birren & Deutchman, 1991, p. 98).

A concern sometimes raised about the writing and reading about one's life is that it may open old wounds long left dormant. Our experience in conducting Guided Autobiography groups suggests that individuals and groups normally gate sensitive information: Individuals tread warily in revealing sensitive material, and the group cushions the emotional responses of the individuals revealing the material in constructive ways. Furthermore, there is generally an information gate-keeping skill acquired as part of the developmental exchange in the group which is reflected in the balance that is reached in which burdensome revealing rarely occurs. Judging how far and how fast to go is generally a skill of normal adults that expresses itself in the group process such that the facilitator rarely needs to address the matter of uncomfortable sharing. However, if it occurs, the revealing participant should be privately encouraged to go more slowly and wait until the time is ripe.

BENEFITS OF PARTICIPATION

Guided Autobiography is not intended to be used as formal therapy; it does, however, have natural therapeutic value, or healing powers that result from the reconciliation of long-standing issues and the insights afforded by supportive group members. It is a meaning-making exercise and provides examples of living for those who participate. As de Vries et al. (1990) have suggested, "The act of telling one's story and listening to the story of others provides models to buffer transitions, to bridge historical times, and to communicate values" (p. 6). Individuals trade in and trade up the old metaphors they have used to characterize themselves (J. E. Birren, 1987).

The benefits of Guided Autobiography extend well beyond producing written accounts of one's life. The life stories of others in the group stimulate old memories. Things forgotten, overlooked, or dimly remembered are brought to mind again. The events, diet, dress styles, and school and work codes of past eras are recalled and provide fresh stimulations for the autobiographical reminiscence. This process of enlargement of past recall is a great advantage of the method over the solitary writing of one's autobiography. For the individual, there is the by-product of making new friends and confidantes who may play active future roles in his or her life; a friendship of depth may even be formed.

In reviewing the literature on human development and autobiography (and life review), J. E. Birren and Deutchman (1991) cited the following advantages: obtaining personal fulfillment and integrating or making sense of a life as it has been lived; maintaining a sense of the continuity of the self, acceptance of one's heritage, and the need to "connect" with ancestors; renewing confidence in one's capacity to adapt; and increasing understanding of one's personal agenda, forming the basis for successful future choices. Areas of cognitive functioning; personality; spirituality; and social, family, and intergenerational interactions are touched by autobiography, helping participants build new skills to meet new demands.

Reedy and J. E. Birren (1980) systematically examined the effects of Guided Autobiography using pre- and post-measurement data from 45 participants. They found that participants showed greater self-acceptance and personal integration (i.e., greater congruence of their real, ideal, and social selves), decreased anxiety and increased energy (i.e., a cathartic and antidepressant effect), and a change in their perceptions of other people after Guided Autobiography. In particular, this latter finding suggests that Guided Autobiography may have an effect on one's sense of social connectedness, willingness to interact with others, and willingness to disclose to others.

RESEARCH

Research Conducted

Research on the Guided Autobiography process and products is in its infancy. Reedy and J. E. Birren (1980) examined personal growth over a course of Guided Autobiography. Hedlund (1987) used Guided Autobiography accounts to examine how individuals developed meaning in life. She used grounded-theory methodology, looked across themes, and found the following primary categories of meaning in life (in order of frequency of assignment): personal development/personal growth, personal relationships, career, belief, service to others, and pleasure. On the basis of her analyses, she proposed (a) that childhood experiences are related to the content of meaning in life in adulthood; (b) that the initial formulation of the meaning-in-life construct occurs between early adolescence and young adulthood; (c) that the earliest form of meaning in life focuses on personal development, and, once personal development issues are resolved, meaning in life remains stable; and (d) that with increased age, the content of meaning in life moves toward sources external to the individual.

de Vries, Bluck, and J. E. Birren (1993) coded written accounts on the theme "Experiences with and ideas about death and dying and other losses" from 54 men and women drawn in equal numbers from young, middle-aged, and older adulthood. Content analysis assessed the extent to which the essays concerned death or dying (i.e., as a subject of discussion) in relation to the self and others or as more abstract conceptions (i.e., as a referent of discussion). Levels of the impact of, involvement with, and acceptance of death and dying were also coded. Each paragraph was also coded for integrative complexity, an information-processing variable ranging from simple to complex. Analyses revealed that for both men and women, discussions of death were both more frequent and more complex than were discussions of dying (perhaps because of greater overall familiarity with the construct of death). Individuals referred to others' death more often and in more simplistic terms than they referred to their own (owing, perhaps, to bereavement stress). The middle-aged participants placed greater emphasis on death than did the older and the younger participants, who allocated proportionately more discussion to dying (perhaps in response to life span and social forces). All discussions were characterized by high impact and involvement and low levels of acceptance. The Guided Autobiography provided a unique opportunity in the examination of death and dying constructs in that the accounts were open-ended and were embedded in and developed over an individual's lifetime of experiences with and reflections on the topic.

Research Potential

The research potential of Guided Autobiography is just becoming apparent. The approach offers a rich source of information not only on the way life is experienced in different eras and places, but also on groups of people, social classes, ethnic groups, gender differences, and victims of life events.

In particular, the contrasts between the life stories of optimum survivors and those of marginal survivors of events and circumstances may be searched for insights into principles of life span development. Increasingly, researchers will be learning about the different ways the course of life is experienced and perceived. Contrasts will increasingly be drawn between, for example, individuals growing up under war conditions and those growing up under peace conditions, or those growing up in urban centers and those growing up in suburban communities. In related ways, the life stories of criminals, gang members, the homeless, creative persons, achievers, and others may be searched for clues about critical experiences and the similarities and differences in patterns of development and aging.

Multiple cohorts may be compared in the ways they view their lives. Presumably, different generations are subject to different pressures (e.g., the Vietnam War, student unrest, recession, and prosperity). Such contextual effects should influence the content of autobiographies written in the different periods of social change or stability. Society or culture provides the interpretations or plots individuals use to explain life experiences. Whether hero plots or victimization plots are dominant in a period should be reflected in the way individuals emplot their lives in their autobiographies. These issues open the way to using autobiographical material to study not only the development of individuals, but also the secular drifts in the interpretations of life afforded by culture and society.

In addition to data on health, social factors, and psychological and motor abilities, autobiographical statements can be obtained sequentially in longitudinal studies of aging. In this way, the internal experience of aging can be related to the externally observed circumstances of life and the state of the individual. Equally important is the opportunity to compare sequential autobiographies of the same individuals to investigate the development of the self over the course of life and how it is experienced at different ages.

This discussion is, in part, intended to make it clear that autobiographical research is affected by the same logical design constraints that affect external measurement and observation. Cohort, sequential changes, and time of measurement are equally relevant matters. Increasingly it is expected that studies of autobiography will use designed sampling of participants to obtain contrast between groups (e.g., those with high and low socioeconomic status, heterosexuals and homosexuals, immigrants and long-term residents). The analysis of such data holds much promise for shedding light on the way life is experienced and interpreted.

SPECIAL APPLICATIONS OF GUIDED AUTOBIOGRAPHY

Several exciting opportunities exist for the Guided Autobiography as a method of life review. For example, new members of a community, church, or home for the aged may particularly benefit from a Guided Autobiography course. They may be relatively isolated, being separated from family members and old friends or neighbors. As an introduction to a new social organization the Guided Autobiography can facilitate friendship and confidante formation. New themes can be introduced into the sequence to serve particular emphases; for example, "My life as a spiritual journey" may be used in a church group or "My life as a learner" may be used in an adult education group.

Guided Autobiography may also be used as an adjunct to bereavement self-help and other support groups in which individuals not only share in the recognition and grief surrounding their loss, but in the reconstruction of their lives given their loss. It is a way of forging new relationships and perspectives on the self. In similar ways, groups of caregivers, as well as those who are terminally ill or suffer with a chronic disability, could share aspects of their lives in an autobiographical experience.

Guided Autobiography also has particular relevance for those in the field of family life education "as the field gives increasing attention to the personal and family needs of older individuals" (de Vries et al., 1990, p. 6). The approach has special potential for facilitating intergenerational communication in families and increasing our understanding of shifting family roles over time and family life transitions such as marriage, the empty nest, retirement, and divorce or separation.

CONCLUSION

This chapter describes the method and uses of Guided Autobiography. It is a semi-structured method for gathering individuals' life stories, their reminiscences of people, events, and emotions. It involves a written component on productive themes of life and a small group process component in which the individual life stories are shared with others.

In 17 years of experience with the method, nine themes have evolved for use that are particularly provocative of significant reminiscence: (1) branching points; (2) family history; (3) career or major life work; (4) role of money; (5) health and body image; (6) loves and hates; (7) sexual identity, sex roles, and sexual experiences; (8) experiences with death and dying; and (9) influences, beliefs, and values that provide meaning in life. The Guided Autobiography is not designed as "therapy" since it is not problem-centered. It does provide, however, an opportunity for reconciliation of long-standing issues and developing insight and integration of the way life has been lived.

Contemporary interest in obtaining information on the way life is experienced by persons of different ages and other characteristics is focusing more attention on the research uses of autobiographical or narrative material. It is the only way of obtaining a view of the inside experiences of life. It is expected that there will be more designed studies using autobiographical materials to shed light on the way people experience growing up and growing old in different eras and circumstances.

APPENDIX*

THEME ASSIGNMENT: HISTORY OF THE MAJOR BRANCHING POINTS IN YOUR LIFE.

Think of your life as a branching tree, as a flowing river which has many points of juncture, or as a trailing plant which puts down roots at various places and then goes on.

What is a branching point? Branching points are events, experiences, happenings in our lives that significantly affect the direction or flow of our lives. Branching points are experiences that shape our lives such that our lives, in some important ways, are not the same as they were before.

What have been the major branching points in your life, from your point of view?

What were the events, experiences, interactions with people and places that have had a major influence or impact on the way your life has flowed?

SENSITIZING QUESTIONS (TO GUIDE BUT NOT TO STRUCTURE YOUR THINKING ABOUT YOUR PERSONAL HISTORY):

About how old were you when the event/experience happened? Place the turning point along a time dimension. That timing of an event is often very important. Did it happen too soon? Were you too young? Did it happen too late? Were you too old, in your view?

Significant people? Who were the important people involved in the turning point? Mother, father, spouse? You alone? Often, people see that the same people are involved again and again in major life turning points.

Emotions and feeling then? What were the feelings, emotions you experienced at the time the branching point occurred? How intense were these feelings? Sometimes our feelings in reaction to an experience are mixed or are changeable (e.g., when a loved one dies who has suffered a long illness, we may feel relieved and terribly sad at the same time).

---

*Adapted from J. E. Birren and D. Deutchman, 1991.

Emotions and feelings now? Sometimes our feelings about an experience or event change over time. People often say that "time heals." What emotions and feelings do you experience as you think about the turning point now?

Personal choice? How much personal choice was involved in this branching point? How much personal control did you have? Was this branching point completely of your choice? Mostly? Only a little? Or was it something that happened that was totally beyond your control (e.g., flood or parents decided to move the family)? If the turning point was not completely within your control, who or what else influenced the occurrence of this branching point?

Consequences? Branching points are branching points because they change our lives in one or many important ways. In your view, in what ways was your life changed or different because of this branching point? What effects, impact, or consequences did this branching point have on your life? Why was this branching point a branching point?

The Linchpins of a Successful Life Review: Structure, Evaluation, and Individuality

Barbara K. Haight
Peter Coleman
Kris Lord

Although Butler's (1963) description of the life review has been a major source of the development of interest in reminiscence work with older people, relatively little of this work has taken an explicitly life review approach. The typical reminiscing intervention has been group work with people in hospital, residential, and day-care centers, in which the sharing of stories about the past takes place, often with the aid of props such as pictures and objects. Yet, a number of studies as well as analyses of the existing literature have established that the life review cannot be equated with general reminiscence (Coleman, 1974, 1986a; Haight, 1991; Merriam, 1980, 1989; Wong & Watt, 1991). The evaluative and integrative nature of the life review give it a purposefulness and force that place it in a different category from most of the reminiscing that occurs within our thoughts and conversations.

Portions of this chapter are based on a research project (HR# E612) funded by the American Association of Retired Persons to determine the key variables in a successful life review.

LIFE REVIEW

Both life review and reminiscing use past memories, but there are more differences than there are similarities between the two interventions (Haight & Burnside, 1993). For example, the goal of the life review is to help older people reach integrity. In the method of life review we have investigated, the process takes 6 weeks. Two people are involved in the process, the reviewer (the person who is reminiscing) and the therapeutic listener (the person conducting the process). At the beginning of the process, the therapeutic listener or person conducting the life review shares the Life Review and Experiencing Form (LREF); see the Appendix to this chapter) and establishes a contract with the reviewer to meet for the next 6 weeks to talk about the past.

The life review is a slice of therapy, but it differs from the psychotherapeutic process in distinct ways. The essential difference is that the therapeutic listener discusses only issues raised by the reviewer. Often, the therapeutic listener recognizes that the reviewer needs to discuss a particular period of life, but if the reviewer does not raise a specific issue, it is not discussed. The therapeutic listener does not dig and probe. The life review requires an awareness of when not to intervene and when to be a good and facilitating listener. Haight and Dias (1992) likened the process to taking out the garbage. In psychotherapy, one keeps going through the garbage, but in life review one wraps up the garbage and takes it out.

Erikson's (1950) model of human development serves as the framework for our model of life review. This framework brings the reviewer through each developmental stage until he or she reaches the final stage and the goal of integrity. Life review facilitates integration in later life. Erikson stated that a person must successfully maneuver each of life's developmental tasks to arrive at the final and complete stage of integrity. He further defined integrity as the acceptance of one's one-and-only life cycle as something that had to be and that by necessity permitted no substitutions. Though Erikson described integrity as the last stage of life, he never stated when integrity happens. Does it happen at age 50 and one remains content for the remainder of life? Or is it an ongoing process, often present but not recognized by its owner? With life continuing for many more years after age 50, integrity may need to be reestablished throughout the years. Linking life review to integrity is a natural progression when one considers the process of life review. However, in his writing, Butler only hinted at the connection between the two. Table 1 shows questions in the LREF that reflect Erikson's model.

When Butler (1974) talked about the life review, he described it as a spontaneous process. When used as a therapeutic intervention, the life review is no longer spontaneous. Rather, it is a directed process in which a therapeutic listener helps an older person instigate and reorganize his or her memories. Through this reorganization, the person makes sense of the past and discovers meanings he or she had not recognized in the present.

Table 1   Erikson's Stages as a Life Review Model

Stage	Life review question
1. Trust vs. mistrust:	Did you always feel cared for?
2. Autonomy vs. shame:	Did you feel well guided through childhood? Do you remember feeling ashamed?
3. Initiative vs. guilt:	Did you enjoy starting new projects (with toys or Scouts)? Did you ever feel guilty as a child?
4. Industry vs. inferiority:	Were you a hardworking student? Did you feel capable of accomplishing most tasks?
5. Identity vs. role confusion:	Did they have cliques in your day? Did you have a sense of belonging?
6. Intimacy vs. isolation:	Do you remember your first attraction? Did you establish a close relationship?
7. Generativity vs. stagnation:	Do you feel like you've helped the next generation?
8. Integrity vs. despair:	On the whole, what kind of life do you think you've had?

Black and Haight (1992) compared the reorganization that occurs in life review to a tapestry. On the wrong side of the tapestry, one sees a mass of tangled threads. They seem to have no purpose and no meaning, tangled as they are at the back of the tapestry, but when the tapestry is turned over, a clear and vibrant picture emerges. Each thread and each color develop the picture and the meaning of the tapestry more clearly. These threads are similar to the singular events of life. The recall of life review helps one to gain meaning from them. In a life review, the listener slowly turns over the tapestry as the reviewer reinterprets his or her life in different ways and finally sees the whole. In essence, the reviewer reaches a gestalt.

Now that we are living longer lives, this reinterpretation may need to happen more than once. Perhaps each time a life crisis occurs, life's events need to be reinterpreted in view of that crisis; to make sense of what has happened, to reweave the tapestry, and to again make the picture brighter and clearer. To the best of our knowledge, no one has researched the need to rereview one's life. To date, research shows that the good effects of a life review last for a year (Haight, 1992a). Perhaps with more research, we shall learn whether the good effects last longer than that or the life review needs to be revisited.

LINCHPINS OF THE LIFE REVIEW

Erikson's (1950) model guides the life review and defines the therapeutic structure, while three linchpins—structure, evaluation, and individuality—provide the basis for the process. First, the process must be structured enough to cover each developmental phase of the life span, from birth to present. Second, evaluation must be a strong component of the life review, to help the reviewer gain insight. Through the weighing and valuing of events, the reviewer begins to absorb the meaning of events for the self and to repaint the life picture. Lastly, individuality (the life review occurring on a one-to-one basis) provides the reviewer with a confidante and a sense of safety for discussing and sharing sensitive issues.

RESEARCH BACKGROUND

The three basic linchpins that assure therapeutic success in life review were identified in a research project funded by the American Association of Retired Persons (Haight & Dias, 1992). This project took place in a variety of nursing homes and highrise apartment buildings for seniors on the southeast coast of the United States. More than 240 subjects participated in the study by joining one of 10 types of groups: eight reminiscing groups and two current events groups.

Five sets of group interventions and five sets of individual interventions acted as 10 unique independent variables. Each intervention was conducted for 6–8 weeks and was preset by the calendar. The intervention groups were as follows:

Structured evaluative life review process: An imposed, structured life review that included an evaluation process and covered life from birth to present.

Structured life review process: An imposed, structured life review that covered life from birth to present, without encouragement to examine feelings or to evaluate events.

Random reminiscing: Reminiscing about randomly selected events without evaluation of feelings.

Evaluative random reminiscing: Reminiscing about randomly selected events with an evaluation component to examine feelings and evaluate events.

Current events: Weekly meetings to talk of the present. *Time* magazine, the newspaper, the radio, and television structured the topics of discussion.

All groups were pre- and post-tested on the four outcome measures.

The pairwise multiple comparisons in Table 2 clearly show the outcomes of comparing one type of process with another. The results indicated that the key variables for a therapeutic reminiscence process were evaluation, structure, and individuality. Thus the best format for therapeutic reminiscing is an individual, structured, evaluative life review process. This process was significantly more therapeutic than all other ways of conducted reminiscing.

Structure

Structure means that reminiscing should cover the whole life span. It is not necessary to proceed in chronological order from birth to present, but it is necessary to cover all the developmental phases and to use all the questions based on Erikson's (1950) model of human development presented in Table 1. If a life span structure is not used, the reviewer may not talk about certain periods that are

Table 2 Pairwise Multiple Comparisons for Dependent Variable Difference Scores in Background Research

Life Satisfaction Index A

Group	IRR	GSLRP	GCE	IERR	ISLRP	GRR	GERR	ICE	GSELRP	ISELRP
Mean Difference Scores	-1.59	-1.50	-0.53	0.67	0.70	0.76	1.18	1.39	1.41	3.05

Rosenberg Self-Esteem Scale

Group	ICE	GRR	GERR	GSLRP	GSELRP	IRR	ISLRP	IERR	GCE	ISELRP
Mean Difference Scores	-0.22	0.82	1.09	1.12	1.23	1.47	1.55	1.56	1.84	3.47

Bradburns Affect Balance Scale

Group	GCE	IRR	GERR	GSLRP	GRR	ISLRP	GSELRP	ICE	IERR	ISELRP
Mean Difference Scores	-1.16	-0.47	-0.45	-0.38	-0.35	0.00	0.36	1.11	1.56	2.53

Beck Depression Inventory

Group	ISLRP	GSLRP	ICE	GERR	GCE	GSELRP	IRR	GRR	IERR	ISELRP
Mean Difference Scores	-0.30	0.56	0.72	0.77	1.21	2.18	2.35	3.71	4.28	5.89

Note: The I and G at the beginning of each group label indicate individual and group work, respectively. RR = random reminiscing; SLRP = structured life review process; CE = current events; ERR = evaluative random reminiscing; SELRP = structured, evaluative life review process. Group means underlined by the same single line are homogeneous, i.e., they are not significantly different at the 0.05 level. Group means not underlined by the same single line are significantly different at the 0.05 level.

troublesome and painful to recall, but, given an opening, he or she may seize the opportunity.

To provide structure, we recommend six visits 1 week apart for 6 weeks. Two visits should focus on childhood, family, and home; two on adolescence and adulthood; and the last two on the summary. The summary is extremely important because this is where the actual integration takes place. The summary encourages evaluation if it has not occurred before that time. As with any process, there are exceptions. If a great deal of repetition, rehearsing, and reintegrating is needed, the process may take longer than six visits.

Evaluation

The key linchpin for therapeutic reminiscing is evaluation. Evaluation is the process of weighing and valuing life's events. For some people, it may be the first time they have introspectively looked at their life. When evaluation occurs, both the reviewer and the therapeutic listener have distinct tasks. The therapeutic listener must guide the reviewer to consider feelings and meanings. For example, the therapeutic listener should ask, "When the event occurred, did you feel proud? [ashamed? guilty?] Describe it. What would you have liked to do differently? How would you change the event?" These questions guide the reviewer to examine and evaluate the life event.

Butler (1963) described the process of evaluating as surveying and reintegrating. Surveying develops insight, and reintegrating creates acceptance. Often, reintegrating requires reframing so that the life event is more acceptable to the reviewer. Reintegrating also can occur with repetition. Consider a particularly troublesome event that needs to be raised and surveyed during each meeting. The repetition of raising this event often serves as its own catharsis. It seems as if finally, after much repetition, the older person can let go of the event. Hence, repetition, as catharsis, is its own kind of evaluation and as such should be encouraged.

Perhaps if people surveyed their own lives more often, they would have an easier time climbing Erikson's developmental ladder. They could begin to mend the hurts as they happen and make real life changes that help them climb the ladder.

Individuality

The last linchpin is the one-to-one process that we call individuality. By emphasizing the one-to-one process, we do not mean to devalue group work. Groups have a very important place and are especially important for socializing new residents to nursing homes. However, for an individual to reveal his or her innermost thoughts and a possibly shameful past, it is necessary to have one listener only. The individual touch provides a more therapeutic milieu.

With trust established, the reviewer feels safe to tell life's story. Often, reviewers feel safer with strangers.

The life review, by its nature, provides the reviewer with a confidante, the therapeutic listener. The intrinsic value of this relationship was recently highlighted in an examination of the life stories of four suicidal women (Haight, unpublished manuscript). Common themes in their lives included dysfunctional families and dysfunctional marriages. Most poignantly, the women were alone, lonely, and lonesome. Never in their lives had they had a confidante. One said, "I was born lonely" and all were truly isolated, possibly because they had never learned to form relationships in their youth, and now they thought it was too late. Thus individuality provides not only privacy, but also intimacy and, for a short time, the presence of a significant other.

TESTING THE PROCESS

The individual, structured life review process is the only life review approach known to have been systematically evaluated in any country. The results of studies evaluating this method in the United States have been promising (Haight, 1988; Haight & Dias, 1992). They illustrate the healing and constructive qualities of the life review and suggest that this particular approach fulfills the original promise seen to lie in the concept described by Butler (1963). But, as with any technique, there are likely to be limitations to its range of applicability. We thought it of particular interest to investigate how successfully the methods that have worked well in an American context would work in a British setting.

Participants and Procedure

The setting chosen for this pilot study was a day center in Southampton, England. The participants were all female and over the age of 60 years, with an average age of 77 years. They attended a craft group for 3 hr a week on either a Monday, Tuesday, or Thursday afternoon. Some lived independently and were brought to the group meetings by a relative. Most lived in sheltered housing or residential care and were transported to the meetings by the Red Cross. The study and interviews were carried out under the supervision of the second author by the third author, a psychology student with experience in both the counseling and education of those with special needs.

Haight's (1988) research served to guide the study. Three groups were formed: a life review group, an attention control group, and a no-contact control group. Participants were allocated to a group depending on which day they came. Mondays provided the no-contact group; Tuesdays, the attention group; and Thursdays the life review group. Allocating the participants to groups in this way meant that there would be no comparing of experience between people receiving different treatments. Six people were selected for each group, matched for age, living circumstances, and general level of health and disability. All those approached agreed to participate.

To the members of the life review group, it was explained that the researcher would be coming to talk with them for six sessions about their life and the things that had happened to them in the past. Members of the attention control group were also visited for six sessions while they were undertaking various craft activities. The researcher chatted about the club and crafts, helped with the threading of needles, played bingo, and generally spent time focused on the current activities and topics of conversation that arose spontaneously. The no-contact group members were not visited for the 6 weeks but received the pre- and post-interviews at the same time as the other two groups.

The pre- and post-test measures chosen to evaluate the intervention were the Southampton Self-Esteem and Sources of Self-Esteem Scale (Coleman, Ivani-Chalian, & Robinson, 1993), a measure specifically developed to assess self-esteem and its perceived sources in older people; the Rosenberg Self-EsteemScale (RSES) (Rosenberg, 1965), one of the most commonly used measures of self-esteem but originally standardized for use with younger people; and the Philadelphia Geriatric Center Morale Scale (Challis & Davies, 1986; Lawton, 1975), one of the most commonly used measures of well-being, which has also been used to demonstrate the beneficial impact of community care in the United Kingdom. The order of presentation of the self-esteem measures was reversed for each alternate participant, although the morale scale was always in the middle. The reversal was to balance out any order effects that might result when working with older people as a result of tiredness, reduced concentration, or impatience.

The life review intervention was administered in the manner described earlier, with each of the 6 participants being interviewed for 1 hr per week for 6 weeks, taking in turn each of the different sections of the LREF.

Results

The life review group showed a significant increase in self-esteem scores after the intervention. Two participants showed particularly marked increases, but all showed some gain. Interestingly, the results obtained with the morale scale were quite different, with no clear overall pattern of change. That the self-esteem and morale measures tapped different dimensions of well-being is suggested by the fact that one of the persons who showed marked improvement on both self-esteem measures actually showed a decrease on the morale score. The gain scores for each group are shown in Table 3.

Neither the attention control group nor the no-contact group showed significant change on any of the indices. (Unfortunately, one member of the attention group who displayed very low self-esteem on the pre-test did not wish to continue with the study, and one member of the no-contact group also

Table 3   Mean Gains in Scores on Outcome Measures in Study of Effectiveness of the Individual, Structured Life Review Process with Seniors

Group	Southampton Self-Esteem and Sources of Self-Esteem Scale	Rosenberg Self-Esteem Scale	Philadelphia Geriatric Center Morale Scale
Experimental (n = 6)	23.3 → 29.0	25.3 → 28.3	38.7 → 40.2
Control (attention) (n = 5)	26.2 → 26.4	29.6 → 29.6	37.6 → 39.8
Control (no contact) (n = 5)	26.8 → 27.2	28.8 → 28.4	40.0 → 41.6

withdrew before the first interview.) Indeed on the self-esteem measures, 85% of the individual scores remained identical over time. However, 70% of the morale scores did improve.

Difference and change between groups were tested statistically using Kruskal Wallis analysis of variance by ranks, resulting in significance at the .05 level for the Southampton self-esteem measure. Even though the numbers in this study were small, it is possible to conclude that the life review intervention had an impact on self-esteem but not on morale. Levels of morale appeared to be more related to continued attendance at the day center.

Discussion

The two cases of marked increase in self-esteem illustrate the value of the present method of life review as intervention. The first was Jean, a woman of 84 years, widowed for 7–8 years and with two sons. She lived in sheltered housing, suffered from angina and arthritis, and was confined to a wheelchair. She had come from a family of eight children. Because her mother had not been able to cope with such a large family, she had given Jean to an aunt, who had had no children of her own and lived at a distance. Jean described her childhood as quiet and lonely, dominated by the fussy attentions of her aunt. When she was 9 or 10, she had saved up the money for a train ticket and ran away back to her mother. After a lot of tears, her mother had let her stay. Regretfully, Jean's mother died early and Jean felt that she never knew her.

Jean impressed the interviewer with the honesty and courage with which she spoke about her past life, and also her sense of humor, which allowed her to relativize her experiences. The improvement in self-esteem did not appear to come from any particular image of herself in the past to which she returned, but rather from having someone to talk to about the painful things.

The second case involved Carol, a woman of 62, one of the youngest participants. Carol also was confined to a wheelchair, the victim of polio in her 20s. She was married and lived in her own home with her husband. She often referred to the death of her mother, whom she loved dearly, when she was in her early teens. She spoke, too, of her unpredictable and often violent father, who physically assaulted his wife, often in front of the children. She stressed how different her own husband was from her father and how lucky she had been.

Although there had been sadness and fear in Carol's childhood, her memories were predominantly of happy and positive events, and she spoke of other relatives and friends who had made her youth and early adulthood an adventure. She concluded that life still had a lot of meaning for her and that she had much to be thankful for. Like Jean, Carol showed striking increases on both of the self-esteem measures, suggesting that something significant had happened during the intervention.

It is possible to see some common ground in the themes covered by the participants whose self-esteem increased as a result of life review intervention. Loss certainly was a major theme. It could be that life review counseling gave participants the opportunity to work through unresolved issues related to loss. It may have been that Jean was able to work further through the feelings associated with her mother's giving her away and her mother's dying "too soon" before she really got to know her (or feel secure?). Loss of mother certainly was a potent and dominant theme that seemed to return time and again for all the participants. The loss of husbands, boyfriends, and other close friends was also potent. Guiding principles on how to live life, including religious faith, were often quoted and derived from their first family, usually a parent. Indeed, it was striking how, despite the structured nature of the life review interviews, which progressed chronologically through the life course, time and again participants went back to childhood and the strong feelings they still had of happiness, sadness, and fear associated with that time.

It could be that reminding oneself of the carefree, untroubled times of childhood is a way to relieve some of the pressure and stress of the present. This is not necessarily an escapist defense, but a way of keeping one's spirits up in order to cope. Even recounting difficult sad times in the past is a reminder that one has survived before. No doubt, much of the working through in the life review occurs at the subconscious level so that it is difficult for the person to identify what has brought about the change, the resolution, the intergration. The empathic and nonjudgmental approach of the listener is thus a vital factor. There is something very powerful about sharing unresolved issues with another person and having them listened to and accepted.

If the things that need to be reworked and integrated tend to come from childhood, it may be because the middle years are more consciously under a person's control. An alternative view is that adult relationships are in fact the most painful to look at and the least well integrated. Perhaps the greatest sensitivity and skills are required of the counselor in helping people to face up to the pain of adult relationships. It may also be that if the process of integration is only just beginning for some participants, they need to integrate the difficulties from their childhood first and only later can move on to integration of adult experiences. If, as Butler (1963) stressed, the life review is a naturally occurring process, this may continue after the formal meetings have ended.

CONCLUSION

We have tested the structured process of life review and used it successfully as a therapeutic intervention in the United States and England. The potential of a structured life review as a universal intervention, excepting cultural differences, is immense. For example, Birren and Deutchman (1991) promoted a structured reminiscence process as a method for writing one's autobiography. Birren's structure is guided by major themes, rather than a developmental ladder, but the end result is a valuing and rewriting of life. Another psychologist, Freeman (1993), has cogently demonstrated the importance of reminiscence to the attainment of truth. Only the passage of time can determine the meanings one should give to the events in one's life, and these meanings are continually evolving. Reminiscences far from being fictions, are necessary to attaining those forms of truth that are unavailable in the flux of the immediate. Literally, we would exist only as bodies and not as selves if we did not have the narrative imagination of memory to tell us who we have been and are.

   In subsequent research on life review as a form of reminiscing, we plan to investigate the impact of the life review intervention over a longer time scale and as a specific intervention for specific problems, such as grieving and depression. Future research is also needed on the influence of different lengths of intervention and the interaction between externally stimulated and spontaneous life review. By keeping in mind that the life review is a precisely detailed phenomenon, different from other reminiscence processes, researchers may begin to examine and appreciate its worth.

APPENDIX: Life Review and Experiencing Form (Haight, 1979)

CHILDHOOD, FAMILY, AND HOME

   1   What is the very first thing you can remember in your life? Go as far back as you can.
   2   What other things can you remember about when you were very young?
   3   What was life like for you as a child?

4   What were your parents like? What were their weaknesses, strengths?

5   Did you have any brothers or sisters? Tell me what each was like.

6   Did someone close to you die when you were growing up?

7   Did someone important to you go away?

8   Do you ever remember being very sick? **Do you remember feeling ashamed?**

9   Do you remember having an accident?

10   Do you remember being in a very dangerous situation? **Did you ever feel guilty as a child?**

11   Was there anything that was important to you that was lost or destroyed?

12   Was church a large part of your life?

13   Did you enjoy being a boy/girl? **Did you ever have an unhappy sexual experience?**

14   **Did you enjoy starting projects as a child (with toys or in Scouts)?**

15   How did you parents get along?

16   How did other people in your home get along? **Did you feel you were guided through childhood?**

17   What was the atmosphere in your home? **Did you always feel cared for?**

18   Were you punished as a child? For what? Who did the punishing? Who was "boss"?

19   When you wanted something from your parents, how did you go about getting it?

20   What kind of person did your parents like the most? The least?

21   Who were you closest to in your family?

22   Who in your family were you most like? In what way?

ADOLESCENCE

1   When you think about yourself and your life as a teenager, what is the first thing you can remember about that time? **Did you feel good about yourself?**

2   What other things stand out in your memory about being a teenager?

3   Who were the important people for you? Tell me about them. Parents, brothers, sisters, friends, teachers, those you were especially close to, those you admired, those you wanted to be like.

4   Did you attend church and youth groups? **Did they have cliques in your day?**

5   Did you go to school? What was the meaning for you? **Were you a hard working student?**

6   Did you work at other jobs during these years? **Did you have a sense of belonging?**

7   Tell me of any hardships you experienced at this time.

8   Do you remember feeling that there wasn't enough food or necessities of life as a child or adolescent?

9   Do you remember feeling left alone, abandoned, not having enough love or care as a child or adolescent?

10   What were the pleasant things about your adolescence?

11   What was the most unpleasant thing about your adolescence?

12   All things considered, would you say you were happy or unhappy as a teenager?

13   Do you remember your first attraction to another person? **Did you establish a close relationship?**

14   How did you feel about sexual activities and your own sexual identity?

ADULTHOOD

1   **Did you do what you were supposed to do in life?**

2   What place did religion play in your life?

3   Now I'd like to talk to you about your life as an adult, starting when you were in your twenties and up to today. Tell me of the most important events that happened in your adulthood.

4   What was life like for you in your twenties and thirties?

5   What kind of person were you? What did you enjoy? **Did you think of yourself as responsible?**

6   Tell me about your work. Did you enjoy your work? Did you earn an adequate living? Did you work hard during those years? Were you appreciated?

7   Did you form significant relationships with other people?

8   Did you marry?

    (yes) What kind of person was your spouse?

    (no) Why not?

    Were you happy with your choice?

9   Do you think marriages get better or worse over time? Were you married more than once?

10   On the whole, would you say you had a happy or unhappy marriage?

11   Was sexual intimacy important to you?

12   What were some of the main difficulties you encountered during your adult years?

    a   Did someone close to you die? Go away?

    b   Were you ever sick? Have an accident?

    c   Did you move often? Change jobs?

    d   Did you ever feel alone? Abandoned?

    e   Did you ever feel need?

13   **Do you think you've helped the next generation?**

SUMMARY

1   On the whole, what kind of life do you thing you've had?

2   If everything were to be the same would you like to live your life over again?

3   If you were going to live your life over again, what would you change? Leave unchanged?

4   We've been talking about your life for quite some time now. Let's discuss your overall feelings and ideas about your life. What would you say the main satisfactions in your life have been? **Try for three. Why were they satisfying?**

5 Everyone has had disappointments. What have been the main disappointments in your life?

6 What was the hardest thing you had to face in your life? Please describe it.

7 What was the happiest period of your life? What about it made it the happiest period? Why is your life less happy now?

8 What was the unhappiest period of your life? Why is your life more happy now?

9 What was the proudest moment in your life?

10 If you could stay the same age all your life, what age would you choose? Why?

11 How do you think you've made out in life? Better or worse than what you hoped for?

12 Let's talk a little about you as you are now. What are the best things about the age you are now?

13 What are the worst things about being the age you are now?

14 What are the most important things to you in your life today?

15 What do you hope will happen to you as you grow older?

16 What do you fear will happen to you as you grow older?

17 Have you enjoyed participating in this review of your life?

NOTE: Questions in boldface are based on Erikson's Model of the Ages of Man. Derived from new questions and two unpublished dissertations:

Gorney, J. (1968). *Experiencing and age: Patterns of reminiscence among the elderly.* Unpublished doctoral dissertation, University of Chicago.

Falk, J. (1969). *The organization of remembered life experience of older people: Its relation to anticipated stress, to subsequent adaptation, and to age.* Unpublished doctoral dissertation, University of Chicago.

Chapter 14

Finding Common Ground and Mutual Social Support Through Reminiscing and Telling One's Story

Howard Iver Thorsheim
Bruce Roberts

When I hear someone else tell of an experience of theirs that I relate to, it's like I find a piece of myself in their story.

Older adults want to participate in community life as contributors. Oriol (1982) identified "opportunities for self-expression in a variety of roles" (p. 59) as a crucial need of elders. Reminiscing and telling one's story, that is, being able to talk about their life experiences with others, is a way for older adults to meet that need.

Our work has been supported in part by grants from the Fulbright Commission, the Norway-Marshall Fund, the American-Scandinavian Foundation, the Blandin Foundation, and St. Olaf College and has involved collaboration with numerous colleagues at the following institutions, which we wish to acknowledge: Akersykehuset Geriatric Department, Oslo, Norway; Diakonhjemmet Høgskole & Sykehuset, Oslo, Norway; Harvard University, Cambridge, Massachusetts; Norwegian Gerontological Institute, Oslo, Norway; Portland Age Wise Senior Community Video Project and Portland State University, Portland, Oregon; University of Oslo Institute of Psychology, Oslo, Norway; St. Olaf College, Northfield, Minnesota; University of Bergen Institute of Psychology and University of Bergen Division for Geriatric Medicine, Bergen, Norway; University of Wales at Cardiff; Ullevål Center for Social Networks and Health of the Norwegian Social Department, Oslo, Norway.

In this chapter, we offer some suggestions to readers who are interested in designing intervention methods to encourage reminiscing and telling one's story that are contextualized for particular groups. Our own experience in developing a process called "bring-a-thing" is used to illustrate some possibilities (Thorsheim & Roberts, 1993).

KEY CONCEPTS

Reminiscing and *telling one's story* have an underlying time continuum along which one may recall and talk about memories. The time focus depends on the stimulus that evokes the telling—it may be anywhere from the distant past to a relatively recent time. In other words, in reminiscing and telling our story, we may focus on long-ago stories as well as on the somewhat more contemporary. *Mutual social support* is the informal help that we give and receive in the form of words and deeds that helps us feel good about ourselves and others. Mutual social support is a two-way street, with benefits of reduced stress and improved mental health experienced by both talker and listener. We are appreciated for who we are and what we can do and may be asked to participate and help in ways we consider important and meaningful. Our *mutual social support network* consists of our relatives, friends, neighbors, and work colleagues. *Empowerment* is closely related to the concept of mutual social support because, like good social support, it involves a sense of well-being and a sense that life has important meaning. In addition, empowerment involves a good sense of identity and the belief that we have some control over areas that personally matter. To feel empowered is to feel a sense of belonging and being accepted. An empowered person cares about others and, reciprocally, is cared about by others. (See J. Rappaport (1990) for a discussion of the theoretical origins of the concept of empowerment.)

THE NEED

The need to effect mutual social support and empowerment by encouraging individuals to reminisce and tell their story is clear from a socioecological perspective (e.g., J. Kelly, 1986; Maton, 1987) at three levels: (a) individual to individual, (b) among family and friends, and (c) in one's neighborhood.

Individual to Individual

As Figure 1 shows, in our 4-year research study of approximately 10,000 persons funded by the National Institute on Drug Abuse (Roberts & Thorsheim, 1986; Thorsheim & Roberts, 1984, 1990a), we found that mutual social support, from both friends and family members, decreases with age across age cohorts.[1]

---

[1] Although our data raise the question whether decreases in social support observed in later life may be seeded as early as age 20, a cohort study such as ours, essentially a between-subjects design, differs from a longitudinal study, which would follow the same subjects throughout life, essentially a within-subject design (e.g., Seim, 1989). Thus we cannot conclude from our data that a developmental effect exists. Our data could reflect the distorting effect of cohort differences, because each cohort may have its own characteristics (e.g., Schaie, 1983).

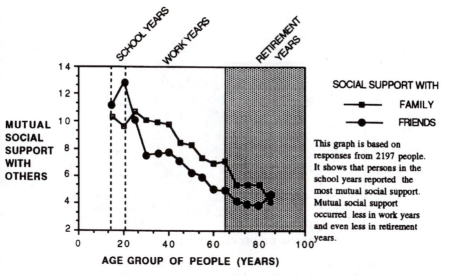

Figure 1 Decrease in mutual social support over the life span. From Thorsheim, H., & Roberts, B. (1990a). Empowerment through storysharing: Communication and reciprocal social support among older persons. In H. Giles, N. Coupland, and J. Wiemann (Eds.) *Communication, health and the elderly* (Fulbright Colloquium Series No. 8, pp. 114–125). London: Manchester University Press.

The mutual-social-support-with-others score in Figure 1 is a total score obtained by summing responses to the following variables from Barrera's scale, the Inventory of Socially Supportive Behaviors (Barrera & Ainlay, 1983): participating in an activity with others, talking with others, sharing something private with others, being told by others that he or she did something well, receiving expressions of esteem from others, and being told by others that he or she is accepted. These are the socially supportive behaviors involved in the activity of reminiscing together or, as we call it, "telling one's story."

Opportunities to tell one's story are dramatically reduced for both older men and older women, but particularly for older men. Figure 2 shows that at the age of retirement (65 in the United States), the cohort of elder men experienced a dramatic drop in the expressions of esteem or respect they received to practically zero, coinciding with loss of daily contact with co-workers (Thorsheim & Roberts, 1992). The women's data did not show nearly such a precipitous drop, although the older cohorts of women did show a decline. These data suggest that opportunities to tell one's story are particularly absent for retired men and constitute an important societal need to be met. Decreased mutual social support may be manifested in (a) fewer opportunities to talk about "what matters" to men, (b) fewer comments of respect or esteem, (c) less confidentiality, (d) loss of reciprocity, and (e) fewer occasions when acknowledgment of competence occurs.

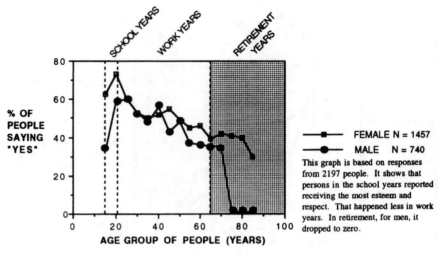

Figure 2   Respondents were asked to check "yes" or "no" to the following statement: "Friends express esteem or respect for a competency or personal quality of mine." ©1992 by Thorsheim & Roberts. From Thorsheim, H. & Roberts, B. (1992, March). *How to help people empower themselves by telling their stories together.* Workshop presented at the 38th Annual Meeting of the American Society on Aging, San Diego, CA.

Such decreases can have serious mental health consequences (Gottlieb, 1981, 1987; Knipscheer, 1991; Lloyd, 1991).

Since Butler's (1963) work with what he termed the "life review," interest in the process people use to tell about and reflect on their life has grown in the research literature. In telling one's story, one may draw on personal life histories and stories of significant life experiences. For example, Beverfelt (1984) and her colleagues have collected personal history accounts from more than 2,000 elderly Norwegians that, together with the results of our research, provide a useful base for new research on telling one's story from a cross-national perspective. Beverfelt reported that elders found sharing of their personal life histories and experiences to be both an enjoyable activity and a means for dealing with current problems, a finding supported by others working in the area of social network stimulation (e.g., Benum, Dalgard, & Sørenson, 1987; Bjelland, Danielsen, Helset, & Thorsen, 1992; Heap, 1990; Jebens, 1990; Knipscheer, 1991; Sauer & Coward, 1985; Støbakk, Bjørnson, Vigsnes, Sandnes, & Øvereng, 1989).

Considering the key role older persons can play in maintaining each other's health (e.g., Becker & Kaufman, 1988), telling one's story is an activity that can give older adults an opportunity to build the networks of mutual social support that are so important in human life (Fossan, 1991; O. C. Rø, personal communication, December 12, 1991). Linked needs are (a) coping with life changes and concerns and (b) improvement in quality of life for elders as well as those who interact with them (Beverfelt, 1990). Both needs call for processes of mutual empowerment

(Thorsheim & Roberts, 1990b). Stories may include community oral histories in which people share their experiences as members of a congregation or other community (Hopewell, 1987), or stories may be related to health and illness, that is, ways to preserve the former and avoid the latter (Kreps, 1989). The stories may be based on skills developed and used in living (e.g., Danielsen, 1990).

Among Family and Friends

For family and friends and, by extension, the broader community, older persons are a resource of wisdom that is significantly underused (e.g., Hagestad, 1987; Dittmann-Kohli & Baltes, 1990; Sternberg, 1990), just as younger persons are an underused resource for elders. Social support networks and their activities are important routes through which elders' life experiences may be shared (e.g., Roberts & Thorsheim, 1994), and through which we can "receive their experiences" to use Myerhoff's (1982) phrase. Elders' and youths' stories provide a different mirror in which both age cohorts can see themselves; however, we need listeners to hear these stories. The accumulated experiences of both young and older persons are available through their stories. Youth and elders need to talk and listen to one another in order to receive the mutual social support that research shows can buffer the stressors of life (Gottlieb, 1981, 1987). For these reasons, we encourage an intergenerational approach to telling one's story.

In One's Neighborhood

The neighborhood is the focus and the nub of our work. By "neighborhood," we mean the lodge, the church, the club, a business or organization, anywhere activities occur in which talking and mutual social support can take place. Such activities can take place, and sometimes do, but they cannot be counted on to happen automatically. Leadership is key to encouraging such activities, given the appropriate empowering tools—the activities, methods, and skills—plus the motivation to encourage such mutually supportive activities. We are dedicated to working with leaders to help them develop those activities, methods, and skills (e.g., Roberts & Thorsheim, 1987, 1988, 1990, 1991a, 1991b, 1994; Thorsheim & Roberts, 1990c, 1993).

Leadership for policy planning, programs, and services can contribute to the empowerment of older persons by creating settings and processes that encourage elders' involvement and participation in their neighborhood. Home and community support services provide social and mental engagement for elders (Kovach, 1991a, 1991b; Melcher, 1988). The research director of the Norwegian Gerontological Institute stated the imperative for leadership: "The responsibility as culture bearers is a challenge to old people. To enable them to participate and use their experience is a challenge to society" (Beverfelt, 1984, p. 233). Support for positive health behavior for elders living at home is the direction of the future, particularly because the percentage of older persons living at home is high and increasing in the United States and other Western countries (Hickey, Dean, & Holstein, 1986; Rø, Hendriksen, Kivela, & Thorslund, 1987). Because the down side of living at home is isolation and loneliness, persons who work with elders should be taught to encourage them to tell their stories (Haight & Olson, 1989; Ingebretsen, 1989). On the up side, support for telling one's story may exist in the form of personal artifacts and pictures at home that serve as cues for remembering experiences (Roberts & Thorsheim, 1994; Thorsheim & Roberts, 1990d, 1993).

It is important to note that activities that encourage telling one's story help combat negative stereotypes about aging and the aged (Langer et al., 1990; Revenson, 1988) as well as stereotypes about individuals who are diverse in other ways, for example, in culture, race, ethnicity, language, gender, life experience, physical ability, socioeconomic background, ways of living, and worldviews (e.g., Howard, 1991). A sign of a healthy human ecology is public policy that supports the development of leadership methods that affirm diversity.

The issues highlighted in this section should lead the reader to ask the questions, "How do we make these activities happen? What are the methods that one might use in these activities?" In the following section, we discuss several methods from which to choose.

POSSIBLE METHODS TO ENCOURAGE TELLING ONE'S STORY

We have been working in several locations in the United States and in Norway to develop and test research-based methods to encourage the activity of telling one's story in diverse groups and to measure the resulting benefits. The focus of this chapter is on how to use such methods to increase empowerment and build social support networks among older persons. Our work to develop methods to encourage telling one's story has been guided by Jim Kelly's counsel to us through the years in various projects. He says to pay attention to contextual uniqueness and to "attend to and learn from community participants" (J. Kelly, 1988, p. 7).

Kelly's work suggests several possible methods that, if pursued, will help you "attend to and learn from" elders who are the community participants. You should choose the methods that are the most salient to you and fit the context of your work. The methods chosen should (a) be the most meaningful to you and the people you will be working with or (b) lead to specific goals you and the people you are working with have set or (c) seem logistically doable.

Initiate Participative Ownership   Form an Elder Advisory Group (or research team) who can help you understand the local context. Identify a process for the Elder Advisory Group. The Elder Advisory Group can be helpful for implementing the findings of your work together. (You may choose to do some of the other possible methods together with members of this advisory group.)

Listen to What the Elders Are Saying   Listen to elders talk and listen for the diverse kinds of issues being shared. Look and listen for stories in the media that refer to elder issues. Listen for the great diversity among elders' issues in terms of core values, sources of meaning and purpose, traditions for working together and the way they are transmitted, and the needs of different age cohorts.

Identify Settings Where Elders Talk   Search for empowered elders. Seek ways to be introduced to them. Meet, talk with, and learn from them. Identify the social settings in which elders are engaged and empowered. Notice the diverse social settings that encourage elders to talk about what is on their minds. These can range from informal but regular coffee or breakfast groups, to physical therapy sessions at the local pool, to an organization of retirees from a local plant. Listen to the Elders Advisory Group, particularly for strategies for understanding and being understood by those who oppose the concept of elder empowerment.

Identify Points of Policy Impact   Identify local and national professionals in gerontology whose work is clearly related to what you are doing. Identify citizens in local and regional communities whose work already enhances elder empowerment and who may be potential partners in your effort. Identify local and national officials who have a potential interest in enhancing elder empowerment and meet to listen to their perspectives. Communicate with the national elder associations as well as professional associations and local corporations who may be invested in elder empowerment.

Identify Informal Social Networks   Identify organizations that promote the concepts of elder renewal and development as core values. Name the mentors and other persons in those informal social networks who value the development of elder empowerment. Identify places that promote informal social networks, such as restaurants, stores, pool halls, bridge clubs; community events; as well as organizations such as elder centers, day activity centers, hospitals, and adult education services. Identify their leaders. Find out what they are doing that they think works well. Find out what they are doing to promote their visibility and to be valued in the community. Connect to voluntary associations and neighborhood organizations as one way to work with formal social structures in the community.

Search for Systemic Variables   Watch for what is working to reduce ageism and economic discrimination. Look for processes and variables that facilitate elder participation—the antecedents and correlates of elders' social integration as well as self-definition and access to community resources.

Identify Multiple System Levels   Use a systems approach or metaperspective to relate the interaction between the individual and collective behavior of elders and assess ways in which elders and social settings are interdependent.

What paths and connections relate to policy formation about elder empowerment? What informal connections exist between elders and external resources? What encourages or discourages boundary spanners, that is, the people who are trying to see through others' eyes? What are the options for and experience with innovative social structures in the community that might bear on what you are planning? Think about how your work can be part of a policy planning and evaluation cycle in the community.

Look for Fortuitous Side Effects from the Methods Chosen   From the methods chosen, watch for side effects at the individual, group, organization, and community levels. To get help in doing this, make use of an Elders Advisory Group. Be on the lookout for side effects among elders' family and friends—their social network. Ask the Elders Advisory Group what is on their mind about various aspects of the methods chosen.

After having made choices among the possible methods for encouraging the telling of one's story, next comes the question as to what is the process for moving from possible methods to actually carrying out the project. We have developed the following logic of inquiry.

ENCOURAGING TELLING ONE'S STORY AMONG ELDERS

Figure 3 summarizes a logic of inquiry of the antecedents, behaviors, and consequent benefits related to encourage elders to tell and listen to one another's stories.

Informal Activities   Participation in informal activities with others makes possible informal, mutually socially supportive interactions.

Telling One's Story   When people gather together for an informal activity, they talk. When people talk with one another, they talk about their experiences in life, as well as what's on their minds at the present time—the mutual process we refer to as telling one's story.

Investment in Community   When people talk with each other, they develop a sense of belonging and then enact certain kinds of behaviors, which we call *investment-in-community behaviors*. These behaviors are good investments because they are good for talker and listener. They include the following:

Belonging   Belonging is often thought of as belonging to an organization, family, or neighborhood. A *psychological sense of belonging* is also generated during informal activities and conversations when one is telling one's story and listening to others, at least for the duration of the activity (e.g., Maslow, 1970).

Naming   People invested in their community know and call each other by name. When people talk together, they learn one another's names and call one

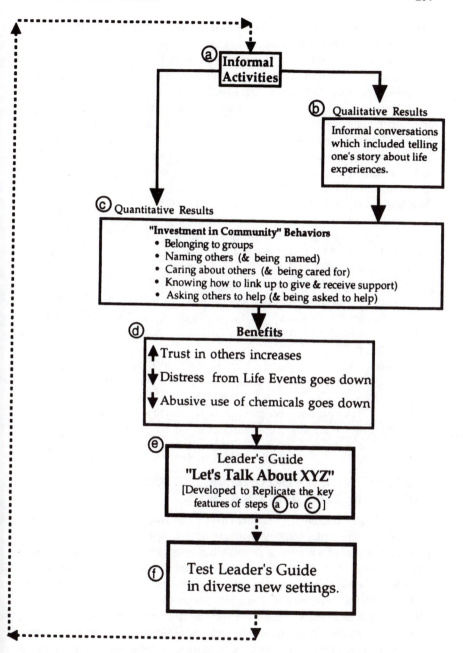

Figure 3 Logic of inquiry followed for development of a reminiscence group leader's guide entitled "Let's Talk about XYZ."

another by name. Being known by name is important to one's identity, meaning, and sense of integrity. There may be a story behind one's name, just as there may be a name to one's story. Our stories may be stories of our own uniqueness and special qualities. Naming leads to knowing and plays a central role in finding common ground and building mutual social support.

Caring   This is the part of the logic of inquiry process that keeps it from being merely mechanical steps. People invested in their community care for one another. When people talk together, it is easier for them to know about and care about each other. Mutual appreciation of and respect for who the other is develops. When we are able to honor our own uniqueness, we may be able to see that the uniqueness of others needs to be honored too. We are part of the diversity; as Maitland (1991) said, "We have a variety of characters within each of us" (p. 177).

Linking   People invested in their community link up to give and receive support. We become more diverse as we age, as Nelson (1992) showed in a meta-analysis of 185 gerontological studies that examined biological, cognitive, personality, and social variables. Theoretically, diversity in a group gives one more opportunity to find common ground with someone.

Asking   People invested in their community ask one another for help. When people talk together, they learn of each other's concerns. "Dialogue is a moment where humans meet to reflect on their reality as they make and remake it" (Shor & Freire, 1987, p. 98).

Benefits   Recent regression analyses showed that persons who manifested high number of investment-in-community behaviors personally realized several very important benefits (Roberts & Thorsheim, 1986). For example, they trusted others more. They experienced less distress from the stressors of life (not necessarily fewer life events that could cause stress, but rather less distress when they occurred). Furthermore, they had a lower incidence of chemical abuse.

ILLUSTRATION OF AN EMPOWERING METHOD TO ENCOURAGE "TELLING ONE'S STORY"

In our work, we have found it helpful to have a very descriptive outline that allows choice but also provides concrete instructions that can be used in their entirety or changed to better fit a particular context. Because we have found this process so helpful, we include at this point a brief discussion of some of the design features considered for our Leader's Guide, which describes a group process titled "Let's Talk About XYZ." The goal of "Let's Talk About XYZ" is a clearly described yet adaptable process to help people tell their stories with each other and, in the process, find and build on common ground. The process includes informal activities that allow for choice and control by participants. "Let's Talk About XYZ" was designed to be attentive to the contextual needs of diverse communities and to encourage persons to tell their stories to one another. The reciprocity of persons both telling and listening is very important.

Adaptablity In "Let's Talk About XYZ," the "XYZ" stands for any topic contextualized to fit the group. For example, it could stand for the name of a neighborhood (e.g., "The Near West Side"), a residence (e.g., "Ebenezer Retirement Residence"), an organization (e.g., "Central Church"), alumni (e.g., "Class of 1963"), people sharing a common work history (e.g., "The Retired Professors' Breakfast Group"), an organization (e.g., "Acme Products Production Team"), or a family reunion (e.g., "The Smith Family"). These are but a few examples of common ground on which people can get together as a group.

Informal Activities Easily Carried Out, Yet Meaningful As a springboard for a group of people to discover their common ground, we use an activity we call "Bring-a-Thing," in which people bring in and talk about personal objects or artifacts. The use of objects, artifacts, or experiences shared in common as vehicles to encourage telling one's story has been described by many others (e.g., Radley, 1990; Thorsheim & Roberts, 1990c) and is discussed in Chapter 11 of this book. The role of objects as tools for bringing forth stories, including how objects may mediate the interaction between two persons,[2] has been the focus of extensive discussion (e.g., Csikszentmihalyi & Rochberg-Halton, 1981).

Choice and Control by Participants Participants choose what they talk about, whether stimuli are from past or present.

Processes Processes that support members' getting to know and call each other by name, having reasons to care about one another, developing skills for linking up with others to give and receive support, and becoming comfortable asking help from others and providing it are empowering.

Clear Language The Leader's Guide has language that includes straightforward steps for the process, avoids jargon, and makes enjoyable reading for participants. Anything less would prevent the intervention from being used, as well as prevent empirical evaluation because of the absence of the independent variable that the process was intended to provide.

Attention to the Contextual Needs of Audiences "Let's Talk About XYZ" has been refined through testing in diverse settings with diverse audiences including persons of various ages, gender, and culture, factors of great importance (e.g., C. Adams, Labouvie-Vief, Hobart, & Dorosz, 1990; Adelman, & Bankoff, 1990; Kleiner & Okeke, 1991).

---

[2]Comment made by Michael Cole June 12, 1993, on email list xlchc@uscd.edu on the topic of subject–object relations.

CONCLUSION

Reminiscing and telling their story help people find common ground with others and thereby engage in a process of mutual social support that is empowering. The need for such a method exists at the level of the individual, family and friends, and the neighborhood.

In this chapter we have suggested several possible tasks, based on the work of J. Kelly (1988), for leaders wishing to develop methods to help persons tell their stories together. These possible tasks were illustrated with design features for a specific intervention method called "Let's Talk About XYZ," part of a Leader's Kit to encourage telling one's story in a group through the use of an object, common experience, or other form of congruence.

Reminiscing and telling one's story put one at "a place where minds meet, where things are not the same to all who see them, where meanings are fluid" (Newman, Griffin, & Cole, 1989, p. ix). What Sarbin (1986) has called "the storied nature of human action" we call reminiscing and telling one's story. It is process of telling with another (narrative interaction), discovering through this interaction what one's own story means (socially constructed meaning), discovering resources in the other's perspective (shared wisdom), naming the feelings associated with one's experiences (affect), and discovering one's own voice while helping another discover his or her's (mutual empowerment). Telling one's story occurs all around us and is a rich resource for those wishing to find common ground in a process of mutual social support.

Chapter 15

Using Reminiscence Interviews for Stress Management in the Medical Setting

Bruce Rybarczyk

It is an inescapable fact about human existence that we are made of our memories: we are what we remember ourselves to be.

E. S. Casey (1989, p. 290)

I begin this chapter with a rationale for using reminiscence interviews to enhance the coping of older patients who are undergoing stressful medical procedures. I then describe two different reminiscence interviews and review and summarize two intervention studies. Finally, I outline future directions for research and recommend other applications in the medical setting.

RATIONALE FOR DEVELOPING A REMINISCENCE APPROACH

Invasive medical procedures are a major stress event for almost all individuals who face them (Auerbach, 1986). Numerous studies document the pervasiveness

This work was partially funded by the Andrus Foundation and the American Cancer Society (Grant IRG-195).

of medi-stress, which causes moderate to high levels of anxiety before and during diagnostic, dental, and surgical procedures, regardless of the routineness of the procedure. This anxiety is typically related to fears about anesthesia, physical pain, loss of control, and the possibility of death (Auerbach, 1986). The anxiety not only is uncomfortable for the patient, but is linked to poorer adjustment and recovery after a medical procedure (Johnston, 1986).

Numerous studies document the effectiveness of various types of psychological interventions in reducing anxiety and facilitating coping among patients facing medical procedures (for a review, see Anderson & Masur, 1983). Outcome effects have ranged from reduced anxiety and increased positive thinking before the procedure to decreased depression, pain, medical complications, and length of stay after a procedure. Methods of intervention include providing factual and sensory information about a procedure, showing videotapes of a patient successfully undergoing a procedure, offering supportive counseling, and teaching patients cognitive coping techniques (e.g., visualization). These interventions attempt to facilitate coping via one of three basic approaches: (a) altering the individual's appraisal of the degree of threat posed by a situation, (b) altering the individual's appraisal of his or her ability to cope with that threat; or (c) reducing the negative emotions that are triggered by the perceived threat (i.e., emotion-focused coping).

The research on stress management interventions for medical and dental patients has focused almost exclusively on children and younger adults. Yet it is older adults who undergo the greatest number of invasive medical procedures. For example, in 1985, persons over the age of 65 were twice as likely to have surgery as any other age group (American College of Surgeons, 1987). In addition, it is older adults who are most vulnerable to the stress of hospitalization and surgery (Davies & Peters, 1983; Irvine, Bagnall, & Smith, 1978), leading to high rates of psychophysiological complications such as depression (Tichener & Levine, 1967), delirium (Seymour, 1986), and loss of appetite (Gillick, Serrell, & Gillick, 1982).

There is also some evidence that conventional stress interventions may not be as effective with older adults as they are with younger adults (Blanchard, Andrasik, Evans, & Hillhouse, 1985; Diamond & Montrose, 1984). In a meta-analysis of the headache treatment literature, for example, Holroyd and Penzien (1986) found a highly significant negative relationship between mean improvement after psychological intervention and the average age of patients. Age accounted for a full 40% of the outcome variance. The only medical procedure intervention study that assessed age as a moderator variable revealed that a standard stress management procedure was not effective with patients over 50 years of age (J. Johnson & Leventhal, 1974). Nonetheless, some stress intervention studies have yielded positive findings with older adults (e.g., Arena, Hightower, & Chong, 1988).

In view of these facts, psychological interventions must be designed that better match the older adults' unique characteristics. A reminiscence approach appears to be an ideal stress intervention approach for older adults. Multisession reminiscence therapy techniques aimed at longer term psychological benefits have already been effective (Haight, 1991). The popularity of reminiscence interventions in the literature testifies to their appeal to older adults, who are reluctant to participate in traditional psychological interventions (Brody, 1985). Another key advantage to reminiscence is that it can be presented to patients as both an inherently enjoyable opportunity to "tell your life story" and as something that may "improve your state of mind." In effect, individuals can participate without acknowledging that they are in need of psychological assistance.

I believe that providing patients with an opportunity to retell their life narrative promotes coping on two different levels. First, on an affective level, reminiscence serves as a buffer against stress-induced anxiety because of its mood-elevating effects. In a basic demonstration of this effect, Fallot (1980) found that interviews in which subjects were prompted to "tell their life story" resulted in more self-reported positive mood changes than did interviews in which older adults were asked to talk about present interests and activities. Second, on a cognitive level, reminiscence that focuses on past accomplishments and triumphs over adversity serves to remind individuals of their coping competencies and resources (Brink, 1979). Bandura's (1986) self-efficacy research has shown that a person's perception of how well he or she is able to complete a task greatly influences how well he or she actually carries out that task. Although research is limited, a pair of studies indicate that there is a link between reminiscence frequency and psychological health (Wong & Watt, 1991) and adjustment to stress (C. N. Lewis, 1971). Thus, a reminiscence intervention may facilitate a patient's natural coping response.

Another advantage of reminiscence interviews is that health professionals of all disciplines as well as volunteers without extensive training in counseling can conduct them. For example, in studies of multisession reminiscence therapy, health care students, nurses, and recreation therapists have been enlisted to provide interventions. Although volunteers have not been employed as peer counselors in the medical setting, hospitals typically have access to numerous older adults who are willing to volunteer their time and talents. Peer counselors can be as effective as professionals when administering structured interventions to the "worried well" who are experiencing situation-related distress (Durlak, 1979). Older counselors, in particular, have been effective in helping their age peers adjust to such stressors as nursing home placement (Scharlach, 1988), retirement (Poser & Engels, 1983; Romaniuk & Priddy, 1980), and widowhood (Silverman, 1974). Peer helpers, as "similar others," are more able to validate patients' experiences and to express empathic understanding (Thoits, 1986). As such, older volunteers may be particularly effective at reminiscence interventions because they share some similar life experiences with the interviewees. Finally, an intervention program staffed by trained volunteers would not cost as much as the stress interventions conducted by nurses, social workers, and psychologists.

The rationale for developing a new approach to stress management that uses reminiscence may be summarized as follows:

1   Older adults are currently undergoing more invasive medical procedures than are persons of any other age group, and this trend will continue for several decades.

2   To date, stress intervention techniques have not been tailored to the needs of older adults, and the few attempts at using standard techniques with this population have been largely unsuccessful.

3   Reminiscence interventions have proven appeal and effectiveness with older adults but have not yet been modified for application to stress events.

4   Even stress interventions that have been demonstrated to be efficacious with younger adults have not been implemented on a routine basis because of a lack of cost-effectiveness. The development of techniques that can be implemented easily by trained volunteers would eliminate this barrier.

TWO VARIATIONS OF THE REMINISCENCE INTERVIEW

On the basis of the preceding rationale, I have conducted a research program to develop and test a 1-hr reminiscence interview to serve as a stress intervention for older medical patients. An initial exploration of the literature led to two approaches to using reminiscence to enhance coping: the Life Experience Interview (LEI) and the Life Challenges Interview (LCI). My intention was to test both interviews to determine which was more effective. However, two studies (described in the next section) indicated that both interviews are efficacious, each having unique advantages and disadvantages.

The two interviews have much in common. In both, the interviewer serves as a participant-listener who directs the patient's telling of the life narrative via chronologically ordered anecdotes. The focus is on positive events only. Both interviews also use a semistructured format, striking a balance between an "I ask the questions, you give the answers" approach, on the one hand and simple free association from topic to topic, on the other. The interviewer is equipped with a list of questions and topics effective in steering the participant toward positive areas. In each case, the interviewer must convey that the goal is not to gather information, but to create a positive psychological experience. In other words, the process is more important than the product (American Association of Retired Persons [AARP], 1989). Haight (1992b) confirmed that the most salutary reminiscence interviews are those that are conducted one on one, proceed in chronological order, and cover personal rather than generational memories.

Life Experience Interview

The simpler of the two interviews is the LEI. This approach is based on the premise that positive feelings elicited by simple interpersonal reminiscing will counteract the anxiety triggered by a stressful situation. This particular life story interview covers topics that usually evoke positive emotions, such as childhood activities, favorite family traditions and holidays, and dating experiences. In contrast to the LCI, no direct effort is made to guide the interviewee toward talking about events that are somehow related to coping.

Five basic rules apply to the LEI:

1   Topics are covered in chronological order, so the interview unfolds as a continuous life story, rather than a series of unconnected anecdotes.
2   The focus is on biographical memories, rather than generational memories.
3   There is an attempt to cover significant life events from all important stages of the life cycle, so that, by the end of the interview, a relatively complete life story has been created.
4   The emphasis is on telling stories with vivid and rich details, rather than merely relating factual information of who, what, and where.
5   Memories that are not often recalled by the patient should be explored.

As evident by these rules, one advantage of this interview is its simplicity; interviewers do not need to be particularly skillful.

Life Challenges Interview

The more advanced LCI builds on the technique used in the LEI interview. The overall goal of this approach is to increase the interviewees' awareness of their coping strengths and resources by directing them to recall past successes in meeting life challenges (e.g., surviving the Great Depression, doing well in school, and getting their first job). Although this approach also invites the interviewee to tell his or her life story, the interviewer steers the participant toward stories that emphasize successfully met challenges.

On an emotional level, the goal of the LCI is to decrease anxiety and increase participants' sense of satisfaction, pride, and accomplishment about their life. On a cognitive level, the goal is to heighten participants' awareness of the strengths and resources they used to meet previous challenges. Patients' increased awareness of their coping resources minimizes their perception that the medical stress they are facing is overwhelming. This conceptualization of the function of LCI is consistent with Bandura's (1986) well-supported theory that a person's perception of how well he or she is able to complete a task (i.e., self-efficacy) greatly influences how well he or she actually carries out that task.

The LCI consists of the following four goals:

1   An LEI interview is conducted as described earlier. This serves as the foundation for the other three goals of the LCI. Roughly 60% of the interview time is spent toward this end.
2   The focus is on reminiscing about life challenges. In this context, challenges are broadly defined and fall into several categories: (a) learning any new skill (e.g., bike riding), (b) achieving something that was valued (e.g., good

grades), (c) making any transition in life (e.g., moving to a new city), and (d) living in a time when there were fewer conveniences and less technology available (e.g., no air conditioning). Approximately 25% of the interview focuses on recalling the events surrounding successfully met challenges.

3   The strengths and resources the patient used to meet the challenges being discussed are underscored. The objective is to identify and reinforce (or validate) the positive attributes that are already a part of the participant's self-concept. Whenever possible, the patient should be prompted to identify his or her positive attributes by a question such as "What qualities do you have that helped you in that situation?" When the patient does not know how to answer the question or is too modest, the interviewer makes a simple observation about an apparent strength or resource (e.g., "You were really determined."). Approximately 10% of the interview is used to pursue this objective.

4   Key lifelong strengths and resources are summarized. The objective is to reinforce key personal attributes that emerged as themes during the course of the interview. This accounts for the final 5% of the total interview time.

The primary disadvantage of the LCI interview is its complexity; the interview must follow all the rules of the LEI while adding three additional therapeutic objectives. In a sense, the interviewer is conducting a simple cognitive therapy intervention in the context of a life history interview.

INITIAL STUDY USING THE TWO INTERVIEWS

Method

In 1987, my professor and I conducted the first stress intervention study using the two reminiscence interviews at McGuire Veterans Administration Hospital in Richmond, Virginia (Rybarczyk, 1988; Rybarczyk & Auerbach, 1990). The 104 veterans who participated (mean age = 65.7 years) were facing a variety of elective surgical procedures, the most common being coronary bypass, prostate resection, and hernia repair. Interviews were conducted the afternoon or evening before the surgical procedure and lasted 45 min to 1 hr. Interviewers were men who were either psychology graduate students (age range = 24–31) or older adults recruited from other volunteer programs (age range = 63–72). Interviewers received 1 hr of individual training, were given a written set of suggested topics to cover, and were given feedback after I had reviewed each interview via audiotape.

Four different groups were compared. One group received the LEI, one group received the LCI, one group received an attention-placebo interview that focused on present interests and activities, and a control group received no intervention. In addition, the effectiveness of the psychology graduate students and the older adult volunteers was compared. Because the interviews were not complicated and capitalized on what is considered to be a natural skill of older adults, I hypothesized that the older adult peer counselors would be as effective as the psychology graduate students.

Contrary to the expectation that only about half of these older male veterans would participate in a psychological intervention, 85% of those who were invited agreed to be in the study. This supported the notion that reminiscence is inherently appealing as a basis for psychological intervention. By and large, the men seemed to view it as an honor that someone was taking an interest in their life story. The original plan was to audiotape the interview solely as a means of monitoring what was happening during the interview, so that feedback could be provided to the interviewers. In retrospect, judging by the comments of the participants, the presence of the recorder seemed to add a sense of importance to the interview.

Results and Discussion

Overall, the results were very encouraging. Subjects who participated in either of the two reminiscence interviews experienced a decrease in anxiety after the interview, compared with an increase in anxiety experienced by subjects who received the attention-placebo interview or no interview (see Figure 1). The anxiety pre-test was given several hours before the interview and the post-test, within an hour after the interview. A four-item version of the State–Trait Anxiety Inventory (STAI; Spielberger, Gorsuch, & Lushene, 1970) was used both times. The attention-placebo group and control group were given the same pre-test and post-test separated by an interval that was equivalent to the other groups.

As hypothesized, in addition to a reduction in anxiety, the LCI and LEI groups scored higher on the Coping Self-Efficacy Inventory than did the other two groups. This scale directly measures the degree of confidence an individual has in his or her coping skills and resources (Rybarczyk & Auerbach, 1990). When interviewer status was factored in, the results showed that the highest scores in

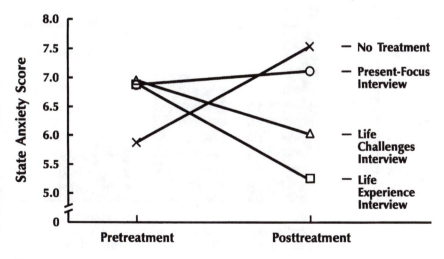

Figure 1 Study 1: Pre- and post-treatment state anxiety scores.

coping self-efficacy occurred in patients who had been interviewed by older volunteers. Thus, the LCI did have the largest positive effect on the patients' awareness of their coping strengths and resources, but only when it was administered by age peers (see Figure 2). Similarly, the interviews conducted by the older volunteers led to greater reductions on the STAI than did those conducted by the graduate students. This finding matched previous research showing that volunteer peer counselors are as effective as professionals when administering structured interventions to the "worried well" (Durlak, 1979). A review of the audiotapes indicated that the better performance of the older male volunteers appeared to be related to the fact that they had lived through the same time period and could directly relate to many of the events being discussed in the interview. A greater level of kinship, trust, and openness between members of the same generation also may have played a role.

The statistically significant differences obtained in these stress intervention studies need to be further evaluated to determine whether they are "clinically significant" (Ludwick-Rosenthal & Neufeld, 1988). One approach to evaluating whether individual patients experienced a tangible benefit from an intervention is to examine the effect size (Cohen, 1977). Using a formula suggested by Hedges and Olkin (1985), we obtained effect sizes of 1.8 and 0.77, respectively, on the measures of state anxiety and coping self-efficacy. According to guidelines proposed by Cohen (1977), these effect sizes can be characterized as very strong. In addition, compared with effect sizes reported for 21 presurgical stress interventions by Suls and Wan (1989) in their meta-analysis, the effects were greater.

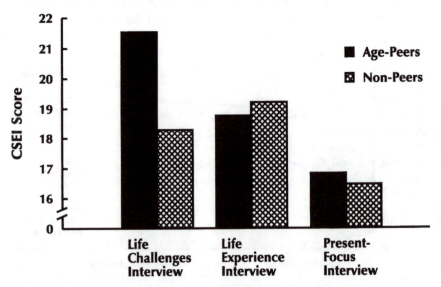

Figure 2   Study 1: Post-treatment scores on the Coping Self-Efficacy Inventory (CSEI).

FOLLOW-UP STUDY

Method

To replicate and extend the findings from the first study, my colleagues and I undertook an 18-month-long study funded by AARP's Andrus Foundation (Rybarczyk, Auerbach, Jorn, Lofland, & Perlman, 1993). This study was conducted at Rush–Presbyterian–St. Luke's Medical Center in Chicago and included 143 patients (mean age = 65 years; 96 men and 47 women). Rather than using a variety of surgical patients, as in the initial study, we included patients who were undergoing the same percutaneous transluminal coronary angioplasty (PTCA) procedure. The PTCA is a very common procedure that involves the insertion and inflation of a balloon-tipped catheter in one or more coronary arteries to compress the plaque that obstructs blood flow. Although technically not a surgical procedure, PTCA is known to be very stressful for patients because of the substantial risks involved and the fact that patients are required to remain conscious and participate during the procedure (Shaw et al., 1986). A homogenous patient sample allowed for measurement of secondary benefits from enhanced coping during and after the PTCA procedure (e.g., pain perception, the nurse's rating of adjustment, use of pain medication, number of days before discharge, and 30-day outcome). In addition, using a procedure that required patients to be awake allowed for the evaluation of coping during the procedure.

The design of this study differed from that of Study 1 in several ways. First, because the first study showed they compared favorably to younger adult volunteers, we used older adult volunteers only. There were 19 volunteers (mean age = 66.2 years; 14 women and 5 men). Second, in lieu of an attention-placebo-interview, a comparison group of patients received a combination of established relaxation training interventions (Aiken & Henrichs, 1971; Corah, Gale, Pace, & Seyrek, 1981), including diaphragmatic breathing, progressive muscle relaxation, and visualization. Third, the training time was increased to 4 hr in the classroom (vs. 1 hr) and a practice session with nonsurgical patients.

On a qualitative level, the social characteristics of the subjects differed substantially from those of the subjects in Study 1. The sample changed from being men who had mostly lived their lives in rural Virginia and West Virginia to older men and women who had been born and raised in a large Midwestern city. In addition, a large subgroup of the Chicago residents had emigrated from Central and Eastern Europe during the 1930s and 1940s. This meant that the stories elicited during the LCI shifted from the burdens of daily farm life or working in coal mines to urban life in Chicago's ethnic neighborhoods and life in "the old country." The inclusion of women and adults as young as 50 years old meant that a broader array of topics and questions had to be developed for the interviews. For instance, we found that women in their 60s who had had professional careers often related rich stories about the challenges they faced as pioneers in the workplace.

Results and Discussion

Although the effect sizes were somewhat attenuated relative to the initial study, several findings support the efficacy of this type of reminiscence intervention. First, both reminiscence interviews led to a significant reduction in state anxiety scores, in contrast to an increase in anxiety scores for the no-treatment group, on the same instrument and at the same measurement points used in the first study. Second, the anxiety reductions obtained as a result of reminiscence were comparable to those obtained as a result of relaxation training (see Figure 3). Third, all three intervention groups reported using more emotion-focused coping, relative to controls, on an abbreviated Ways of Coping Checklist. Lastly, patients in all three intervention groups reported greater satisfaction with the preparation for and scheduling of the angioplasty procedure than did controls. Thus, the hospital as a whole was perceived as providing better services to these patients. (All effect sizes were in the moderate to strong range according to Cohen's, 1977, criteria.)

As in Study 1, a pair of findings also confirmed the unique effect of the LCI on the appraisal aspect of coping. The LCI group reported significantly more positive thinking on a validated measure of positive and negative self-statements (Kendall et al., 1979) than did controls. In addition, only the LCI subjects had significantly higher scores on the coping self-efficacy measure than did the controls. The other two intervention groups scored higher than controls but less than the LCI subjects, and neither difference was significant. Both of these findings support the hypothesis that a reminiscence interview focused on challenge events stimulates increases in patients' awareness of their coping abilities.

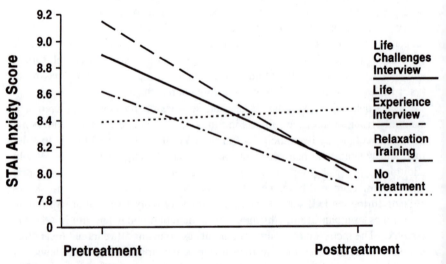

Figure 3   Study 2: Pre- and post-treatment state anxiety scores on the State–Trait Anxiety Inventory (STAI).

In contrast to the range of positive findings on measures of coping, there were no demonstrable secondary benefits of the reminiscence interventions. Secondary benefits are medical and quasi-medical benefits that appear after the intervention and presumably derive from the improved coping of the patient. In this study, there were no positive findings for a nurse rating of adjustment during the PTCA procedure, for perception of pain during the PTCA, for post-PTCA use of pain medication, for number of days betweeen PTCA and discharge, and for quality of life and psychological adjustment 30 days after the procedure.

The lack of secondary medical benefits has two plausible explanations. First, it may be that coping interventions of this type only enhance psychological coping and do not cross the mind–body barrier to provide medical benefits per se. Since the PTCA procedure is relatively routine and not very physically demanding, it may not have provided enough of an opportunity for this crossover. A second explanation for the lack of findings in the area of medical benefits is that the benefits did exist but could not be detected with our crude measurements and a methodology that looked for differences across randomly assigned groups. Previous stress intervention research has been mixed in terms of demonstrating a connection between patients' level of coping and various medical outcomes (Anderson & Masur, 1983). When they have been demonstrated, these effects have often been small and have required sophisticated assessment techniques (e.g., immunological tests and standardized observer rating scales) not used in this study. In future reminiscence intervention studies, my colleagues and I will attempt to demonstrate secondary benefits in patients undergoing a more physically demanding medical procedure than PTCA, with an eye toward improving the measurement of these benefits.

As in Study 1, the gender, educational status, and age of the patient had no influence on the efficacy of the reminiscence interventions. Study 2 included women as well as men and patients who were as young as 50. This lends support to the idea that the benefits of reminiscence cut across gender and age barriers. Borden (1992) has posited that "life narrative" interventions can play a key role in helping younger adult patients adjust to catastrophic medical illness. Although the reminiscence literature of the past 20 years generally assumes that reminiscence makes a *unique* contribution to psychological adjustment in the latter portion of the life cycle, several studies suggest that this may not be the case (Hyland & Ackerman, 1988; Merriam & Cross, 1982; Romaniuk & Romaniuk, 1983).

Finally, one very encouraging finding with regard to the efficacy of the reminiscence interviews was the exceptional results obtained by a subset of volunteers in both studies. For instance, in Study 2 when the results from the most effective 4 volunteers from the LEI and LCI groups (2 in each) were examined separately, the 22 subjects they interviewed showed an average decrease of 2.2 points on the STAI. In contrast, the average anxiety decrease for the remaining 49 subjects interviewed by the other 12 volunteers was 0.4. The variability among the volunteers who provided the relaxation training was negligible. Thus, the results of reminiscence interviews may be improved substantially by both using a more stringent criteria for selecting volunteers and improving the training.

SUMMARY OF THE RESEARCH FINDINGS

The present studies demonstrate that reminiscence interviews are effective tools for enhancing the coping of older medical patients. The important findings were as follows:

1 Both studies showed that the two types of reminiscence interviews significantly reduced the anxiety of patients facing an invasive medical procedure. Patients who received reminiscence interviews had greater anxiety reductions than did those who received no intervention in both studies.

2 In Study 1, a comparison interview covering current interests and activities did not reduce anxiety. This finding demonstrates that the effects of reminiscence interviews go beyond those obtained from basic emotional support.

3 In Study 2, patients who received either of the two reminiscence interviews had anxiety reductions that were equivalent to those experienced by patients who received a relaxation training intervention. The relaxation training used was a state-of-the-art coping intervention often used in the medical setting.

4 In both studies, the LCI had a significant positive effect on coping self-efficacy when compared with other interventions. These findings indicate that the LCI has a unique and specific impact on patients' beliefs regarding their coping strengths and resources.

5 In Study 2, patients who received the LCI reported more positive thinking during the medical procedure than did controls. This finding is presumably linked to the unique effect of the LCI on the appraisal aspect of coping.

6 In Study 2, both reminiscence interviews and relaxation training had significant positive effects on patient satisfaction when compared with controls. Given the limited costs to the hospital for implementing a volunteer program, this appears to be an important finding from a patient care and customer satisfaction perspective.

7 In both studies, no measurable medical or quasi-medical benefits were found for any of the interventions. This aspect of outcome is difficult to measure and will be given higher priority in future studies.

8 The effect sizes of the reminiscence interventions in both studies were in the moderate to strong range and compared favorably with those of other stress interventions reported by Suls and Wan (1989).

9 Older volunteers who worked in either of the two studies reported a very high level of satisfaction with their participation in the program. When appropriate supervision is provided, this type of program provides volunteers with a rare and enriching opportunity to serve as a peer counselor in the medical setting.

In summary, the interviews appeared to provide important benefits to the patient, the hospital, and even the volunteers (on the basis of their subjective reports). Put another way, this type of program is a win-win-win proposition from the standpoint of each group involved. Future studies should focus on replicating these findings and testing the degree to which improved coping has an impact on medical outcomes and longer term aspects of adjustment to surgery.

FUTURE DIRECTIONS

I believe that the reminiscence interviews described herein would be effective with different types of patients facing a variety of stressful medical situations. For example, the interviews can be administered to patients who are in different stages of coping with an illness and treatment, such as patients who are receiving chemotherapy or kidney dialysis, or patients who are undergoing rehabilitation after a disabling injury, such as hip fracture. In terms of age groups, although reminiscence appears to be ideally suited to middle-aged and older patients, Borden (1992) has presented clinical vignettes that support the use of life narrative interviews with young adults adjusting to life-threatening illnesses such as AIDS.

Reminiscence interviews can also be modified to suit the situation. For instance, they can be given as a one-shot interview or a series of interviews. A single interview probably serves best when the patient is facing a circumscribed medical procedure, whereas a series of interviews would fit a patient who is undergoing a long-term medical procedure (e.g., kidney dialysis or chemotherapy) that requires an extended coping effort. In addition, the interviewers could be either hospital staff members who address the psychological needs of patients as part of their role (e.g., nurses, recreation therapists, social workers, and psychologists) or volunteers who have an interest in counseling work with patients.

Further studies need to be conducted to determine the efficacy of reminiscence interventions for nonsurgical types of "medi-stress." Currently, in a study funded by the American Cancer Society, a series of three LCI interviews is being provided to lung cancer patients during the first several weeks of a 14-week protocol of combined chemotherapy and radiation therapy. I hypothesized that this extended intervention will have a positive impact on psychological adjustment during the course of medical treatment as well as quality of life after medical treatment. Lastly, to facilitate replication of the intervention described in this chapter, a comprehensive practitioners' guidebook for health care professionals of all disciplines is in preparation (Rybarczyk, in preparation).

Part Four

Applications

How has reminiscence been used in practice and research to date? This section highlights various uses of the life story in different countries, showing the widespread use of the modality.

From Canada, Watt and Cappeliez suggest reminiscence interventions as a treatment for depression. They particularly recommend the use of the integrative and instrumental types of reminiscence. They postulate that the integrative type will help individuals develop a positive picture of themselves, whereas the instrumental style of reminiscence, particularly adaptive coping appraisals, will mediate stress and therefore prevent depression.

From Great Britain, Woods and McKiernan report on the use of reminiscence with people with cognitive deficits. There have been few reports of individual reminiscence work with this population, they state, but the potential is there. Perhaps their contribution and helpful hints will encourage others interested in working with this population.

From Australia, Viney reports on the use of reminiscence in psychotherapy. She describes its power and, with some poignant case studies, shows the way people link past events together to get a clearer picture of themselves. Her incorporation of reminiscence into her practice echoes many of the recommendations made in earlier chapters.

From the United States, Sherman discusses the use of oral reminiscence in groups, advocating the use of written and oral reminiscence together, much as is done in Guided Autobiography described in Chapter 12. Hence, applications and methods agree showing a coming together in the field rather than the years of separateness in the past.

Davis reports on a national volunteer program for reminiscing in the United States directed by the American Association of Retired Persons (AARP). This program uses volunteers and well-thought-out educational materials available from AARP. With these aids, anyone can begin such a program.

Webster and Haight conclude the book by trying to make sense of the past 35 years of research and practice, pointing out differences and similarities . The use of common terms by all future researchers is recommended, and future directions for research are specified.

Chapter 16

Reminiscence Interventions for the Treatment of Depression in Older Adults

Lisa M. Watt
Philippe Cappeliez

DEVELOPMENT OF REMINISCENCE AS A THERAPEUTIC INTERVENTION

Butler's (1963) introduction of the life review concept initiated the now wide-spread interest in the adaptive function of reminiscing in later life (for reviews, see Haight, 1991; Webster & Cappeliez, 1993). According to Butler, a life review follows the onset of a crisis, such as a significant loss or the realization of approaching death. The crisis prompts the resurgence of memories of past experiences, particularly unresolved conflicts. Through reconsideration of these experiences, a revised or expanded understanding of the self and the meaning of one's life may be achieved. Successful reconsideration of the past and its integration into the present are thought to lead ultimately to personality reorganization, characterized by wisdom and serenity, and to greater adaptation to the demands of later life. If the process of life review is unsuccessful, however, individuals may experience guilt, anxiety, and depression. Butler's concept of the life review offers both an explanation for the function of reminiscence in late life and a rationale for the use of reminiscence as a therapeutic intervention for older adults who are experiencing adaptational difficulties. In particular, his formulation suggests that life review can reduce the probability that life crises will trigger depression and anxiety by helping individuals develop a positive view of themselves, their abilities, and the purpose of their life.

Empirical investigations of the adaptive function of reminiscence therapy have focused primarily on samples of nonclinical participants seeking a personal growth experience or nursing home residents presenting some degree of cognitive or physical impairment. These studies provide support both for (e.g., Harp Scates, Randolph, Gutsch, & Knight, 1986–86; Lappe, 1987; Rattenbury & Stones, 1989; Rybarczyk & Auerbach, 1990; Sherman, 1987) and against (e.g., Bender, Cooper, & Howe, 1983; Schafer, Berghorn, Holmes, & Quadagno, 1986) the effectiveness of reminiscence as a clinical intervention. Reminiscence therapy has rarely been studied with focused clinical samples, such as depressed older adults. Niederehe (in press) identified three controlled studies that provided mixed results concerning the effects of reminiscence intervention on depression (Fry, 1983; Goldwasser, Auerbach, & Harkins, 1987; Perotta & Meacham, 1981–82).

The ambiguity concerning the usefulness of reminiscence as a therapeutic modality stems from the lack of a clear specification of the psychological processes involved in reminiscence that contribute to particular adaptive goals, such as the reduction of anxiety, guilt, or depression. As a result, practitioners have implemented unstructured, nonspecific reminiscence interventions with the aim of achieving a wide variety of therapeutic outcomes (e.g., reduced anxiety and depression and increased cognitive functioning, psychological well-being, and life satisfaction). To assess adequately the effectiveness of reminiscence interventions, however, clinicians need to identify the components of the reminiscing process that play a critical role in achieving a specific adaptive goal for a specific clinical problem.

In recent research, Wong and Watt (1991; Watt & Wong, 1991) identified specific reminiscence processes that are associated with adaptation. They conceptualized reminiscence as a multidimensional construct that comprises at least six different types of reminiscence, each of which serves a different adaptive function. Two types of reminiscence—integrative (focused on a constructive reappraisal of the past) and instrumental (centered on memories of past problem-solving experiences and coping activities)—appear to be associated with indices of psychological well-being and mental and physical health. As described by Wong and Watt, the integrative and instrumental types of reminiscence involve cognitive content and processes thought to be related to the onset and maintenance of depression (e.g., self-evaluation, causal attribution for events, appraisal of personal coping resources, and selection of coping strategies). In this chapter, we present a theory supporting the therapeutic value of instrumental and integrative reminiscence for alleviating depression in older adults by integrating our understanding of reminiscence processes with contemporary cognitive models of depression. This fine-grained analysis of the relationship between reminiscence and the relief of depressive symptomatology is aimed at identifying the critical components of an effective reminiscence intervention with depressed older adults. This knowledge will enable evaluation of the effectiveness of reminiscence therapy in reducing depressive symptomatology.

REMINISCENCE AND COGNITIVE MODELS OF DEPRESSION

Cognitive processes have been identified as key players in the etiology, maintenance, and treatment of depression (e.g., Abramson, Alloy, & Metalsky, 1988; Abramson, Seligman, & Teasdale, 1978; Beck, Rush, Shaw, & Emery, 1979; DeRubeis & Beck, 1988; Folkman & Lazarus, 1986). The great variability in emotional response to stressful encounters among individuals underscores the important mediating role of cognitive processes. This variability is thought to result from differences in the way individuals interpret stressful events and evaluate their capacity to deal with them, rather than from the stressfulness of the situation itself (Billings & Moos, 1982; Hammen, 1988). Cognitive theories of depression differ in terms of the cognitive processes they deem to be critical in the development and maintenance of depression. Research that attempts to detail the cognitive appraisals and coping responses that mediate between stressors and depression in the day-to-day adaptational tasks of living (e.g., Folkman & Lazarus, 1986; Rohde, Lewinsohn, Tilson, & Seeley, 1990) offers a useful framework for elucidating the effect of instrumental reminiscence on the alleviation of depression. Models that focus on negative evaluations of the self, the world, and the future (Beck, 1967; Beck et al., 1979) and approaches that emphasize dysfunctional causal attributions for negative events (Abramson et al., 1988) provide tools for understanding the potential impact of integrative reminiscence on the relief of depressive symptomatology.

Instrumental Reminiscence and the Mediation of Depressive Symptomatology: A Stress and Coping Approach

The psychosocial model of depression proposed by Billings and Moos (1982, 1985) is a useful framework for conceptualizing the onset and maintenance of depression (e.g., Cappeliez, 1993). This model assumes that depression results from an interplay involving the situational demands experienced by an individual, the individual's cognitive appraisal of the coping resources available to meet these demands, and the individual's responses to the stressors. When a potentially stressful event is encountered, individuals first evaluate the importance of the event in terms of their own, or important others', well-being. They next evaluate what, if anything, can be done to overcome or prevent harm or to improve the prospects of benefit. These primary and secondary appraisals converge to determine whether the individual regards the person–environment transaction as significant to his or her well-being and, if so, whether it is primarily threatening (containing the possibility of harm or loss) or challenging (holding the possibility of mastery or benefit) (Lazarus & Folkman, 1984). Challenge appraisals (in which individuals see the situation as something they can change or cope with) typically initiate active, problem-focused coping responses, which are associated with freedom or relief from depression in older adults (Cappeliez & Blanchet, 1986; Folkman, Lazarus, Dunkel-Schetter, DeLongis, & Gruen, 1986; Foster & Gallagher, 1986; Fry, 1993; Gerbaux, Vézina, Hardy, & Gendron, 1988; Vézina & Bourque, 1984, 1985). Individuals' appraisals of stressors and their coping responses to them are determined by their personal resources and the resources available in their environment. Personal resources such as self-esteem, self-efficacy, a sense of personal meaning, adaptive beliefs about personal control, and rewarding commitments and values can diminish the probability of depression's developing by reducing the perceived frequency or intensity of stressful situations or by facilitating the use of functional coping strategies (Bandura, 1977; Fry, 1989, 1993; Lazarus & DeLongis, 1983; Pearlin, Lieberman, Menaghen, & Mullen, 1981). In turn, depression can have a negative impact on each of the aforementioned resources.

Instrumental reminiscence involves recollections of past coping activities, including memories of plans developed to solve difficult situations, goal-directed activities, and the achievement of one's own goals or goals one helped others meet (Watt & Wong, 1991; Wong & Watt, 1991). Recollection of instrumental memories can help depressed clients to (a) recognize and develop coping resources that have been identified as important aspects of adaptive coping with depression (e.g., self-esteem, self-efficacy, and positive control beliefs); (b) implement coping strategies that promote challenge-oriented appraisals and an active, problem-focused approach to current problem-solving; and (c) identify concrete, specific coping strategies that have been effective in the past and may be productively applied to current stressors (e.g., seeking social support in times of crisis).

Coping Resources   Self-esteem and efficacy/control beliefs are personal resources that play an important role in the coping process because they support people's belief that they can control or deal effectively with ongoing stressors. When individuals believe they are capable of managing negative events in their environment, they are less likely to appraise these events as threatening and more likely to appraise them as challenges that can be coped with effectively (Lazarus & Folkman, 1984). These challenge-oriented appraisals lead individuals to take active, problem-focused approaches to alter situations. For example, in a study of community-dwelling elders, Fry (1993) found that perceptions of self-efficacy lead to greater problem-solving initiatives and integration of social support, moderating the effects of negative experiences. In contrast, low perceived self-efficacy and self-esteem have been found to be negatively related to psychological adjustment and effective coping (Abler & Fretz, 1988; Holahan & Holahan, 1987; Taylor, 1983; Woodward & Wallston, 1987). When individuals believe they are unable to deal effectively with a difficult experience, they typically view the stressor as a threat and use escape or avoidant coping activities, such as wishing the problem would disappear. Through their impact on adaptive coping, self-esteem and efficacy/control beliefs serve to mediate between the experience of stress and the onset of depression (Billings & Moos, 1982, 1985; Cappeliez, 1993).

Instrumental reminiscence may exert a positive effect on individuals' self-esteem and efficacy/control beliefs via recall of mastery experiences in which the individuals acted effectively and competently to control their environment. This goal may be obtained by recalling episodes of successful past coping, with a focus on individuals' crucial contribution to the achievement. For example, individuals may recall times when they responded efficiently to a crisis, such as an illness in the family, or when they developed solutions to long-term stressors, such as being denied the opportunity to pursue educational ambitions because of financial hardship. The concrete and vivid nature of these memories may have a greater impact on people's perceptions of their control/efficacy and self-esteem, as well as their subsequent behaviors, than do abstract discussions about level of control and how to exert it.

Appraisal Strategies In addition to promoting positive control and self-efficacy beliefs, instrumental reminiscence can foster adaptive coping in that memories may be used to highlight specific strategies that promote challenge appraisals and an active, problem-focused approach to coping. Through this process, individuals can rediscover important coping strategies within their own experience. For example, a major feature of adaptive coping is to renounce or relegate to the periphery of importance those roles and commitments that are no longer rewarding and to invest in other roles more in tune with one's current conditions of living (Pearlin, 1980). Throughout life, failed ambitions and dreams, changes in the environment in which one acts, and changes in energy and resources available to a one necessitate major shifts in long-standing commitments. If these changes in priority are not accomplished when they are required, individuals may continue to struggle without reward, experiencing a loss of morale and reductions in adaptation (Lazarus & DeLongis, 1983). The importance of taking stock of past roles and commitments and reevaluating them in the light of present circumstances to identify the appropriate goal in a current coping episode can be highlighted and reinforced in examples of past successful coping recalled by the client.

Other problem-solving skills that promote challenge appraisals and an active, problem-focused orientation to coping may also be illustrated through the client's own recollections. For example, defining the aspects of a stressful situation that can be changed and those that cannot, brainstorming alternative solutions to problems, and deciding on an appropriate solution are all essential features of coping that individuals can recognize in themselves through reminiscence. Nezu, Nezu, and Perri (1989) have presented guidelines for the use of problem-solving therapy for depression, and these guidelines can be adapted for the work with reminiscence. By illustrating the importance of identifying the possibilities for change and adaptation that exist in a stressful situation and the development of appropriate and meaningful goals in coping activities, instrumental memories make stressors manageable. The threatening and overwhelming nature of stressors is thus reduced, enabling clients to address negative experiences with a challenge orientation and a dynamic approach to problem solving.

Coping Responses Instrumental reminiscence can have a positive impact on current coping practices by influencing the type of coping responses that are selected. Recent research indicates that older adults who successfully cope with depression use an active, problem-solving approach (Cappeliez & Blanchet, 1986; Foster & Gallagher, 1986; Fry, 1993; Gerbaux et al., 1988; Vézina & Bourque, 1984, 1985). Folkman and Lazarus (1986) described problem-focused coping as a strategy that involves the individual in a deliberate goal-oriented effort to alter the situation (e.g., "I knew what had to be done, so I doubled my efforts to make things work"), coupled with an analytic approach to solving the problem (e.g., "I made a plan of action and followed it" or "I came up with a couple of different solutions to the problem"). Instrumental reminiscence, with its focus on the recall of successful problem-solving strategies used in the past that can be applied to current problematic situations, encourages individuals to use the active, problem-focused coping responses that have been identified as antidepressive.

In addition to focusing the individual on doing something to alter the situation, recollection of past, effective strategies provides the individual with specific strategies to apply. For example, an individual may recall bartering his or her services during the Great Depression and subsequently implement this problem-solving activity as a viable solution to a current reduction in income due to retirement. Furthermore, reviewing past coping activities normalizes the experience of environmental stressors and the requirement that they be coped with as a continuous process in which clients have participated successfully throughout life. The idea that coping is an expected part of living gives some meaning to coping efforts and is likely to initiate more active and less avoidant coping activities (Wong, 1989). In addition to encouraging problem-focused coping activities and appropriate goal setting, successful application of past problem-solving skills should also contribute to an enhanced sense of control and self-esteem as individuals gain evidence of their current ability to act effectively. Thus, application of these skills promotes self-esteem and personal control, which, in turn, encourage positive, challenge-oriented appraisals and more problem-focused and less escape–avoidance coping responses, thereby resulting in the creation of a positive feedback loop. Fry (1989, 1993) has provided support for this conjecture in a demonstration of reciprocal influences between engagement in problem solving and self-efficacy. Casey and Grant (1993) have also noted that reminiscence that focuses on valuable accomplishments can help individuals regain a sense of control, purpose, and self-efficacy in the present.

Integrative Reminiscence and the Mediation of Depressive Symptomatology: A Cognitive Approach

From a cognitive perspective, patterns of thinking that predispose individuals to depression are formed early in life, and derive from personal experiences, identification with important others, and perceptions of the attitudes of other people toward the self (Beck, 1967; Beck & Greenberg, 1986; Beck et al., 1979). Early interactions that emphasize rigid and perfectionistic achievement and reinforce the importance of others' evaluation of one's personal worth are thought to predispose individuals to develop limited sources of self-worth and an over-reliance on external feedback for feelings of self-esteem. In this environment, individuals learn to judge themselves harshly and interpret frustrations, failures, and losses as evidence of negative characteristics such as unworthiness or ineptitude. The self-critical judgments crystallize into core dysfunctional beliefs, such as "I am unlovable" or "I am incapable." These latent depressogenic belief systems are typically activated by situations analogous to the experience responsible for embedding a negative belief (e.g., failure or loss). When the schema is activated, the propensity toward self-criticism and self-evaluation based on external standards dominates individuals' thinking, leading to the systematic interpretation of circumstances in a negative way, even when more plausible explanations are available or evidence contradicting the negative interpretation exists. As part of this process of negative interpretation, individuals make logical errors in the conceptualization of experience; for example, they overgeneralize from a single negative incident or selectively attend to a negative detail and ignore any positive aspects of a situation (Beck, 1967; Beck & Greenberg, 1986; Beck et al., 1979). Each cognitive error and distortion confirm the negative schema, precipitating a downward spiral in which the person's thinking style becomes less differentiated and the person is less and less able to explore alternative, more adaptive explanations for life events. Eventually, individuals vulnerable to depression lose the ability to view their negative thoughts with objectivity, and three main cognitive patterns are activated that cause individuals to see themselves ("I am worthless"), their world ("Life is miserable"), and their future ("It is hopeless") in a negative manner. Depressive symptoms such as social withdrawal, sadness, and loss of motivation and interest are considered to be the consequences of the activation of the negative cognitive triad (Beck, 1967; Beck & Greenberg, 1986; Beck et al., 1979).

Like Beck's (1967) model of depression, the hopelessness paradigm (Alloy, Hartlage, & Abramson, 1988) is a diathesis–stress model that proposes that depression results from the interaction between negative life experiences and inter-pretations of those events. From this perspective, an expectation of hopeless-ness—the belief that highly aversive outcomes are probable and no response can be made to alter their probability—is viewed as the primary cause of depression. This hopelessness develops as a result of attributing the occurrence of important negative life events to stable, global causes. An individual who consistently applies these attributions of causality will develop hopelessness and depressive symptoms when confronted with negative experiences (Abramson et al., 1978; Alloy et al., 1988).

The primary goal of the cognitive treatment of depression is to train clients to alter the thoughts that maintain their depressed mood and lie beneath their lack of motivation, low activity level, and other symptoms (Beck & Greenberg, 1986). A variety of cognitive and behavioral techniques are used to achieve this end, including activity scheduling; disconfirmation of distorted views of the self that support the negative cognitive and behavioral set; analysis and modification of maladaptive beliefs and assumptions about the world; and a balanced, realistic reattribution of responsibility in situations of client self-blame and self-criticism (Beck, 1967; Beck & Greenberg, 1986; Beck et al., 1979).

Integrative reminiscence is similar to a successful life review as described by Butler (1963). It is a process of self-discovery in which individuals attempt to accept negative events in the past, resolve past conflicts, and reconcile the discrepancy between the ideal and reality (J. E. Birren, 1964; Lieberman & Tobin, 1983). Furthermore, it is aimed at helping people identify a pattern of continuity between the past and present (Lieberman & Tobin, 1983) and find meaning and worth in their life as they lived it (Butler, 1963; Erikson, 1980; Wong, 1989). Like cognitive therapy, integrative reminiscence deals with individuals' beliefs about themselves, their attitudes toward and assumptions about the world, and the attributions they make about the causes of the nega-tive events in their life. As such, integrative recollections deal directly with the negative thoughts and schematic information-processing styles that support the negative mood and behavioral symptoms of depression. Distorted views of the self and the tacit rules for the interpretation of experience that are con-tained in individuals' schemas are modified through the reconstructive nature of integrative reminiscence processes. Integrative recollections do not involve simple recall of bygone events; rather, past experiences are endowed with meaning and significance as a result of interpretation of those events in the light of current knowledge, perspective, and concerns (e.g., Webster & Young, 1988; Yang & Rehm, 1993). Past unresolved experiences of failure or loss and negative conclusions about the self and the future can thus be reinterpreted in an adaptive fashion within the context of evidence that disconfirms negative beliefs and through application of information-processing strategies that em-phasize positive interpretations of events.

Disconfirmation of Negative Self-Beliefs   The life review provides the client with the opportunity to examine evidence that may disconfirm negative self-evaluations associated with depression. To counteract the tendency of many depressed persons to ignore major pieces of information and center on those that support their dysfunctional views, the therapist can help these clients seek fuller, more detailed accounts of events and correspondingly fuller interpretations to help them structure alternative ways of perceiving past events. As individuals review both good and bad experiences within the context of their entire lifetime, the negative impact of any given hardship, failure to act at an optimal level, or negative comparison with others may be dispersed by recognition of good actions taken and happy events experienced. Both the sheer number of positive and negative experiences that fill the life span, and the fact that failures in one domain, such as career, may be offset by accomplishments in another arena, such as family life, reduce the probability of the client's committing cognitive errors such as selective abstraction and magnification/minimization. Individuals may thus disconfirm global, negative evaluations of the self that are associated with depression and begin to develop a realistic, adaptive view of the self that incorporates both positive and negative attributes. Furthermore, recollection of difficult past experiences that have been resolved over time can also provide concrete evidence that challenges the depressed individual's belief in his or her negative qualities and the hopeless attitude that circumstances will never improve or be resolved in the future.

Development of Alternative Explanations for Self-Blame and Self-Criticism
In addition to disconfirming clients' negative beliefs about themselves and the future, integrative reminiscence can interrupt the systematic interpretation of events in a negative fashion that results when depressogenic schemata are activated. In particular, integrative reminiscence provides the opportunity for a balanced, realistic reattribution of responsibility in situations of self-blame and self-criticism.

Individuals develop beliefs about their own worth that are based on evaluations of how responsibly and appropriately they have acted. These moral evaluations are concerned with whether one did what one ought to have done in a given circumstance, and stand in contrast to causal evaluations, which involve examining why events occurred (Brewin, 1986). Integrative reminiscence engages moral evaluations as individuals question the appropriateness of their actions when they attempt to reconcile guilt and blame associated with past conflicts and wrongdoings and attempt to come to terms with the discrepancy between the ideal and the real self (J. E. Birren & Hedlund, 1987; Butler, 1974).

Social comparison has also been identified in the literature as an important source of self-evaluation (Festinger, 1954). Social comparison involves an evaluation of whether one measures up to the abilities observed in others and whether one experiences more negative events than others because of one's own personal failings (e.g., Lewinsohn, Mischel, Chaplain, & Barton, 1980). Comparisons of the self against others are made during integrative reminiscence when individuals try to measure the impact of their accomplishments and understand the meaning of negative events in their lives (Butler, 1974). In addition, integrative reminiscence addresses social comparisons during the resolution of conflicts, such as jealousy, within relationships. To the extent that these experiences remain unresolved, they will contribute to the client's negative view of him- or herself. Furthermore, attribution of the causes of these experiences to stable and global factors will increase the likelihood that the client will form an expectation of hopelessness and hence depression (Alloy et al., 1988).

Integrative reminiscence gives clients the opportunity to review the causes and consequences of many negative events they have experienced during their lifetimes. From a nonjudgmental, middle-ground position, they can be prompted to identify their spontaneous attributions as well as alternative attributions. The life review format provides some distancing from the personal and often emotionally charged material and locates the life story within its historical context. This distance may permit individuals to think in a relativistic fashion about their actions and accomplishments. Negative social comparisons and moral evaluations may be short-circuited by recognition of mediating factors that may have led to differential experiences for each individual. For example, an elderly woman may ascribe her failure to obtain a teaching position to the difficult economic times experienced during the Great Depression, rather than to personal failings or to the "fact" that others always get better breaks than she. The different temporal and contextual guidelines provided by the life review may afford elderly individuals the opportunity to reinterpret their experiences without making negative personal or social judgments (Blanchard-Fields, 1990; Labouvie-Vief, 1982; Labouvie-Vief, Hakim-Larson, Devoe, & Schoeberlein, 1989; Webster & Young, 1988). In other words, individuals engage in the developoment of a new set of beliefs about themselves that are less absolutistic and reflect openness to alternative explanations (Riegel, 1973, 1975).

Identification of Internal Guidelines for the Evaluation of Self-Worth One factor that has been identified as contributing to a vulnerability to depression is the reliance on external sources of information about self-worth (Beck & Greenberg, 1986). To the extent that individuals fail to develop internal guidelines for determining their success and value, their sense of self remains fragile and vulnerable to changing circumstances. The life review process invites an interpretation of experience that is dynamic; participatory; and governed by standards that reflect personal interests, motivations, and philosophies. The life review provides a forum for individuals to interpret life according to their own emerging standards. As clients weave the stories of their lives, they reinterpret episodes in terms of the meaning they hold for them, rather than whether they are objectively right or wrong, good or bad (Bruner, 1986; Gergen & Gergen, 1986). For example, the failure to act effectively to avoid an accident may be taken as a learning experience that has stood the person in good stead over the years. A divorce may be interpreted as the impetus that led to a voyage of self-discovery for the individual. In both cases, the ability to view the events of the past from the perspective of their role in the life story provides the individual with alternatives to self-recrimination and unfavorable comparison with others. Through the development of a set of subjective, self-affirming assumptions, the individual is able to reinterpret his or her experience in terms of its personal meaning and significance, rather than its negative reflection on the self (Labouvie-Vief, 1982; Labouvie-Vief et al., 1989).

Development of Sources of Self-Worth   A restricted number of sources of self-worth is another vulnerability factor for the development of depression. In particular, early interactions focusing on rigid and perfectionistic achievement predispose individuals to regard achievement as the central source of self-worth and self-esteem. The drive toward identifying meaning in life that is one of the hallmarks of integrative reminiscence may provide individuals who are vulnerable to depression with additional sources of self-worth, thereby providing them with increased protection against the onset of depression. For example, Butler (1963) emphasized that sources of self-esteem and self-worth such as the development of personal values and commitments, the identification of spiritual or philosophical meaning, and the recognition of one's place in intergenerational continuity are outcomes of a successful life review.

CONCLUSION

By integrating our understanding of reminiscence processes with contemporary cognitive models of depression, we have presented a theory supporting the therapeutic value of reminiscence for the alleviation of depression in older adults. Two types of reminiscence—integrative (focused on a constructive reappraisal of the past) and instrumental (centered on memories of past problem-solving experiences and coping activities)—appear to have promise as effective therapeutic approaches with depressed older adults. In particular, we have identified the use of adaptive coping appraisals and strategies that are thought to mediate between the experience of stress and the development of depression as a key therapeutic component of instrumental reminiscence. Elements of integrative reminiscence that may play a role in recovery from depression center on the development of positive beliefs about the self and attributions about one's role in negative events. This model provides a framework for both the development of effective clinical interventions and the evaluation of the hypothesized links between reminiscence therapy and alleviation of depressive symptomatology. We are currently testing these links in a controlled prospective study of the impact of integrative and instrumental reminiscence on the relief of depression in older adults.

In addition to the specific therapeutic benefits offered by instrumental and integrative reminiscence, the use of memories as a therapeutic modality per se may be particularly beneficial to depressed older clients for several reasons. First, reminiscing is a familiar activity to older adults, and therefore the use of personal recollections as a forum for therapeutic work may be less threatening and more appealing than other forms of therapy. Second, the use of personal memories provides older clients with the sense that their experience is important to their current adaptation—that relief from depression does not require them to abandon the past and learn new approaches to living that are not consonant with their experience. Rather, clients are provided with a sense of normalcy and competency through the use and analysis of their own experience. Finally, the focus on reestablishing a positive view of the past provides clients with feelings of self-worth and self-esteem as they begin to accept, respect, and enjoy what they have been and done in their lifetime. It is likely that the combination of a nonthreatening approach and the promotion of a sense of normalcy, competence, and esteem within the therapeutic relationship will promote increased commitment and motivation to participate in therapy, setting the stage for acceptance and implementation of the particular therapeutic strategies offered by integrative and instrumental reminiscence.

Chapter 17

Evaluating the Impact of Reminiscence on Older People with Dementia

Bob Woods
Fionnuala McKiernan

Dementia refers to a global decline in cognitive abilities, self-care functioning, judgment, and day-to-day living skills. It is thought to arise from a number of conditions, most notably Alzheimer's disease and multi-infarct dementia. Increasingly these categories are being refined, reflecting for example, that what we have in recent years considered to be Alzheimer's disease has included a substantial number of people suffering from other conditions, such as Lewy body disease. The dementias have an increasing prevalence with age, so that whereas 5% of the over-65 years age group might suffer from some form of dementia, this figure increases dramatically to around 20% of the over-80 group. Dementias are usually characterized as progressive, with memory difficulty the first, early, insidious indications that something is amiss. A person with severe dementia usually needs a massive input of care and supervision, with communication extremely difficult. We are thus considering in this chapter a number of related, but different conditions, with further individual differences in the degree of severity of the condition. We should also add that, as Kitwood (1990) has eloquently pointed out, what is seen in dementia is an interaction between the changes in the person's brain that relate to the underlying condition and important factors in the physical and social environment surrounding the person; for example, an unstimulating or, worse, devaluing environment might reduce the function of a person with dementia to an even lower level than his or her neurological impairment would dictate. When readers are considering the impact of reminiscence on people suffering from dementia, they need to keep these individual differences in mind and consider both the severity of the person's condition and the environmental context in which he or she functions.

Reminiscence work makes intuitive sense to those providing care for people with dementia in the earlier stages, because in the early stages it is often noted that the person's recent memory is more obviously impaired than his or her memory for the past. Thus the person will not remember what he or she ate for breakfast but will apparently recall clearly events from childhood. Detailed investigations of memory functioning in people with Alzheimer's disease have, perhaps surprisingly, not identified a particular sparing of retrieval from remote memory (Morris & Kopelman, 1986). However, personal memories may be somewhat more accessible than the relatively neutral events and items assessed in tests of remote memory. They are more likely to have been rehearsed and reconstructed on a number of occasions during the person's life; they are more likely to have strong affective associations, enhancing their memorability; and some personal memories may have been so thoroughly learned that they have become part of the person's automatic function (e.g., the person's name or well-rehearsed songs and rhymes). It is also clear from the research on Alzheimer's disease that retrieval is often enhanced by offering the person appropriate cues or prompts, and this may offer another avenue for assisting the person with dementia to reminisce.

In evaluations of reminiscence work, the effects on the care provider as well as on the dementia sufferer should be considered. Most older people with dementia live at home, often being cared for by their spouse, an adult child, or other relative. Few studies have examined the effect of reminiscence work on family members (Davies, 1981, being an exception). Some professionals providing care in day-care and residential care settings have shown a hunger for therapies that they can use with people with dementia, perhaps as a way of staving off their feelings of powerlessness in dealing with a progressive, deteriorating condition. This has led to enthusiasm for approaches such as reality orientation (Holden & Woods, 1988) and validation therapy (Feil, 1993) as well as reminiscence work. The extent to which these and other strategies bring about significant lasting changes in staff behavior and attitudes is of considerable interest. There is concern that at times these approaches are taken up with rather more enthusiasm than skill and knowledge, leading to demoralization of staff as their high expectations are quickly dashed. It is important, then, to evaluate carefully what has actually been carried out in the implementation of any such program in working with people with dementia, as there is great variation in approach.

Although there are a few reports of individual reminiscence work with people with dementia (Woods, Portnoy, Head, & Jones, 1992; Gibson, 1994), group applications have been the norm to date, so our focus here is mainly on group reminiscence work. Thornton and Brotchie's (1987) review of the reminiscence literature identified only two published studies investigating the use of reminiscence with people with dementia (Kiernat, 1979; Baines, Saxby, & Ehlert, 1987). Although there have been some studies since, it is important to emphasize that this literature is at an early stage of development and that a great deal of discussion is based on anecdotal accounts as much as empirical data. The positive nature of these qualitative accounts is encouraging in the development of this work.

Some researchers have argued that reminiscence work is inappropriate for those with a dementia. For example, Burnside (1978) suggested that its reliance on verbal content and lack of structure make reminiscence unsuitable for these clients. It is unclear whether the relative scarcity of work in this area implies that such a view has become pervasive; difficulties in evaluation have probably also contributed to the lack of evaluative studies.

EMPIRICAL STUDIES

In an early published study, Kiernat (1979) evaluated the effects of a group reminiscence activity on three groups of nursing home residents ($N = 23$) over a 10-week period. Residents were offered 20 sessions that lasted 45 min to an hour. Attendance was quite variable, and slightly less than half of the sample attended three fourths or more of the sessions. Interestingly, it was these frequent attenders who showed most improvement on a rating scale of behavior in the nursing home. Methodological difficulties make it difficult to draw conclusions from this study, but it is worth noting that qualitative records taken during the groups showed that many group members enjoyed and responded to the activity, with a number showing behavioral improvements during the time. Group members gradually began to address one another and respond spontaneously, as opposed to communicating only with staff. Two of the three nursing homes continued the groups after the study ended. There seemed to be a suggestion that some individuals responded better than others.

In a controlled study, Goldwasser, Auerbach, and Harkins (1987) compared the effects of reminiscence group therapy and supportive group therapy with a no-treatment control condition. There were 9 nursing home residents with a clinical diagnosis of dementia in each group. The range of impairment was broad. The therapy groups met twice weekly for 30 min for 5 weeks. The reminiscence group had a schedule of topics from the past, whereas the supportive group therapy focused on current or future events and issues. The results showed no significant changes on measures of behavioral or cognitive functioning, although there was a tendency for the reminiscence group's scores on the Mini-Mental State Examination to improve immediately after the intervention and to have decreased slightly at follow-up; the other two groups showed less change. For the reminiscence group, there was a significant improvement in scores on the Beck Depression Inventory immediately after the intervention, with a sharp decline at follow-up 6 weeks later. The other two groups showed little change. The initial depression scores for the reminiscence group were higher than those of the other two groups, which did allow more room for improvement. At a qualitative level, Goldwasser et al. reported the positive impact on group members of finding that they had common experiences and histories, and described how this enhanced mutual support and respect. They suggested that this may have contributed to the decrease in negative affect.

A number of other important issues are also raised by Goldwasser et al.'s (1987) study. The relatively short-term effect seen in the reminiscence group and its sharp decline at follow-up suggest that such groups may need to be im-plemented on an ongoing basis if they are to be beneficial. Subjective reports indicated that those who responded most to the reminiscence work were the less impaired subjects; the effects on those with severe impairment were reported to be more limited. In addition, the less impaired residents sometimes resented being included with the more impaired, an issue requiring further investigation. Gold-wasser et al. also suggested that short-term subtle mood changes after particular sessions deserved further investigation and may help to elucidate the effects of different components of the intervention, including different topic areas.

Baines et al. (1987) compared the effects of reminiscence and reality orienta-tion in a controlled study of 15 confused older people in a residential setting. A crossover design was used for the two experimental groups, and, in addition, there was an untreated control group. The effects of the group work on staff were measured in addition to those on the residents' cognitive and behavioral function. The participants were described as having a moderate to severe degree of cogni-tive impairment. In each treatment condition, groups were held for a half hour a day for 4 weeks.

The attendance rates were high for both groups, and the authors gained the qualitative impression that residents found them to be enjoyable and stimulating. As membership became more established, an increase in spontaneity and expres-sion of emotion was noted. The most significant effects on behavioral and cogni-tive measures overall were found for the group who attended a reality orientation session first, followed by a reminiscence session. However, both therapy groups showed less decline in mental ability scores than did the nonintervention group over the 4-month period of the study. Other differences between the three groups were not significant at this point.

The most important finding of Baines et al.'s (1987) study, however, is the effects of the group work on staff. Both the reminiscence and reality orientation intervention groups were associated with a significant increase in staff knowledge of the participants' personal histories. The groups were also continued spontane-ously by the units, showing evidence of a positive effect on staff enthusiasm in the longer term. Clearly, if such group work does have a positive effect on staff attitudes and job satisfaction, which have implications for the residents' quality of life, this may be a particularly important outcome. There was the further interesting indication that the positive effects on intervention group members may have rubbed off on roommates who were in the no-treatment control group. This may have limited the size of the intervention effect, but, more important, may suggest that reminiscence work may enhance the social environment of the setting.

Clearly, Baines et al.'s (1987) study does not provide specific evidence of the positive effects of reminiscence for older confused people, because similar results were obtained for the reality orientation group. Indeed, the group who received reality orientation before reminiscence appeared to do better than the group who received the two interventions in the reverse order. However, this finding might have been due to differences between the groups; there is clearly a need for replication of this work. The notion that reminiscence work may have more impact if preceded by reality orientation is interesting, but needs further exploration.

In another comparative study, Head, Portnoy, and Woods (1990) contrasted the effectiveness of reminiscence work with that of alternative group activities for people with dementia in two different settings. Their results showed that the interventions had quite different impacts on the staff and participants at each setting. The groups differed in membership and approach, but whereas in a hospital setting there was a significant increase in contributions made by group members during reminiscence compared with the other group activities offered, there was no such difference between the number of contributions made during the two activities in a community setting. The latter setting was a specialist day center which seemed to provide a generally more stimulating environment than the activity center in a large geriatric hospital provided. Head et al. suggested that in the community center there was stronger competition from the alternative activities, which tended to engage participants much more than those offered in the hospital setting. Similarly, the effects on staff were significant only in the hospital setting, where there was a gradual increase in the number of times a staff member addressed the older people and a corresponding decline in communications with other members of staff, which had predominated initially. It would appear that the impact of reminiscence group work needs to be evaluated within the context in which it is carried out. Goldwasser et al. (1987) suggested that reminiscence may have a particularly positive and powerful impact in institutional settings where people may lack a sense of their own identity and value, and the results from Head et al.'s study lend some support to this view.

Bender (1994) has been working on providing reminiscence group work for people with severe dementia over some years. In the context of this program, McKiernan and Yardley (1991) reported on the results of three of these groups in three different settings: a long-stay ward in a traditional psychiatric hospital, a long-stay ward in a community hospital, and a community day hospital. Each group was composed of 6 members with dementia, and the staff to client ratio was

1:2. Generally, the degree of disability was very severe, with the day patients being slightly less impaired. Group members had considerable difficulty under-standing and expressing themselves verbally. Thus the membership of these groups, in contrast with that of the other studies described, was composed much more of people with very severe deficits. In Table 1, the average total level of engagement for each group during reminiscence intervention is compared with the average engagement levels for the group members on their unit at the same time on a day when a reminiscence group was not operating.

As Table 1 indicates, the levels of engagement were statistically significantly higher within the groups than on the ward. Clearly, people with even a very severe degree of cognitive deficit can become engaged in, and involved with, a complex verbal group activity. Whatever the specific effects of reminiscence, there seems little doubt that it can provide a meaningful, appropriate, and stimulating activity for people with even very severe impairment. The attendance rates (97%, 96%, and 86% for the long-stay ward in the traditional hospital, the long-stay ward in the community hospital, and the community day hospital, respectively) provide indirect evidence of members' interest in the group work. However, again, it is in the qualitative data that the most striking effects emerge. One woman, for exam-ple, in making unexpected and spontaneous contributions to the group, demon-strated a wicked sense of humor that had not been observed previously.

Morton and Bleathman (1991) used reminiscence therapy groups as a com-parison in their evaluation of validation therapy. After a 10-week baseline period, 20 weeks of validation group work were followed by 10 weeks of reminiscence therapy. Both groups were held for 1 hr weekly, and the 5 participants were studied individually, although only 3 residents completed the study. Analysis of verbal interactions for 1 hr in the afternoon after group sessions showed an interesting pattern. Two of the 3 residents showed an increase in postsession verbal interaction during the validation therapy period and a decline in the remi-niscence period, whereas for the other subject, the opposite occurred. Morton and Bleathman suggested that this indicates that both approaches may be differentially effective for different individuals. Such comparisons between different group work approaches would be useful, but at present we are only beginning to scratch the surface of this area.

Table 1   Levels of Engagement of Patients with Severe Dementia in Reminiscence Groups and in Normal Ward Activities at Three Settings

Activity	Group 1: Traditional psychiatric hospital long-stay ward	Group 2: Community hospital long-stay ward	Group 3: Community day hospital
Reminiscence group	72%	63%	80%
Ward	29%	39%	33%

In an invaluable account, Gibson (1994) reported the effects of "general" reminiscence work in groups of 6–10 people in four residential homes and two day centers. Twenty-five groups were studied in total. Some groups were specifically for people with a dementia, and others included people with dementia together with people without cognitive impairment. Written and tape-recorded records of group sessions were analyzed. These indicated that in mixed groups, people with dementia showed pleasure and enjoyment and the difficult behavior they exhibited outside the group was rarely seen within the group. The effects on some individuals outside the group, as recorded by staff, included reduced restlessness and agitation and improved appetite. In those groups that included only people with dementia, communication tended to be between the facilitators and members rather than between members. Large, unstructured groups of people with dementia did not show much response; small groups seemed to be much more effective. Although the detailed reactions of the unimpaired members of the mixed groups were not reported, these individuals were described as tolerant of and encouraging to those with dementia; to some extent, the reaction may depend on the degree of impairment of the person with dementia.

Gibson (1994) went on to report the effects of individual reminiscence work with people with dementia in a series of five case studies. Nursing homes were asked to select particularly "troubled or troubling" residents for the study. Eight stages of work were involved: obtaining the support of management; identifying the person; observing; compiling a detailed life history; planning the special work, including a care plan; implementing the plan, evaluating the outcomes, and continuing the work and generalizing from it.

Detailed personal histories were obtained from various sources and used in a practical and very individual way, on the basis of the results of Gibson's initial work. The aim was to use "life-history as a working tool to enrich the quality of social exchange in the present" (Gibson, 1994, p. 58). For example, relevant trips and activities were planned and opportunities for meaningful social interaction increased. The environment was individualized according to the person's style. The effects on the individuals included increased sociability and decreased aggression and demanding behavior.

Staff were also very positive about the impact of the work, and changes in behavior and attitude were noted. The work seemed to bring out the "personhood" of each individual and demanded a personal response from the staff. The potential of this individual work merits further exploration. Gibson (1994) suggested that such work requires a degree of careful planning and thought beyond that required for reminiscence work generally.

INTEGRATION AND CONCLUSIONS

It seems from the literature that research on the effectiveness of reminiscence for people with dementia remains at an early stage. However, it does seem clear that people with even severe dementia can be stimulated by reminiscence work both on a group and on an individual basis. The literature does not support the view that reminiscence is inappropriate for those who have a degree of memory impairment. However, whether the impact of reminiscence work is due to the specific effect of reminiscence, as opposed to a more general effect of participation in a structured, appropriate, stimulating activity, remains to be established. The beneficial impact on staff may be the path by which the most beneficial results accrue to the long-term quality of the client's life. There is clear evidence that staff change their behavior in response to the experience of participating in reminiscence work. In two of the studies reviewed, the staff spontaneously continued the groups initiated by the researchers. It appears that this type of work creates a degree of enthusiasm in staff and has a face validity that enables it to continue. The possible carryover effect from participants to nonparticipants sharing their setting, observed by Baines et al. (1987) is an interesting possibility that could be investigated further.

The importance of context in the evaluation of the effects of reminiscence work cannot be underestimated. It appears from Head et al.'s (1990) study that the impact of reminiscence work differs according to the setting. It may be that the therapeutic potential of reminiscence is greater in an institutionalized and im-poverished setting where residents have greater need to remind themselves of their identities and their past lives and require activities that help them do so.

Closely related is the question of whether reminiscence may in fact be considered to be a therapy. Bender (1994) made some interesting contributions to this debate. He argued that reminiscence work cannot be viewed as therapy because it does not meet a number of criteria for therapy in its more formal sense. However, he considered the benefits of its nontherapy effects, including stimula-tion, enjoyment, and rehabilitation of communication and social skills to be extremely useful and significant. He also proposed that reminiscence work should be seen as a means to various ends, for example, stimulation or therapeutic goals such as repairing damaged identities, rather than as an end in itself. This seems to us to be a constructive view that opens up the area and places the perhaps sterile question as to whether reminiscence is in fact a therapy in its rightful place.

However, the question remains as to the beneficial effects that reminiscence work may have under certain conditions. It seems to have the potential to have a positive effect on participants' lives, at least for a brief period. Although there does not appear to be a strong case for proposing reminiscence work as a therapy in its own right, it may be an important activity with therapeutic potential, particularly for those in poorer quality environments. Evidence of the impact of individual reminiscence work is difficult to find, but the potential highlighted by Gibson (1994) seems exciting. The most therapeutic work may indeed occur on an individual basis, through the medium of working on the individual's life history (cf. Woods et al., 1992). This should be distinguished from life review therapy in that it does not necessarily involve the evaluative aspect that is central to the life review process. Life history work with people with dementia focuses not so much on changing the person's view of him- or herself, but on helping caregivers to see the whole person, "within the perspective of a whole long life and not just as they were in the present, demented, difficult and often demanding" (Gibson, p. 58). The pathway to change is then through changing the caregiver's perception of the person with dementia, in the hope that this change will lead to change in the caregiver's behavior toward and interactions with the person. As Gibson illustrated, changes in caregivers' perceptions may have profound effects on the quality of life of the individual person with dementia.

PRACTICAL ISSUES AND APPLICATIONS

In a number of the articles reviewed herein, the authors suggested important practical considerations for running reminiscence groups for people with dementia. The guidelines presented in this section are based on the suggestions of Head et al. (1990) and McKiernan and Yardley (1991). In many ways, group work with people with severe cognitive impairment does not differ from any other form of group work. However, there does seem to be some agreement as to the importance of certain practical considerations for such groups. McKiernan and Yardley suggested that these considerations are important, first, because of the need for stimuli to be powerful enough to overcome the limitations on information processing that result from cognitive deficits, and, second, because of the high level of anxiety in people who are having great difficulty making sense of their world, particularly when faced with in a new situation. Staff may also experience this anxiety in what may be new circumstances with new expectations. Most of the following points attempt to address these two factors.

1 Careful planning for the full number of sessions and in detail for each session is essential.

2 A participant:facilitator ratio of 2:1 is required if the quality of the activity is to be maintained in groups in which the level of impairment is severe. Normally, a group would have two to six members.

3 The facilitators, the seating, the setting, and the routine of the meetings should remain consistent throughout the life of the group to maximize the chances of establishing a group identity.

4 Multisensory triggers, such as objects, activities, and particularly music, seem much more effective than more abstract materials such as photographs and slides. Too many stimuli may be counterproductive.

5 Ideally, the triggers are of specific relevance to participants' personal histories. To this end, a personal history for each participant should be collected as part of the preliminary planning.

6 The length of sessions should not be too long. Generally, 30–40 min is adequate. Long sessions can become aversive to clients.

7 A presession cup of tea or coffee can serve an important function in settling people down and orienting them to the group.

8 Sufficient time for staff briefing and debriefing is particularly important for such groups, which place emotionally taxing demands on group workers.

9 Advance staff training that focuses on some of the issues of clients with cognitive deficits and of group work in general may decrease anxiety in staff. However, Bender (1994) argued that on-the-job training and supervision are most effective for this type of specialized work.

10 Elderly people with sensory problems such as severe hearing loss or visual impairment may respond better to individual work than to group work. If these persons are included in a group, special thought must be given as to how they can keep track of what is happening (e.g., microphone and loop system or staff members sitting next to them and passing on information).

Above all, elderly people require the same sensitivity of approach as any other group. There will be individual differences—as Coleman (1986a) indicated, not all older people enjoy reminiscing, and not all wish to take part in group work. The person with dementia may feel he or she is being asked to share his or her personal life with complete strangers in a reminiscence group. Trusting relationships may take longer to develop. Leaders should beware of pursuing personal information overzealously; it is better to ask a more general question and allow the person to choose how much to share than to charge into personal areas and thereby intimidate the person. Preparation is vital, to ensure as far as possible that areas of trauma and upset for a particular group member are not inadvertently raised in this group setting where they cannot be adequately handled. One of the issues for supervision is how to recognize such sensitive areas and ensure that in one-to-one work the person receives appropriate support, without restricting the group to discussing only happy events. Of course, "the good old days" for many of these clients were marked by real hardship and suffering that they may wish to share with others. It is not the unhappiness of the event, but whether the wound has healed, that must be carefully judged, and the person's family will often be able to give some guidance in this area, as in others.

CONCLUSION

The potential for the use of reminiscence with people with dementia is relatively untapped. The few written reports on the topic speak positively of the use of reminiscence with this population. Gibson (1994) stated that the gains are small but are so rewarding when they occur that one must not hestiate to use reminiscence with this group. Whether reminiscence serves as therapy or stimulation for this group remains an argument. It does seem to make sense that the use of the past would be therapeutic for this population, who are often stuck in the past and cannot understand the present.

Chapter 18

Reminiscence in Psychotherapy with the Elderly: Telling and Retelling Their Stories

Linda L. Viney

In this chapter, I show how the elderly can benefit from reminiscence in psychotherapy. The form of therapy is personal construct therapy. From this constructivist perspective, the elderly are seen as having lost many of their earlier sources (e.g., spouses and friends) of confirmation of the stories that day by day maintain their identity, integrate their experiences, and gain them the acknowledgment of others. These stories can be self-limiting or self-empowering. The elderly's self-powerment is achieved through direct confirmation of such stories by the therapist.

In this chapter, I first explore the power of the stories of the elderly and show how the elderly are often cut off from that power. Then the role of reminiscence as a source of story confirmation is considered. Personal construct therapy for the elderly that focuses on storytelling is next described, with concepts defined as self-empowering or self-limiting and storytelling and retelling considered. Finally, the courses of storytelling therapy with 3 elderly clients for whom reminiscence was central—withdrawn Mr. N., bereaved Mrs. Z, and dying Mrs. T—are described.

THE POWER OF THE STORIES OF THE ELDERLY

What do I mean when I use this concept of story? A story enables people to link together the events they experience, using their customary ways of viewing things, that is, their personal constructs (G. A. Kelly, 1955), to do so. This linking often occurs over time (Sarbin, 1986). Integration is therefore a defining characteristic of stories, or narratives, but it can vary from being tight and inflexible to loose and easily changed over time. Good or bad stories can be identified, not so much in terms of the degree of integration they provide, but in terms of the paths of living they open or close for those who tell them. Another important aspect of the story is its context. Each story has a storyteller who chooses to tell a particular story from among a number of stories and to tell it in a particular way, to a particular person, in a particular setting.

The stories that are important to understanding the elderly are centered primarily on the self, but they also help the elderly to make sense of other people in relation to the self (Dennett, 1983). There are therefore personal, social, and cultural aspects to each story. The personal aspects of a story include the elder's presentation of him- or herself to others, as well as of the events that are most important to him or her. The story also helps the elder meet some psychological needs, such as preserving self-esteem or allocating responsibility. Stories also have implications for emotion and action and the linking of the present and past in order to anticipate the future. The most important social aspects of the story are its context, the sources of confirmation or validation for it, and how it allocates power to the teller and to other people. Its major cultural aspects lie in the information that is shared through it and the values implicit in it.

Our stories have at least four major implications for how we live our lives. First, and perhaps most important, they help us to develop and maintain a sense of identity (H. White, 1980). We know best who we are when we tell stories in which we play active roles. These stories help to fill out the many different ways in which we can live, and they can remind us of our own resources. Important too is the hearing of stories about ourselves, or at least stories that *could* be ours, from other people. If we lived in a culture in which none of our stories were told, we would soon lose any sense of identity (Mair, 1990).

Second, stories provide us with guidance on how to live our lives. They enable us to recognize our own existences, unleash our abilities, and continue to broaden our focus on the world. They also give us opportunities to acknowledge and make use of our similarities to others, while maintaining our sense of uniqueness. They permit us to prepare for the future. When people's stories no longer provide them with this guide, problems in living become apparent (Viney, 1989a). Elderly people who are depressed are an example. Their view of themselves, as presented in their stories, is mainly negative and self-critical. Their focus on the world has narrowed. They feel helpless and alienated from others. They are hopeless and therefore unable to plan effectively for the future. Such stories make living very difficult, indeed.

Third, our stories enable us to place order on the sometimes chaotic events of our lives. They hold our experiences in sequence for us, so that we can move in a planned fashion through them and are not overwhelmed by them. They also give us the opportunity to link present, past, and future events together. Such sequencing gives us the chance to reflect on what we have done and to draw general conclusions from it. Psychologists have paid particular attention to the stories people develop to account for why events occur as they do. There is, however, a much wider range of accounts available from people. For example, some stories focus on the purposes and goals of people in their causal explanations.

Fourth, getting others to listen to our stories gives us more power than we might otherwise have (McAdams, 1985). This is partly because the narrator's role is one of active agent and because of the personal resources that our stories remind us we have (Berger, 1989). It is also because of the social contexts in which these stories are heard. When people are invited to tell their stories, this is often an indication that they have sufficient power to ensure that that invitation occurs. Moreover, when their story is listened to, they are given an opportunity to contribute to the shared interpretation of events that occurs in that social context. The people whose stories are heard within a culture contribute to framing how that culture sees itself and its problems. That is why there is so much competition for a voice in newspapers, radio, and television. People whose stories are not heard lack influence. They must seek more power by working to get their stories heard.

What kinds of stories about the elderly are found in newspapers and on television? A survey of Australian newspapers I conducted showed them to be horrifyingly barren of stories that could serve as sources of identity and self-esteem for the elderly. The national and metropolitan papers gave no space to stories about the elderly, unless they had died. There was no mention of them in the international and local news sections, entertainment section, or sports section or even in the advertisements. It was only in the free local papers, supported completely by advertising, that some stories about the elderly appeared. In these papers, the news included the 100th anniversary of the Soccer Club reunion of old members and a comunity-based program to provide a bridge between young and old. The entertainment sections provided, for example, accounts of the Combined Pensioners' Card Day.

The only story I could find that portrayed the elderly in an active, rather than passive role involved a recently set-up Grandmothers' Club. Its aim was to build friendships with disabled children. Only in this story were elderly portrayed as competent. In much broader and more rigorous surveys of the papers, magazines, and television, others have also found references to the elderly to be rare (Berman & Sokowska-Ashcroft, 1986; Loupland, Couplan, & Giles, 1991; Ward, 1984). Giles (1991) reported that the media provide many hints to the elderly that they are excluded from storytelling. For example, even when a story about an elderly person who is competent and happy is told, it is presented in such a way as to make it both uncommon and unexpected. For example, the headline: "Life Is Great at 98!" implies that it ought not to be.

REMINISCENCE AS A SOURCE OF CONFIRMATION

Although reminiscence is not limited to the elderly, as the authors of other chapters of this book have shown, it has been observed to be prevalent in and also characteristic of them (Richter, 1986). These observations have led to many functions being ascribed to reminiscence. Prior to Butler's (1963) work, the predominantly negative aspects of reminiscing by the elderly had been emphasized (Sherman, 1987). Later writers stressed the adaptational functions of reminiscence. Butler and M. I. Lewis (1977; Lewis & Butler, 1974) emphasized the life review function of reminiscence in relation to the aged. Their writings have given rise to experimental studies of the parameters of reminiscence and to the use of reminiscence as a therapeutic tool (Coleman, 1986a, 1986b). Butler defined the life review form of reminiscence as a common mental process marked by the return to awareness of past experiences. Threat is often part of these experiences. The therapeutic use of reminiscence is now becoming more common (Agnew, 1986; Webster & Young, 1988; D. White & Ingersoll, 1989).

My colleagues and I have provided a personal construct theory account of this phenomenon of reminiscence (Viney, Benjamin, & Preston, 1988–89). Over a lifetime, the elderly have formed construct systems to interpret the meaning of their lives and the world around them. The constructs have enabled them to predict, with varying degrees of accuracy, the external results of behavior based on these constructs and their own psychological comfort or discomfort resulting from this behavior. The elderly experience changes in technology, culture, and values at the same time they are dealing with personal change and loss. Like any other people overloaded with invalidating information, the elderly tend to tighten their long established constructs in order to defend against what seems incongruous to them, and they resort to reminiscence to provide some of the missing validation for their constructs.

PERSONAL CONSTRUCT STORY RETELLING
THERAPY FOR THE ELDERLY

Two sets of criteria are useful to the therapist listening evaluatively to the stories of elderly clients. They concern the functions these stories fulfill and the content of the stories (Viney, 1989a). A story provides a sequence of personal constructs that together form a theme. Stories integrate different constructs and events to achieve a whole, and that whole has a meaning different from the meanings of its separate constructs. First, then, stories should integrate or pull together separate elements. Second, stories should be internally consistent and cohesive. Third, they should provide this integration of constructs and events over time, in order to give their teller a sense of continuity. A story should integrate present, past, and future.

The content of elders' stories is just as important. Their stories need to include predictions about the outcomes of actions that are precise and feasible enough to make appropriate action by clients possible. They also need to be optimistic enough to make it possible. Stories without hope make life for those who tell them very difficult.

There is, unfortunately, much in the lives of the elderly that can lead to hopelessness and thus to stories that are self-limiting for their teller (Viney, 1993). Such self-limiting content needs to be listened to by therapists in assessment of clients prior to therapy. For example, their physical functioning is often not as good as it used to be, even if only in terms of increased tiredness and a lack of energy. Their cognitive functioning is different from when they were younger: It is slower and perhaps less organized, because of their less organized life-style. Depression has been considered a frequent problem for the elderly and suicide can be associated with this. Elderly people can also have problems with drugs, through taking many medications simultaneously and underestimating the effects alcohol will have on them as they age, especially if alcohol is taken with medication. Many elderly people lack partners for sexual activities. This can be another source of hopelessness. So, too, can be the rapid pace of change.

However, there are other areas of content in elderly clients' stories for which therapists can listen to find answers to the self-defeating content. These are areas of self-empowering content and there are four of them (Viney, 1993). First, elderly people's acknowledgement of their own control, competence, and other abilities often gives them evidence of their capacity to cope effectively with whatever assails them. So too does self-actualization, by allowing growth, determination of the meaning in life, and establishment of the identity and integrity of the self. Religious beliefs are another source of self-empowering stories. Finally, there are family and friends who, at many degrees of intimacy and geographical closeness, provide support for and confirmation of many of these stories.

The hub of personal construct therapy is meaning, that is, meanings created and organized into construct systems (G. A. Kelly, 1967). People are seen as flexible and having several levels of awareness. When their constructs are validated, they experience good feelings, and when they are not, they do not. Clients and therapists come together to share meanings in a constructive dialogue, involving the interaction of two construct systems (Guidano, 1991). As they work in therapy, clients test the validity of their systems, making clearer their implications for emotions and action and extending the number of paths open to them (Epting, 1984; G. A. Kelly, 1969; Neimeyer, 1967). Such is the therapeutic process of reconstruction. Therapists working with clients validate some parts of their construct systems and invalidate others, with some changes resulting in clients' patterns of construing.

In such therapy, then, the client and therapist tell their stories: the therapist, about therapy, and the client, about the self and his or her world. The reconstruction of those stories then begins. Both participants take part in these reconstructions, so that therapy becomes the shared retelling of stories (Viney, 1989b). Because the stories therapists tell in therapy are mostly about therapy, they may change less than those of the clients, but they do change (Fransella & Dalton, 1990). Clients are often the first to tell their tales, which are marked by sad and frustrated content and by discontinuities, which therapists help them to reconstrue. Reconstruction occurs, of course, only when a close, trusting relationship between client and therapist has developed. Often, clients are reluctant to tell their stories or are not aware of the full story they are telling; they need help from the therapist to make that story explicit (Viney, Benjamin, & Preston, 1990). Therapists, however, are responsible for making clients' stories that are relevant to therapy sufficiently clear for clients to understand them. They are also responsible for the stories clients carry away about clients and therapists.

Story retelling is a highly appropriate form of therapy for the elderly (Viney, 1993). Their many life events have given them plenty of stories to draw from and a more distanced perspective on those stories than they would have had when younger. They can construe loosely and reflectively and, at their age, are able to relate stories that they might have been too ashamed to tell when they were younger. Reminiscence—telling stories from the past—comes naturally to people toward the end of the life span. And, as I suggested earlier, one reason they reminisce may be that, with the deaths of friends, neighbors, and loved ones, they have lost so many sources of confirmation of their personal constructs. By telling their own stories themselves, they can provide their own confirmation. This may be why storytelling comes naturally to many of them. Taking stock is also a common and age-appropriate activity, involving an element of evaluation. Thus story retelling may also be said to be a natural process for the elderly.

THREE ELDERLY CLIENTS' USE OF REMINISCENCE IN THEIR STORYTELLING THERAPY

Highlights of therapy with 3 elderly clients who were referred to our Psychological Services Unit are presented in this section to show how reminiscence allowed them to reclaim some of their old self-empowering stories, together with their old sources of confirmation for them. I chose these clients because they were dealing with three of the most common events the elderly have to deal with: their withdrawal from others (Anderson, 1985; Natale, 1986), the loss of a loved one (Essa, 1986; Raphael, 1984), and their own death (Rinaldi & Kearl, 1990; Stedeford, 1984).

Withdrawn Mr. N

Mr. N, at 86, was a pensioner living in a pleasant hostel unit, with his family readily available. He was referred to us because of his anxiety and depression. His wife had died 18 months before. Only 3 years before, she had, after brain surgery, suffered from dementia, and he had been successful in finding good nursing home accommodation for her and hostel accommodation for himself in the same retirement village. When he first came to the village, he sang in its choir and played indoor bowls, making several friends of his own age. Recently, however, he had withdrawn both physically and psychologically. When his therapist first saw him, which was in his unit, he was in his pajamas in bed. He felt cold; his eyes were expressionless, and his face seemed to have fallen in. "I don't want to live. I don't care what happens to me. They can do what they want." He was in the grip of despair, severe anxiety, and lack of faith in self and others. He was withdrawn and inert as a result of his serious concerns about the future.

Reminiscence provided Mr. N an opportunity to retell this anxiety-based story. This was especially useful with Mr. N because his withdrawal in the face of his anxieties about the future made more client-dependent techniques, such as relaxation inappropriate. At first, however, the therapist's invitations for Mr. N to "Tell me about the old days" were ignored. However, when he eventually did begin to talk, it was about an early job he had in the mine, looking after the pit ponies. He talked a little about how hard the conditions were for workers, but, on the positive side, about how that job had actually kept him from having to go underground. An example of Mr. N's reminiscence follows.

Therapist: You were pleased to have that job then?

Mr. N: Oh yes. Those ponies and I got to know one another pretty well and I was glad to be working on top. Our family sometimes got lucky like that, but other times I can remember hard times for us. When my older brother left school, they had no job for him at all. He would have been glad to go underground. He tried and tried but he couldn't get anyone to give him work. So I was the lucky one, but you don't appreciate things like that when you are young. . . .

And I remember how bad my old mum felt when they wouldn't let her go to communion at our church. Well, they'd let her go to church but not take communion because she hadn't done all the right things first. She used to come home and cry sometimes, the bastards. . . .

And Dad, he got thrown out of a few places too. It was mostly pubs, where they felt he'd had too much to drink. Well, maybe he had. I didn't follow him down that road, and I'm glad about that too.

In subsequent therapy sessions, for which he would get dressed, he explored many events in his early family life, often repeating himself. The common theme that emerged from these reminiscences was one of rejection, not necessarily of himself, but of other family members. He dwelt many times, for example, on how his mother had been refused communion by the Anglican Church because she was not a communicating member. He later related this to his relationship with his two estranged sons. He was becoming able to move easily between these events, seeing their loose links and the choices they represented for him. One day, however, his therapist arrived to find that Mr. N had withdrawn back to his bed. His therapist discussed with him the choice he now had available to him: essentially between "lying down" and dying or "standing up and being counted" and living. She left his room for him to make a decision; an hour later he emerged, showered and shaved and ready for lunch in the dining room. On her next visit, she found him up, talkative and cheerful about his son, who had come to see him. "I did some painting yesterday. It was alright. I painted mountains and a sun. It was supposed to be our states of mind. Come and I'll show you." Mr. N used reminiscence to explore loosely the issues that were important to him.

Bereaved Mrs. Z

Mrs. Z was referred to our therapy team because of the possibility of some debilitating depression as a result of her second husband's having died of cancer only a year earlier. The Zs had arrived together from Spain 6 years before, having been then married for 20 years. Mrs. Z had also had a small stroke more recently. She cried almost continually during the first two therapy sessions, in despair and lamentation over the loss of a perfect partner. She talked, through her sobs, of how generous her husband, Mariano, had been with her, how caring and how gentlemanly. She also spoke of how difficult she found it to be alone in their house and how she dreaded the long nights. She felt herself to be extremely lonely and isolated, and was regretting that they had not had children together. It later transpired that she alone had made this choice, for reasons that will become apparent. Her son from her first marriage was still in Spain. She received some support from her priest and congregation, as well as God, but felt much guilt about her choice to not have children.

Although Mrs. Z still had extensive family both in Australia and Spain, she did not regard most of them as supportive, because of the pressure she experienced from them to spend her newly inherited money on them or at least leave it to them when she died. They were also trying to encourage her, she reported, to sell the house of which she was so proud. Most of them she considered to be greedy, although later she came to identify some family who were "needy" and so, she felt, more deserving of her help. As therapy progressed also, her earlier idealization of her husband became much more realistic. It seemed that since they had been in Australia he had often been as she had described, but back home in Spain he had been mean, demanding, and patriarchal. She referred to him as "a tyrant" and confessed that she had refused to have children with him, even though he wanted them, because she had not wanted to mix their genes. Now, she said, she thought she could have raised their children to be more like her than him.

At the beginning of her therapy, two stories seemed to hold particular importance for Mrs. Z. The first set dealt with her despair and isolation. The "My life is over" set of stories trapped her into giving up all hope for the future and so also giving up any reason to make an effort. The other set of stories, "I am alone," was based on the assumption that, if she did try to reach out to others, there would be no one there. Her continuing despair and isolation could have been ensured by these stories. Her second and somewhat contradictory set of stories assumed that such reaching out might be possible, but only by giving and not by receiving. These stories were "I must be good" and "I must help others." Therefore she could meet her own expectations of being "good" only by giving to others.

When Mrs. Z's therapist began to explore with her the meanings "independence" held for her, they were confused and involved both positive and negative emotions. This proved, in part, to be because Mariano had encouraged her to be independent, but only as he was dying, and her meanings were confused with his. He had, as her reminiscences began to show, treated her almost as a vassal before they came to Australia, and she did not want to have that kind of relationship with her family. The reminiscences provided opportunities to come to grips with the anger she had been experiencing at Mariano. They also gave her the chance to again get in touch with some old sources of support for some of her more useful stories of independence. This reminiscence also gave her the opportunity to mourn the loss of the parts of her relationship with Mariano that had been good and express more fully her sadness. An example of her reminiscences follows.

Mrs. Z: This is the day, the exact day my husband died. It brings back so much to me. Tears of course. My Mariano and I were so close and yet it was an almost suffocating closeness. He used to assume so much, that he left me little room for myself. He was an infuriating man who never listened to what I said. Living with Mariano was difficult and I would try to make with him a decision about our house, say whether we should get new curtains and he would take it out of my hands. He was a pig at times.

Yet at others he and I worked together well. That is what I miss and will go on missing is a companion for my lonely hours. Mariano was a very good companion, whether we were working together or just relaxing. Sometimes at night still I sit and cry and cry when I think of the companionship I have lost.

The mornings are better now though, I suppose because I didn't see so much of Mariano then. I'm beginning to remember my work with the church, I had been helping out with St. Vincent de Paul, and I know I was of some use there. So perhaps, when I feel a bit better physically, I can go back to that. There is also a church group that we belonged to, that I know I was able to support; and maybe I can start that again too?

Mrs. Z's further explanation of some alternative stories of independence was encouraged by working through some of her most feared aspects of independence and encouraging her to try them out in actuality, for example, traveling alone and negotiating with her health professionals.

On all of the goals her therapist had anticipated their dealing with, Mrs. Z showed some gain. She was still saddened by the loss of her husband, but she had done some effective mourning, especially in expressing her anger about him. Her stories about her own independence were much clearer and more feasible, and she was taking some of the independent actions she had most feared. To replace her stories about loneliness and life's being over she had developed a range of alternatives that were well supported by friends, church acquaintances, an exercise group, and even by God. Her sense of being alone had lessened, but she was still crying a little when alone to express her sadness. Her "disabled" self had become a much more healthy and active self, taking responsibility for monitoring and maintaining her own health. As for being responsible for others, she had been able to achieve a more realistic assessment of the needs of her family and free herself from constructs that required her to help them financially. She was even able to reconstrue her relationship with God to feel more "cared about" and "secure."

Dying Mrs. F

Mrs. F was referred for therapy as she was dying of breast cancer in a general hospital. She was 69 years of age. This cancer had made its original appearance in her breast more than 9 years earlier, but a combination of surgery and other treatments had kept it in remission. Mrs. F reported having felt obliged, for a long time, to care for whichever members of her family needed care. When her father, for example, was ill for years before his death, it was she, not her three brothers and sisters, who looked after him. Her mother, in her late 80s, was now becoming more frail and needing more supervision. And she, even with her cancer, was finding herself providing this care. Her husband had recently become depressed, and she was finding this difficult to deal with.

At the time of referral, Mrs. F was living in a family situation with very few resources to help her adjust to the nearness of death for her. She was also being hospitalized frequently for short periods. Her husband was depressed. Her mother was frail. Her brothers and sisters had, for decades, been confirming her in the role of supporter and comforter to the rest of them. Even her grown daughters she saw as still reliant on her. After her first bout with cancer, it was not herself but her daughter she reported as needing to "stand on her own two feet." The very person in the family who would have been the one to support and be with her was Mrs. F herself!

One of Mrs. F's most central constructs seemed, not surprisingly, to focus on her being "a caring and capable person." These constructs had been repeatedly validated by her family and friends. They had enabled her to live a full and rewarding life; however, they could provide a trap for her in death. Because they had been so important to her, she was needing to hang on to them as other certainties let her down. Even in her relationship with God, in which many otherwise active and capable people allow themselves to be supported, she saw herself as "more of a doer than a taker." Central to her relationship with God was "being a giver of my time" to help others. Thus even in this relationship, some changes in construing were needed to help her approach her death with dignity.

Mrs. F proved to be confused by the need to change, in some ways at least, her most central construct of herself as a carer. She felt, by this time, too ill and weak, for example, to care for her mother, but she was not ready to acknowledge that another member of the family could take on this role in her place. In fact, she clung more closely to the family carer role when she described how her sister could not take on the responsibility of their mother because "she is really an alcoholic." However, while talking with her therapist, she began to rehearse handing over that responsibility, and by the end of that session she had done so in imagination, if not yet in fact. She had thus loosened her construing of her family roles considerably. It may have been that her ability to share her feelings with her therapist encouraged her to reconstrue herself in a role more suited to her recently altered circumstances. She became able to discuss her sister's role in her mother's care with other family members.

Another therapeutic process that may have helped Mrs. F get to this point of reconstruction was a "balancing of the books" that her therapist had undertaken with her through reminiscence. An example of such a life review reminiscence follows.

Mrs. F: When I first found I had cancer I coped with it well. And then I found I had advanced secondary breast cancer and that did knock me through a loop, after thinking I had beaten the disease. But it wasn't to be. So I was wondering, where the devil is the justice in the world, you know, after all that. And I thought, well, at least I can cope with it, more so than somebody else; so that was why it was put on my shoulders.

And now you talk about "balancing the books." Well, I have done a lot for other people. With my family, it has always been, "Joyce will cope, let's get Joyce to deal with it." And so I've been the one to look after my mother, my father, my sister, my daughters and even my husband. I haven't begrudged this because I felt that it was what God had given me my strength for.

Therapist: You've given so much to your family and to God through your church work, you may now feel that you can let your family and God give back to you.

Mrs. F: That's the sort of person I am though. When I know I can be of use to others, I don't hold myself back from giving.

Therapist: And now that you have less strength . . .

Mrs. F: It is hard to change something so central in my life. . . . Well, I guess I have done my bit. Perhaps I could leave my sister to cope with our mother, but . . .

It was when Mrs. F realized how much she had done for others, through the church, for example, that she began to accept that she did not need to go on "doing for" God, but could afford to think a little about what He might do for her. This led her to think about her own death as a part of life, with its books balanced. She also began to consider death as an alternative with advantages compared with the diminished life she was currently experiencing.

REMINISCENCE IN PSYCHOTHERAPY WITH THE ELDERLY: SOME REFLECTIONS

Reminiscence in psychotherapy with the elderly focuses on the types of stories elderly clients are telling themselves, that is, whether they are self-limiting or self-promoting. Self-limiting stories need retelling through story reconstruction. Self-promoting stories may lack current sources of confirmation and they can be easily lost. Reminiscence in therapy involves identification of family members and friends who were the original sources of confirmation of the stories, resulting not only in these persons' reliving in the client's mind, but in a sharing of them with the therapist. Self-empowering stories may thus be promoted in the elderly to replace more damaging stories.

Chapter 19

Differential Effects of Oral and Written Reminiscence in the Elderly

Edmund Sherman

The use of oral reminiscence in groups has been an established part of gerontological practice for many years, and its application has served many purposes, including enjoyment, socialization, development of friendships, enhancement of morale and life satisfaction, and the treatment of depression.

I have used oral reminiscence for all these purposes, with differential results or effects. A number of these effects were not necessarily in line with the planned purposes of the applied reminiscence. It was largely these varied effects that gave me the idea of incorporating written journal methods into oral reminiscence group practice.

Effects that differed from the ostensible purposes occurred in eight reminiscence groups that were held as part of a demonstration study funded by the American Association of Retired Person's Andrus Foundation (Sherman, 1987). The primary purpose of the study was to determine whether getting older persons together in reminiscence groups would help them develop friendships that could increase their social support in the community. Ten group reminiscence sessions of 1½ hr each were held in four different community settings, three senior apartment dwellings, and one community center. In one setting, members from two different reminiscence groups who had completed the 10 sessions merged to form a mutual support group. They called themselves a "coping group" because they were coping with multiple losses of friends, family, pets, belongings, and so on when they had to move into a newly constructed senior apartment complex.

However, even in the six groups in the other three study settings, there were usually 2 or 3 of the 8–12 group participants who were coping with losses or current emotional adjustment problems or were engaged in an active life review process (Butler, 1963). The content of their reminiscence frequently differed from that of the majority of the other group members in that it was sometimes more hesitant, painful, and personal. Therefore, it was as though the mutual enjoyment and socialization features of the groups were at cross-purposes with the current needs of a few members.

Over the years, I and graduate social work students in my department have run reminiscence groups in many different community settings (e.g., senior citizen centers, senior apartments, and community service centers) and have generally found a few persons who were using the group reminiscence experience for somewhat different personal purposes than the majority of group members.

These impressions from group reminiscence practice were substantiated in a survey conducted on a sample ($N = 100$) drawn from a range of urban and suburban senior centers (Sherman & Peak, 1991). On Romaniuk and Romaniuk's (1981) Reminiscence Uses Scale 12% of the sample indicated that they were engaged in the coping kind of reminiscence noted above, and 13% indicated they were engaged in an active life review process. The Romaniuks found these two types of reminiscence, which they called Current Problem Solving and Existential/Self-Understanding, respectively, along with a third type, or factor, which they called Self-Regard/Image Enhancement, in a factor analysis of the responses from their sample ($N = 91$). The self-regard/image enhancement type of reminiscence was used by a much larger proportion of the sample and was more pleasant and positive in terms of memory content than the other two types. The frequencies of use of the various types of reminiscence that we found in our survey were equivalent to the figures found by the Romaniuks in a very similar sample of community-dwelling elders (Sherman & Peak, 1991).

These figures raise the issue of how one can facilitate coping and life review processes for certain individuals in reminiscence groups without negatively impacting the overall group process. On the basis of a review of the practice and empirical literature on written reminiscence, I hypothesized that the incorporation of written reminiscence methods into the group process might address that issue. Therefore, the question I investigated was, Does written reminiscence differ in its effects from conventional oral reminiscence when applied in a group context? *Effects* refers to current mood or morale, general life adjustment, and the reminiscence process itself.

ORAL VERSUS WRITTEN REMINISCENCE

The operational definition of reminiscence I used in my investigation of oral versus written reminiscence was taken from Romaniuk and Romaniuk (1981), whose research on the functions and types of reminiscence provided the basic classification scheme for much of the data reported herein. They simply took the following definition of reminiscence from Webster's dictionary (1988): "The process or practice of thinking or telling about past experiences." When groups of older adults get together to reminisce and to share memories, it is obviously the oral practice of telling, rather than the interior process of thinking, that tends to predominate. This conversational process of mutual telling and sharing of experiences from the past is what makes group reminiscence such a natural ice-breaker in social situations among the elderly, leading to new friendships and enjoyment.

One of the first efforts to incorporate written reminiscence into an essentially oral group format with the elderly was undertaken by Myerhoff and Tufte (1975) with what they called the "life history technique." They found it helpful to give group members notebooks to record their memories, "dreams, concerns, fears, philosophical and polemical pieces" (Myerhoff & Tufte, p. 543). They felt these records would give evidence of the importance of the members' recollections, and, although the intent was not therapeutic, "occasionally the depths plumbed and the re-evaluations accomplished might earn them that label" (i.e., therapeutic label) (Myerhoff & Tufte, 1975, p. 543).

Since then, there have been empirical studies indicating that writing about past experiences such as traumas, losses, and illnesses can have a healing effect on individuals of various ages (Pennebaker & Beall, 1986). However, most of the writing done by the elderly in groups has been geared toward producing a written record of life histories or autobiographies. On the basis of their research and practice with autobiography groups, J. E. Birren and Deutchman (1991) have found several important reasons for incorporating writing into group reminiscence formats:

> The writing process itself is a stimulus to further recall. As thoughts are put on paper, rearranged, and read, related memories are elicited. The perspective of the self as a reader also provides the person with a unique opportunity to obtain a degree of separation from the material. This helps to open the door for the emergence of new perspectives on the past, the perspective of the more distant and mature present.
>
> By writing one's thoughts down before sharing with the group, a person is, in a sense, rehearsing. He or she can plan what will be shared with the group, homing in on the experiences that were most important. Without this opportunity, the account of memories might ramble, and the person's time to share with the group might be taken up by less meaningful recall. Similarly, a person has the opportunity to review his or her life theme and determine what will and will not be shared with the group. This protects the individual's right to monitor the developmental exchange and not to share what he or she feels is too personal or painful. (p. 57)

Another approach to such writing in groups is the intensive journal workshops method developed by Progoff (1975). It is a well-established and widely used method that incorporates an internal dialogue technique that I used in the present comparative group study. I chose to use a similar personal-journal approach conjointly with oral reminiscence in a group and compare it to a pure oral reminiscence group, rather than conduct a purely written life history or autobiography group.

There were several reasons for this choice. The first was that both life history and the autobiography groups are geared toward a specific written product at the end, a document, perhaps to be shared with or bequeathed to children, grandchildren, or others. In contrast, the journal is more personal and private, less structured, to be used in any way the person sees fit, without regard to spelling, grammar, or ultimate reading by others. Second, life histories and autobiographies tend to be linear in structure, that is, chronicles of a life from childhood to old age. This constrains the group process to some extent, as members spend a considerable amount of group time reading to each other. The journal method is more flexible and adaptive to the group process, since the writing is purely personal and does not have to be shared with the group unless the writer wishes. Consequently, less group time is taken up by oral reading. The written entries can also be about any personal concern, past or present, regardless of what life stage the group might be discussing at the time, allowing the individual greater flexibility in addressing concerns of the moment. It should be noted that even when a person is presently coping with a loss, that loss occurred in the past and that invariably involves reminiscence.

METHOD

The original purpose of the present study was basically to conduct an oral/journal reminiscence group concurrently with a purely oral reminiscence group and compare them on certain pre- and post-test measures to test for possible differential changes and effects. An unforeseen opportunity presented itself to obtain comparable outcome data from several autobiography groups that were coming to closure in Sarasota, Florida, just as arrangements for the basic study were being carried out. Arrangements were made to distribute and collect questionnaires containing the basic study instruments from the group participants. Although pre-test data were not available from these groups, I felt that comparable outcome data from the autobiography groups would provide valuable additional information for this exploration of oral and written reminiscence.

While the questionnaires from the autobiography groups were being returned and processed, the oral and oral/journal groups were being selected from among attendees in a senior service program in an Albany, New York, community center. Plans for the two groups were announced in advance, and I met with about 30 older persons from the center who expressed an interest in participating in either

group. After the study was described to them, 25 persons volunteered to participate, 13 of whom were randomly assigned to the oral reminiscence group and 12
of whom were assigned to the oral/journal reminiscence group.

Subjects

Given the exploratory and largely practice-oriented nature of this study, demographic data were restricted to age, gender, and marital status. No questions were
asked about race, ethnicity, social class, etc., because there was no intention to
represent, or generalize to, any larger population.

Of the 13 volunteers assigned to the oral reminiscence group, 9 were women.
Seven of the volunteers were widowed, 5 were married, and 1 had never married.
They ranged in age from 65 to 79 years, with a mean of 71.6 years ($SD = 4.03$). Of
the 12 volunteers assigned to the oral/journal group, 8 were women. Seven
members of the oral/journal group were widowed, 4 were married, and 1 was
divorced. Their ages ranged from 66 to 79 years, with a mean of 71.9 years ($SD =
3.48$). Two women stopped attending the oral reminiscence group, and another
woman left the oral/journal group, so that 11 members remained in each group at
the end of the eight planned sessions.

A total of 49 out of 58 people in the six autobiography groups completed
questionnaires. Of these, 38 were women. Of these volunteers, 29 were widowed,
11 were married, 3 were divorced, and 6 had never married. Their ages ranged
from 61 to 89 years, with a mean of 75.6 ($SD = 7.85$). Thus, the autobiography
group members had a wider range of ages than the other two groups had and were
somewhat older. They also had somewhat higher ratios of women to men and
widowed to married persons. However, none of these differences from the oral
and oral/journal reminiscence groups were significant (.05 level).

Measures

The instrument used to measure mood or current sense of psychological well-
being was Bradburn's (1969) Affect-Balance Scale (ABS). This 10-item scale is
based on self-reported feelings experienced "during the past few weeks." Five
positive items (e.g., "pleased" and "excited about something") are balanced by
five negative items (e.g., "bored," "depressed," and "very lonely"), and in this
study the items were scored cumulatively in the positive direction (0 to 10). The
ABS has been used extensively with older populations and shows acceptable
reliability and validity (George & Bearon, 1980).

The measure of late-life adjustment used was the Ego Integrity Scale (Boylin,
Gordon, & Nehrke, 1976) because it was developed and operationalized on the
basis of Erikson's (1963) ego integrity concept. The 10-item scale reflects Erikson's descriptions of feelings and attitudes characteristic of the two alternative
solutions to the final stage of development: ego integrity or despair. Five of the

items represent a positive resolution (integrity), and 5 items represent a negative resolution (despair). They were scored on a 5-point Likert scale from *strongly agree* to *strongly disagree* with *neither agree nor disagree* in the middle. The five ego integrity items were

1 "I am satisfied with my life so far."
2 "I am willing to take responsibility for my decisions."
3 "I would not change my life if I lived it over."
4 "I am proud of what I have done."
5 "I accept myself the way I am."

The five despair items were

1 "I worry about getting old."
2 "I regret the mistakes I've made."
3 "I am discontented with life."
4 "Life is too short."
5 "I wish I could change myself."

Support for the validity and reliability of the Ego Integrity Scale was published by Walaskay, Whitbourne, and Nehrke (1983).

It should be added that the Ego Integrity Scale was originally used with an all-male sample (Boylin et al., 1976). However, Sherman and Peak (1991) found no significance between men ($n = 25$) and women ($n = 75$) on integrity scores in a survey of a sample very similar demographically to the present study sample, which also showed no significant differences between the sexes.

Romaniuk and Romaniuk's Reminiscences Uses Scale (1981), a 13-item, three-factor scale of the uses or functions of reminiscence, asks respondents if they have engaged in each use when talking or thinking about the past. Measures of the frequency of interpersonal (oral, public) reminiscing and of intrapersonal (private) reminiscing were also administered.

Group Procedures

I conducted both the oral and the oral/journal reminiscence groups on different days of the week for eight sessions each over the same 2-month period. The sessions lasted 1½ hr each and followed essentially the same format. At the beginning of each session, I introduced a reminiscence topic that reflected a developmental stage of the life cycle, such as first memory, first day at school, first date, and so on. Members were encouraged to share their memories, but they were also reassured that this was purely voluntary so they should not feel pressured to share or discuss anything that made them uncomfortable. Both groups began with early childhood and moved on to later childhood, adolescence, adulthood, middle age, and senior adulthood in chronological progression over the eight sessions.

The members of the oral/journal group were given a looseleaf notebook in which to make entries during sessions. The entries were made after there had been some open discussion and sharing of memories about the life period under consideration. The members would be asked to sit quietly, with their eyes closed, to feel the content of the period just discussed. They were instructed to relax and let imagery, impressions, feelings, or symbols form in their minds. Then, when they were ready, they were to record the entry without regard to grammar, organization, or spelling. After 5–10 min of this, I asked whether anyone wanted to share impressions or memories that were evoked by the exercise.

In addition to this exercise, the members of the oral/journal group engaged in an internal "dialogue with persons" in which they would pick someone, living or dead, of importance to them during the stage of life currently under discussion. They were asked to relax, close their eyes, and imagine talking to that person. They were asked to write in their notebooks what they would have said to that person as they remembered him or her in that stage, then write that person's response, and continue the dialogue in this way. A variation on this was to have members talk with themselves as they remembered themselves at a younger stage of life (e.g., childhood or adolescence). This exercise elicited many insightful and amusing responses in the members.

In middle and later adulthood sessions, group members were asked to choose an activity they cared about and write down their thoughts and feelings about their relationship to it. This was called a "dialogue with works" (Progoff, 1975).

Thus, members in the oral/journal group would make two or three reflective and introspective entry episodes during each session, and they were encouraged to continue writing in their journals between sessions if there was anything they wanted to expand on or explore. In the last sessions they were asked to identify meaningful emotional, physical, occupational, and relational milestones in lives so as to give a sense of continuity and a picture of their lives as a whole.

The autobiography groups varied from 8 to 10 sessions, and much more time was devoted to writing and reading personal entries aloud to one another than was the case in the oral/journal group, which still consisted mostly of oral reminiscence. On average, about a third of the time in the oral/journal group was spent on the writing exercises.

Because I led both groups and had hypothesized that the journal method would facilitate coping and life review processes without negatively impacting the overall group process, I had to guard against experimenter bias. I made every effort not to be more enthusiastic about the oral/journal group procedures than those of the oral group. Ultimately, however, there is no definitive way of knowing whether some experimenter bias entered the process.

RESULTS

I used nonparametric tests to test for significant differences among the three groups, because prior research has shown that instruments measuring subjective well-being, such as the ABS and the Ego Integrity Scale, tend to elicit a response bias that skews results toward higher scores (Stock, Okun, & Benin, 1986). That did, in fact, occur in this study, as can be seen from the mean ABS and Ego Integrity Scale scores shown in Table 1.

The ABS has a midpoint of 5 and the Ego Integrity Scale a midpoint score of 25, but the means of all three groups exceeded these midpoints. Rather than make any unwarranted assumptions about the population distribution or the level of measurement of the scales, I opted to perform nonparametric tests to determine significant difference in scores between the groups and from pre-test to post-test.

There were no significant differences between the oral/journal and oral groups' mean ABS scores. However, the oral/journal and oral interventions had differential effects on ego integrity scores. The mean integrity score for the oral/journal group increased significantly from pre- to post-test measures, whereas the oral group's essentially remained the same. Table 2 shows that the increase in ego integrity scores was significantly greater for the oral/journal group than for the oral group at post-test.

Regarding the findings on the post-test-only measure of ego integrity in the autobiography group, it is of interest that this group showed significantly ($p =$ .039) higher ego integrity scores than the oral group but not the oral/journal group at outcome, according to the Mann-Whitney two-sample test. On the other hand,

Table 1   Pre- and Post-Test Scores in the Oral, Journal, and Autobiography Groups

Group type	Pre-test	Post-test
Oral reminiscence ($n = 11$)		
Affect-Balance Scale		
M	7.36	7.73
SD	2.11	2.19
Ego Integrity Scale		
M	34.27	34.00
SD	3.98	4.71
Journal reminiscence ($n = 11$)		
Affect-Balance Scale		
M	7.27	8.45
SD	2.37	1.37
Ego Integrity Scale		
M	34.36	36.54
SD	6.56	5.48
Autobiography ($n = 49$)		
Affect-Balance Scale		
M	—	8.18
SD	—	1.52
Ego Integrity Scale		
M	—	36.76
SD	—	4.63

Table 2   Change Scores on Outcome Variables in the Oral and Oral/Journal Reminiscence Groups

Measure	Change score		Z^a	p
	Oral	Oral/ Journal		
Affect-balance	-0.36^b	−1.18	1.05	.293
Ego integrity	0.27	−2.18	2.30	.022

[a] Z = score conversions from the Mann-Whitney two-sample test.

[b] Negative scores indicate change toward higher scores.

the autobiography group's mean ABS score was not significantly different from the means of the oral and oral/journal groups at outcome.

An analysis of the differences and changes in the uses, types, and frequency of reminiscence also showed some interesting results. There was an expected shift from pre-test to post-test in the uses of enjoyable, image-enhancing reminiscence in both the oral and oral/journal groups. More persons in both groups were using reminiscence to lift spirits, to be entertaining or amusing, etc.

There were no marked changes in the use of the problem-solving type of reminiscence by either group. However, there was a marked difference between the two groups in the use of the existential or life review type of reminiscence. The oral group showed no perceptible change from pre- to post-test, but the oral/ journal group showed a significant ($p = .021$) increase in combined responses to the items tapping the use of reminiscence "to solve past troubles" and "to arrive at a better understanding of your past life and yourself."

There was a difference in the use of private (intrapersonal) reminiscence between the two groups, with no increase in private reminiscence reported by the oral group members but a clear increase in its use among the oral/journal group members. This appeared to be related to the more private and introspective kinds of reminiscence entailed by the journal entries made during and in between group sessions.

DISCUSSION

The results indicate that the oral and oral/journal group interventions had some similar as well as differential effects. The most notable differential effect involved ego integrity scores. When the changes in the pre- and post-scores of the oral/ journal group were analyzed more closely on a case-by-case basis, it became clear that 3 people in the group accounted for much of the change. It was evident from their group participation and their self-reports that 2 of them (1 man and 1 woman) were going through an active life review process and the third (a widow) was still coping with the loss of a spouse after a prolonged illness. These 3 members showed marked positive changes in their scores on the self and life satisfaction items in the integrity scale and showed commensurate changes in the use of life review reminiscence dealing with self-understanding and resolving past problems. It is also significant that these same 3 participants tended to use the journal for entries between sessions more than the other participants and intended to continue with the journal when the group ended.

It is also of interest that the oral/journal group's mean integrity score at outcome was similar to that of the autobiography groups. Whether this was due largely to the fact that written reminiscence is used in both journals and autobiographies cannot be known, because pre-test data were lacking for the autobiography groups. Yet, this does suggest that the written reminiscence done in journal groups does not suffer in comparison to the written reminiscence done in autobiography groups.

Despite the limitations and exploratory nature of this study, it does appear that written reminiscence can be effectively incorporated into an essentially oral reminiscence group with evident beneficial effects. Of course, one needs to use written reminiscence selectively. Not all elderly persons would be comfortable with the journal approach. They might be concerned about their own level of literacy and use of written language, even though this is kept private within their own personal journals. The present sample was, after all, a largely young-old (under 75) group of people who were relatively well educated, active, intellectually curious, and open to new experiences. One might question whether an old-old (over 75) group would be as open to this approach. Yet, it should be noted that a large proportion of participants in the autobiography groups were over 75, and their ABS and ego integrity scores were comparable to those of the oral/journal group.

CONCLUSION

The present study yielded several interesting results. First, oral/journal reminiscence had a greater effect on Ego Integrity Scale scores than did purely oral reminiscence, at least for selected individuals in the oral/journal reminiscence group. Second, use of the journal facilitated coping and life review processes in selected individuals in the oral/journal group, without negatively impacting the overall group process. Third, all members of the oral/journal group reported that writing entries in their journals stimulated their recall and enhanced their oral memory sharing in the group reminiscence process. Given these findings, practitioners would do well to consider the advantages of including journals in their work with oral reminiscence groups in community, and even institutional, settings.

Finding Meaning in Memories: The American Association of Retired Persons' Reminiscence Program

Betty Davis

My mother was so angry with me when I placed her in a nursing home that she would not speak to me when I visited her. A reminiscence volunteer visited with her several times and soon she had her laughing and sharing her life story. Then she got the two of us to start reminiscing together. Mother and I were able to share many memories together—happy times and difficult times. She only lived three months more and because of that reminiscence volunteer we had a meaningful three months.

I visited an older gentleman who was lonely and depressed. He had been a baker. After several months of reminiscing, he perked up and started participating in activities at the senior center. He now offers cake-decorating courses on a regular basis at the center.

HISTORY OF THE PROGRAM

Earl Kragnes, a staff member at the American Association of Retired Persons (AARP), began the AARP Reminiscence Program in 1983. He was concerned that churches and synagogues were not responding to people in institutional settings who were unable to get to organized religious services or programs. He was also motivated by Butler's (1963) writing on the value of reminiscence and the need for attentive listeners. Kragnes began thinking about and planning how AARP volunteers could fill this need. After considerable work, the AARP Reminiscence Program was born.

A core group of appointed AARP reminiscence volunteers were trained to help local communities organize programs and give 9-hr training sessions to volunteers who would make a commitment to visit an isolated older person once a week for 6 months. The training sessions were followed by monthly volunteer support meetings. AARP paid the costs of travel, food, lodging, and training materials.

In 1993, after 10 years of volunteer-supported involvement, AARP felt the "reminiscence seed" had been planted. The reminiscence volunteers retired; however, the reminiscence training materials remain available for purchase. Many communities have trained people who organize programs in their areas. A booklet entitled *The Power of Memories: Creative Uses of Reminiscence,* published in 1992 by AARP, highlights unique programs throughout the country that can be replicated. Information on ordering materials is presented at the end of this chapter.

DESCRIPTION OF THE REMINISCENCE PROGRAM

The Reminiscence Program effectively reaches lonely and isolated older people in many different settings. Sharing the stories that make up their lives helps people to feel valued and to feel their lives have mattered. Although the AARP Reminiscence Program focuses on older people, reminiscence can serve all ages—hospice and hospital patients, troubled youth, etc. It also helps families to communicate better.

To interest communities, AARP's reminiscence volunteer organizers made outreach efforts to local areas. When several people from a community indicated they were interested in reminiscence, the organizer worked with them to plan an organizational meeting. At this meeting, the reminiscence organizer gave a 2-hr presentation explaining the value of reminiscence and the responsibilities of the participating organizations. If the community voted to start a program, the organizer made recommendations to the local community on organizing a steering committee and planning for a volunteer training session.

Once the training event was organized, an AARP reminiscence trainer arrived to give the training, which consisted of three sessions of 3 hours each. AARP supplied all the training materials and films. The training covered topics such as myths about aging, active listening, triggers to encourage reminiscing, open-ended questions, how to talk with someone who is grieving, and how to make the first visit.

After training, each local reminiscence volunteer was matched with someone who needed a visitor. Four weeks after the training, the local reminiscence steering committee held a follow-up session with their volunteers to review what they learned and to hear about successes and difficult situations. In return for the AARP assistance, the community steering committee made a commitment to hold training sessions with their own local trainer every 6 months to train new volunteers. AARP continued to supply training materials and technical assistance.

IMPLEMENTING THE REMINISCENCE PROGRAM

Older people are uniquely qualified to develop and run a community Reminiscence Program. This activity is an interesting and rewarding way for them to provide an important service. The following are steps for developing a community Reminiscence Program and some suggestions for overcoming troublesome areas.

Gathering of Information about the AARP Reminiscence Program   The AARP Gerontological Resource Information Center (202-434-6240) loans the Reminiscence Training Kit through interlibrary loan. This training kit gives information on the formation and training involved in developing a Reminiscence Program. If you wish to have a kit of your own, it can be purchased (see the Appendix at the end of the chapter). You may have heard about trainings in a nearby community and may be able to borrow their training kit. Someone from that community might be willing to be a speaker or trainer for your community. For information, write AARP, Reminiscence Program, 601 E St. NW, Washington, DC 20049.

Identification of Interest in a Reminiscence Program   There may be several people in a community who think a Reminiscence Program would be valuable, but it is important to evaluate the other volunteer activities existing in the community, especially if the community is small. Ask some preliminary questions, such as

Are there so many volunteer activities in this community that the pool of existing volunteers is already drained?

Could the Reminiscence Program be part of another program, such as the Retired Senior Volunteer Program (RSVP)?

Could the Reminiscence Program be an activity sponsored by several churches as an ecumenical endeavor?

Introductory Meeting with Members of Interested Groups   Keep in mind that your program will be more successful if you involve people and organizations in the very beginning, so they can be part of the design and decision making. Look at the makeup of nationalities, ethnic groups, and religious groups in your community and ensure that the introductory meeting includes representatives from all these groups. Men are frequently underrepresented, so find ways to include men's groups. Do not overlook people with disabilities; they can be excellent reminiscence visitors.

Describe the concept and value of reminiscence to the group. Show the slide show or video that is included in the training kit. Discuss the value of having one person visit an isolated person for 6 months and indicate that this is what would be asked of volunteers.

If the group decides to start a Reminiscence Program, include as many groups as possible on the steering committee. This committee handles the details of the training—time, place, refreshments, equipment, recruiting of volunteers, publicity, and so on. Choose several trainers, if possible, from different organizations. The availability of at least two trainers at all times is an important component of the program. Most trainers enjoy doing trainings together; the trainings are more interesting; the trainers motivate each other; and—most important—if one is ill or moves away, the program doesn't falter.

Training of Volunteers   The AARP *Reminiscence Training Guide* includes a section entitled "Important Considerations for the Reminiscence Trainer," that offers many helpful suggestions on organizing and presenting the training and ensuring good attendance. The following items are worth stressing:

- Charge a small registration fee. People seem to value something they have to pay for and are more apt to attend the training if they have paid a fee.
- Send volunteers letters of confirmation with a brief description of the training and complete information about time and place. Stress the importance of attending all three sessions and the follow-up fourth session. Let them know you will assign them someone to visit.
- Call all participants the day before the training to remind them of the time and place. This is time consuming, but it pays off in better attendance. It is disappointing to have no-shows after all the effort of planning. Perhaps several volunteers can make the phone calls.
- Training is most effective for volunteers if it is given in three sessions of 3 hours each. (We gave trainings for professionals in 1-day sessions but found that after 6 hours, volunteers' saturation point had been reached.) Volunteers who are not used to sitting in classes do much better if sessions are shorter. By having 3 sessions, more information is retained because participants can practice the new reminiscence techniques, share results, and read and discuss assignments. Participants find the training is fun and enjoy returning for each session.
- Fifteen to 20 participants is best. The training uses experiential learning to teach the necessary listening and interviewing skills. With fewer than 10 people, the discussion is not as varied. With more than 20, the group is too large for everyone to share.

Volunteer Assignments   Develop a plan before the training begins on how to assign volunteers. Volunteer visitors will be asked to visit homebound or institutionalized older people for a period of at least 6 months. Sometimes the length of time is reduced because of illness or death, but often the reminiscence volunteers want to continue longer because close friendships develop. Let volunteers know they can request a change if the match is not good. Gather names from participating organizations and make assignments in the volunteer's geographical area of preference.

Assignments can be made immediately after the third training session, or arrangements can be made to take the volunteer to introduce him or her to the person they will be visiting. Having an agency staff person introduce the volunteer is very helpful. The isolated person is less apprehensive about trusting the new volunteer, and the reminiscence volunteer is not as shy about the first visit. Be aware that sometimes volunteers drop out of the program because they fear making the first visit.

Follow-Up Session   One month after the third training session, a follow-up session should be held. When making the arrangements for the training, also make arrangements for the follow-up session. During all three training sessions, stress the date of the follow-up session and the importance of attendance. This is a time for volunteers to share their experiences and talk about the positives and negatives of the visiting.

Some volunteers have difficulty with smells and clutter in a person's home or nursing home. They may also have difficulty leaving at the end of a visit—they may be asked to stay longer or run errands. To prevent burnout, the volunteer should make sure to spend time only visiting, not running errands. Volunteers who do not do this may soon feel they are giving more time than they want to give to the program. The reminiscence visit is what is important. Try to find other volunteers to do the additional tasks.

Ongoing Meetings   Periodic sharing and evaluation sessions should be scheduled on a monthly basis to support volunteers. The steering committee or the trainers should coordinate these sessions. One of our most successful programs includes a monthly brown bag lunch meeting so volunteers and employed steering committee members can participate. Often, the steering committee schedules a business meeting before or after the volunteer meeting. Speakers can be invited, and some programs have a yearly volunteer recognition pot-luck supper. Individuals who are being visited may enjoy an invitation to the recognition supper as well.

Volunteer Follow-Up   Check on all newly trained volunteers within 2 weeks after training. As mentioned earlier, a volunteer may experience cold feet and can be helped to make that first visit through an introduction by an agency staff person or a buddy on the first visit. Many volunteers are lost if early contact is not made by the steering committee.

Ongoing follow-up is important because the volunteers need recognition and support. If the volunteer's client dies or no longer can have a visitor, or if the match is not good, follow-up helps in reassignment. Those trained volunteers are valuable, so don't lose them! Develop a volunteer tracking system early.

Steering Committee Meetings   Every community is unique. Develop a program that serves your community best. Help the Reminiscence Program develop an identity and get community recognition to keep volunteers involved. (See Publicity and Media Coverage for additional tips.)

Ongoing Trainings   Set the date for the next training soon after a training is completed. The future of the program rests on recruiting and training more volunteers. Ideally, the steering committee and organizations should recruit and train volunteers every 5–6 months. The value of the program is characterized in the following vignette. A trainee in one of our reminiscence trainings stood up at the end of the training to share this with the group:

> I am losing my eyesight and have been feeling very depressed and useless. This training has shown me that I can still be a valuable person. I can make reminiscence visits and help lonely people feel cared about. Thank you for helping me find some purpose in life!

The reminiscence training is valuable to the volunteers in many ways. Many who have taken the training are amazed at how helpful the reminiscence techniques are with their own family members. This can be a fun workshop for family members visiting a loved one in the nursing home. It could be titled, "What do you say after you say 'hello'?"

Special friendships develop between some volunteers and reminiscers. The volunteer hears interesting history and stories of courageous acts. The volunteer can use the lessons learned in his or her own life. Several of our volunteers have been asked to speak at memorial services of their reminiscers because they knew stories that the family didn't know. Volunteers feel very honored to be asked.

The reminiscence training stresses the importance of confidentiality. Volunteers hear about sensitive issues that they should hold in confidence. Even "funny" stories shared at a gathering may not be amusing to the older person or family member.

Volunteer Recognition   Recognition and appreciation of the volunteers are very important. Volunteers can be recognized annually with plaques and creative gifts, along with recognition of the number of hours served. This makes interesting news for local papers and publicizes your program.

Publicity and Media Coverage   Media coverage cannot be stressed enough. Designate one volunteer as the "media volunteer." Invite media people to participate in the trainings. They may not stay for the entire training, but they get a much better sense of the program if they attend even one session. We have had a number of reporters stay for the whole training.

The media will be more interested in reminiscence stories during traditional times of family gatherings. For example, during the holidays, place an article in the newspaper on the value of reminiscing and some suggested questions that families can ask each other. Or submit an article telling families how to do a video or audio interview with an older family member to save for posterity.

Local cable stations are often interested in reminiscence interviews with people from the community. One of our volunteers gathered four female members of her family who represented four generations and did a reminiscence session on her local cable station during the Christmas season. The youngest was her 7-year-old granddaughter.

Placement of a reminiscer's biography in the local library can make an interesting local news story.

Articles about reminiscence trainings and stories about individual volunteers bring attention not only to the Reminiscence Program, but also to the organizations that participate. Organizations and volunteers feel proud when their program is recognized at parties and gatherings.

Leadership   Committed leadership that gives volunteers attention and follow-up helps a volunteer program thrive. Staff at health care and social service organizations are stretched to the maximum and don't usually have time to give the volunteers the extra attention they need. Volunteers may have the time, so it is helpful to find several talented and committed volunteers to manage this program. Sharing tasks with several organizations allows more organizations to feel ownership, and this builds a stronger program.

CONCLUSION

A Reminiscence Program can benefit the volunteers, the reminiscers, and the community in many ways. Rewarding friendships form, history is preserved, people feel valued, and depression and loneliness are averted. This program can draw a community together and help build links that, in turn, facilitate community problem solving. One AARP Reminiscence Program volunteer said it best: "Reminiscence helps people build bridges of understanding across generations and between cultures. In reminiscing together, people who might otherwise be strangers see and enjoy their common humanity."

APPENDIX: MATERIALS ON THE REMINISCENCE PROGRAM THAT MAY BE ORDERED FROM THE AMERICAN ASSOCIATION OF RETIRED PERSONS

The American Association of Retired Persons (AARP) no longer funds volunteers to present trainings but the following materials are available. Please be sure to indicate stock number when ordering.

The Power of Memories: Creative Uses of Reminiscence (D14930)—This 11-page booklet describes creative uses of reminiscence in a variety of settings and with different populations. One copy is available free of charge from AARP Fulfillment, 601 E St. NW, Washington, DC 20049.

Reminiscence: Reaching Back, Moving Forward (D13186)—This brochure describes the benefits and techniques of reviewing past experiences. It includes a number of questions and triggers to prompt remembering and lists resources for reminiscence activities. It is available free from AARP Fulfillment, 601 E St. NW, Washington, DC 20049.

Reminiscence: Finding Meaning in Memories—Training Kit (D13403)—This kit includes a step-by-step training guide to help trainers give a 2- or 9-hr experiential training on the value and techniques of reminiscence. It is designed so that the training can be adapted for volunteer visitors, nurses, hospice staff, nurses aides, activity directors, family members, and others who work with older people. The kit includes a *Trainers Guide,* a video, and 10 resource material books for participants. Available for $30 from AARP, Program Resources Dept., P.O. Box 51040, Station R, Washington, DC 20091.

Chapter 21

Memory Lane Milestones: Progress in Reminiscence Definition and Classification

Jeffrey D. Webster
Barbara K. Haight

The universe of reminiscence investigation is simultaneously exploding and imploding. Researchers and practitioners are looking both outside their immediate areas, seeking connections to related domains of work such as narratives and autobiographical memory, and also within the area to examine more closely fundamental issues of concept definition, psychometrics, and how reminiscence differs from other forms of memorial discourse. As Butler illustrates in the Foreword, the area has grown in many ways, emerging from its clinical roots to inform and be informed by other mainstream academic disciplines. This is an exciting, challenging, and sometimes frustrating time for some, as this growth and divergence occur prior to the resolution of some thorny and persistent methodological and conceptual problems.

As indicated by the division of this book into Theory, Research, Methods, and Applications sections, specialized areas of interest continue to expand. As areas of expertise develop, however, there is the inevitable tradeoff of depth for breadth. As we become further engrossed in a specific pursuit, we lose sight of the aims and discoveries of our colleagues addressing the same issue from different vantage points. Although tunnel vision is certainly not unique to the reminiscence research arena, long-standing disputes concerning, for instance, the therapeutic efficacy of reminiscence interventions (e.g., Middleton & Buchanan, 1993), call our attention to the need to examine such existing tensions.

Some of this tension results from our relative ignorance of developments that occur in different subareas. We simply do not have the time to immerse ourselves in literature that does not bear directly on our own current research interests. This is an understandable and benign form of neglect. There seems to exist, however, a more deeply rooted reason for the persistence of tension between divisions of reminiscence research. Because of differences in training, philosophy, and research agenda, there remains the traditional schism between experimental and clinical branches, with proponents of each somewhat skeptical, if not dismissive, of the conclusions of each other. As stated in the Preface, drawing our attention to this problem places us in jeopardy because we run the risk of perpetuating the very antipathies we are trying to dismantle. Each subarea is like a sibling in a larger family with a shared heritage. Each brings to bear certain strengths and inherent weaknesses. Together, our cumulative resources provide a solid family foundation even in the face of sibling squabbles.

This book purposely brings together representatives of some of these growing divisions to foster a constructive interchange of ideas. This is not an easy task, and the difficulties inherent can be illustrated with a story. With apologies to Aesop, consider the following brief parable.

Once upon a time an old man, a Mr. Otto Biawg-Raphe, grew tired and lonely spending time without the cheerful comfort of his family. Being a person of action, Mr. Biawg-Raphe calls all his wayward children, demanding, and getting, a convening of the clan for a family picnic. At the outing, each child brings a contribution to distribute the burden of the preparations equally. His oldest daughter from his first marriage, Thera Pea, brings some fresh-baked, whole wheat buns. They taste great, are good for you, and leave everyone feeling sort of warm and nurtured. His youngest son from his second marriage brings the expected roast beef. Reese Urch was always a meat-and-potatoes kind of guy, and he has carefully and precisely followed cooking instructions, removing the meat from the barbeque when the thermometer reached .05. This renders the roast a little overdone for some tastes, necessitating much chewing and swallowing. As usual, there always seems to be disagreement about whether gnawing on the bone is healthy, but all present acknowledge the importance of the salubrious effects of this food group. After finishing, everyone feels somehow stronger. May Thawds, always the inventive one and Thera Pea's twin sister, thoughtfully brings fancy dishes, cutlery, napkins, condiments, and other assorted picnic accoutrements, which allows for easy access to the culinary delights provided by her other siblings. All gathered are amazed at May's inventiveness and her abilities to discover and apply wonderful and effective ways for enjoying the sumptuous repast. Finally, Theo Ree, forever the deep thinker and Reese's big brother, brings an exotic dessert that serves to tantalize everyone's imagination and appetite. With the first bite they discover a symphony of tastes in an airy concoction that, at first blush, seems to bear little relation to the basic fare served earlier. As they go back for second and third helpings, however, the family realizes how Theo's contribution pulls many of the flavors, textures, and spices from the other foods into some type of coherent balance, a culinary unification at a higher level.

Finally sated, the family settles on a blanket by the stream and attempts to catch one another up on their lives. As the discussion proceeds, Mr. Biawg-Raphe's smile at his seemingly happily reunited family slowly fades as he realizes there exists an undercurrent of tension between the siblings. It isn't that they dislike one another—in fact, the camaraderie seems quite high and genuine. It is just that with a prolonged separation combined with the historical accident of having different mothers, each child has matured and become increasingly entrenched in his or her own work and families of procreation, with all the pulls, strains, and attractions that entails. In his wisdom, Otto accepts the divergent interests of his progeny, recognizing that family members tend to drift apart when interests and backgrounds propel them in different directions. He must be thankful, he muses, that at least the family can still come together and learn from one another.

The above parable is a metaphor for both the current state of reminiscence research and this book. Clinicians continue to make claims based on evidence that experimental researchers consider equivocal at best. Researchers continue to conduct projects without clear theoretical foundations. Theoretical conceptions (e.g., ego integrity) continue to be vaguely defined and resistant to contrary experimental findings. Therapists remain somewhat disdainful of the quantitative, positivist approach used by experimentalists. And so it goes. Given these less than optimal family dynamics, we sought to provide a forum wherein each family member could place their achievements alongside the successes of their siblings. Perhaps, like Mr. Biawg-Raphe, we should not expect total rapproachment. Nevertheless, seeing the strength in our diversity will enable us to incorporate findings across some subareas and should allow for an assimilation of ideas at a more general level.

In this concluding chapter, we address the following issues. First, we try to define reminiscence via comparison with related concepts that are often used interchangeably, and inappropriately, with it. Second, we identify promising taxonomies of reminiscence functions. Finally, we suggest areas for future research.

REMINISCENCE: WHAT IT IS AND WHAT IT IS NOT

One of the long-standing issues in reminiscence research is the lack of conceptual clarity concerning the nature of reminiscence and its corollary, the inability to arrive at, or at least agree on, an operational definition (Merriam, 1980; Webster & Cappeliez, 1993). Some conflicting findings based on earlier research can surely be traced to the fact that people thought they were ostensibly examining an evaluative type of reminiscence, such as the life review, when in fact they were really investigating simple reminiscence. Persons have used life review and reminiscence interchangeably, and several related concepts, such as personal narratives and autobiography, are sometimes seen as synonymous. In this section, we attempt to identify similarities and differences between selected terms and simple reminiscence by contrasting them along several dimensions. This will of necessity be a crude and subjective exercise. We harbor no fantasies that we will achieve consensus. What we hope to do, realistically, is have the discussion serve as a preliminary position, a foil against which readers can react, elaborate, and refine. As Butler notes in the Foreword, perhaps life review and reminiscence are not amenable to rigid and precise definitions. Nevertheless, it is probably a productive exercise to see whether and how simple reminiscence overlaps with related terms. To this end, we discuss the following five dimensions along which each concept can be rated as high, medium, and low: spontaneity, structure, evaluation, frequency, and comprehensiveness. The concepts we compare are reminiscence, life review, autobiographical memory, and narrative. Table 1 lists the positions for each concept along all five dimensions.

Reminiscence

Reminiscence, as a phenomenon, is high in spontaneity. A variety of props or themes can begin the process with any group of people. For example, one lady in a coffee klatch group pulled out some dance programs from hops (dances) that she had attended at West Point. These dance programs generated a lively discussion regarding old gowns, old beaus, and old good times. Everyone had something to say, and the reminiscence event was unplanned.

In reminiscence, there is little structure; people can skip from one event to another at any given time. Words describing one event may set off talk of a different event in another person because one similar word served as a reminder to that other person. Reminiscence can be fun, and the spontaneity and lack of structure found in reminiscence actually make it the modality of choice in group work (Haight & Dias, 1992).

Reminiscence can contain the element of evaluation, but evaluation is not an integral part of reminiscence. The evaluation can also be internal and not shared with others and can occur at any time either during or after the reminiscence. Because it can occur in isolation, the outcome is not always positive and there is not a lot of working through. The presence or absence of evaluation in reminis-

Table 1   Five Dimensions of Recall

Type of recall	Spontaneity	Structure	Evaluation	Frequency	Comprehension
Reminiscence	High	Low	Medium	High	Low
Life review	Medium	High	High	Low	High
Autobiography	Low	High	Medium-high	Low	Medium
Narrative	Medium-high	Low-medium	Low	Low-medium	Low

cence is probably more dependent on individual personality traits than on anything provided by the modality.

The frequency of reminiscence is highly variable across individuals, but if we consider average rates, the frequency is very high across both gender and age groups. Partly as a function of the spontaneous nature of reminiscing, we turn to the past in many public and private contexts. The fact that there is such a large variability in reminiscence frequency, however, suggests that one avenue of future research is the explication of individual differences (see Future Directions section).

Finally, reminiscence is rated low on comprehensiveness. Simple reminiscence involves the recall of relatively independent, isolated episodes from our past. There is no necessary logic, sequence, or theme to simple reminiscence. There is no systematic exploration of developmental blocks of time, no attempts to place the recalled memory within a broader psychosocial context. Of course, one memory can elicit several more, but subsequent recall is just as likely to lead in different directions than toward some teleological goal.

Life Review

Life review differs from simple reminiscence on many of these dimensions. The spontaneity of the life review is lower than that of simple reminiscence because fewer and more specific triggers are required to elicit it. Many authors contend that the life review is triggered by external life events, generally (although not exclusively) of a crisis or transitional nature. Stressful disruptions (e.g., death, divorce, or unemployment) or developmental milestones may prompt a reassessment of past accomplishments, values, and goals. Such periodic self-reassessments are built into many life span theories.

The life review is also more structured and comprehensive than simple reminiscence. In a life review, there is more apt to be a sequential recounting from childhood to the present or an identification and systematic elaboration of developmental concerns. Certainly, more territory is covered in a life review and one gains an appreciation for the magnitude of one's life.

There is also a greater effort to evaluate the recalled memories in order to derive a sense of meaning and purpose to one's life. This necessarily entails working through painful emotional episodes as well as positive, self-enhancing memories. Evaluation involves renegotiating the meaning of memories given their psychosociocultural origins. Seen from a current vantage point, perhaps through a new construct system (see Chapter 18), previous sources of anger, shame, embarrassment, guilt, and other assorted negative emotions can be reconstrued in more positive terms. Webster and Young (1988) have suggested that a comprehensive life review entails the recall, evaluation, and synthesis of positive and negative memories. Recall, or simple reminiscence, is therefore only one part of the life review process.

Autobiography

By its nature, writing an autobiography must be a planned event. Some inner spontaneous urge may instigate the need to write an autobiography, but the process itself is planned. The trigger for writing down one's life story is probably quite formal and specific (e.g., grandchildren request a family history) and therefore occurs infrequently.

The autobiography is a highly structured enterprise covering major life themes such as love, money, work, and family. These do not necessarily follow a chronological or developmental sequence more characteristic of a life review.

Autobiography includes, but does not require, evaluation. However, it is probably impossible to write about the choices one has made in life without evaluating them. By virtue of the topics covered, evaluation occurs, but, again, it can take place in isolation or in the group when one reads what one has written. When the autobiography is shared with a group, there is a group effect that helps the individual reintegrate and accept questionable events.

The autobiography, like the life review, is comprehensive. Although the approach is different and not developmental, looking at themes such as love should cover the entire life span, including parental love, sibling love, the love of a significant other, a mother's love for a child, or the love of close friends. In both approaches, one's life is placed in some context that in turn provides meaning and direction to it.

Narrative

Narrative is telling a story and passing down facts. Narrative can be spontaneously prompted by a need in either the listener or the storyteller, or it can be triggered by external events in the environment. Narrative has its own internal logic and structure, and the stories we tell conform closely to societally sanctioned templates. Western culture has standard story formats in which protaganists encounter and resolve problems in a sequential order from beginning to middle to end. Often, our stories are shaped and reshaped to fit, for instance, a comedy, tragedy, or adventure format.

The frequency of the narrative depends on need as well. However, when compared with simple reminiscence, the narrative is less spontaneous, more structured, and less frequent. The narrative might be comprehensive about a single fact, but it is not comprehensive in terms of a whole life. Narrative is more of a technique for passing down information.

TAXONOMIES OF REMINISCENCE FUNCTIONS

Despite these differences, many members of the family are talking a common language. A clear example of this is the recognition of different types of reminiscence and the potentially divergent psychological consequences they might have.

Several authors have devised taxonomies of reminiscence and elaborated their functions. Table 2 lists examples from recent efforts.

It is clear from even a cursory examination of Table 2 that we have made significant strides in moving away from global, unidimensional conceptions of reminiscence to multifaceted, multipurpose conceptions. These differentiated and specific taxonomies have already borne fruit in terms of the identification of which types of reminiscence are associated, for example, with successful aging (e.g., Chapters 2 and 16 in this volume; Wong & Watt, 1991). What is encouraging about this development is that regardless of methods of data collection and analysis (e.g., quantitative vs. qualitative) and orientation (e.g., clinical vs. experimental), a clear overlap between, and sometimes virtual replication of, categories of reminiscence functions is emerging. This speaks well of the convergent validity of these divisions of reminiscence uses and empirically substantiates many functions of reminiscence that clinicians have intuitively identified in working with clients. What are some of these functions?

As early as 1974, Coleman introduced a preliminary taxonomy of reminiscence functions. Simple reminiscence involves recalling past events so that having the past present as a significant element in one's mental life is a continual source of strength to the self. Informative reminiscence involves applying the relevant experiences of the past to the present to facilitate a teaching relationship. Finally, according to Coleman, the life review involves "analyzing memories of one's life to integrate a proper image of oneself in the face of death" (p. 283).

In the early 1980s, two other tripartite taxonomies joined Coleman's. LoGerfo (1981) suggested that informative reminiscence entailed a pleasurable form of recollection, perhaps contributing to mood enhancement; evaluative reminiscence involved attempts at reconciliation with past conflicts and failures; and, finally, obsessive reminiscence was manifested in an unproductive rehashing of remorseful memories.

Romaniuk and Romaniuk (1981) found three factors in a factor analysis of responses to a 13-item questionnaire. Self-Regard/Image Enhancement served to bolster feelings of self-worth and elevate mood. This would be similar to LoGerfo's informative and Coleman's simple types of reminiscence. Present Problem-Solving is an adaptive form of reminiscing in which memories of past efforts and strategies that were effective in overcoming obstacles serve to reinforce the reminiscer's sense of mastery and skill for dealing with a current stressor. This type does not have a clear parallel with either of the other two taxonomies. Finally, Existential/Self-Understanding shares much with Coleman's life review type of reminiscing (although the latter is more comprehensive), whereas LoGerfo's evaluative type is a stronger match.

These early attempts to differentiate reminiscence served the important purpose of illustrating that not all forms of reminiscence are equally adaptive. This provided clues as to why the ostensible therapeutic value of reminiscing was equivocal when tested empirically.

Table 2 Taxonomy of Recall

Authors	Function: To discover meaning and continuity	To draw on past experiences to solve present problems and to cope	To provide an instructive story	To provide a descriptive story	To dwell on good old days to escape from present	To obsess about unresolved disturbing events in the past	To prepare for death	To maintain memories of significant others	
Beaton (1980)	Affirming					Despairing			Negating
Coleman (1974)	Life review		Informative	Simple					
Kovach (Chap. 8)		Validating			Deprecating and glorifying	Lamenting			
LoGerfo (1981)	Evaluative			Informative		Obsessive			
McMahon & Rhudick (1967)	Life review								

Source	Therapeutic		Informative		Enjoyment			
Merriam (1993a, Chapter 6 in this volume)								
Romaniuk & Romaniuk (1981)	Existential Self-understanding	Present problem solving			Self-regard Image enhancement			
Rybarczyk (Chap. 15)		Challenge interview			General reminiscence interview			
Sherman (Chap. 19)	Life review reminiscing	Adapting and coping	Narrative		Enhancing	Reparative and retentive		
Watt & Wong (1991)	Integrative	Instrumental	Trans-missive	Narrative	Escapist	Obsessive		
Webster (1993, 1994b)	Identity	Problem solving	Teach/inform	Conversation	Boredom reduction	Bitterness revival	Death preparation	Intimacy maintenance

Much of the discourse of the past 30 years might have been avoided if we had started with a taxonomy in 1963. For example, Beaton (1980) adopted the terms *affirming,* meaning *integrative* and *despairing,* meaning *obsessive,* and then added a new term, *negating,* that referred to a form of denial. McMahon and Rhudick (1967) discussed two types of reminiscence used by their sample of veterans: life review, equal to integrative reminiscence, and depreciating and glorifying reminiscence, which in our opinion relates to Watt and Wong's escapist, Webster's boredom reduction, and Sherman's enhancing types of reminiscence. Sherman presented five different types, all relating to types in the taxonomy of either Wong or Webster, as Table 2 shows.

Kovach has examined reminiscence qualitatively, and her chapter in this book (Chapter 8) is very helpful to understanding the meaning of validating and lamenting types of reminiscence. For example, the validating type of reminiscence contains joy, past-to-present comparisons, and positive self-appraisals. It seems that validating reminiscence, although categorized as instrumental, also subsumes a small amount of narrative and may be integrative. On the other hand, lamenting reminiscence contains regrets, lack of choice, and difficulties. Not only is it obsessive, it may also be escapist. The difference in interpretation may come from comparing a type of reminiscer with kinds of reminiscence, an important point for making Table 2 a useful instrument.

Rounding out tri-dimensional classifications, Merriam (1993a; Chapter 6 in this book) reports on a factor-analytic study that identified three types of reminiscence based on a 17-item questionnaire. In Chapter 6, Merriam writes that therapeutic reminiscence reflects "coping with life's problems, an effort to understand oneself, and the work involved in Butler's life review" (p. 82). Informative reminiscence clearly reflects Coleman's (1986) notion of the storytelling function of reminiscence. Finally, an enjoyment factor emerged that is close to Coleman's simple and LoGerfo's informative types of reminiscence.

In the early 1990s, two classification schemes were developed based on qualitative coding of reminiscence transcripts (Wong & Watt, 1991) and factor-analytic studies of questionnaire responses (Webster, 1993, 1994). These recent classification schemes are more comprehensive and differentiated than earlier approaches, encompassing and adding to the previous categories. Wong and Watt (1991) identified six types of reminiscence: integrative, instrumental, transmissive, narrative, escapist, and obsessive. As Wong illustrates in Chapter 2, integrative reminiscence concerns conflict resolution and reconciliation, an acceptance of the self and others, a sense of meaning and self-worth, and the integration of past and present. This shares properties of Coleman's life review, LoGerfo's evaluative, the Romaniuks' existential/self-understanding, and Merriam's therapeutic types of reminiscence. Instrumental reminiscence involves drawing on memories of past plans, goal-directed activities, and episodes of successful coping to help solve a current problem. As such, it is virtually identical to the Romaniuks' present problem-solving type of reminiscence. Transmissive reminiscence involves recounting of past events with the purpose of instructing or entertaining the listener. This equates with both Coleman's and Merriam's informative type of reminiscence. Escapist reminiscence involves a defensive recapturing of pleasant memories to glorify the past and deprecate the present. This shares certain characteristics with LoGerfo's informative type of reminiscence, with its properties of mood elevation, and overlaps somewhat with Merriam's enjoyment type of reminiscence. Obsessive reminiscence is characterized by persistent rumination about unpleasant past events. As such, it maps precisely onto LoGerfo's obsessive type of reminiscence. Finally, narrative reminiscence involves a bare account of autobiographical facts unembellished by any type of interpretive or evaluative stance. This does not have an obvious and direct connection with earlier taxonomies.

Recently, Webster (1993) factor-analyzed the responses of more than 700 subjects on the 43-item Reminiscence Functions Scale (RFS). A replication study (Webster, 1994b) based on 399 subjects confirmed the earlier factor structure with an extension of one factor. In total, the RFS consists of eight factors: Boredom Reduction, Death Preparation, Identity, Problem-Solving, Conversation, Intimacy Maintenance, Bitterness Revival, and Teach/Inform. Boredom Reduction refers to reminiscence that serves as a generally pleasant form of arousal during times when one is unoccupied or one's environment lacks stimulation. This is somewhat similar to Wong and Watt's escapist type of reminiscence, although it does not necessarily entail a deprecation of the present. Death Preparation represents reminiscence that functions to reduce fears of impending death and help one face thoughts of one's mortality with relative equanimity. As a separate function, death preparation does not appear in any other taxonomy, but it is generally seen as one function of the life review. Identity refers to reminiscing with the purpose of establishing and maintaining a coherent sense of self, direction, and meaning in life. This is similar to Wong and Watt's integrative reminiscence, the Romaniuks' existential/self-understanding reminiscence, and parts of Merriam's therapeutic types of reminiscence. Problem Solving represents reminiscence in which one reviews past coping strategies and problem situations to see that one is capable of dealing with current stressors. This corresponds to both Wong and Watt's instrumental type of reminiscence and the Romaniuk's present problem-solving type of reminiscence. Conversation reminiscence serves a social function by bringing new and old acquaintances together via shared memories. This is a relatively nonevaluative type of reminiscence without any intention of purposely teaching others moral or life lessons. It is similar to Wong and Watt's narrative type of reminiscence, although the former does have the specific aim of facilitating social discourse. Intimacy Maintenance reflects reminiscence that has as its aim the resurrection and maintenance of a mental model of a person who is no longer a part of the reminiscer's life. It involves keeping alive the memory of a significant other who, for whatever reason, is separated from the reminiscer. As a relatively discrete functional category, Intimacy Maintenance does not have a corresponding category in other taxonomies. Bitterness Revival represents reminiscing that is purposely focused on memories with a heavy negative valence. They serve to keep old injustices, either real or imagined, fresh in our minds. There are clear parallels here to the Romaniuks' and Wong and Watt's obsessive types of reminiscence. Finally, Teach/Inform reflects the use of memories to teach or inform others about life in a different time, with the purpose of passing on cultural/familial knowledge deemed useful in facilitating another's adjustment or decision making. It is identical to the categories proposed by the Romaniuks of the same name and to Wong and Watt's transmissive and Coleman's informative types of reminiscence.

Clearly, we have made some headway on categorizing reminiscence into relatively specific and comprehensive functions. The consistency with which certain dimensions appear (e.g., problem solving), coupled with the continued assimilation of categories of earlier taxonomies into later schemes, bolsters our confidence that these are real functional categories and not simply methodological artifacts or idiosyncratic findings. The taxonomies of both Wong and Watt and Webster incorporate all of the previous dimensions and have extended the number of independent, discrete functions close to the outer boundary.

FUTURE DIRECTIONS

There are many possible directions for future research. We concentrate on those suggested by the projects described in this volume. First, researchers, theorists, clinicians, and practitioners must adopt a common language, or at least explicitly state what type of reminiscence they are investigating. We hope the taxonomy of terms in Table 2 will help in this regard. A clear description of the process used in a study will help readers make meaningful comparisons between approaches. For example, Haight's process of life review is a 6-hr intervention, whereas, Rybar-czyk's challenge reminiscing intervention requires 1–2 hr. Practitioners reading these results can then decide the type of intervention they wish to use. A clear description of the process may also help clarify results. For instance, group work often uses longer interventions than does one-on-one work, and group research usually has positive outcomes. These results may lead the reader to think that group reminiscence is more effective than individual reminiscing. However, it should be obvious that in this situation, length of treatment is confounded with type (i.e., group vs. individual) of intervention format.

We now have several carefully constructed measures of reminiscence types, functions, and content. Researchers should examine these measures to see which is the most appropriate for their needs. As results based on the same measure accrue, a more meaningful comparison of findings is possible. These tools need further refinement and cross-validation, which will only come with further use. Being ourselves developers of some of these instruments, we clearly have a vested interest in this subject. The point remains, however, that researchers no longer need to create measures on the fly.

We also need more model building. Fry's work is an excellent example of the type of conceptual framework that can advance the field. Perhaps research can be conducted to test aspects of her model or other models. The very general Eriksonian framework within which much reminiscence research has been conducted is simply too amorphous to provide specific answers unless and until more precise measures are created.

Several contributors to this book have discussed interesting findings in relation to gender and age. These individual difference variables have been relatively unexplored, as have personality factors. If there is a latitude in reminiscence behavior that is not accounted for by age, differences due to sex and personality variables may help us account for certain conflicting findings. Webster (1994), for instance, recently reported that personality traits (e.g., neuroticism) accounted for more variance than did age in certain reminiscence dimensions.

The incidence of reminiscence use and enjoyment, then, may stem in no small part from these individual difference variables. Others that have not been examined systematically are family dynamics and cultural variability. It is possible that parent–child transactions that include talking about and valuing the past produce a relatively enduring trait in which the adult enjoys and engages in reminiscence to a greater extent than individuals who had not been exposed to reminiscing in their childhood. It would be interesting and instructive to see what the developmental precursors are for reminiscence. In a similar vein, do cultures with strong oral traditions (e.g., Native Americans) engage in reminiscing more or less frequently than other cultures? Would certain religious groups with strong oral traditions (e.g., Jews) reminisce more frequently on Wong and Watt's transmissive or Webster's Teach/Inform function of reminiscence relative to other groups?

Finally, researchers need to look at the effect of reminiscence on the people conducting the process. Some practitioners report that those conducting the reminiscence process have changed their attitudes toward their clients. To date, reminiscence has been used as an intervention only to improve affective outcomes in clients. If it also has potential for changing the attitudes of caregivers, this possible use needs to be explored and exploited. Perhaps reminiscence dyads between caregiver and dementia sufferers would reestablish affectional bonds and alleviate to a small degree the burden of caregiver stress.

CONCLUSION

We have come a long way, but in some sense are still beginning, our journey. There are many fascinating questions left unanswered, many prompted by the findings reported in this volume. We are beginning to amass a critical amount of data and can make the following claim with assurance: *Reminiscence is a multi-facted, multipurpose, naturally occurring mental phenomenon manifested across the life span in a variety of forms and contexts.* Given the emerging conceptual clarity, availability of assessment tools, and specific research questions, the future vitality of reminiscence research and application seems guaranteed.

References

Abler, R. M., & Fretz, B. (1988). Self-efficacy and competence in independent living among oldest old persons. *Journal of Gerontology, 43,* 138–143.

Abramson, L. Y., Alloy, L. B., & Metalsky, G. I. (1988). The cognitive diathesis-stress theories of depression: Toward an adequate evaluation of the theories' validities. In L. B. Alloy (Ed.), *Cognitive processes in depression.* New York: Guilford Press.

Abramson, L. Y., Seligman, M. E. P., & Teasdale, J. D. (1978). Learned helplessness in humans: Critique and reformulation. *Journal of Abnormal Psychology, 87,* 49–74.

Adams, C. (1991). Qualitative age differences in memory for text: A life-span developmental perspective. *Psychology and Aging, 3,* 323–336.

Adams, C., Labouvie-Vief, G., Hobart, C. J., & Dorosz, M. (1990). Adult age differences in story recall style. *Journal of Gerontology, 45,* 12–27.

Adams, D. L. (1969). Analysis of a life satisfaction index. *Journal of Gerontology, 24,* 470–475.

Adams, J. (1991a). Human biography: A personal approach . . . open learning programme part 1. *Nursing Times, 87*(25), vii.

Adams, J. (1991b). Professional development module P2: Human biography—A personal approach. *Nursing Times, 87*), i–viii.

Adelman, M. B., & Bankoff, E. (1990). Life-span concerns: Implications for mid-life adult singles. In H. Giles, N. Coupland, & J. Weimann (Eds.), *Communication, health, and the elderly* (Fulbright Colloquium Series No. 8, pp. 64–91). Manchester, England: University of Manchester Press.

Adler, A. (1957). *Understanding human nature.* Greenwich, CT: Fawcett. (Original work published 1927)

Adler, A. (1958). *What life should mean to you.* New York: G. P. Putnam's Sons.

Agnew, D. P. (1986). Psychotherapy of the elderly: The life validation approach in psychotherapy with elderly patients. *Journal of Geriatric Psychiatry, 16,* 87–92.

Aiken, L. H., & Henrichs, T. F. (1971). Systematic relaxation as a nursing intervention technique with open heart surgery patients. *Nursing Research, 20,* 212–217.

Alloy, L. B., Hartlage, S., & Abramson, L. Y. (1988). Testing the cognitive diathesis-stress theories of depression: Issues of research design, conceptualization, and assessment. In L. B. Alloy (Ed.), *Cognitive processes in depression.* New York: Guilford Press.

American Association of Retired Persons. (1989). *Reminiscence: Finding meaning in memories. Training guide.* Washington, DC: Author.

American Association of Retired Persons. *Reminiscence: Reaching back, moving forward.* Washington, DC: Author.

American Association of Retired Persons. (1992). *The power of memories: Creative uses of reminiscence.* Washington, DC: Author.

American College of Surgeons. (1987). *Socio-economic factbook for surgery 1987.* Chicago: Author.

Anderson, K. O., & Masur, F. T. (1984). Psychological preparation for invasive medical and dental procedures. *Journal of Behavioral Medicine, 6,* 1–40.

Andersson, L. (1985). Intervention against loneliness in a group of elderly women. An impact evaluation. *Social Science and Medicine, 20,* 355–364.

Aranda, M. (1990). Culture-friendly services for Latino elders. *Generations, 14,* 55–57.

Arena, J. G., Hightower, N. E., & Chong, G. C. (1988). Relaxation therapy for tension headache in the elderly: A prospective study. *Psychology and Aging, 3,* 96–98.

Aronoff, J., & Wilson, J. P. (1985). *Personality in the social process.* Hillsdale, NJ: Erlbaum.

Auerbach, S. M. (1986). Assumptions of crisis theory and a temporal model of crisis intervention. In S. M. Auerbach & A. Stohlberg (Eds.), *Crisis intervention with children and families* (pp. 3–37). Washington, DC: Hemisphere.

Baines, S., Saxby, P., & Ehlert, K. (1987). Reality orientation and reminiscence therapy: A controlled cross-over study of elderly confused people. *British Journal of Psychiatry, 151,* 222–231.

Baker-Brown, G., Ballard, E., Bluck, S., de Vries, B., Suedfeld, P., & Tetlock, P. (1992). The conceptual/integrative complexity scoring manual. In C. Smith (Ed.), *Motivation and personality: Handbook of content analytic procedures* (pp. 401–418). New York: Cambridge University Press.

Ballard, E. J. (1982). Canadian Prime Ministers: Complexity in political crises. *Canadian Psychology, 24,* 125–129.

Baltes, P. (1987). Theoretical propositions of life-span developmental psychology: On the dynamics between growth and decline. *Developmental Psychology, 23,* 611–626.

Bandura, A. (1977). Self-efficacy: Toward a unifying theory of behaviour change. *Psychological Review, 84,* 191–215.

Bandura, A. (1981). Self-referent thought: A developmental analysis of self-efficacy. In J. H. Flavell & L. Ross (Eds.), *Social cognitive development: Frontiers and possible futures.* New York: Cambridge University Press.

Bandura, A. (1986). Self-efficacy mechanism in physiological activation and health-promoting behavior. In J. Madden IV, S. Matthysse, & J. Barchas (Eds.), *Adaptation, learning, and affect* (pp. 1–51). New York: Raven Press.

Barclay (1986).

Barclay, C. (1988). Schematization of autobiographical memory. In D. C. Rubin (Ed.), *Autobiographical memory* (pp. 82–99). Cambridge: Cambridge University Press.

Barclay & Hodges (1987). *Content and structure in autobiographical memory.* Unpublished manuscript, University of Rochester, Rochester, NY.

Barclay, C. R., & Wellman, H. (1986). Accuracies and inaccuracies in autobiographical memories. *Journal of Memory and Language, 25,* 93–103.

Barrera, M., & Ainlay, S. (1983). The structure of social support: A conceptual and empirical analysis. *American Journal of Community Psychology, 11,* 133–157.

Bartlett, F. C. (1932). *Remembering: A study in experimental and social psychology.* Cambridge: Cambridge University Press.

Baruch, G. K., Biener, L., & Barnett, R. C. (1987). Women and gender in research on work and family stress. *American Psychologist, 42,* 130–136.

Beaton, S. R. (1980). Reminiscence in old age. *Nursing Forum, 19,* 271–283.

Beaton, S. (1991). Styles of reminiscence and ego development of older women residing in long-term care settings. *International Journal of Aging and Human Development, 32,* 53–63.

Beck, A. T. (1967). *Depression: Clinical, experimental, and theoretical aspects.* New York: Harper & Row.

Beck, A. T., & Beamesderfer, A. (1974). Assessment of depression: The Depression Inventory. In P. Pichot (Ed.), *Psychological measurements in psychopharmacology: Modern problems in pharmacopsychiatry* (Vol. 7).

Beck, A. T., & Greenberg, R. L. (1986). Cognitive therapy in the treatment of depression. In N. Hoffman (Ed.), *Foundations of cognitive therapy: Theoretical methods and practical applications.* New York: Plenum Press.

Beck, A. T., Rush, A. J., Shaw, B. F., & Emery, G. (1979). *Cognitive therapy of depression.* New York: Guilford Press.

Becker, G., & Kaufman, S. (1988). Old age, rehabilitation, and research: A review of the issues. *The Gerontologist, 28,* 459–468.

Belenky, M. F., Clinchy, B. M., Goldberger, N. R., & Tarule, J. M. (1986). *Women's ways of knowing: The development of self, voice, and mind.* New York: Basic Books.

Bender, M. (1994). An interesting confusion: What can we do with reminiscence groupwork? In J. Bornat (Ed.), *Reminiscence reviewed: Evaluations, achievements, perspectives* (pp. 32–45). Buckingham, England: Open University Press.

Bender, M. P., Cooper, A. E., & Howe, A. (1983). *The utility of reminiscence groups in old people's homes.* London: Borough of Newham.

Benum, K., Dalgard, O. S., & Sørensen, T. (1987). Social network stimulation: Health promotion in a high-risk group of middle-aged women. *Acta Psychiatrica Scandinavica, 337,* 33–41.

Berger, J. W. (1989). Developing the story in psychotherapy. *American Journal of Psychotherapy, 43,* 248–259.

Berman, L., & Sokowska-Ashcroft, I. (1986). The old in language and literature. *Language and Communication, 6,* 139–144.

Beverfelt, E. (1984). Old people remember: A contribution to society. *Educational Gerontology, 10,* 233–244.

Beverfelt, E. (1990). *The public authorities' contributions to families caring for elderly people* (Gerontological Report No. 10-90). Oslo, Norway: Norwegian Gerontological Institute.

Billings, A. G., & Moos, R. H. (1981). The role of coping responses and social resources in attenuating stress of life events. *Journal of Behavioral Medicine, 4,* 139–157.

Billings, A. G., & Moos, R. H. (1982). Psychosocial theory and research on depression: An integrative framework and review. *Clinical Psychology Review, 2,* 213–237.

Billings, A. G., & Moos, R. H. (1985). Psychosocial stressors, coping, and depression. In E. E. Beckman & W. R. Leber (Eds.), *Handbook of depression: Treatment, assessment, and research* (pp. 940–974). Homewood, IL: Dorsey Press.

Birren, J. E. (1964). *The psychology of aging.* Englewood Cliffs, NJ: Prentice-Hall.

Birren, J. E. (1987, May). The best of all stories. *Psychology Today, 21,* p. 74.

Birren, J. E., & Deutchman, D. E. (1991). *Guiding autobiography groups for older adults: Exploring the fabric of life.* Baltimore, MD: Johns Hopkins University Press.

Birren, J. E., & Hedlund, B. (1987). Contributions of autobiography to developmental psychology. In N. Isenberg (Ed.), *Contemporary topics in developmental psychology* (pp. 1–39, 394–415). New York: Wiley.

Bjelland, A. K., Danielsen, K., Helset, A., & Thorsen, K. (1992). *Livsløp og livshistorier* [Life course and life stories] (Gerontological Report 4-1992). Oslo, Norway: Norwegian Gerontological Institute.

Black, G., & Haight, B. K. (1992). Integrality as a holistic framework for the life-review process. *Holistic Nurse Practitioner, 7*(1), 7–15.

Blanchard, E. B., Andrasik, F., Evans, D. D., & Hillhouse, J. (1985). Biofeedback and relaxation treatments for headache in the elderly: A caution and a challenge. *Biofeedback and Self-Regulation, 10*(1), 69–73.

Blanchard-Fields, F. (1990). Postformal reasoning in a socioemotional context. In M. L. Commons, J. D. Sinnott, F. A. Richards, & C. Armon (Eds.), *Adult development: Comparisons and applications of developmental models* (Vol. 1). New York: Praeger.

Boden, D., & Bielby, D. (1983). The past as resource: A conversational analysis of elderly talk. *Human Development, 26,* 308–319.

Boggs, D., & Leptak, J. (1991). Life review among senior citizens as a product of drama. *Educational Gerontology, 17,* 239–246.

Borden, W. (1992). Narrative perspectives in psychosocial intervention following adverse life events. *Social Work, 37,* 135–141.

Botella, L., & Feixas, G. (1992–93). The autobiographical group: A tool for the reconstruction of past life experience with the aged. *International Journal of Aging and Human Development, 36,* 303–319.

Bowlby, J. (1986). Attachment, life-span, and old-age. In J. Munnichs & B. Miesen (Eds.), *Attachment, life-span, and old-age* (pp. 9–19).

Boylin, W., Gordon, S. K., & Nehrke, M. F. (1976). Reminiscing and ego integrity in institutionalized elderly males. *The Gerontologist, 16,* 118–124.

Bradburn, N. M. (1969). *The structure of psychological well-being.* Chicago: Aldine.

Bramlett, M., & Gueldner, S. (1993). Reminiscence: A viable option to enhance power in elders. *Clinical Nurse Specialist, 7,* 68–74.

Brewer, W. (1986). What is autobiographical memory? In D. Rubin (Ed.), *Autobiographical memory.* Cambridge, England: Cambridge University Press.

Brewin, C. R. (1986). Internal attribution and self-esteem in depression: A theoretical note. *Cognitive Therapy and Research, 10,* 469–475.

Brink, T. L. (1979). *Geriatric psychotherapy.* New York: Human Sciences Press.

Brody, E. M. (1985). *Mental and physical health practices of older people.* New York: Springer Publishing Company.

Brown, G., & Harris, J. (1978). *Social origins of depression: A study of psychiatric disorder in women.* New York: Free Press.

Bruner, J. (1986). *Actual minds, possible worlds.* Cambridge, England: Cambridge University Press.

Bruner, J. (1987). Life as narrative. *Social Research, 54*(1), 11–32.

Buhler, C. (1933). *Der lebenslauf als psycholgisches problem.* Göttingen, Germany: Hogrefe.

Burnside, I. *Teaching reminiscence interventions.* Manuscript submitted for publication.

Burnside, I. M. (1978). Reminiscence and group therapy with the aged. In I. M. Burnside (Ed.), *Working with the elderly: Group processes and techniques.* New York: Duxbury Press.

Burnside, I. (1990a). Reminiscence: An independent nursing intervention for the elderly. *Issues in Mental Health Nursing, 11,* 33–48.

Burnside, I. (1990b). *The effect of reminiscence groups on fatigue, affect, and life satisfaction in older women.* Unpublished doctoral dissertation, School of Nursing, University of Texas at Austin, Austin, TX.

Burnside, I. (1993). Themes in reminiscence groups with older women. *International Journal of Aging and Human Development, 37,* 177–189.

Burnside, I. (1994). Group work with the cognitively impaired. In I. Burnside & M. G. Schmidt (Eds.), *Working with older persons: Group process and techniques* (3rd ed.). Boston: Jones & Bartlett.

Burnside, I., & Haight, B. K. (1992). Reminiscence and life review: Analyzing each concept. *Journal of Advanced Nursing, 17,* 855–862.

Burnside, I., & Haight, B. K. (1994). Protocols for reminiscence and life review. *Nurse Practitioner, 19,* 55–61.

Butler, R. N. (1963). The life review: An interpretation of reminiscence in the aged. *Psychiatry, 26,* 65–76.

Butler, R. (1964). The life review: An interpretation of reminiscence in the aged. In R. Kastenbaum (Ed.), *New thoughts on aging.* New York: Springer Publishing Company.

Butler, R. N. (1974). Successful aging and the role of the life review. *Journal of the American Geriatrics Society, 22,* 529–535.

Butler, R. N. (1975). *Why survive? Being old in America.* New York: Harper & Row.

Butler, R. N., & Lewis, M. I. (1977). *Aging and mental health.* St. Louis, MO: C. V. Mosby.

Cameron, P. (1972). The generation gap: Time orientation. *The Gerontologist, 12*(11), 117–119.

Cappeliez, P. (1993). Depression in elderly persons: Prevalence, predictors, and psychological intervention. In P. Cappeliez & R. J. Flynn (Eds.), *Depression and the social environment: Research and intervention with neglected populations* (pp. 332–368). Montreal, Quebec, Canada: McGill-Queen's University Press.

Cappeliez, P., & Blanchet, D. (1986). Les strategies d'adaptation des personnes agees aux prises avec des sentiments depressifs. *Revue Canadienne du Viellissement, 5,* 125–134.

Casey, D. A., & Grant, R. W. (1993). Cognitive therapy with depressed elderly inpatients. In J. H. Wright, M. E. Thase, A. T. Beck, & J. W. Ludgate (Eds.), *Cognitive therapy with inpatients: Developing a cognitive milieu* (pp. 295–314). New York: Guilford Press.

Casey, E. S. (1989). *Remembering: A phenomenological study.* Bloomington, IN: Indiana University Press.

Challis, D., & Davies, B. (1986). *Case management in community care.* London: Gower.

Chandler, M. J. (1987). The Othello effect: Essay on the emergence and eclipse of skeptical doubt. *Human Development, 30,* 137–159.

Clements, W. M. (1982). Therapeutic functions of recreation in reminiscence with aging persons. In M. L. Teague, R. D. MacWeil, & G. L. Hutzhuser (Eds.), *Perspectives on leisure and aging.* Columbia, MO: University of Missouri Press.

Cohen, J. (1977). *Statistical power analysis for the behavioral sciences.* San Diego, CA: Academic Press.

Cohler, B. (1982). Personal narrative and life course. In P. Baltes & O. Brim (Eds.), *Life-span development and behavior* (Vol. 4, pp. 205–241). San Diego, CA: Academic Press.

Coleman, P. G. (1974). Measuring reminiscence characteristics from conversation as adaptive features of old age. *International Journal of Aging and Human Development, 5,* 281–294.

Coleman, P. G. (1986a). *Aging and reminiscence processes: Social and clinical implications.* New York: Wiley.

Coleman, P. (1986b). Issues in the therapeutic use of reminiscence in elderly people. In I. Hanley & M. Gilhooley (Eds.), *Psychological therapies for elderly people.* London: Croom Helm.

Coleman, P. (1991). Ageing and life history: The meaning of reminiscence in late life. *Sociological Review* (Monograph), *37,* 120–143.

Coleman, P. G., Ivani-Chalian, C., & Robinson, M. (1993). Self-esteem and its sources: Stability and change in later life. *Ageing and Society, 13,* 171–192.

Cook, E. A. (1988). *The effect of reminiscence group therapy on depressed institutionalized elders.* Unpublished doctoral dissertation, School of Nursing, University of Texas at Austin, Austin, TX.

Cook, E. (1991). The effects of reminiscence on psychological measures of ego integrity in elderly nursing home residents. *Archives of Psychiatric Nursing, 5,* 292–298.

Corah, N. L., Gale, E. N., Pace, L. F., & Seyrek, S. K. (1981). Relaxation and muscle programming as a means of reducing psychological stress during dental procedures. *Journal of the American Dental Association, 103,* 232–234.

Costa, P., & Kastenbaum, R. (1967). Some aspects of memories and ambitions in centenarians. *Journal of Genetic Psychology, 110,* 3–16.

Costa, P. T., & McCrae, R. R. (1985). *The NEO Personality Inventory.* Odessa, FL: Psychological Assessment Resources.

Costa, P. T., McCrae, R. R., & Zonderman, A. B. (1987). Environmental and dispositional influences on well-being: Longitudinal follow-up of an American national sample. *British Journal of Psychology, 78,* 299–306.

Crose, R. (1990). Reviewing the past in the here and now: Using gestalt therapy techniques with life review. *Journal of Mental Health Counseling, 12,* 279–287.

Csikszentimihalyi, M., & Beattie, O. V. (1979). Life themes: A theoretical and empirical explanation of their origins and effects. *Journal of Humanistic Psychology, 19,* 45–63.

Csikszentimihalyi, M., & Rochberg-Halton, E. (1981). *The meaning of things: Domestic symbols and the self.* New York: Cambridge University Press.

Danielsen, K. (1990). *De gammeldagse piker: Eldre kvinner forteller om sitt liv* [Girls of olden times: Elder women tell about their lives]. Oslo, Norway: Pax Forlag.

David, D. (1990). Reminiscence, adaptation, and social context in old age. *International Journal of Aging and Human Development, 30,* 175–188.

Davies, A. D. M. (1981). Neither wife nor widow: An intervention with the wife of a chronically handicapped man during hospital visits. *Behaviour Research & Therapy, 19,* 449–451.

Davies, A. D. M., & Peters, M. (1983). Stresses of hospitalization in the elderly: Nurses' and patients' perceptions. *Journal of Advanced Nursing, 8,* 99–105.

DeGenova, M. (1991). Elderly life review therapy: A Bowen approach. *American Journal of Family Therapy, 19,* 160–166.

Dennett, D. C. (1983). The self as a center of narrative gravity. In D. L. Johnson & P. M. Cole (Eds.), *Consciousness and self.* New York: Praeger.

Dennis, H. (1994). Remotivation therapy. In I. Burnside (Ed.), *Working with the elderly: Group process and techniques* (3rd ed.). Boston: Jones & Bartlett.

DeRubeis, R. J., & Beck, A. T. (1988). Cognitive therapy. In K. S. Dobson (Ed.), *Handbook of cognitive-behavioral therapies.* New York: Guilford Press.

de Vries, B., Birren, J. E., & Deutchman, D. E. (1990). Adult development through Guided Autobiography: The family context. *Family Relations, 39,* 3–7.

de Vries, B., Bluck, S., & Birren, J. E. (1993). The understanding of death and dying in a life-span perspective. *The Gerontologist, 33,* 366–372.

de Vries, B., & Walker, L. J. (1987). Complexity theory and attitudes toward capital punishment: A structural analysis. *Personality and Social Psychology Bulletin, 13,* 448–457.

Diamond, S., & Montrose, D. (1984). The value in biofeedback in the treatment of chronic headache: A four-year retrospective study. *Headache, 24,* 5–18.

Dietsche, L. M. (1979). Facilitating the life review through group reminiscence. *Journal of Gerontological Nursing, 5*(4), 43–46.

Disch, R. (1988). Twenty-five years of the life review. *Journal of Gerontological Social Work, 12,* (3/4).

Dittmann-Kohli, F., & Baltes, P. B. (1990). Toward a neofunctionalist conception of adult intellectual development: Wisdom as a prototypical case of intellectual growth. In C. Alexander & E. Langer (Eds.), *Higher stages of human development* (pp. 54–78). New York: Oxford University Press.

Drabble, M. (1992). *The gates of ivory.* New York: Viking Penguin.

Durlak, J. A. (1979). Comparative effectiveness of paraprofessionals and professional helpers. *Psychological Bulletin, 86,* 80–92.

Edwards, M. (1990). Poetry: Vehicle for retrospection and delight. *Generations, 14,* 61–62.

Epting, F. R. (1984). *Personal construct counseling and psychotherapy.* New York: Wiley.

Erikson, E. (1950). *Childhood and society.* New York: W. W. Norton.

Erikson, E. H. (1959). *Identity and the life cycle.* New York: International Universities Press.

Erikson, E. (1963). *Childhood and society* (2nd ed.). New York: W. W. Norton.

Erikson, E. (1968). *Identity: Youth and crisis.* New York: W. W. Norton.

Erikson, E. H. (1980). *Identity and the life cycle.* New York: W. W. Norton.

Erikson, E. H. (1982). *The life cycle completed: A review.* New York: W. W. Norton.

Erikson, E. H., Erikson, J. M., & Kivnick, H. G. (1986). *Vital involvements in old age.* New York: W. W. Norton.

Essa, M. (1986). Grief as a crisis: Psychotherapeutic interventions with the elderly bereaved. *American Journal of Psychotherapy, 40,* 243–251.

Eysenck, H. J., & Eysenck, S. (1969). *Personality structure and measurement.* London: EDITS.

Falk, J. (1969). *The organization of remembered life experience of older people: Its relation to anticipated stress, to subsequent adaptation, and to age.* Unpublished doctoral dissertation, University of Chicago.

Fallot, R. (1980). The impact on mood of verbal reminiscing in later adulthood. *International Journal of Aging and Human Development, 10,* 385–400.

Fassinger, R. E. (1990). Causal models of career choice in two samples of college women. *Journal of Vocational Behavior, 36,* 225–248.

Feil, N. (1993). *The validation breakthrough: Simple techniques for communicating with people with "Alzheimer's type dementia."* Baltimore, MD: Health Professions Press.

Festinger, L. (1954). A theory of social comparison processes. *Human Relations, 7,* 117–140.

Field, D. (1989, July). *Recollections of the personal past and psychological well-being in old age.* Paper presented at the Fourteenth International Congress of Gerontology, Acapulco, Mexico.

Fishman, S. (1992). Relationships among an older adult's life review, ego integrity, and death anxiety. *International Psychogeriatrics, 4,* 267–277.

Fitzgerald, J. M. (1986). Autobiographical memory: A developmental perspective. In D. C. Rubin (Ed.), *Autobiographical memory* (pp. 122–133). Cambridge, England: Cambridge University Press.

Fivush, R., & Reese, E. (1992). The social construction of autobiographical memory. In M. A. Conway, D. C. Rubin, H. Spinnler, & W. A. Wagenaar (Eds.), *Theoretical perspectives on autobiographical memory.* Dordrecht, The Netherlands: Kluwer Academic Publishers.

Folkman, S., & Lazarus, R. S. (1986). Stress processes and depressive symptomatology. *Journal of Abnormal Psychology, 95,* 107–113.

Folkman, S., Lazarus, R. S., Dunkel-Schetter, C., DeLongis, A., & Gruen, R. (1986). The dynamics of a stressful encounter: Cognitive appraisal, coping, and encounter outcomes. *Journal of Personality and Social Psychology, 50,* 992–1003.

Folkman, S., Lazarus, R. S., Pimley, S., & Novacek, J. (1987). Age differences in stress and coping processes. *Psychology and Aging, 2,* 171–184.

Folstein, M., Folstein, S., & McHugh, P. (1975). "Mini-Mental State": A practical method for grading the cognitive states of patients for the clinician. *Journal of Psychiatric Research, 12,* 189–198.

Forrest, M. (1990). Reminiscence therapy in a Scottish hospital. *Health Libraries Review, 7,* 69–72.

Fossan, G. (Ed.). (1991). *Overbehandler eller underbehandler vi vare gamle?* [Do we overtreat or undertreat our elderly?] Oslo, Norway: Apothekernes Laboratorium.

Foster, J. M., & Gallagher, D. (1986). An exploratory study comparing depressed and nondepressed elders' coping strategies. *Journal of Gerontology, 41,* 91–93.

Fransella, F., & Dalton, P. (1990). *Personal construct counseling in action.* Newbury Park, CA: Sage.

Freeman, M. (1993). *Rewriting the self: History, memory, narrative.* London: Routledge.

Freud, A. (1936). *Das Ich und die Abwehrmechanismen.* London: Imago.

Fromholt, P., & Larsen, S. (1991). Autobiographical memory in normal aging and primary degenerative dementia (dementia of Alzheimer type). *Journal of Gerontology, 3,* 85–91.

Fromm, E. (1947). *Man for himself: Inquiry into the psychology of ethics.* New York: Holt, Rinehart & Winston.

Fry, P. S. (1983). Structured and unstructured reminiscence training and depression among the elderly. *Clinical Gerontologist, 1*(3), 15–37.

Fry, P. S. (1986). *Depression, stress, and adaptations in the elderly: Psychological assessment and interventions.* Rockville, MD: Aspen Publishers.

Fry, P. S. (1989). Mediators of stress in older adults: Conceptual and integrative frameworks. *Canadian Psychology, 30,* 636–649.

Fry, P. S. (1990). A factor-analytic investigation of elderly individuals' death and dying concerns and their coping responses. *Journal of Clinical Psychology, 46,* 25–40.

Fry, P. S. (1990b). Zero-order correlations among path model variables in a pilot study of the impact of agentic traits on reminiscence styles. Unpublished paper, The University of Calgary, Calgary, Alberta.

Fry, P. S. (1991a). Individual differences in reminiscence among older adults: Predictors of frequency and pleasantness ratings of reminiscence activity. *International Journal of Aging and Human Development, 33,* 311–326.

Fry, P. S. (1991b). Assessment of private speech of older adults in relation to depression. In R. Diaz & L. Berk (Eds.), *Private speech: From social interaction to self-regulation* (pp. 267–284). Hillsdale, NJ: Erlbaum.

Fry, P. S. (1993). Mediation of depression in community-based elders. In P. Cappeliez & R. J. Flynn (Eds.), *Depression and the social environment: Research and intervention with neglected populations* (pp. 369–394). Montreal, Quebec, Canada: McGill-Queen's University Press.

Fry, P. S., Slivinske, L. R., & Fitch, V. L. (1989). Power, control, and well-being of the elderly: A critical reconstruction. In P. S. Fry (Ed.), *Psychological perspectives of helplessness and control in the elderly* (pp. 319–338). Amsterdam, The Netherlands: Elsevier.

Galassie, F. (1991). A life-review workshop for gay and lesbian elders. Journal of Gerontological Social Work, 16, 75–86.

Gatchel, R. J., & Mears, F. G. (1982). *Personality: Theory, assessment, and research.* New York: St. Martin's Press.

George, L., & Bearon, L. B. (1980). *Quality of life in older persons: Meaning and measurement.* New York: Human Sciences Press.

Gerbaux, S., Vézina, J., Hardy, J., & Gendron, C. (1988, October). *Appraisal, hassles, coping responses, and depression: A model.* Paper presented at the annual meeting of the Canadian Association on Gerontology, Halifax, Nova Scotia.

Gergen, K., & Gergen, M. (1983). Narrative of the self. In T. R. Sarbin & K. E. Scheibe (Eds.), *Studies in social identity* (pp. 254–273). New York: Praeger.

Gergen, K. J., & Gergen, M. M. (1986). Narrative form and the construction of psychological science. In T. R. Sarbin (Ed.), *Narrative psychology: The storied nature of human conduct.* New York: Praeger.

Gibson, F. (1994). What can reminiscence contribute to people with dementia? In J. Bornat (Ed.), *Reminiscence reviewed: Evaluations, achievements, perspectives* (pp. 46–60). Buckingham, England: Open University Press.

Giles, H. (1991). "Gosh, you don't look it!" A sociolinguistic construction of aging. *The Psychologist, 4,* 99–119.

Gillick, M. R., Serrell, N. A., & Gillick, L. S. (1982). Adverse consequences of hospitalization in the elderly. *Social Sciences and Medicine, 16,* 1033–1038.

Gilligan, C. (1982). *In a different voice: Psychological theory and women's development.* Cambridge, MA: Harvard University Press.

Giltinan, J. (1990). Using life review to facilitate self-actualization in elderly women. *Gerontology & Geriatrics Education, 10,* 75–83.

Goldwasser, A. N., Auerbach, S. M., & Harkins, S. W. (1987). Cognitive, affective, and behavioral effects of reminiscence group therapy on demented elderly. *International Journal of Aging and Human Development, 25,* 209–222.

Gorney, J. (1968). *Experiencing and age: Patterns of reminiscence among the elderly.* Unpublished doctoral dissertation, University of Chicago.

Gottlieb, B. (1981). *Social networks and social support.* Beverly Hills, CA: Sage.

Gottlieb, B. (1987). Using social support to protect and promote health. *Journal of Primary Prevention, 8,* 49–70.

Greenwald, A. G. (1980). The totalitarian ego: Fabrication and revision of personal history. *American Psychologist, 35,* 603–618.

Guidauo, J. E. (1991). *A redefinition of cognitive therapy.* New York: Guilford.

Habermas, J. (1984). *The theory of communicative action: Volume 1. Reason and the rationalization of society.* Boston: Beacon Press.

Hagberg, B., Samuelsson, G., Lindberg, B., & Dehlin, O. (1991). Stability and change of personality in old age and its relation to survival. *Journal of Gerontology, 6,* 285–291.

Hagestad, G. (1987). Able elderly in the family context: Changes, chances, and challenges. *The Gerontologist, 27,* 417–422.

Haight, B. K. (1979). *The therapeutic role of the life review in the elderly.* Master's Thesis, University of Kansas, Kansas City, Kansas.

Haight, B. K. (1988). The therapeutic role of a structured life review process in homebound elderly subjects. *Journal of Gerontology, 43*(2), 40–44.

Haight, B. K. (1991). Reminiscing: The state of the art as a basis for practice. *International Journal of Aging and Human Development, 33,* 1–32.

Haight, B. K. (1992a). Long-term effects of a structured life review process. *Journal of Gerontology, 47,* 312–315.

Haight, B. K., & Burnside, I. (1992). Clinical outlook: Reminiscence and life review: Conducting the processes. *Journal of Gerontological Nursing, 18*(2), 39–42.

Haight, B. K., & Burnside, I. (1993). Reminiscence and life review: Explaining the differences. *Archives of Psychiatric Nursing, 7,* 91–98.

Haight, B. K., & Dias, J. K. (1992). Examining key variables in selected reminiscing modalities. *International Psychogeriatrics, 4*(Suppl. 2), 279–290.

Haight, B. K., & Olson, M. (1989, January/February). Teaching home health aides the use of life review. *Journal of Nursing Staff Development*, pp. 110–116.

Hamilton, D. B. (1985). Reminiscence therapy. In G. Bulecheck & J. McCloskey (Eds.), *Nursing interventions: Treatments for nursing diagnosis* (pp. 139–151). Philadelphia: W. B. Saunders.

Hamilton, D. B. (1992). Reminiscence therapy. In G. Bulechek & J. McCloskey (Eds.), *Nursing interventions: Essential nursing treatments* (pp. 292–303). Philadelphia:. W. B. Saunders.

Hammen, C. (1988). Depression and cognitions about personal stressful events. In L. B. Alloy (Ed.), *Cognitive processes in depression*. New York: Guilford Press.

Harp Scates, S. K., Randolph, D. L., Gutsch, K. U., & Knight, H. V. (1985–86). Effects of cognitive-behavioral, reminiscence, and activity treatments on life satisfaction and anxiety in the elderly. *International Journal of Aging and Human Development, 22*, 141–146.

Harvey, J. H., Flannery, R., & Morgan, M. (1986). Vivid memories of vivid loves gone by. *Journal of Social and Personal Relationships, 3*, 359–373.

Havighurst, R., & Glasser, R. (1972). An exploratory study of reminiscence. *Journal of Gerontology, 27*, 245–253.

Head, D., Portnoy, S., & Woods, R. T. (1990). The impact of reminiscence groups in two different settings. *International Journal of Geriatric Psychiatry, 5*, 295–302.

Heady, B., & Wearing, A. (1988). The sense of relative superiority—central to well-being. *Social Indicators Research, 20*, 497–516.

Heap, K. (1990). *Samtalen i eldreomsorgen: Kommunikasjon, minner, kriser, sorg* [Conversation in the care of elders: Communication, memories, crises, and sorrow]. Oslo, Norway: Kommuneforlaget.

Hedges, L. V., & Olkin, I. (1985). *Statistical methods for meta-analysis*. San Diego, CA: Academic Press.

Hedlund, B. L. (1987). *The development of meaning in life in adulthood*. Unpublished doctoral dissertation, University of Southern California, Los Angeles.

Herth, K. A. (1989). The root of it all: Genograms as a nursing assessment tool. *Journal of Gerontological Nursing, 15*(12), 32–37.

Herth, K. A. (1993). Hope in older adults in community and institutional settings. *Issues in Mental Health Nursing, 14*, 139–159.

Hessel, D. (1977). *Maggie Kuhn on aging: A dialogue*. Philadelphia: Westminster Press.

Hewett, L., Asamen, J., & Dietch, J. (1991). Group reminiscence with nursing home residents. *Clinical Gerontologist, 10*, 69–72.

Hickey, T., Dean, K., & Holstein, B. E. (1986). Emerging trends in gerontology and geriatrics: Implications for the self-care of the elderly. *Social Science and Medicine, 23*, 1363–1369.

Holahan, C. K., & Holahan, C. J. (1987). Self-efficacy, social support, and depression in aging: A longitudinal analysis. *Journal of Gerontology, 42*, 65–68.

Holden, U. P., & Woods, R. T. (1988). *Reality orientation: Psychological approaches to the "confused" elderly* (2nd ed.). Edinburgh: Churchill Livingstone.

Holmes, T. H., & Rahe, R. H. (1967). The Social Readjustment Rating Scale. *Journal of Psychosomatic Research, 14*, 121–132.

Holroyd, K. A., & Penzien, D. B. (1986). Client variables and the behavioral treatment of recurrent tension headache: A meta-analytic review. *Journal of Behavioral Medicine, 9,* 515–535.

Hopewell, J. F. (1987). Storytelling. In *Congregations: Stories and structures* (pp. 140–149). Philadelphia: Fortress Press.

Horacek, B. J. (1977). Life review: A pastoral counseling technique. In J. A. Thorson & T. C. Cook, Jr. (Eds.), *Spiritual well-being of the elderly.* Springfield, IL: Charles C Thomas.

Howard, G. S. (1991). Culture tales: A narrative approach to thinking, cross-cultural psychology, and psychotherapy. *American Psychologist,* 187–197.

Hunter, J. E., Gerbing, D. W., Cohen, S. H., & Nicol, T. S. (1980). *PACKAGE 1980: A system of FORTRAN routines for the analysis of correlational data.* Waco, TX: Academic Computing Services, Baylor University.

Husserl, E. (1965). Phenomenology and the crisis of philosophy. In Q. Lauer (Ed. and trans.), *Philosophy as rigorous science/Philosophy and the crisis of European man.* New York: Harper Torchbooks.

Hyland, D. T., & Ackerman, A. M. (1988). Reminiscence and autobiographical memory in the study of the personal past. *Journal of Gerontology, 43,* 35–39.

Ingebretsen, R. (1989). *Mine, dine, og våre erfaringer: Samtalegrupper for pårørende til aldersdemente* [My, your, and our experiences: Conversation groups for family members of patients with senile dementia] (Gerontological Report No. 6-1989). Oslo, Norway: Norwegian Gerontological Institute.

Ingersoll, B., & Goodman, L. (1983). A reminiscence group for institutionalized elderly. In M. Rosenbaum (Ed.), *Handbook for short-term therapy groups.* New York: McGraw-Hill.

Ingersoll-Dayton, B., & Arndt, B. (1990). Use of the genogram with the elderly and their families. *Journal of Gerontological Social Work, 15,* 105–121.

Irvine, R. E., Bagnall, M. K., & Smith, B. J. (1978). *The older patient.* London: Hodder & Stoughton.

Janis, I. L. (1958). *Psychological stress.* New York: Wiley.

Jebens, A. (1990). Fra tradisjonelle ledete grupper til selvtreningsgrupper [From traditionally led groups to self-training groups]. Oslo, Norway: Diakonhjemmets Sykehus.

Johnson, B. (1993, August 16). Native Americans critical of land run celebration: Say settlement of Oklahoma devastated tribes. *The Buffalo News,* p. A-7.

Johnson, J., & Leventhal, H. (1974). Effects of accurate expectations and behavioral instructions on reactions during a noxious medical examination. *Journal of Personality and Social Psychology, 29,* 710–718.

Johnston, M. (1986). Pre-operative emotional states and post-operative recovery. In F. G. Guggenheim (Ed.), *Psychological aspects of surgery* (pp. 1–22). New York: Karger.

Kalantzis, M., & Cope, W. (1992, November 4). Multiculturalism may prove to be the key issue of our epoch. *Chronicle of Higher Education,* pp. B-3, B-5.

Kaminsky, M. (1984). *The uses of reminiscence: New ways of working with older adults.* New York: Haworth Press.

Kantor, J. R. (1933). *A survey of the science of psychology.* Bloomington, IN: Principia Press.

Kelly, G. A. (1955). *The psychology of personal constructs.* New York: W. W. Norton.

Kelly, G. A. (1967). A psychology of the optimal man. In A. H. Mahrer (Ed.), *The goals of psychotherapy*. New York: Appleton-Century-Crofts.

Kelly, G. A. (1969). Personal construct theory and the psychotherapeutic interview. In B. Maher (Ed.), *Clinical psychology and personality*. New York: Wiley.

Kelly, J. (1986). An ecological paradigm: Defining mental health as a preventive service. In R. E. Hess & J. G. Kelly (Eds.), *Prevention in human services. The ecology of prevention: Illustrating mental health consultation* (pp. 1–36). New York: Haworth Press.

Kelly, J. (1988). *Guide to conducting prevention research in communities*. New York: Haworth Press.

Kendall, P. C., Williams, L., Pechacek, T. F., Graham, L. E., Shisslak, C., & Herzoff, N. (1979). Cognitive-behavioral and patient education interventions in cardiac catheterization procedures: The Palo Alto Medical Psychology Project. *Journal of Consulting and Clinical Psychology, 47,* 49–58.

Kessler-Harris, A. (1992, October 21). Multiculturalism can strengthen, not undermine, a common culture. *Chronicle of Higher Education,* pp. B-3, B-7.

Kiernat, J. M. (1979). The use of life review activity with confused nursing home residents. *American Journal of Occupational Therapy, 33,* 306–310.

Kiernat, J. M. (1983). Retrospection as a life span concept. *Physical and Occupational Therapy in Geriatrics, 3*(2), 35–48.

King, K. (1979). *Reminiscing group experiences with aging people.* Unpublished master's thesis, School of Nursing, University of Utah, Salt Lake City, UT.

King, K. (1984). Reminiscing, dying, and counseling: A contextual approach. In I. Burnside (Ed.), *Working with the elderly: Group process and techniques* (2nd ed.). Belmont, CA: Wadsworth.

King, P. M., Kitchener, K. S., Davison, M. L., Parker, C. A., & Wood, P. K. (1983). The justification of beliefs in young adults: A longitudinal study. *Human Development, 26,* 106–116.

Kirchmeyer, C. (1992). Perceptions of nonwork to work spillover: Challenging the common view of conflict-ridden domain relationships. *Basic & Applied Social Psychology, 13,* 231–250.

Kitwood, T. (1990). The dialectics of dementia: With particular reference to Alzheimer's disease. *Ageing & Society, 10,* 177–196.

Kleiner, R. J., & Okeke, B. I. (1991). Advances in field theory: New approaches and methods in cross-cultural research. *Journal of Cross-Cultural Psychology, 22,* 509–524.

Knipscheer, K. (1991, September). *Aging, social environment, and social support.* Paper presented at the Second European Congress of Gerontology, Madrid, Spain.

Koestner, R., Franz, C., & Weinberger, J. (1990). The family origins of empathic concern: A 26-year longitudinal study. *Journal of Personality and Social Psychology, 58,* 709–717.

Kovach, C. R. (1987). *Reminiscence: Themes and affect.* Unpublished pilot study.

Kovach, C. (1990). Promise and problems in reminiscence research. *Journal of Gerontological Nursing, 16,* 10–14.

Kovach, C. (1991a). Content analysis of reminiscences of elderly women. *Research in Nursing and Health, 14,* 287–295.

Kovach, C. (1991b). Reminiscence: A closer look at content. *Issues in Mental Health Nursing, 12,* 193–204.

Kovach, C. (1991c). Reminiscence: Exploring the origins, processes, and consequences. *Nursing Forum, 26,* 14–20.

Kovach, C. (1991d). Reminiscence behavior: An empirical exploration. *Journal of Gerontological Nursing, 17,* 23–28.

Kovach, C. (1993). Development and testing of the Autobiographical Memory Coding Tool. *Journal of Advanced Nursing, 18,* 669–674.

Kozma, A., & Stones, M. J. (1987). Social desirability in measures of subjective well-being: A systematic evaluation. *Journal of Gerontology, 42,* 56–59.

Kozma, A., & Stones, M. J. (1988). Social desirability in measures of subjective well-being: Age comparisons. *Social Indicators Research, 20,* 1–14.

Kozma, A., Stones, M. J., & McNeil, K. (1991). *Subjective well-being in later life.* Toronto, Ontario, Canada: Butterworths.

Kozma, A., Stone, S., Stones, M. J., Hannah, T. E., & McNeil, J. K. (1990). Long- and short-term affective states in happiness. *Social Indicators Research, 22,* 119–138.

Kreps, G. (1989). Communication and health. In E. B. Ray & L. Donohew (Eds.), *Communication in health care contexts: A systems perspective* (pp. 187–203). Hillsdale, NJ: Erlbaum.

Kuhn, M. (1977). In D. Hessel (Ed.), *Maggie Kuhn on aging: A dialogue* (p. 34). Philadelphia: Westminster Press.

Labouvie-Vief, G. (1982). Dynamic development and mature autonomy. *Human Development, 25,* 161–191.

Labouvie-Vief, G., Hakim-Larson, J., DeVoe, M., & Schoeberlein, S. (1989). Emotions and self-regulation: A life span view. *Human Development, 32,* 279–299.

Langer, E., Chanowitz, B., Palmerino, M., Jacobs, S., Rhodes, M., & Thayer, P. (1990). Nonsequential development and aging. In C. N. Alexander & E. J. Langer (Eds.), *Higher stages of human development* (pp. 114–136). New York: Oxford University Press.

Lappe, J. M. (1987). Reminiscing: The life review therapy. *Journal of Gerontological Nursing, 13,* 12–16.

Lashley, M. (1992). Reminiscence: A biblical basis for telling our stories. *Journal of Christian Nursing, 9,* 4–8.

Lashley, M. (1993). The painful side of reminiscence. *Geriatric Nursing, 14,* 138–141.

Lawton, M. P. (1975). The Philadelphia Geriatric Center Morale Scale: A revision. *Journal of Gerontology, 30,* 85–89.

Lazarus, R. S. (1966). *Psychological stress and the coping process.* New York: McGraw-Hill.

Lazarus, R. S., & DeLongis, A. (1983). Psychological stress and coping in aging. *American Psychologist, 38,* 245–254.

Lazarus, R. S., & Folkman, S. (1984). *Stress, appraisal, and coping.* New York: Springer Publishing Company.

Lefcourt, H. M. (1976). *Locus of control.* Hillsdale, NJ: Erlbaum.

Lefcourt, H. M., & Martin, R. A. (1986). *Humor and life stress: Antidote to adversity.* New York: Springer-Verlag.

Lerner, M. J. (1980). *The belief in a just world.* New York: Plenum.

Lewinsohn, P. M., Mischel, W., Chaplain, W., & Barton, R. (1980). Social competence and depression: The role of illusory self-perception? *Journal of Abnormal Psychology, 89,* 203–212.

Lewis, C. N. (1971). Reminiscing and self-concept in old age. *Journal of Gerontology, 26,* 240–243.

Lewis, M. I., & Butler, R. N. (1974). Life review therapy: Putting memories to work in individual and group psychotherapy. *Geriatrics, 29,* 165–173.

Liang, J. (1984). Dimensions of the Life Satisfaction Index A: A structural formulation. *Journal of Gerontology, 39,* 613–622.

Lieberman, M. A., & Falk, J. (1971). The remembered past as a source of data for research on the life cycle. *Human Development, 14,* 132–141.

Lieberman, M. A., & Tobin, S. S. (1983). *The experience of old age: Stress, coping, and survival.* New York: Basic Books.

Linton, M. (1986). Ways of searching and the contents of memory. In D. C. Rubin (Ed.), *Autobiographical memory* (pp. 50–67). Cambridge, England: Cambridge University Press.

Lloyd, P. (1991). The empowerment of elderly people. *Journal of Aging Studies, 5,* 125–135.

Loftus, E. F. (1993). The reality of repressed memories. *American Psychologist, 48,* 518–537.

Loupland, N., Couplan, J., & Giles, H. (Eds.). (1991). *Sociolinguistics and the elderly: Discourse, identity, and ageing.* Oxford, England: Blackwell.

Lowenthal, M., Thurnher, M., & Chiriboga, D. (1975). *Four stages of life.* San Francisco: Jossey-Bass.

Lowenthal, R., & Marrazzo, R. (1990). Milestoning: Evoking memories for resocialization through group reminiscence. *The Gerontologist, 30,* 269–272.

Luborsky, M. (1993). The romance with personal meaning in gerontology: Cultural aspects of life themes. *The Gerontologist, 33,* 445–452.

Ludwick-Rosenthal, R., & Neufeld, R. W. J. (1988). Stress management during noxious medical procedures: An evaluative review of outcome studies. *Psychological Bulletin, 104,* 326–342.

Mackay, C., Cox, T., Burrows, G., & Lazzerini, T. (1978). An inventory for the measurement of self-reported stress and arousal. *British Journal of Social and Clinical Psychology, 17,* 283–282.

MacLean, M. J., & Chown, S. M. (1988). Just world beliefs and attitudes toward helping elderly people: A comparison of British and Canadian university students. *International Journal of Aging and Human Development, 26,* 249–259.

Mac Crae, H. (1990). Older women and identity maintenance in later life. *Canadian Journal on Aging, 9,* 248–267.

Magee, J. J. (1988a). *A professional's guide to older adults' life review: Releasing the peace within.* Lexington, MA: Lexington Books.

Magee, J. J. (1988b). Using poetry as an aid to life review. *Activities, Adaptation, and Aging, 12,* 91–100.

Magee, J. (1991). Using metaphors in life review groups to empower shame-driven older adults. *Activities, Adaptation, and Aging, 16,* 19–30.

Mair, J. M. M. (1990). Telling psychological tales. *International Journal of Personal Construct Psychology, 3,* 27–36.

Maitland, D. (1991). *Aging as counterculture: A vocation for the later years.* New York: Pilgrim Press.

Markus, H. (1977). Self-schemata and processing information about the self. *Journal of Personality and Social Psychology, 35,* 63–78.

Martin, P. (1991). Life patterns and age styles in older adults. *International Journal of Aging and Human Development, 32,* 289–302.

Martin, P., & Smyer, M. (1990). The experience of micro and macro events: A life-span analysis. *Research on Aging, 12,* 294–310.

Maslow, A. (1970). *Motivation and personality* (2nd ed.). New York: Harper & Row.

Maton, K. (1987). Patterns and psychological correlates of material support: The bidirectionality hypothesis. *American Journal of Community Psychology, 15,* 185–207.

Matteson, M. A., & Munsat, E. M. (1982). Group reminiscing with elderly clients. *Issues in Mental Health Nursing, 4,* 177–189.

McAdams, D. (1985). *Power, intimacy, and the life story: Personological inquiries into identity.* Homewood, IL: Dorsey Press.

McAllister, C. (1990). Materials for reminiscence. *Health Libraries Review, 7,* 120–122.

McCarthy, T. (1981). *The critical theory of Jurgen Habermas.* Cambridge, MA: MIT Press.

McCloskey, L. (1990). The silent heart sings. *Generations, 14,* 63–65.

McKiernan, F., & Yardley, G. (1991, June). Why bother? Can reminiscence groupwork be effective for elderly people with severe dementia? *PSIGE Newsletter,* pp. 14–17.

McMahon, A. W., & Rhudick, P. J. (1964). Reminiscing: Adaptational significance in the aged. *Archives of General Psychiatry, 10,* 292–298.

McMordie, N. R., & Blom, S. (1979). Life review therapy: Psychotherapy for the elderly. *Perspectives in Psychiatric Care, 17*(4), 162–166.

McNeil, J. K., Stones, M. J., Kozma, A., & Andres, D. (1994). Age differences in mood: Structure, mean level, and diurnal variation. *Canadian Journal on Aging, 13,* 201–220.

Meacham, J. A. (1972). The development of memory abilities in the individual and society. *Human Development, 15,* 205–228.

Meacham, J. A. (1980). Research on remembering: Interrogation or conversation, mono- logue or dialogue? *Human Development, 23,* 236–245.

Meacham, J. A. (1988). Interpersonal relations and prospective remembering. In M. M. Grune- berg, P. Morris, & R. N. Sykes (Eds.), *Practical aspects of memory: Current research and issues* (Vol. 1, pp. 354–359). New York: Wiley.

Meacham, J. A. (1992). Cooperative action and reconstructing the personal past as func- tions of autobiographical remembering. In R. L. West & J. D. Sinnott (Eds.), *Everyday memory and aging: Current research and methodology* (pp. 259–269). New York: Springer-Verlag.

Meer, B., & Baker, J. (1966). The Stockton Geriatric Rating Scale. *Journal of Gerontology, 41,* 85–90.

Melcher, J. (1988). Keeping our elderly out of institutions by putting them back in their homes. *American Psychologist, 43,* 643–647.

Merriam, S. B. (1980). The concept and function of reminiscence: A review of the research. *The Gerontologist, 20,* 604–609.

Merriam, S. B. (1989). The structure of simple reminiscence. *The Gerontologist, 29,* 761–767.

Merriam, S. B. (1993a). Butler's life review: How universal is it? *International Journal of Aging and Human Development, 37,* 163–175.

Merriam, S. B. (1993b). The uses of reminiscence in older adulthood. *Educational Gerontology, 19,* 441–450.

Merriam, S. B., & Cross, L. H. (1981). Aging, reminiscence, and life satisfaction. *Activities, Adaptation, and Aging, 8,* 275–290.

Merriam, S. B., & Cross, L. (1982). Adulthood and reminiscence: A descriptive study. *Educational Gerontology, 8,* 275–290.

Merriam, S. B., Martin, P., Adkins, G., & Poon, L. (in press). Centenarians: Their memories and future ambitions. *International Journal of Aging and Human Development.*

Molinari, V., & Reichlin, R. E. (1984–85). Life review reminiscence in the elderly: A review of the literature. *International Journal of Aging and Human Development, 20,* 81–92.

Molloy, G., & Bramwell, L. (1991). The life history process: Is it useful? *Perspectives, 15,* 12–15.

Moody, H. R. (1988a). Toward a critical gerontology: The contribution of the humanities to theories of aging. In J. E. Birren & V. L. Bengtson (Eds.), *Emergent theories of aging* (pp. 19–40). New York: Springer Publishing Company.

Moody, H. R. (1988b). Twenty-five years of the life review: Where did we come from? Where are we going? *Journal of Gerontological Social Work, 12,* 7–21.

Moore, B. (1992). Reminiscing therapy: A CNS intervention. *Clinical Nurse Specialist, 6,* 170–173.

Moore, R. G., Watts, F. N., & Williams, J. M. (1988). The specificity of personal memories in depression. *British Journal of Clinical Psychology, 27,* 275–276.

Morris, R. G., & Kopelman, M. D. (1986). The memory deficits in Alzheimer-type dementia: A review. *Quarterly Journal of Experimental Psychology, 38A,* 575–602.

Morton, I., & Bleathman, C. (1991). The effectiveness of validation therapy in dementia: A pilot study. *International Journal of Geriatric Psychiatry, 6,* 327–330.

Moum, T. (1988). Yea-saying and mood-of-the-day effects in self-reported quality of life. *Social Indicators Research, 20,* 117–140.

Mudrack, P. E. (1990). Machiavellianism and locus of control: A meta-analytic review. *Journal of Social Psychology, 130,* 125–126.

Myerhoff, B. (1982). Life history among the elderly: Performance, visibility, and remembering. In J. Ruby (Ed.), *A crack in the mirror: Reflexive perspectives in anthropology* (pp. 99–117). Philadelphia: University of Pennsylvania Press.

Myerhoff, B. G., & Tufte, V. (1975). Life history as integration: An essay on an experiential model. *The Gerontologist, 15,* 541–543.

Natale, S. M. (1986). Loneliness and the ageing client: Psychotherapeutic considerations. *Psychotherapy Patient, 2,* 77–93.

Nash, J. R. (1976). *Darkest hours.* Chicago: Nelson-Hall.

Neimeyer, R. A. (1987). An orientation to personal construct therapy. In R. A. Neimeyer & G. J. Neimeyer (Eds.), *Personal construct therapy casebook.* New York: Springer Publishing Company.

Neisser, U. (1967). *Cognitive psychology.* New York: Appleton-Century-Crofts.

Nekanda-Trepka, C. J. (1984). Perfectionism and the threat to self-esteem in clinical anxiety. In R. Schwartz (Ed.), *The self in anxiety, stress, and depression*. Amsterdam: North Holland Elsevier.

Nelson, E. A. (1992). Aged heterogeneity: Fact or fiction? *The Gerontologist, 32,* 17–23.

Neugarten, B. L. (1970). Dynamics of transition to old age. *Journal of Geriatric Psychiatry, 4,* 71–87.

Neugarten, B., & Gutmann, D. (1958). Age-sex roles and personality in middle age: A thematic apperception study. *Psychological Monographs, 72,* No. 470.

Neugarten, B. L., Havighurst, R. J., & Tobin, S. S. (1961). The measurement of life satisfaction. *Journal of Gerontology, 16,* 134–143.

Nevisn, A. (1938). *Gateway to history.*

Newbern, V. (1992). Sharing the memories: The value of reminiscence as a research tool. *Journal of Gerontological Nursing, 18,* 13–18.

Newman, D., Griffin, P., & Cole, M. (1989). *The construction zone* (p. ix). Cambridge, England: Cambridge University Press.

Nezu, A. M., Nezu, C. M., & Blissett, S. E. (1988). Sense of humor as a moderator of the relation between stressful events and psychological distress: A prospective analysis. *Journal of Personality and Social Psychology, 54,* 520–525.

Nezu, A. M., Nezu, C. M., & Perri, M. G. (1989). *Problem-solving therapy for depression: Theory, research, and clinical guidelines.* New York: Wiley.

Niederehe, G. (in press). Psychosocial therapies with depressed older adults. In L. S. Schneider, C. F. Reynolds, B. D. Lebowitz, & Friedhoff (Eds.), *Diagnosis and treatment of depression in late life: Results of the NIH Consensus Development Conference.* St. Louis, MO: Mosby.

Norusis, M. J. (1990). *SPSS/PC+4.0 base manual.* Chicago: SPSS Inc.

Nyman, G. E., & Marke, S. (1958). *Medisinskt frageschema.* Lund, Sweden: Lund University.

Oriol, W. E. (1982). *Aging in all nations: A special report on the United Nations World Assembly on Aging, including the text of the International Action Program on Aging.* Washington, DC: National Council on the Aging, Inc.

Peachey, N. (1992). Helping the elderly person resolve integrity versus despair. *Perspectives in Psychiatric Care, 28,* 29–30.

Pearlin, L. I. (1980). Life strains and psychological distress among adults. In N. J. Smelser & E. H. Erikson (Eds.), *Themes of love and work in adulthood.* Cambridge, MA: Harvard University Press.

Pearlin, L. I., Lieberman, M. A., Menaghen, E. G., & Mullan, J. T. (1981). The stress process. *Journal of Health and Social Behaviour, 22,* 337–356.

Pennebaker, J. W., & Beall, S. (1986). Confronting a traumatic event: Toward an understanding of inhibition and disease. *Journal of Abnormal Psychology, 95,* 274–281.

Perkins, D. V. (1982). The assessment of stress using life events scales. In L. Goldberger & S. Breznitz (Eds.), *Handbook of stress: Theoretical and clinical aspects* (pp. 320–331). New York: Free Press.

Perotta, P., & Meacham, J. A. (1981–82). Can a reminiscing intervention alter depression and self-esteem? *International Journal of Aging and Human Development, 14,* 23–29.

Peterson, B. E., & Stewart, A. J. (1993). Generativity and social motives in young adults. *Journal of Personality and Social Psychology, 65,* 186–198.

Phair, L., & Elsey, I. (1990). Sharing memories. *Nursing Times, 86,* 50–52.

Piaget, J. (1926). *Language and thought of the child.* New York: Harcourt, Brace.

Pietrukowicz, M., & Johnson, M. (1991). Using life histories to individualize nursing home staff attitudes toward residents. *The Gerontologist, 31,* 102–106.

Poon, L. (Ed.). (1992). The Georgia centenarian study [Special issue]. *International Journal of Aging and Human Development.*

Porter, C., & Suedfeld, P. (1981). Integrative complexity in the correspondence of literary figures: Effects of personal and societal stress. *Journal of Personality and Social Psychology, 40,* 321–330.

Poser, E. G., & Engels, M. L. (1983). Self-efficacy assessment and peer group assistance in a preretirement intervention. *Educational Gerontology, 9,* 159–169.

Progoff, I. (1975). *At a journal workshop.* New York: Dialogue House Library.

Rabkin, J. G. (1980). Stressful life events and schizophrenia: A review of the research literature. *Psychological Bulletin, 87,* 408–425.

Radley, A. (1990). Artifacts, memory, and a sense of the past. In D. Middleton & D. Edwards, *Collective remembering.* Newbury Park, CA: Sage.

Raphael, B. (1984). Allowing ego integrity through life review. *Journal of Religion and Ageing, 2,* 1–11.

Rappaport, H., Enrich, K., & Wilson, A. (1982). Ego integrity and temporality: Psychoanalytic and existential perspectives. *Journal of Humanistic Psychology, 22,* 53–70.

Rappaport, H., Enrich, K., & Wilson, A. (1985). Relation between ego identity and temporal perspective. *Journal of Personality and Social Psychology, 48,* 1609–1620.

Rappaport, J. (1990). Research methods and the empowerment social agenda. In P. Tolan, C. Keys, F. Chertok, & L. Jason (Eds.), *Researching community psychology: Issues of theory and methods* (pp. 51–63). Washington, DC: American Psychological Association.

Rattenbury, C. (1991). *A large-scale longitudinal study of the therapeutic value of reminiscence intervention with elderly institutionalized adults.* Unpublished doctoral thesis, Memorial University of Newfoundland, St. John's, Newfoundland, Canada.

Rattenbury, C., & Stones, M. J. (1989). A controlled evaluation of reminiscence and current topics discussion groups in a nursing home context. *The Gerontologist, 29,* 768–771.

Reed, D. M., & Cobble, R. (1986). Tools for reminiscence with veterans. *Clinical Gerontologist, 4*(4), 53–57.

Reed, P. G. (1991). Toward a nursing theory of self-transcendance: Deductive reformulation using developmental theories. *Advances in Nursing Science, 13*(4), 64–77.

Reedy, M. N., & Birren, J. E. (1980). *Life review through guided autobiography.* Paper presented at the annual meeting of the American Psychological Association, Montreal, Quebec, Canada.

Reese, E., & Fivush, R. (1993). Parental styles of talking about the past. *Developmental Psychology, 29,* 596–606.

Reid, D. W. (1984). Participatory control and the chronic-illness adjustment process. In H. Lefcourt (Ed.), *Research with the locus of control construct: Extensions and limitations* (Vol. 3, pp. 361–389. New York: Academic Press.

Reiff, R., & Sheerer, M. (1959). *Memory and hypnotic age regression.* New York: International Universities Press.

Revenson, T. (1988). Epilogue: The social constructions of aging revisited. *The Community Psychologist, 22,* 13–14.

Richter, R. L. (1986). Allowing ego integrity through life review. *Journal of Religion and Ageing, 2,* 1–11.

Riegel, K. (1973). Dialectic operations: The final period of cognitive development. *Human Development, 16,* 346–370.

Riegel, K. (1975). Adult life crises: A dialectical interpretation of development. In N. Datan & L. H. Ginsberg (Eds.), *Life-span developmental psychology: Normative life crises.* San Diego, CA: Academic Press.

Rinaldi, A., & Kearl, M. C. (1990). The hospice farewell: Ideological perspective of its professional practitioners. *Omega, 21,* 283–300.

Rø, O. C., Hendriksen, C., Kivela, S., & Thorslund, M. (1987). Intervention studies among elderly people. *Scandinavian Journal of Primary Health Care, 5,* 163–168.

Roberts, B., & Thorsheim, H. (1982). The approach of social ecology: A partnership of support and empowerment. *Journal of Primary Prevention, 3,* 139–143.

Roberts, B., & Thorsheim, H. (1986). *A partnership approach to consultation: The process and results of a major primary prevention field experiment* (Vol 4, pp. 151–186). Prevention in Human Services Series. New York: Haworth Press.

Roberts, B., & Thorsheim, H. (1987). *Empowering leadership.* Northfield, MN: St. Olaf's College.

Roberts, B., & Thorsheim, H. (1988, August). *Church congregations as mediating structures for empowering people: A field research project to reduce distress and problem use of alcohol.* Paper presented at the annual meeting of the American Psychological Association, Atlanta, GA.

Roberts, B., & Thorsheim, H. (1990). The Dakota LEADer's project: A test of empowering approaches to leadership. *The Community Psychologist, 25.*

Roberts, B., & Thorsheim, H. (1991a). Reciprocal ministry: A transforming vision of help and leadership. In R. E. Hess, K. I. Maton, & K. I. Pargament (Eds.), *Religion and prevention in mental health: Community intervention* (pp. 51–67). New York: Haworth Press.

Roberts, B., & Thorsheim, H. (1991b). Translating empowerment and disempowerment into everyday action and meaning. *The Community Psychologist, 25,* 24–28.

Roberts, B., & Thorsheim, H. (1994). Finding common ground between generations: A bring-a-thing process (video). In T. Taylor (Producer), *Who is telling your story?* Portland, OR: Age Wise Senior Community Video Project.

Rodin, J., Timko, C., & Harris, S. (1985). The construct of control: Biological and psychological correlates. In M. P. Lawton & G. L. Maddox (Eds.), *Annual review of gerontology and geriatrics* (Vol. 5, pp. 3–55). New York: Springer Publishing Company.

Rodriguez, A. (1990). *A descriptive study of selected props used to elicit memories in elders.* Unpublished master's thesis, School of Nursing, University of Texas at Austin, Austin, TX.

Rohde, P., Lewinsohn, P. M., Tilson, M., & Seeley, J. R. (1990). Dimensionality of coping and its relation to depression. *Journal of Personality and Social Psychology, 58,* 499–511.

Romaniuk, M. (1981). Review: Reminiscence and the second half of life. *Experimental Aging Research, 7,* 315–336.

Romaniuk, M., & Priddy, J. (1980). Widowhood and peer counseling. *Counseling and Values, 24,* 195–203.

Romaniuk, M., & Romaniuk, J. G. (1981). Looking back: An analysis of reminiscence functions and triggers. *Experimental Aging Research, 7,* 477–489.

Romaniuk, M., & Romaniuk, J. G. (1983). Life events and reminiscence: A comparison of the memories of young and old adults. *Imagination, Cognition, and Personality, 2,* 125–136.

Rosenberg, M. (1965). *Society and adolescent self-image.* Princeton, NJ: Princeton University Press.

Rosenmayr, L. (1979). Biography and identity. In T. K. Hareven & K. J. Addams (Eds.), *Aging and life course transitions: An interdisciplinary perspective* (pp. 27–53). New York: Guilford Press.

Rosenmayr, L., & Majce, G. (1978). Die soziale Benachteiligung. In L. Rosenmayr & H. Rosenmayr (Eds.), *Der alte Mensch in der Gesellschaft.* Reinbek: Rowohlt.

Rosenthal, C. J. (1987). The comforter: Providing personal advice and emotional support to generations in the family. *Canadian Journal on Aging, 6,* 228–239.

Ross, B. M. (1991). *Remembering the personal past: Descriptions of autobiographical memory.* New York: Oxford University Press.

Ross, H. (1990). Lesson of life. *Geriatric Nursing, 11,* 274–275.

Ross, M., & Holmberg, D. (1992). Are wives' memories for events in relationships more vivid than their husbands' memories? *Journal of Social and Personal Relationships, 9,* 585–604.

Rowe, D. (1982). *The construction of life and death.* New York: Wiley.

Rubin, D. D., Wetzler, S. E., & Nebes, R. D. (1986). Autobiographical memory across the life span. In D. C. Rubin (Ed.), *Autobiographical memory* (pp. 202–221). Cambridge, England: Cambridge University Press.

Runyan, W. M. (1984). *Life histories and psychobiography: Explorations in theory and method.* New York: Oxford University Press.

Russell, G. M., & Jorgenson, D. O. (1978). Religious group membership, locus of control, and dogmatism. *Psychological Reports, 42,* 1099–1102.

Rybarczyk, B. D. (1988). Two types of reminiscence interviews for coping enhancement: A presurgical intervention tailored for older adults. *Dissertation Abstracts International, 49,* 4021B. (University Microfilms No. 88-26,976)

Rybarczyk, B. D. (in preparation). *The reminiscence interview: A new approach to stress intervention in the medical setting.* New York: Springer Publishing Company.

Rybarczyk, B. D., & Auerbach, S. M. (1990). Reminiscence interviews as stress management interventions for older patients undergoing surgery. *The Gerontologist, 30,* 522–528.

Rybarczyk, B. D., Auerbach, S., Jorn, M., Lofland, K., & Perlman, M. (1993). Using volunteers and reminiscence to help older adults cope with an invasive medical procedure: A follow-up study. *Behavior, Health, and Aging, 3,* 147–162.

Ryff, C. D. (1986). The subjective construction of self and society: An agenda for life-span research. In V. W. Marshall (Ed.), *Later life: The social psychology of aging* (pp. 33–74). Beverly Hills, CA: Sage.

Ryff, C. D., & Essex, M. J. (1992). The interpretation of life experience and well-being: The sample case of relocation. *Psychology and Aging, 4,* 507–517.

Sarbin, T. R. (Ed.). (1986). *Narrative psychology: The storied nature of human conduct* (p. vii). New York: Praeger.

Sauer, W. J., & Coward, R. C. (Eds.). (1985). *Social support networks and the care of the elderly.* New York: Springer Publishing Company.

Schafer, D. E., Berghorn, F. J., Holmes, D. S., & Quadagno, J. S. (1986). The effects of reminiscing on the perceived control and social relations of institutionalized elderly. *Activities, Adaptation, and Aging, 8,* 95–110.

Schaie, K. W. (1983). The Seattle longitudinal study: A twenty-one year investigation of psychometric intelligence. In K. W. Schaie (Ed.), *Longitudinal studies of adult psychological development.* New York: Guilford Press.

Schaie, K. W., & Willis, S. L. (1991). *Adult development and aging.* New York: Harper-Collins.

Scharlach, A. E. (1988). Peer counseling training for nursing home residents. *The Gerontologist, 28,* 499–502.

Schindler, R. (1992). Silences: Helping elderly holocaust victims deal with the past. *International Journal of Aging and Human Development, 35,* 243–252.

Schulz, R. (1976). Effects of control and predictability on the physical and psychological well-being of the institutionalized aged. *Journal of Personality and Social Psychology, 33,* 563–573.

Seim, S. (1989). *Teenagers become adult and elderly.* (Gerontological Report No. 5-1989). Oslo, Norway: Norwegian Gerontological Institute.

Seligman, M. E. (1975). *Helplessness: On depression, development, and death.* San Francisco: Freeman.

Selye, H. (1956). *The stress of life.* New York: McGraw-Hill.

Shaw, R. E., Cohen, F., Fishman-Rosen, J., Murphy, M. C., Stertzer, S. H., Clark, D. A., & Myler, R. K. (1986). Psychological predictors of psychosocial and medical outcomes in patients undergoing coronary angioplasty. *Psychosomatic Medicine, 48,* 582–597.

Sherman, E. (1987). Reminiscence groups for community elderly. *The Gerontologist, 27,* 569–572.

Sherman, E. (1991). Reminiscentia: Cherished objects as memorabilia in late-life reminiscence. *International Journal of Aging and Human Development, 33,* 89–100.

Sherman, E., & Peak, T. (1991). Patterns of reminiscence and the assessment of late life adjustment. *Journal of Gerontological Social Work, 16,* 59–74.

Shor, I., & Freire, P. (1987). *A pedagogy for liberation.* New York: Bergin & Garvey.

Silverman, P. (1974). *Helping each other in widowhood.* New York: Health Sciences Press.

Sinnott, J. D. (1984). Postformal reasoning: The relativistic stage. In M. I. Commons, F. A. Richards, & C. Armon (Eds.), *Beyond formal operations: Late adolescent and adult cognitive development* (pp. 298–325). New York: Praeger.

Slivinske, L. R., & Fitch, V. L. (1987). The effect of control enhancing interventions on the well-being of elderly individuals living in retirement communities. *The Gerontologist, 27,* 176–181.

Smith, G., & Carlsson, I. (1990). *The creative process.* Madison, CT: International Universities Press.

Smith, G. J. W., & Nyman, G. E. (1961). A serial tachistoscopic experiment and its clinical application. *Acta Psychol., 18,* 67–84.

Smith, R. P., Woodward, N. J., Wallston, B. S., Wallston, K. A., Rye, P., & Zylstra, M. (1988). Health care implications of desire and expectancy of control in elderly adults. *Journal of Gerontology, 43,* 1–7.

Sperbeck, D. J. (1982). *Age and personality effects on autobiographical memory in adulthood.* Unpublished doctoral dissertation, University of Rochester, Rochester, NY.

Spielberger, C. D., Gorsuch, R., & Lushene, R. L. (1970). *Manual for the State–Trait Anxiety Inventory.* Palo Alto, CA: Consulting Psychologists Press.

Staudinger, U. M. (1989). *The study of life review: An approach to the investigation of intellectual development across the life span* (Studien und berichte 47). Germany: Max-Planck-Institut fur Bildungsforschung.

Staudinger, U. M., Smith, J., & Baltes, P. (1992). Wisdom-related knowledge in a life review task: Age differences and the role of professional specialization. *Psychology and Aging, 7,* 271–281.

Stedeford, A. (1984). *Facing death.* London: Heinemann.

Steiger, J. H. (1989). *EzPATH: A supplementary module for SYSTAT and SYGRAPH.* Evanston, IL: SYSTAT.

Sternberg, R. (1990). *Wisdom: Its nature, origins, and development.* Cambridge, England: Cambridge University Press.

Stevens-Ratchford, R. (1993). The effect of life review reminiscence activities on depression and self-esteem in older adults. *American Journal of Occupational Therapy, 47,* 413–420.

Støbakk, R., Bjørnson, L. J., Vigsnes, B., Sandnes, K., & Øvereng, A. (1989). *The Newtork Project: Fourth half-year concluding report.* Oslo, Norway: Diakon-hjemmets Sykehuset.

Stock, W. A., Okun, M. A., & Benin, M. (1986). Structure of subjective well-being among the elderly. *Psychology and Aging, 1,* 91–102.

Stones, M. J. (1976). Response set and the Eysenck Personality Inventory. *Journal of Clinical Psychology, 32,* 568–571.

Stones, M. J. (1977). A further study of response set and the Eysenck Personality Inventory. *Journal of Clinical Psychology, 33,* 147–150.

Stones, M. J., Ivany, G., & Kozma, A. (1994). Anticipating attendance in reminiscence therapy. *Social Indicators Research, 32,* 251–264.

Stones, M. J., & Kozma, A. (1986a). "Happy are they who are happy . . .": A test between two causal models of relationships between happiness and its correlates. *Experimental Aging Research, 12,* 23–29.

Stones, M. J., & Kozma, A. (1986b). Happiness and activities as propensities. *Journal of Gerontology, 41,* 85–90.

Stones, M. J., & Kozma, A. (1989). Multidimensional assessment of the elderly via a microcomputer: The SENOTS program and battery. *Psychology and Aging, 4,* 113–118.

Stones, M. J., & Kozma, A. (1991). A magical model of happiness. *Social Indicators Research, 25,* 31–50.

Stones, M. J., Rattenbury, C., & Kozma, A. (1994). Application of a nonlinear mathematical model to data on a successful therapeutic intervention. *Social Indicators Research, 31,* 47–62.

Straker, G., & Jacobson, R. S. (1981). Aggression, emotional maladjustment, and empathy in the abused child. *Developmental Psychology, 17,* 762–765.

Suedfeld, P., & Bluck, S. (1993). Changes in integrative complexity accompanying significant life events: Historical evidence. *Journal of Personality and Social Psychology, 64,* 124–130.

Suedfeld, P., & Piedrahita, L. E. (1984). Intimations of mortality: Integrative simplifications as a precursor of death. *Journal of Personality and Social Psychology, 47,* 848–852.

Suedfeld, P., & Tetlock, P. (1977). Integrative complexity of communications in international crises. *Journal of Conflict Resolution, 21,* 169–184.

Suedfeld, P., Tetlock, P., & Streufert, S. (1992). Conceptual/integrative complexity. In C. P. Smith (Ed.), *Motivation and personality: Handbook of thematic content analysis* (pp. 393–400). Cambridge, England: Cambridge University Press.

Suls, J., & Wan, C. K. (1989). Effects of sensory and procedural information on coping with stressful medical procedures and pain: A meta-analysis. *Journal of Consulting and Clinical Psychology, 57,* 372–379.

Taft, L. B., & Nehrke, M. F. (1990). Reminiscence, life review, and ego integrity in nursing home residents. *International Journal of Aging and Human Development, 30,* 189–196.

Tarman, V. I. (1988). Autobiography: The negotiation of a life-time. *International Journal of Aging and Human Development, 27,* 171–191.

Taulbee, L. R. (1986). Reality orientation and clinical practice. In I. Burnside (Ed.), *Working with the elderly: Group process and techniques* (pp. 177–186). Boston: Jones & Bartlett.

Taylor, S. E. (1983). Adjustment to threatening events: A theory of cognitive adaptation. *American Psychologist, 38,* 1161–1173.

Taylor, S. E., & Brown, J. D. (1988). Illusion and well-being: A social psychological perspective on mental health. *Psychological Bulletin, 103,* 193–210.

Tesser, A., & Campbell, J. (1982). Self-evaluation maintenance and the perception of friends and strangers. *Journal of Personality, 50,* 261–279.

Tetlock, P. (1984). Cognitive style and political belief systems in the British House of Commons. *Journal of Personality and Social Psychology, 46,* 365–375.

Thoits, P. A. (1983). Dimensions of life events that influence psychological distress: An evaluation and synthesis of the literature. In H. B. Kaplan (Ed.), *Psychosocial stress: Trends in theory and research* (pp. 33–103). San Diego, CA: Academic Press.

Thoits, P. (1986). Social support as coping assistance. *Journal of Consulting and Clinical Psychology, 54,* 416–423.

Thornton, S., & Brotchie, J. (1987). Reminiscence: A critical review of the empirical literature. *British Journal of Clinical Psychology, 26,* 93–111.

Thorsheim, H., & Roberts, B. (1984). *Substance abuse prevention: A social ecology approach* (NIDA Report No. 1-R01-DA-02671). Washington, DC: National Institute on Drug Abuse.

Thorsheim, H., & Roberts, B. (1990a). Empowerment through reminiscing: Communication and reciprocal social support among elders. In H. Giles, N. Coupland, & J. Wiemann (Eds.), *Communication, health, and the elderly* (Fulbright Colloquium Series, No. 8, pp. 114–125). Manchester, England: University of Manchester Press.

Thorsheim, H., & Roberts, B. (1990b, April). *Storytelling.* Presented at the Working Invitational Conference, "Values Baseline Measures in Long-Term Care," University of Minnesota, Minneapolis, MN.

Thorsheim, H., & Roberts, B. (1990c). *Elders as consultants: The Lifestories Program* (video). Northfield, MN: Media Services, St. Olaf College.

Thorsheim, H., & Roberts, B. (1990d). *Reminiscing together: Ways to help us keep mentally fit as we grow older.* Minneapolis, MN: CompCare.

Thorsheim, H., & Roberts, B. (1992). How to help people empower themselves by telling their stories together. Workshop presented at the 38th annual meeting of the American Society on Aging, San Diego, CA.

Thorsheim, H., & Roberts, B. (1993). *Telling one's story: Leader's kit.* Unpublished manuscript, St. Olaf's College, Northfield, MN.

Tichener, J. L., & Levine, N. (1967). Psychiatry and surgery. In A. M. Freedman & H. I. Kaplan (Eds.), *Comprehensive textbook of psychiatry* (Vol. 1). Baltimore: Williams & Wilkins.

Tornstam, L. (1989). Gero-transcendance: A reformulation of engagement theory. *Aging, 1,* 55–63.

Ulanov, A. B. (1981). Aging: On the way to one's end. In W. M. Clements (Ed.), *Ministry with the aging.* New York: Harper & Row.

Vézina, J., & Bourque, P. (1984). The relationship between cognitive structure and symptoms of depression in the elderly. *Cognitive Therapy and Research, 8,* 29–36.

Vézina, J., & Bourque, P. (1985). Les stratégies comportementales adoptées par les personnes âgées devant les sentiments dépressifs. *Revue Canadienne du Vieillissement, 4,* 161–169.

Viney, L. L. (1989a). *Images of illness* (2nd ed). Malabar, FL: Krieger.

Viney, L. L. (1989b). Psychotherapy as shared reconstruction. *International Journal of Personal Construct Psychology, 3,* 423–442.

Viney, L. L. (1992). Goals in psychotherapy: Some reflections of a constructivisit therapist. In L. Leitner & G. Dunnett (Eds.), *Critical issues in personal construct therapy.* Malabar, FL: Krieger.

Viney, L. L. (1993). *Life stories: Personal construct therapy with the elderly.* Chichester, England: Wiley.

Viney, L. L., Benjamin, Y. N., & Preston, C. (1988–89). Mourning and reminiscence: Parallel psychotherapeutic processes for the elderly. *International Journal of Aging and Human Development, 28,* 237–249.

Viney, L. L., Benjamin, Y. N., & Preston, C. (1990). Personal construct therapy for the elderly. *Journal of Cognitive Psychotherapy, 4,* 211–224.

Vinokur, A., & Caplan, R. D. (1986). Cognitive and affective components of life events: Their relations and effects on well-being. *American Journal of Community Psychology, 14,* 351–370.

Vinokur, A., & Selzer, M. (1975). Desirable versus undesirable life events: Their relationship to stress and mental distress. *Journal of Personality and Social Psychology, 32,* 329–337.

Vygotsky, L. S. (1978). *Mind and society.* Cambridge, MA: Harvard University Press.

Walaskay, M., Whitbourne, S., & Nehrke, M. (1983). Construction and validation of an ego integrity status interview. *International Journal of Aging and Human Development, 18,* 61–72.

Wallace, J. (1992). Reconsidering the life review: The social construction of talk about the past. *Gerontologist, 32,* 120–125.

Walsh, W. H. (1967). *Philosophy of history: An introduction.* New York: Harper & Row.

Ward, R. A. (1984). The marginality and salience of being old: When is age relevant? *The Gerontologist, 24,* 227–237.

Waters, E. (1990). The life review: Strategies for working with individuals and groups. *Journal of Mental Health Counseling, 12,* 270–278.

Watt, L., & Wong, P. T. P. (1990). A new taxonomy of reminiscence and its therapeutic implications. *Journal of Gerontological Social Work, 16*.

Watt, L., & Wong, P. (1991). A taxonomy of reminiscence and therapeutic implications. *Journal of Mental Health Counseling, 12*, 270–278.

Weber, R. P. (1985). *Basic content analysis.* Beverly Hills, CA: Sage.

Webster's Ninth New Collegiate Dictionary (1988). Springfield, MA: Merriam Company.

Webster, J. D. (1992). *Predictors of reminiscence: A lifespan perspective.* Poster presented at the annual meeting of the Canadian Psychological Association, Quebec City, Quebec, Canada.

Webster, J. D. (1993). Construction and validation of the Reminiscence Functions Scale. *Journal of Gerontology, 48*, 256–262.

Webster, J. D. (1994). Predictors of reminiscence: A lifespan perspective. *Canadian Journal on Aging, 13*, 66–78.

Webster, J. D., & Cappeliez, P. (1993). Reminiscence and autobiographical memory: Complementary contexts for cognitive aging research. *Developmental Review, 13*, 54–91.

Webster, J. D., & Young, R. A. (1988). Process variables of the life review: Counseling implications. *International Journal of Aging and Human Development, 26*, 315–323.

Wechsler, D. (1981). *Wechsler Adult Intellligence Scale—Revised: Manual.* New York: Psychological Corporation.

Weenolsen, P. (1986). What's it all mean?: We never stop asking. *APA Monitor,* p. 20.

Wetterau, B. (1990). *Book of chronologies.* New York: Stonesong Press.

White, D., & Ingersoll, D. (1989). Life review groups: Helping their members with an unhappy life. *Clinical Gerontologist, 8*, 47–50.

White, H. (1980). The value of narrativity in the representation of reality. *Critical Inquiry, 7*, 5–28.

Wholihan, D. (1992). The value of reminiscence in hospice care. *American Journal of Hospice and Palliative Care, 9*, 33–35.

Williams, N. (1967). *Chronology of the modern world: 1763 to the present time.* New York: David McKay.

Winkler, K. J. (1993, January 20). Encyclopedia of U.S. social history marks the field's coming of age. *Chronicle of Higher Education,* pp. A-7, A-8.

Wolf, M. (1990). The call to vocation: Life histories of elderly religious women. *International Journal of Aging and Human Development, 31*, 197–203.

Wong, P. T. P. (1989). Personal meaning and successful aging. *Canadian Psychology, 30*, 516–525.

Wong, P. T. P. (1991). Social support functions of group reminiscence. *Canadian Journal of Community Health, 10*, 151–161.

Wong, P. T. P. (1992). Control is a double-edged sword. *Canadian Journal of Behavioural Science, 24*, 143–146.

Wong, P. T. P. (1993). Effective management of life stress: The resource-congruence model. *Stress Medicine, 9*, 51–60.

Wong, P. T. P., & Sproule, C. F. (1984). Attributional analysis of locus of control and the Trent Attribution Profile (TAP). In H. M. Lefcourt (Ed.), *Research with the locus of control construct: Vol. 3. Limitation and extensions.* San Diego, CA: Academic Press.

Wong, P. T. P., & Watt, L. M. (1991). What types of reminiscence are associated with successful aging? *Psychology and Aging, 6,* 272–279.

Wood, V., Wylie, M., & Sheafor, B. (1969). An analysis of a short self-report measure of life satisfaction: Correlation with rater judgments. *Journal of Gerontology, 24,* 465–469.

Woodhouse, L. (1992). Women with jagged edges: Voices from a culture of substance abuse. *Qualitative Health Research, 2,* 262–281.

Woods, R. T., Portnoy, S., Head, D., & Jones, G. (1992). Reminiscence and life-review with persons with dementia: Which way forward? In G. Jones & B. Miesen (Eds.), *Caregiving in dementia* (pp. 137–161). London: Routledge.

Woodward, N. J., & Wallston, B. S. (1987). Age and health care beliefs: Self-efficacy as a mediator of low desire for control. *Psychology and Aging, 2,* 3–8.

Woodworth, R. S., & Schlosberg, H. (1954). *Experimental psychology.* New York: Holt, Rinehart & Winston.

World Health Organization. (1977). *International Classification of Diseases: Volume 1.* Geneva, Switzerland: Author.

Yalom, I. (1970). *The theory and practice of group psychotherapy.* New York: Basic Books.

Yang, J. A., & Rehm, L. P. (1993). A study of autobiographical memories in depressed and nondepressed elderly individuals. *International Journal of Aging and Human Development, 36,* 39–55.

Youssef, F. A. (1990). The impact of group reminiscence counseling on a depressed elderly population. *Nurse Practitioner, 15,* 32–38.

Zetterberg, H. (1977). *Arbete, livsstil, och motivation.* Stockholm, Sweden: SAF.

Index

AARP (*see* American Association of Retired Persons Reminiscence Program)
ABS (*see* Affect-Balance Scale)
Accomplishments, past, 207
Activity, goal-directed, 25
Adaptation, 125, 221, 224
  memories and, 23–24
  negative, 50
  positive, 50
Adaptive function, of reminiscence therapy, 222
Adaptive processes of reminiscence, 29–35
Adolescence, 69–70, 99, 191
Adults
  age-differences in reminiscence, 90
  elderly, (*see* Elderly)
  middle-age, 90, 173
  questions, for Life Review and Experiencing Form, 191–192
  young, 90, 173, 215

Affect-Balance Scale (ABS), 259, 262
Age
  adult differences in reminiscence functions, 91–95
  categories, 96–100
  differences, 127–137
  group, 169
  life events and, 125
  ranges, 88
  specificity, of life review, 124
  telling one's own story and, 195–196
Agentic traits, 52, 55, 56, 58
Aging, successful, 18, 24–25, 29–35, 221–222, 279
AIDS, 217
Alcohol, 247
Alzheimer's disease, 233, 234
AMCT (*see* Autobiographical memory coding tool)

American Association of Retired Persons Reminiscence Program
  description, 266–267
  follow-up, 269–270
  history of, 265–266
  implementing, 267–271
  materials for, 272
  meetings, 267–270
  training guide, 268
  training kit, 267, 272
Anaclitic depression, 72
Anecdotes, 27
Anticipation, 125–126, 128
Anxiety, 19, 33, 64
Anxiety reduction, 222, 248–250
Appraisals, 223–224
  challenge-oriented, 224, 226
  of personal coping resources, 222
  positive self-appraisals, 111, 112, 119, 120
  strategies, 225–226
Asking, 202
Autobiographical memories, 71, 101, 103–105, 109
Autobiographical Memory Coding Tool (AMCT), 115–122
  development, 106
  testing, 106
  using, 107–115
    classifying themes, 114–115
    coding of data, 110–113
    deleting units that don't refer to past, 110
    delineating units of analysis, 108–110
    identifying dominant themes, 113–114
Autobiographical memory thematic dictionary, 110, 111
Autobiographical memory themes, 119
Autobiography, 276
  comparison with other types of recall, 276
  comprehensiveness, 278
  defined, 165
  evaluation, 278
  guided (see Guided autobiography)
  structure, 278

Beck Depression Inventory, 235–236
Belonging, 200
Benefectance, 135
Benefits, 202
Bereavement, 34, 175, 250–252

Birren, James E., 54, 70, 75, 90, 124, 165–177, 189, 229, 257
Bitterness revival, 94–95, 122, 283–284
Bittersweet memories, 162
Blando, John A., 123–137
Boredom reduction, 92, 94, 98, 101, 122, 283
Bradburn's Affect Balance Scale, 82
Branching points, 176
Bring-a-thing, 194, 203
Burnout, 56
Burnside, Irene, 5, 14, 21, 153–163

Cancer, 217
Cappeliez, Philippe, 50, 55, 123, 124, 219, 221–232, 275
Career achievement, 33
Caring, 202
Centenarians, 80–88
Challenge events, appraisals, 224, 226
Chemotherapy, 217
Childhood, 69–70, 190
Children, 89–90
Choices theme, 111, 113, 119, 120
Chronological pattern, 154
Closure, 122
Coding
  of data in AMCT, 110–113
  guidelines, 28–29
  of reminiscence transcripts, 282
Cognitive impairment, 142–144
Cognitive models, of depression, 223–231
Cognitive treatment, for depression, 227–231
Cohorts, 169–170, 174
Coleman, Peter, 5, 18, 49, 54, 82, 83, 123, 179–192, 246, 280, 282, 283
Columbia Adult Health Inventory, 65
Community based studies, 140–142
Competence, sense of, 33
Comprehensiveness
  of autobiography, 278
  of reminiscence, 277
Compulsive behavior, 64
Confidence, of group, 169
Confirmation, 243, 246
Consensual analysis, 109–110
Constructs, personal, 246–248
Content analysis, 173
  frequency counts, 108
  molecular approach, 108
  quantitative approaches, 108–109

weighting, 108
Context
  defined, 109
  of stories/narratives, 244
Control, 33, 125
Conversation, 99, 122, 283
Conversion, 94–95
Coping, 21, 58
  capacity, 62, 65
  emotion-focused, 206, 214
  group, 256
  interventions, 206
  problem-focused approach, 225–226
  promotion by retelling life narrative, 207
  resources, 224–225
  responses, 226–227
Coping Self-Efficacy Inventory (CSEI), 211, 212
Cornell Medical Index, 65
Counseling, peer, 207
Creativity, 74–75
CSEI (*see* Coping Self-Efficacy Inventory)
Culture, 20, 25, 197
Current Problem Solving and Existential/Self-Understanding, 256

Davis, Betty, 265–272
Daycare center, adult, 186–189, 234, 237
de Vries, Brian, 123–137, 165–177
Death, 19, 173
Death preparation, 58, 94, 98, 122, 252–254, 279, 283
Dementia
  brain changes in, 233–234
  defined, 233
  life review therapy, 240–241
  prevalence, 233
  reminiscence work for, 234–235, 240
    effectiveness, 239–240
    empirical studies, 235–239
    practical issues/applications of group therapy, 241–242
Depression, 19, 20, 64, 82
  cognitive models, 223–231
  instrumental reminiscence for, 223–227
  reminiscence for, 231–232
  therapy
    reminiscence, development of, 221–223, 247
    storytelling in, 248–250

Depressogenic schemata, 229
Deutchman, Donna E., 70, 75, 165–177, 257
Developmental exchange, 170
Dialogue with works, 261
Diathesis-stress model, 227–228
Difficulties theme, 111, 118, 119, 120
Diseases, 147
Disruptive stress hypothesis, 126
Dominant themes, 113–114, 121
Dying (*see* Death)

Effects, context, 256
Efficacy/control beliefs, 224, 225
Ego
  development, 19
  integrity, 19, 20, 29–30
Ego Integrity Scale, 259–260, 262, 264
Elderly, 18, 19, 173
  adaptive functioning of, 49
  confirmation, 246
  cumulative deprivation, 74
  inferiority feelings and, 33
  oldest old, 79–88
  reminiscence styles, psychosocial variables/health outcomes and, 50–52
  stories, power of, 244–246
  stress intervention, 206–208
  universal occurrence of reminiscence in, 77
Elderly Advisory Board, 198
Empowerment, 194
  mutual, 196–197
  self, 243, 247, 248, 254
Engagement, 20, 238
Escapist reminiscence, 26–27, 50–53, 121
Evaluation
  in autobiography, 278
  in life review, 277
  reminiscence, 276–277
Events, defined, 109
Existential/self understanding reminiscence, 279, 282, 283

Facilitator, group, 170–171
Family
  comforter, 101
  development, toxic issues in, 168
  mutual social support among, 197
  therapy, 21
Feedback, group, 169

Females, 90
Financial security
Fixations, 61
Flashbulb memory, 154
Frequency
  of narrative, 278
  of reminiscence, 277
Friends
  in group, 169
  mutual social support among, 197
Frustration, 33
Fry, P. S., 1, 9, 19, 20, 49–60, 224, 226, 285

Gays, 21
Gender
  differences, 95, 100–102, 126, 127–137
  life review and, 124
Genograms, 156–157
Geriatric Depression Screening Scale, 82
Gero-transcedence, 160
Gestalt techniques, 20
Goal-directed activities, 282
Goals, 224
Graduate students, 212, 219
Group
  autobiography, process for, 169–170
  composition, 169
  confidence/trust of, 169
  experience, power of, 170
  facilitator, 170–171
  friendships in, 169
  interventions, 139–140
    AARP Reminiscence Program (*see* American Association of Retired Persons Reminiscence Program)
    general, 239
    for increasing social support, 255–256
    introduction of themes, 155
    props, 158–159
    theme/prop usage guidelines, 161–162
  mutual support, 256
  process, problematic circumstances and, 171–172
  reality orientation, 153
  reminiscence, 19
Guided autobiography, 20, 165
  benefits of participation, 172–173
  content or products of, 165–166
  group facilitator and, 170–171
  method, 166

overview of process, 166–167
potential for research, 174
research, 173
rules, 170
special applications, 175
structured nature, 166
theme assignment, 176
themes, 166, 167–168, 175
Guilt reduction, 222

Hagberg, Bo, 61–75
Haight, Barbara K., 1, 3–21, 49, 53, 54, 72, 73, 82, 155, 179–192, 198, 221, 273–286
Happiness scales, 141–142
Health and Daily Living Scale, 82
Health outcomes
  long-term, 56–57
  negative, 50–53
  psychosocial variables/reminiscence styles and, 50–52
Hendrix, Shirley, 3–21
Hermeneutics, 165
History, philosophy of, 38–43
Homosexuality, 21
Hope objects, 158
Hopelessness, 227–228, 247
Hospitals, 237–238
Hostility, 33

Idea unit, 108
Identity/problem solving, 94–95, 122, 283
Immersion, 122
Inferiority complex, 33
Instrumental reminiscence, 25, 57, 121, 231
  for depression, 223–227
  functions of, 32–35
Integration, in stories/narratives, 244
Integrative complexity, life events and, 126
Integrative reminiscence, 24–25, 57, 121, 231, 282
  for depression, 227–231
  functions, 29–32
Integrity
  defined, 180
  life review and, 180
Interviews
  Life Challenge, 209–210, 213, 214, 216
  Life Experience, 208–212
  reminiscence (*see* Reminiscence interviews)

Intimacy maintenance, 94, 99, 122, 283
Investment-in-community behaviors, 200, 202

Journal method, 258–264
Joys theme, 111, 115, 119, 120

Kidney dialysis, 217
Koh's Block Design test, 64
Kovach, Christine R., 5, 6, 10, 18, 20, 103–122
Kozma, Albert, 139–150

Labels, 18
Lack of choice theme, 111, 117, 119
Lamenting, 18, 20, 114–115, 121, 282
LCI (*see* Life Challenge Interview)
Leadership, for AARP Reminiscence Program, 271
LEI (*see* Life Experience Interview)
Lesbians, 21
"Let's Talk About XYZ," 201, 202–203
Lewy body disease, 233
Life Challenge Interview (LCI), 209–214, 216
Life events, 124–126
    affective dimensions, 125
    complexity, 130–134
    integrative complexity and, 126
    major and minor, 125
    number of, 129
    properties, 125
    type and evaluation of, 129–130
    uncontrollable, 125
Life Experience Interview (LEI), 208–212
Life history, 1, 3, 20
    individual, to increase sociability, 239
    periods, 65, 107
    phenomenological perspective, 62
    prospective, 62
    report, 64
    retrospective, 61–62
    technique, 257
Life review, 18–19, 20, 221, 275–276, 277
    (*See also* Guided autobiography)
    active, 30–31, 256
    age and gender differences, 127–137
    age specificity, 124
    background, 123–124
    cognitive processes of, 31–32
    comparison with other types of recall, 276
    defined, 30
    for dementia, 240–241
    evaluation, 181, 183–185, 277
    goal of, 180
    individuality, 181, 185
    integrity and, 180
    life events, 124–126
    linchpins, 181–185
    problem-solving aspect, 30
    rudiments, 153
    structure, 181, 183, 277
    testing of process, 188–189
    versus psychotherapy, 180
    versus reminiscing, 179–181
Life Review and Experiencing Form (LREF), 180, 181, 190–192
Life review theory, stages of, 180–181
Life satisfaction, 82
Life span, 18, 61
Life stages, 118, 139
Life themes, 18
Life-style, 65
Linking, 202
Locus of control, 57, 58, 60, 65, 70
Lord, Kris, 179–192
LREF (*see* Life Review and Experiencing Form)

McKiernan, Fionnuala, 219, 233–242
Mastery, sense of, 32–35
Meacham, John A., 1, 37–48, 49, 141
Meanings
    defined, 109
    involvement, 20
    making history of, 40–43
    personal construct therapy and, 247
Measurement
    by content analysis, 105–107
    methodological difficulties, 103
    problems, 103
Media coverage, of AARP Reminiscence Program, 270–271
Medical procedures
    follow-up, 213–217
    invasive, 205–208
    reminiscence approach, rationale for developing, 205–208
Memories
    accuracy of, 39–40
    bitter, 92, 100
    constructing meaning of, 42–43

Memories (*continued*)
  discovering meaning of, 40–42
  painful, 20
  positive, 20
  reconstructive, 31
  search of, 31
  social construction of, 43–48
Memory impairment
  in dementia, 233, 234
  reminiscence work and, 240
Men, 195–196
Mental health, 125, 222
Merriam, Sharan B., 11, 79–88, 90, 100, 122, 124, 275, 281, 282, 283
Metaphors, 20
Methods, 20–21
  intensive journals, 258–264
  structured (*see* Guided Autobiography; Life history; Life review)
Milestoning, 20
Mini-Mental State Examination, 235
Mood enhancement, 279
Morale, 82
Multicultural group, 156
Multiculturalism, 39, 45, 88
Multi-infarct dementia, 233
MUMS, 142, 145
MUNSH, 140, 142, 143, 145, 148, 149
Mutual social support, 194
  among family and friends, 197
  groups, 256
  individual to individual, 194–197
  neighborhood, 197–198
  network, 194

Naming, 200, 202
Narrative reminiscence, 27–28, 121, 276, 278
  comparison with other types of recall, 276
Native Americans, 46
Neighborhood, mutual social support in, 197–198
Neugarten's Life Satisfaction Index, 82
Neuroticism, 62
Neutral/informative recall, 110, 111
Nonparametric tests, 261
Nonrelated theme, 154
Nurses, 145, 207

Nursing home residents, 21, 140, 144–146, 222, 235–239
Nursing interventions, 18

Obsessive reminiscence, 27, 50–53, 121
Oh phenomenon, 169
Openness, 19, 230
Oral reminiscence, 255
  versus written reminiscence, 257–264

Past-to-present comparisons theme, 111, 116, 118, 119, 120
Peer counseling, 207
Percutaneous transluminal coronary angioplasty, 213–217
Personal construct, 243
  meanings and, 247
  story retelling, for elderly, 246–248
  theory, 246
Personal meaning, 32, 224
Personal narrative (*see* Narrative reminiscence)
Personality
  construct, 62
  reorganization, 221
  traits, 18, 49–50
    neuroticism, 62
    openness, 19, 230
Philadelphia Geriatric Center Moral Scale (PGCMS), 186
Philosophy, history, 38–43
Photographs, 139, 159–160
Poetry, to evoke life review, 20–21
Positivism, 38, 61
The Power of Memories: Creative Uses of Reminiscence, 266, 272
Preconstructs, adaptive versus maladaptive, 75
Predictability, 125–126
Present-status assessment, 64
Problem-solving skills, 35
Problem-solving tool, reminiscence as, 98–99
Projection, 64
Props, 139, 153, 158–159
  advantages/disadvantages, 161
  defined, 158
  evocative materials, 158
  guidelines for use in group intervention, 161–162
  memorabilia, 158

objects, 158
personal artifacts, 158
precautions, 161
relics of past, 158
selection, 159–160
successful, 160–161
visual aids, 158
Protocols, 155
Psychological interventions, for medically-related stress, 206
Psychosocial model of depression, 223
Psychosocial variables, reminiscence
styles/health outcomes and, 50–52
Psychosomatic symptoms, 56
Psychotherapy
reminiscence in, 243, 248–254
versus life review, 180
Publicity, for AARP Reminiscence Program,
270–271

Rappaport Time Line, 127
Rattenbury, Christine, 139–150, 222
Reality orientation, 235–239
Reality orientation groups, 153
Recall
dimensions of, 276
types (*see* Autobiography; Life review; Narrative; Reminiscence)
Recreation therapists, conduction of reminiscence interviews, 207
Red Cross day center, 186–189
Regressive behavior, 64
Regrets theme, 111, 116, 119, 120
Relationships, friends, 169, 197
Religious beliefs, self-empowering stories and,
247
Reminiscence, 194, 275–276, 285–286
(*See also* Lamenting; Validating)
adaptive processes, 29–35
benefits, 49–50
comparison with other types of recall, 276
comprehensiveness, 277
conceptual model, 54–60
data collection, 4
defined, 257
elicitation, 20–21
(*See also* Methods)
escapist, 26–27, 282
evaluative, 279

forms, 20
frequency, 277
function-based types, 121–122
informative, 282, 283
instrumental, 25, 35, 222, 282
integrative, 24–25, 222, 282
kinds or types of, 18, 20
narrative, 27–28, 282, 283
in nursing home, 144–146
obsessive, 27, 282, 283, 284
oldest old and, 79–88
published articles, types of, 17
research, 19–20
satisfactory, 19
scholarly discussion, 4–17
simple, 277, 279
structure, 122
styles, 18, 50–51
taxonomy, 24–29
themes, 20
therapeutic efficacy and, 50
transmissive, 25–26, 282–283
variability, 20
versus reality orientation for nursing home
residents, 235–239
written, 257–264
*Reminiscence: Finding Meaning in Memories-
Training Kit,* 267, 272
*Reminiscence: Reaching Back, Moving For-
ward,* 272
Reminiscence function, 20, 21
bitterness revival, 94–95, 122, 283–284
boredom reduction, 92, 94, 98, 101, 122, 283
conversation, 122, 283
death preparation, 58, 94, 98, 122, 252–254,
279, 283
identity, 94–95, 122, 283
intimacy maintenance, 94, 99, 122, 283
problem solving, 94–95, 122, 283
taxonomies, 278–284
teach/inform, 94–95, 100, 101, 122, 283
Reminiscence Function Scale (RFS), 18, 283
age-related differences, 91–100
factors, description of, 92
gender differences, 100–102
reliability, 92
validity, 92–93
Reminiscence interviews
advantages, 207
bias in, 107

Reminiscence interviews (*continued*)
  conduction, 207
  with older adults, 106–107
  variations, 208–210
Reminiscence units, 120, 121
Reminiscence Uses Questionnaire, 256
Research
  division between experimental and clinical
      branches, 274–275
  future directions, 284–285
  guided autobiography, 173–174
  lack of conceptual clarity and, 275
Residential care settings, 234
Responsibility, 125
Retirement satisfaction, 63, 64
RFS (*see* Reminiscence Function Scale)
Roberts, Bruce, 193–204
Rosenberg Self-Esteem Scale (RSES), 186
Rybarczyk, Bruce, 11, 19, 205–217, 222, 281

Scarcity hypothesis, 57
Secondary gain mechanisms, 72
Selection, 122
Self
  actualization, 247
  affirmation, 31
  appraisals, positive, 111, 112, 119, 120
  beliefs, negative, 229
  blame, 55, 229–230
  concept, 29, 30, 121
  criticism, 227, 229–230
  deception, 31
  disclosure, 170
  discovery, 231
  efficacy, 207, 209, 224, 227
  empowerment, 243, 247, 248, 254
  esteem, 19, 49, 56, 57, 58, 60, 121, 188, 224,
      225, 227
  evaluation, 227
  identity, 34
  importance, 26–27
  limitation, 247
  recrimination, 231
  regard, 256, 279
  schemas, 29–30, 32, 121
  transcendence, 160
  understanding, 58
  worth, 105, 230–231
SENOTS, 140, 144, 147, 148, 149
Sensitizing questions, 176–177

Sensory impairments, 242
Sexual abuse, repressed memories of, 42–43
Sexual orientation, 21
Sherman, Edmund, 11–12, 20, 141, 222, 255–
      264, 281
Social comparison, 229–230
Social connections theme, 111, 114, 119, 120
Social construction, of memories, 43–48
Social interaction, impact over lifetime, 63–75
Social Readjustment Rating Scale (SRRS),
      125
Social support, 255
Southampton Self-Esteem and Sources of Self-
      Esteem Scale, 186, 187
Speculative perspective, 41
State-Trait Anxiety Inventory (STAI), 211
Statistics
  ANOVA, 93, 129, 130, 132–134
  Kruskal Wallis analysis of variance by ranks,
      187
  MANOVA, 93, 144
Stereotypes, 198
Stones, M. J., 139–150, 222
Stories
  (*See also* Narrative reminiscence)
  context, 244
  functions, 244–245
  power, 244–246
Storytelling/retelling, 194, 243
  age and, 195
  for elderly, appropriateness of, 248
  elderly clients' use of reminiscence in, 248–
      254
  encouragement, empowerment method of,
      200–203
  personal construct, for elderly, 246–248
  prior tasks, 198–200
Stress
  and adaptation, 125
  medically-related, 205–206
Stress management, 206–208
Structure
  of autobiography, 278
  in life review, 277
  in reminiscence, 276
Subjective life history report, 70
Subtheme, 154
SYSTAT/EZPATH, 68

Terminal drop, 126

Themes
  autobiographical memory, 119
  career, 33
  death, dying & losses, 173
  defined, 153
  dominant, 121
  effectiveness, 156, 158
  to elicit reminiscence, 158
  in group intervention
    advantages/disadvantages, 156
    guidelines for, 161–162
    reasons for introducing, 155
  guiding, 166, 167–168, 175
  major branching point, 176
  non-related, 154
  protocols and, 155
  selection, 153
  sub-themes, 154
  trigger themes, 154, 241
  types, 155–156
Therapeutic effectiveness, 50, 146–150
Thorsheim, Howard Iver, 193–204
Time lines, 155, 157
Topics
  (See also Themes)
  Burnside's list, 158
  current, 153–154
  past events, 157
Total equation model, 57
Trait theory of conceptual complexity, 126
Transmissive reminiscence, 25–26, 121
Trauma, 21
Trigger themes, 154, 241
Trust, 169, 212, 242

Undesirability, 125
United Nations World Assembly on Aging, 193
Units of analysis, 108–110
Uses of Reminiscence Scale, 260

Validating, 18, 20, 114–115, 247, 282

frequency of reminiscence units, 121
  interpretations, 104–105, 118
  themes, 110
Value pluralism model, 136
Veracity, of personal memories, 105
Veterans, 210–211
Videotapes, 206
Viney, Linda L., 219, 243–254
Volunteers
  assignments, 268–269
  follow-up, 269
  recognition, 270
  training of, 268

Walker, Lawrence J., 123–137
War-time memories, 162
Watt, Lisa M., 13, 24, 31, 35, 49, 50, 53, 54, 57,
    121, 124, 179, 207, 219, 221–232, 281,
    282, 283
Ways of Coping Checklist, 214
Webster, Jeffrey Dean, 49, 50, 54, 55, 89–102,
    121–122, 123, 124, 230, 273–286
Well-being, psychological, 49
Wisdom, 18, 26, 29, 30, 90, 221
Withdrawal, 122
Women
  age, telling one's own story and, 195–196
  autobiographical memories, 103–104
  props and, 160
  reciprocal interpersonal relationships and, 101
  substance abusers, 21
  wisdom-related knowledge, 18
Wong, Paul T. P., 1, 13, 23–35, 50, 53, 54, 55,
    57, 121, 124, 179, 207, 222, 224, 228,
    281, 282, 283
Woods, Bob, 219, 233–242
Written reminiscence, versus oral reminiscence,
    257–264

Ziegamik effect, 136